Germany,
The Wall and Berlin:

Internal Politics
During An International Crisis

By

JOHN W. KELLER, Ph.D.

Professor of International Relations
California State College in Pennsylvania

Foreword by Dr. Hans Kohn

Center for Advanced Studies
Wesleyan University

VANTAGE PRESS
NEW YORK WASHINGTON HOLLYWOOD

FIRST EDITION

Published by Vantage Press, Inc.
120 West 31st Street, New York 1, N.Y.

Manufactured in the United States of America

To my wife Kay Bullion Keller
for her untiring assistance, understanding
and encouragement

FOREWORD

Professor John W. Keller of California State College has written a useful chronicle of the development and fluctuations of German public opinion as expressed by German politicians and in German periodicals concerning the future of Berlin and the foreign policy to be followed by West Germany. Students of recent German history and politics will find here many half-forgotten events and utterances of the last fifteen years, which are interesting to recall.

The book appropriately ends with the ratification of the Franco-German treaty of friendship in May, 1963—the climactic achievement of the Adenauer era. Hardly nine months have passed since then, yet in many ways the scene has changed. To mention only a few of those changes: Dr. Adenauer has been replaced—much against his wish—by Dr. Ludwig Erhard as Federal Chancellor; General de Gaulle and the late President John F. Kennedy have each visited Germany and have, each in his turn, aroused great enthusiasm among the German public; the rift between Soviet Russian Communism and Chinese Communism has deepened; Communist states and parties have been able to assert to a large degree their independence from Moscow or Peking; President Lyndon B. Johnson and Premier Nikita Khrushchev have assured mankind of their and their nations' will to peace and readiness to ease the tensions along the road started with the treaty ban on nuclear testing of July, 1963; and General de Gaulle has reiterated his conviction that the post-1945 world situation has ended by his diplomatic recognition of Communist China—an important step in his foreign policy, undertaken in violation of the Franco-German treaty and without previous consultation with the West German Government. Under these circumstances the German situation, too, may change and lead toward greater stabilization, which may, in turn, cause a "liberalization" of the Communist regime in the

German Democratic Republic, following the example of almost all other Communist states of central Eastern Europe. A new chapter in the post-war history of the German people may then begin.

Meanwhile it is a great comfort for the West and for its liberal traditions that the by far larger part of Germany, felicitously organized in the German Federal Republic, has developed, especially since the assertion of democratic public opinion in Germany in protest against the Government's attitudes in the *Spiegel* Affair (discussed in detail in Professor Keller's study), in a democratic way. The same profound democratic feeling animates the population of West Berlin. In 1940, when the large majority of Germans enthusiastically supported the National Socialist regime, and when Berlin was the capital of a victorious Great German Reich, no one would have believed this post-1945 development possible. Even the regime of German Communists in the much smaller part of Germany controlled by them can not be regarded as a deterioration from the point of view of liberty and humanity compared with the National Socialist regime which it replaced. Thus the war which Germany under National Socialist leadership conducted in 1939 and the following years against democracy and communism, in the deeply rooted conviction of the triumph of its superior nature over the two equally despised adversaries, ended unexpectedly in the creation of a large and prosperous democracy and a small and much less economically developed Communist state on the territory of the former German Reich.

Only the future will tell whether and how these two German states will find common interests on which to cooperate and to unite. Then, hopefully, the wall dividing Berlin will belong to the past.

On this recent past, and on German internal politics during the crisis of the Berlin wall, the interested reader will find much pertinent information in Professor Keller's book.

Center for Advanced Studies   HANS KOHN
Wesleyan University
Middletown, Connecticut

Contents

Foreword by Dr. Hans Kohn

Part I *Nature of Berlin Crisis*

Part II *The Berlin Wall: August 13-20, 1961*

Part III *Reactions to Events of 13 August 1961*

Part IV *German Parliamentary Elections of 17 September 1961*

Part V *Protracted Conflict*

PART I.

NATURE OF BERLIN CRISIS

Chapter 1

ORIGINS OF THE BERLIN CRISIS IN WORLD WAR II

I

The Focus of Crisis

Berlin is bound to be a focus of crisis between East and West for a long time to come. Rooted in geographic and embedded in diplomatic shufflings since World War II the real issues of Berlin suggest no easy solution. The origins of the diplomatic blunder go back to World War II, to the year 1943. World public opinion then regarded Germans as Huns, as a nation guilty of genocide and bent on crushing democracy as a degenerate system of government.

Why did the U.S. Army not take Berlin in 1945? Why did the Allies not insist on land approaches to the Berlin capital if they were to govern, occupy and administer the city in conjunction with the Soviets? At the Moscow Conference of Foreign Ministers in 1943 it was decided to set up a European Advisory Commission in London to consider plans for the postwar Allied occupation of Germany. Early in 1943 powerful German armies were in strong positions in Europe. British generals and diplomats were rightly hesitant about a premature landing of Anglo-American forces, lest a mass slaughter entail a Pyrrhic victory. A channel landing even if successful might permit a Russian break through the Nazi forces in the East. In that case the Russians might even push to the Rhine or beyond. The British therefore favored negotiations with the Russians for an agreement on the occupation of Germany by Russian troops east of the Elbe and Anglo-American troops west of the river.[1] Though formerly the Eastern boundary of Germany, the eastward push of the Teutonic Knights in 1225 made the Elbe River practically the center of Germany.

This dividing line had the support of President Roosevelt and some of the military echelons and was later confirmed at the wartime conference of Teheran. The basic agreement over occupation zones was signed in London on 12 September 1944 by representatives of the three great powers. It specifically set aside Greater Berlin as a separate area to be occupied and administered jointly by all three powers, but not part of any one occupation zone. Months of negotiations with the Russians in Berlin failed to produce any written agreement for access to the Reich capital, located 110 miles inside the Soviet Zone of Occupation.[2]

In 1944 the psychology of hatred of Nazi Germany was no small factor in bringing about this arrangement, which present-day critics with 20 per cent hindsight vision so strongly denounce. American forces might have captured both Berlin and Prague were it not for the implicit feeling that Berlin should not be the capital of postwar Germany. This was in spite of the fact that Nazism originally emerged in Bavaria and not in Prussia. In a paper read before the American Historical Association in Boston in December, 1949, Sergeant Pogue of the Army Historical Division pointed out that in 1945 many Americans had a repugnance to the seat of Nazi power and secretly hoped the Russians would reach Berlin before the Americans, who were too courteous and considerate to mete out the kind of punishment the Nazis deserved.

Neither General Eisenhower nor General Bradley regarded Berlin as militarily important enough to justify the sacrifice of a hundred thousand American lives to capture it. Eisenhower was misinformed by Military Intelligence as to the number of American casualties it would cost to take Berlin.[3]

President Roosevelt, partly owing to the precarious state of his health, authorized General Eisenhower as theater commander to make the decision whether to capture Berlin. Unfortunately this was a political decision which might better have been made by a civilian official. During the 1952 presidential campaign former President Truman charged that General Eisenhower was responsible for leaving Berlin isolated 110 miles inside the Soviet Zone with no written guarantee of right of access. Granting that the Western armies could have taken Berlin, the Supreme Commander, General Eisenhower, believed they could be more usefully employed against the major German forces elsewhere.[4] He advised Stalin that he proposed to make the main American thrust along the Erfurt-Leipzig-Dresden Line just north of the Czech border instead of driving on Berlin. Churchill immediately wired Eisenhower on 31 March 1945: "If we deliberately leave Berlin to them [the Russians] even if it should be in our grasp, the double event may strengthen their conviction, already apparent, that they have done everything. Further, I do not consider myself that Berlin has lost its military and certainly not its political significance."[5]

On 5 April 1945 Churchill wired President Roosevelt that he did not want to lower General Eisenhower's prestige with the Russian Commanders, but continued:

All we sought was a little time to consider the far-reaching change desired by General Eisenhower in his plans that had been concerted by the combined chiefs of staff at Yalta and had received your and my joint approval. . . . General Eisenhower . . . now wishes to shift the axis somewhat to the southward and strike through Leipzig. . . . He withdraws the Ninth U.S. Army from the northern group of armies. . . .

I say quite frankly Berlin remains of high strategic importance. Nothing will exert a psychological feeling of despair upon all German forces equal to that of the fall of Berlin. . . . If they (the Russians) also take Berlin, will not their impression that they have been the overwhelming contributor to our common victory be unduly imprinted on their minds, and may this not lead them into a mood which will raise grave and formidable difficulties in the future? I consider further that from a political standpoint we should march as far East into Germany as possible, and that should Berlin be within our grasp, we should certainly take it.[6]

Churchill also sent a telegram to General Eisenhower on 28 March 1945 complaining that the General had sent a telegram direct to Stalin changing military strategy. Two weeks later President Roosevelt was dead, and no one was in position to reverse General Eisenhower. Here were the decisive military, diplomatic and psychological factors behind the Berlin Crisis.

The occupation plan agreed to by Churchill, Roosevelt and Stalin and implemented by a British Cabinet Committee, headed by Clement Atlee, recommended a totally disarmed and occupied Germany. It called for the division of Germany into three Occupation Zones: Britain in the northwest, the United States in the south and southwest and Russia in the east. All three powers would occupy Berlin and govern it jointly. The Western Allies gave in to Stalin's demand that East Prussia be cut off from Germany with part of it going to the USSR and the remainder under Polish administration.

President Truman ordered American troops back from the Elbe into their own Occupation Zone in return for promises of the Russians that they would permit Allied forces to join in the occupation of Berlin. In June 1945 General Eisenhower and Robert Murphy of the State Department flew into Berlin for their first meeting with the Russians to organize a Four-Power Government for Germany and Berlin. Marshal Zhukov insisted that he could not discuss the question of Allied access to Berlin until General Patton's troops were evacuated from the states of Thuringia and Saxony. Despite Churchill's pleas that our forces remain as a means of pressure on the USSR, they were evacuated by order of President Truman prior to the Potsdam Conference in July and August, 1945.

The Soviets agreed to designate certain highway, rail, water and air routes linking Berlin and the Allied Occupation Zones in West Germany. This agreement on access was not a written, but oral agreement, although both sides made memoranda of the conversations with Marshal Zhukov. Berlin, an enclave deep within the Soviet Zone, was in the words of President Roosevelt a test tube of American ability to cooperate with the Soviet Union. Roosevelt had always hoped that cooperation in Berlin might lead to worldwide cooperation.[7] Stalin said the most difficult postwar problems would be disagreements among ourselves. Only an hour before he died President Roosevelt in a trans-Atlantic telephone conversation with Churchill said he would minimize the Russian problem because we always have that problem.

20

MAPS

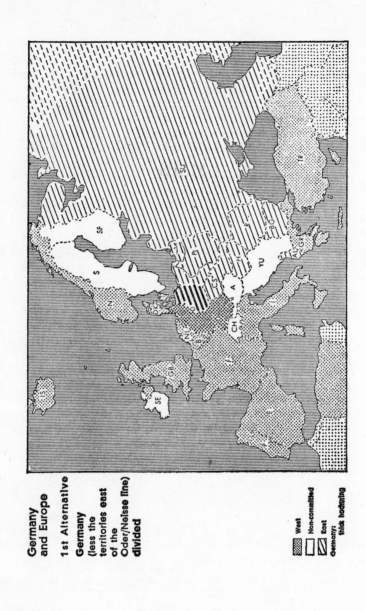

Germany
and Europe

1st Alternative

Germany
(less the
territories east
of the
Oder/Neisse line)
divided

West
Non-committed
East
Germany: thick hatching

Western Bloc countries Non-committed countries Eastern Bloc countries

POPULATION
1954 census
⬆ = 10 million

ELECTRICITY
1954 production
= 10 thousand million kw/h

HARD COAL
1954 winnings
= 25 million t

RAW STEEL
1954 production
I = 2,500,000 t

These statistics refer only to the European countries, including, however, Russia and Turkey in Asia and the French territories in Algeria. The statistics pertaining to Germany do not include the disputed territories east of the Oder-Neisse line, which are shown on the sketches by dotted lines.

Copyright 1956: Siegler & Co. K. G., Bonn-Vienna-Zurich

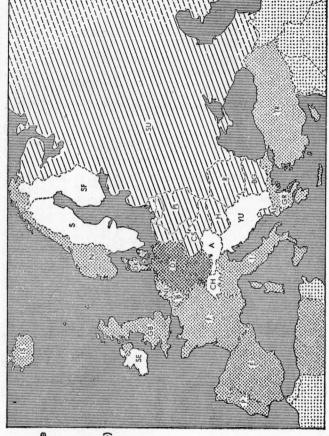

Germany and Europe

2nd Alternative

Germany
(less the territories east of the Oder/Neisse line)
completely allied with the West

West

Non-committed

East

Germany: thick hachuring

Black symbols
refer to Germany

POPULATION

1954 census

⬦ = 10 million

Western Bloc countries

Non-committed countries

Eastern Bloc countries

ELECTRICITY

1954 production

= 10 thousand million kwh

HARD COAL

1954 winnings

= 25 million t

RAW STEEL

1954 production

= 2,500,000 t

These statistics refer only to the European countries, including, however, Russia and Turkey in Asia and the French territories in Algeria. The statistics pertaining to Germany do not include the disputed territories east of the Oder-Neisse line, which are shown on the sketches by dotted lines.

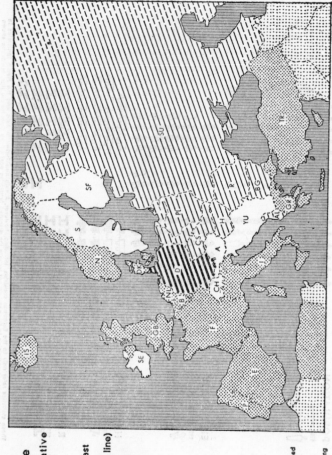

Germany and Europe

3rd Alternative

Germany (less the territories east of the Oder/Neisse line)

completely allied with the East

West

Non-committed

East

Germany: thick hachuring

Black symbols refer to Germany

| | Western Bloc countries | Non-committed countries | Eastern Bloc countries |

POPULATION

1954 census

⬦ = 10 million

ELECTRICITY

1954 production

⚡ = 10 thousand million kw/h

HARD COAL

1954 winnings

= 25 million t

RAW STEEL

1954 production

= 2,500,000 t

These statistics refer only to the European countries, including, however, Russia and Turkey in Asia and the French territories in Algeria. The statistics pertaining to Germany do not include the disputed territories east of the Oder-Neisse line, which are shown on the sketches by dotted lines.

Copyright 1956: Siegler & Co. K. G., Bonn - Vienna - Zurich

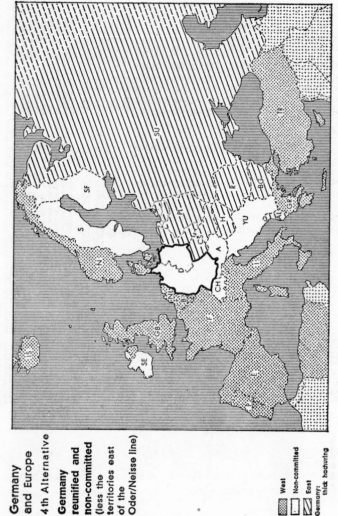

**Germany
and Europe**

4th Alternative

**Germany
reunified and
non-committed**
(less the
territories east
of the
Oder/Neisse line)

West

Non-committed

East

Germany:
thick hachuring

Black symbols
refer to Germany

| | Western Bloc countries | Non-committed countries | Eastern Bloc countries |

POPULATION

1954 census

= 10 million

ELECTRICITY

1954 production

= 10 thousand million kwh

HARD COAL

1954 winnings

= 25 million t

RAW STEEL

1954 production

= 2,500,000 t

These statistics refer only to the European countries, including, however, Russia and Turkey in Asia and the French territories in Algeria. The statistics pertaining to Germany do not include the disputed territories east of the Oder-Neisse line, which are shown on the sketches by dotted lines. Drawn on the basis of an idea put forward by H. Siegler; edited by W. Krallert.

Copyright 1956: Siegler & Co. K. G., Bonn-Vienna-Zurich

II

Potsdam Protocol

Having liberated Europe including Germany from the terror of Nazi tyranny, the Allied Nations were most determined that Germany should never again be permitted to endanger world peace. They therefore agreed on the total defeat of Germany, its complete disarmament and occupation by Allied Military forces. The Potsdam Conference of July 17-August 2, 1945 generalized the historic experience of the struggle waged by European peoples against German militarism. At Potsdam the Heads of State of the United States, Great Britain and the USSR reached agreement on the four D's—demilitarization, denazification, democratization and decentralization of Germany. On the first two there was real cooperation; the others resulted in continued misunderstanding and vituperation, worsened by hate, fear and mistrust.

Demilitarization meant complete disarmament and the elimination or control of all German industry that could be used for military production in order that:

All German land, naval and air forces, the S.S., S.A. and Gestapo with all their organizations, staffs and institutions, including the general staff, officers' corps, reserve corps, military schools, war veterans' organizations and all of her military and quasi-military organizations . . . shall be abolished . . . to prevent the revival or reorganization of German militarism and Nazism.

All arms, ammunition and implements of war and all specialized facilities for their production shall be held at the disposal of the Allies or destroyed.[8]

The aims of these provisions of the Potsdam Protocol were:

To convince the German people that they have suffered a total military defeat and that they cannot escape responsibility for what they have brought upon themselves . . . to dissolve all Nazi institutions, to insure against their

30

revival, to prevent all Nazi and militarist activity or propaganda; and to prepare for the eventful reconstruction of German life on a democratic basis and for eventual peaceful cooperation in international life by Germany.[9]

Under the Potsdam agreement democratic institutions were to evolve at the grass roots level through the election of local councils. As soon as practicable, elections were to be held for local, district and state (*Land*) governments; but occupation authorities were instructed to license only democratic political parties. In order to eliminate Germany's war potential, production of metals, chemicals and machinery necessary to a war, economy was to be rigidly controlled and restricted to Germany's approved postwar peacetime needs. German economy was to be decentralized in order to eliminate excessive concentration of economic power as exemplified by cartels, trusts and other monopolizers.[10]

Although the Soviets signed the Potsdam agreement, they evidently counted on the United States losing interest in Germany and leaving it open to Soviet political development, with a single-party government in Berlin controlled by the all-Russian Communist Party from Moscow.[11] Even after these Soviet objectives became crystal clear, the Western Allies at the Moscow Conference in 1947 made a last effort to follow the terms of the Potsdam agreement. Here it became obvious that Molotov did not want German unification. Stalin realized now that the Potsdam agreement to make Germany an "economic entity" would be bad for Russia because a unified economy would have produced a united, healthy German nation.

Meanwhile the Soviets violated the Potsdam provisions for restoring German political life on the democratic basis of freedom of choice. On the contrary they imposed totalitarian Communist control in their Zone of East Germany.[12] That is, they appointed seasoned German Communists to key posts. These German Communists, backed by Russia, began to destroy all opposition. They used the device of the single ticket chosen by Communists and compelled the Social Democratic Party to merge with the Communist Party in the Socialist Unity Party (SED). Although this trick failed in the Berlin elections of 1946, it worked in the Soviet Zone. This became the basic political instrument of Com-

31

munist control by the party of Walter Ulbricht, a key German Communist trained in the Lenin Institute in Moscow.

In the meantime the Soviets were imposing Communist control on the States of central Europe: Poland, Rumania, Hungary, Bulgaria and Albania. These tactics were flagrant violations of pledges of free elections made by Stalin in the Yalta Declarations on Poland and liberated Europe. Moreover, the Soviets prevented the implementation of the Potsdam agreement for treating Germany as an "economic entity." First, they refused to open zonal borders to travel by Germans. Secondly, they looted the Eastern Zone as they had Berlin before the arrival of the Allies and commandeered and shipped Eastward most of the agricultural yield of their Zone.[13] In 1948 came the decision of British and American officials to merge their Occupation Zones and effect currency reforms in order to curb ruinous inflation, to promote European recovery and to prevent enslaving the German people. The Soviets responded to these economic reforms by a series of obstructive measures, culminating in the Berlin Blockade of 1948-49. German Communists staged riots in Berlin to protest Allied introduction of West German currency reforms in Berlin on 23 June 1948. The following day the Soviets closed all land and water routes between Berlin and the Western Occupation Zones 110 miles away. Here was an undisguised attempt to seal off Berlin, to force the Western Allies out of the city and to starve the Berlin populace into submission to Communism.

The resolute courage and moral fiber of leading citizens of Berlin who refused to abandon their city strengthened the convictions of General Clay, who then obtained permission from Washington for the Airlift to supply Berlin.[14] The hardships and suffering from cold and hunger endured by Berliners helped to restore respect for the German people by world public opinion. The Berlin Blockade cemented a lasting friendship among Berliners, Americans and their Allies. After 11 months of the Airlift, the Soviets apparently realized the failure of their design to oust the Western Powers and monopolize all Berlin. On 4 May 1949 they signed a Four-Power agreement providing that:

All restrictions imposed since 1 March 1949 by the Government of the USSR on communications, transport and trade between Berlin and the Western Zones of Germany and between the Eastern Zone and the Western Zones will be removed on 12 May 1949.[15]

III

Great Debate Over German Rearmament, 1950-51

Continued cold war was bound to raise the question of German rearmament. If the problem had been simply one of control of German militarism, demilitarization, dismantling, decartelization and democratization set forth in the Potsdam agreements might have borne fruit. Stalin once told Roosevelt and Churchill that:

The danger in the future is the possibility of conflicts among ourselves. If there is unity, then the danger from Germany will not be great. . . . It is not hard to keep unity in times of war, since there is a joint aim to defeat the common enemy. The difficult task will come after the war when diverse interests tend to divide the Allies. It is our duty to see that our relations in peacetime are as strong as they have been in War.[16]

As the years passed by the East-West conflict developed into a deadlock. Apart from considerations of Soviet intransigeance, the overwhelming reason for this was the strategic importance of Germany in central Europe. Any geopolitical analysis of the German problem must emphasize that neither the United States nor the USSR could afford to permit its opponent in the East-West struggle to control a united Germany with its 70 millions of highly skilled people and enormous industrial potential. "If Germany were added to the already extensive Soviet sphere, the entire Eurasian land mass with its vast resources of men and materials would be within the Kremlin's grasp. Then the island outposts of Britain and Japan would be directly threatened and the peace, security and well-being of the Western Hemisphere would be in jeopardy." [17] From the Russian viewpoint defense of the USSR would hinge on the nature of the

33

decision on Germany. A strong rearmed Germany would be opposed by a defense minded Russia, the same as the West would oppose an aggressive regime in Russia, although the latter would seek control over Germany to achieve the very thing the United States would avoid. In any case East and West bargaining for high stakes are confronted with three aspects of the German problem: Oder-Neisse lands, unity and control.

The partition of Germany was not intended to be permanent by the victorious powers, but resulted from later disagreements. A related problem was that of control of German military power that twice within the twentieth century involved the Western powers in a Herculean conflict. "While this aspect of a settlement may not appear urgent to Washington, it is one that is not taken lightly in Paris, the Hague and Brussels, not to mention Moscow and Eastern Europe."[18] Although strategic military considerations weigh heavily in Washington and Moscow, these factors alone cannot decide the future of Germany. The German people themselves and the peoples of Europe are both deeply concerned with the outcome.

The United States in 1946 offered Moscow a 25-year treaty, guaranteeing against German attack and even then when East-West relations had not yet deteriorated as in the cold war, the offer was rejected by the Kremlin. After the Czech coup d'etat in February, 1948 Britain, France, Belgium, the Netherlands and Luxembourg signed a 50-year defense alliance, the Brussels Treaty. In June, 1948 the U.S. Senate adopted the Vandenburg Resolution supporting the principle of American association with such regional security alliances as were sanctioned under Article 51 of the U.N. Charter. This resolution resulted in negotiations, which led to the formation of the North Atlantic Treaty Organization (NATO), signed in April, 1949. In the fall of 1949 a committee of NATO worked on a defense strategy for the alliance against a grim background of unilateral measures to sharpen the division of Germany, the tactics pulled on Czechoslovakia in 1948 and Communist gains in Asia along with steadily increasing Soviet pressures on Berlin and the newly created West German Federal Republic.[19]

It was the beleaguered city of Berlin at the crossroads of the East-West conflict, which dramatized before world public opinion and German opinion the nature of the power struggle. Apart from the "creeping blockade" of January 1950 aimed at undermining the economy of West Berlin, came a violent propaganda campaign to frighten Berliners into submission. Moreover, the Soviets began training East Germans in the so called "People's Police." As a result units of battalion strength were stationed in Berlin and armed not with ordinary police weapons, but infantry weapons under the very eyes of West Berliners. Two days after the Communist invasion of South Korea (25 June 1950), Soviet propaganda media were informing the German people that:

> Korea was a test case for the planned American attack upon the so called "German Democratic Republic" (DDR). Within a few days the Communist-controlled press and radio were reiterating the legend that the United States had planned a new world war and that American intervention in Korea was part of a design to establish a ring of military bases around Asia as a preliminary to aggression against Manchuria, China and the USSR.[20]

The purpose of this study is not merely to repeat the running account of East-West measures and counter-measures of the next decade, which is all recorded, but rather to deal with internal politics during an international crisis. As stated above, strategic military considerations may, and indeed do, weigh heavily in Washington and Moscow, but they alone cannot decide the future of Germany. Rather the German people as well as European people have a stake in the final outcome. With this idea in mind, let us examine a fair cross-section of West German public opinion on the issue of German rearmament in the year 1950. The problem here is to determine whether German opposition to rearmament in 1950 was anti-American, anti-Western European or merely a logical continuation of past traditions and policies, as modified by the experiences of two World Wars.

In the early 1950's American demands for German rearmament were based primarily on the all too vivid memory of the fighting qualities of Nazi armies and a dream of turning them to a better use. The fundamental question to ask is do the Germans really want guns? Are they Western enough to be willing to

35

die for the West? Chancellor Adenauer was thoroughly Western and from 1949 was eager to integrate Western Germany into Western Europe. He was backed by two traditional pillars of German conservatism—the Roman Catholic Church and the industrial magnates of the Ruhr. In fact he was accused by deputies in the West German Parliament of turning his back on Eastern Germany prematurely.[21]

In a full-dress debate on rearmament in the West German Parliament (*Bundestag*) on 8 November 1950, Dr. Kurt Schumacher, leader of the opposition Social Democratic Party (SPD), berated Adenauer for offering to rearm Germany without Allied guarantees of equality and for making commitments to the Allies before the German people even had a chance to vote on the question.[22] Except for very small radical parties, the only real opposition to the West German Government in the early 1950's was that of the Social Democrats. Their moderate policy of opposition then—long before the later switch to a sort of bipartisan foreign policy, heralded by the Bad-Godesberg program of 1960—was entirely consistent with the rules of parliamentary, democratic government. Socialist opposition did not endanger the Bonn Republic as did the right wing opposition of the early Weimar Republic, which mitigated against the whole concept of democracy. The Bonn Government is not the Weimar Republic.[23] The great paradox of the Weimar period was militarism in an era of pacifism. To contravene this pacifism a Fascist political movement was required. According to Ernst Hans Fried the only type of militarism German officers could establish in an era of pacifism was the degenerate Nazi type.[24]

On 15 October 1950 Reverend Martin Niemoeller addressed 15,000 churchmen and appealed to the Bonn Government not to create a *fait accompli* without first ascertaining the will of the German people on the issue of rearmament. His appeal was echoed by the *Bruderrat*, which represents the type of Confessional Church which so courageously opposed National Socialism. Gustav Heinemann, President of the German Evangelical Church, resigned from the Bonn Cabinet over Adenauer's rearmament policy and called for a popular plebiscite before any rearming of West Germany was undertaken.[25]

Mounting pressures calling for an expression of the German people on the issue of rearmament proved decisive in the state

(*Länder*) elections in Hesse and Württemberg-Baden in November, 1950. Later, when General Eisenhower, Commander of the proposed West European army, considered the question of German divisions a political-diplomatic problem, Dr. Schumacher (Chairman of the SPD) thought he had shown the greatest understanding for the Social Democratic view of German rearmament. At the same time Dr. Schumacher rejected any cooperation with the Communist Party in a so called "peace front."[26] In August, 1950 the Communist-dominated National Congress of the National Front held in East Berlin was hymning "national resistance" through the National Front in the fight for German unity, an all-German Government, a peace treaty and the withdrawal of occupation troops.[27] The SPD Chairman simply stated that the German Communists could best show their sympathy with the Social Democrats by supporting the cause of freedom in the Soviet Zone of Occupation.

While the Allies in Berlin in November, 1950 enforced their garrisons with American infantry and British tanks and gave machine-guns to the West Berlin police, the Social Democrats in West Germany won important election victories. In the *Land* (state) elections of Hesse they gained 47 of the 80 seats in the *Landtag,* while in Württemberg-Baden the Socialists replaced the Christian Democrats as the principal party.[28] The important losses were those suffered by the large Christian Democratic Party of Adenauer. Social Democratic gains were attributed primarily to the anti-rearmament campaign of the SPD Party, although there were other factors such as the strong influence of Reverend Martin Niemoeller and the proximity of the Iron Curtain only a hundred miles away. Yet even a month prior to these elections, the distaste for war-making was confirmed by an expert public-opinion survey submitted to the U.S. High Commissioner in October, 1950 by Dr. George Katona of Michigan University:

A very substantial part of the German population is opposed to what the army has meant to Germans for about one hundred years. . . . Especially many of those who have served as privates in Germany's armed forces repeat over and over: 'I shall never again serve under my old officers.' [29]

37

The remarkable fact about German voters except for the refugees is the orderly and consistent way they vote their class or religious interests in normal times. For instance the combined share of the Socialists (SPD) and Communists (KPD) in the total vote remained constant since 1928 (about 36 per cent) and the Social Democratic Party's position as the major working class party was confirmed.[30] In the Berlin elections of November, 1950 the Social Democrats polled a third fewer votes than they did in 1948, but were still the strongest party. The 1950 vote reflected the return to normal politics rather than any real shift in public opinion. In fact this election was the nearest to normal since the year 1932. After all the 1948 elections in Berlin were held under Russian pressure when every West Berliner wanted to be sure of voting against the Russians. Therefore, the Social Democrats gained because of their known strength. The SPD polled 64.5 per cent of the total vote as against only 19.4 for the CDU and 16.1 for the Free Democratic Party. Then in 1950 Berlin voters returned to their normal voting habits and voted their traditional parties.[31]

A London *Times* editorial stressed local issues in these elections and refused to admit that the German people were, therefore, against rearmament.[32] Beneath the surface, however, the debate in public and parliament revealed that a huge body of the German people wanted no part in rearmament. Germans frequently observed to occupation authorities that "demilitarization was your greatest success."[33] The German correspondent of the British newspaper, *New Statesman and Nation* found Germans of all classes—laborers, teachers, clerks and civil servants—all untrue to their warlike, bellicose traditions and repelled by the very idea of war. After travelling up and down Germany he found "the younger ex-officers . . . unanimous in their reluctance ever again to wear the uniform."[34] Regardless of the opinions of the older ex-officers or of big Ruhr industrialists expecting to profit from rearmament, it is significant that popular illustrated weeklies were competing with one another in publishing anti-war statements by ex-German war heroes. Equally significant was the nation-wide appeal of German women, sponsored by the Hamburg *Frauenring* (Women's Circle) and its 21 subsidiary Unions, the Protestant and Catholic Unions Globe, the Federation of

38

Professional Women and Women's Auxiliaries of the chief political parties:

> We mothers protest against Germany's rearmament because armed conflict would be tantamount to suicide. . . . We demand that no decision about West German rearmament be taken without first referring it to the vote of the nation, including its mothers.[35]

In Hannover, Germany on 25 December 1950 an independent weekly news magazine, *Der Spiegel,* found a large majority of its German readers opposed to West German rearmament. Of the 33,000 readers who answered the questionnaire:

85% did not want to become soldiers;
60.8% opposed the creation of voluntary troop units;
82.6% voted against compulsory military service; and
95.5% opposed the French plan to restrict German contingents to small units with no war ministry. Even if West Germany were given full equality with other nations in a European army,
68.4% would still oppose German rearmament.[36]

Four days later the *U.S. News and World Report* for 29 December 1950 reported that among the discoveries made by Secretary of State Acheson on his quick trip to Brussels was that war with Russia turned on the arming of Western Germany. . . . and that European diplomats thought the United States had blundered by making four mistakes:

1) The first U.S. mistake was to spring the plan to raise 10 West German divisions without first getting France's agreement. As a result France balked and forced both a compromise and a delay on the United States.
2) The second mistake of the U.S. was to brush off French objections as based primarily on fear of Germany.
3) The third mistake was to assume ready acceptance by West Germany of U.S. plans. West Germans were not at all enthusiastic about facing the Russians. The long

U.S.-French debate, moreover, gave German politicians a golden opportunity to boost the price the Allies must pay Germans for rearming.

4) The fourth U.S. mistake was the apparent assumption that Soviet opposition was a bluff or not too risky. To Europeans it does not look that way.[37]

One month later, on 27 January 1951, the East German Government (DDR) made a new proposal for German unity to Dr. Gustav Heinemann, President of the German Evangelical Churches in Germany and former Minister of the Interior in Adenauer's Cabinet in Bonn. The main parts of this proposal were:

1) disbanding of the East German People's Police and abandonment of plans to rearm West Germany;
2) withdrawal of all foreign troops in Germany;
3) unification of Germany through an election held under international auspices;
4) establishment of a neutral German state.[38]

Not only did the Soviet Government offer large concessions for the abandonment of West German armaments, but the Soviet offers had great attraction in Germany and France. In a public-opinion poll conducted by U.S. Officials, Germans were asked whether West Germany ought to line up with the Western Allies in a military and political alliance, or try to unite with East Germany and stay neutral. The vote was about 50-50.[39]

According to a special dispatch to the New York Times for 13 February 1951, leaders of Adenauer's Coalition Government and the Social Democratic Opposition in West Germany agreed to demand that the Council of Foreign Ministers of the three Western Powers and Russia authorize secret-ballot elections for an all-German parliament.[40] Earlier in February, 1951 the German Social Democratic leader, Kurt Schumacher, challenged the opinion of the French Deputy High Commissioner for Germany, Berard, that German participation in a European army implied no breach of the Potsdam agreement and, therefore, no provocation of Russia. Schumacher pointed out that "a breach of the

Potsdam agreement was a matter of legal definition and provocation of Russia was a matter of diplomatic judgment."[41]

Fred W. Riggs found many motives for German opposition to rearmament such as war-weariness, the bitter experiences of totalitarianism and a fear that rearmament would reinstate reactionary nationalists and lead to civil war between East and West Germans without any promise of German unity, national sovereignty or military security.[42] Any attempt to enlist volunteers in the face of such overwhelming opposition, it was fared, might result in the arming of mercenaries, adventurers and neo-Nazis that would be no asset to the democratic cause. In his report to Congress General Eisenhower stated, "I certainly . . . want no unwilling contingents, no soldiers serving in the position of the Hessians . . . (in the American Revolution) in any army of my command."[43]

IV

East-West Stalemate, 1951-1959

Closely related to the proposals for German rearmament was the problem of how either side could insure against a resurgence of German military might that twice in the twentieth century had engulfed the democratic world and overturned the status quo and peace of Europe. "In the Brussels Pact of 1948 defense of Europe still meant chiefly defense against Germany."[44] Immediately after the Korean War began the young Bonn Democracy was confronted with the ominous issue of rearmament, just as it was getting its feet on the ground. The three-year delay of the French National Assembly in ratifying the European Defense Community (later called West European Union) led to many concessions to the French, such as the Coal and Steel Authority to prevent mobilization of Germany industry for war against Western Europe. Likewise the European Defense Community was planned to prevent the unilateral use of German military power. Nevertheless, all these arrangements to assure France, Belgium and Holland were regarded with suspicion in Central and Eastern Europe.

The Paris Conference of Foreign Ministers broke up in June,

1951 after its failure in 74 sessions to reach any agreement over armaments or the German problem. In violation of agreements with its Allies, Soviet Russia had erected within its occupation zone a Communistic regime, which finally emerged as a pseudo-state dependent on Moscow, the so called "German Democratic Republic," *Deutsche Demokratische Republik* (DDR). After the failure of the Paris Conference of Foreign Ministers to agree on a solution for the German problem, Chancellor Adenauer issued a Government Declaration on 27 September 1951. It contained 14 basic principles for all-German elections to be carried out by a neutral commission. This Declaration was unanimously voted by the Bundestag, with the exception of the small German Communist Party (KPD), which was later outlawed (1956) by the High Court in Karlsruhe. This Declaration expressed the viewpoint of both the Federal Government and the Bundestag as follows:

> The primary aim of the policy of the Federal Government is and remains the re-establishment of German unity in a free and united Europe. This unity must emerge from the free choice of the whole German people. The Federal Government, therefore, has proposed in its Declaration of 9 March 1951 the holding of free, universal, equal, secret and direct elections in all of Germany for a Constitutional National Assembly. . . . In all these proposals for free elections the Federal Government has not followed the proposals of the Soviet Occupation Power. The officials of the Soviet Zone have rejected our proposals.[45]

Although this Declaration of the West German Federal Government won the support of the three Western Occupation Powers, of the United Nations General Assembly and of its political committee by a vote of 45 to 6 with 8 abstentions on 19/20 December 1951, the Soviet Zone Government rejected the plan. It refused permission to the UN Investigating Commission to enter the Zone on the grounds of its illegality and of attempted interference with "the internal plans of the German people." The Soviets also argued that the UN Commission was incompetent because by international agreement only the Four

Occupation Powers could exercise control functions in Germany. After the series of East-West deadlocks over efforts to settle the German problem, the Soviet Note of 10 March 1952 came as a surprise to the Three Western Powers represented in the Allied Control Council. To avoid over-simplification, the main Soviet proposals were as follows:

1) Partition would be ended and a unified Germany would have the opportunity to develop as an independent, democratic, peace-loving state.

2) Simultaneously the military forces of the Occupation Powers must all be removed from Germany one year after the signing of a peace treaty. All foreign military bases on German territory must be liquidated.

3) Democratic rights must be guaranteed to all the German people and to all persons living within German jurisdiction, with no discrimination because of race, sex, speech or religion, who are guaranteed human rights and the basic freedoms, including freedom of speech, press and religion, the freedom of political convictions and the freedom of assembly.

4) Freedom of activity must be guaranteed to democratic parties and organizations in Germany. They must have the right to choose freely their activities and to hold congresses and assemblies and enjoy freedom of press and publications.

5) Organizations which are hostile to democracy and the cause of peace can not exist on German territory.

6) All former members of the German army, including officers and generals and all former Nazis, except those who after a court trial suffer punishment for their misdeeds must be guaranteed the same civic and political rights as all other German citizens for participation in the building of a peaceful, democratic Germany.

7) Germany obligates herself to enter no coalition or military alliance which is directed against any state which has engaged its military forces in the war against Germany.

8) The territory of Germany is determined by the borders which were established by the Great Powers through resolutions of the Potsdam Conference.

9) There would be no limitations placed on Germany's peacetime economy which should tend to raise living standards. Likewise there should be no restrictions on Germany's commerce with foreign lands and her access to world markets.

10) Germany will be permitted to have her own national defense forces (land, air and sea), which are required for her defense.

11) Germany will be permitted to produce war materials and equipment whose quantity and type dare not go beyond her frontiers. What military forces will be required for Germany's defense will be determined by peace treaty.

12) The nations which have signed a peace treaty with Germany would support her application for admission to the United Nations.[46]

These principles for a German peace treaty were contained in a long accompanying text, which stated that the implementation of a peace treaty should result from cooperation with Germany, represented by an all-German Government. The accompanying text stated that the need to speed up the signing of a peace treaty was dictated by the danger that the rebirth of German militarism would not be removed because the corresponding resolutions of the Potsdam Conference were still not carried out. Therefore, a peace treaty with Germany must guarantee against any possible rebirth of German militarism and aggression.

The world as it awoke on the morning of 11 March 1952 was confronted by this Kremlin offer. Were the proposals meant seriously or were they only beautiful words? Discussion of the Soviet Note continued several weeks. An editorial in the Swiss conservative paper, *Neue Züricher Zeitung*, expressed the idea that the Russian draft had great surprises for Germans as well as some of the Western nations and appeared at first to contain some alluring offers. Discussion of the first days after reception of the Note completely dominated the press, which subjected Moscow's proposals to serious cross-examination.

Neue Züricher Zeitung added:

One can not rule out the possibility that the judgment of skeptical prognosis (it is only a case of variation of a long familiar theme) will finally be confirmed. . . . One certainly has the right to recall how many dramatic and largely staged actions of Soviet foreign policy have already been shattered in the tactics of their author in the course of negotiations or already broken up in the propaganda arena, although Moscow previously on the basis of the greatest urgency of existing problems and in certain cases with naive partners had announced the expectation that the goals strived for were within reach.[47]

The first press reaction focused on three items of interpretation of great national significance for the German people:

1) The timing of the note occasioned mistrust. The signing of the treaties of the European Defense Community and the debate over ratification in the German Bundestag and the French National Assembly had just taken place. Was the note from Moscow intended merely to delay European integration at the last hour?[48] This was evidently the view of Chancellor Adenauer, who rejected the note peremptorily the very next day and was sharply criticized for this not only by opposition deputies, but by a member of his own CDU fraction, Dr. Ferdinand Friedensberg, who at the CDU Party Congress of 27-29 April 1956 criticized Adenauer's foreign policy and called for more friendly relations with the Soviet Union.
2) The Soviet Note made no mention at all of German elections. It was, however, the demand for free all-German elections which had been raised repeatedly by all parties in the Bundestag as the first step toward reunification.
3) The Soviet Note was directed toward the Potsdam agreements. Did it thereby demand recognition of the Oder-Neisse Border? Heretofore, all parties in the Bundestag had always opposed recognition of this so called "Frontier" arbitrarily created by Soviet Russia.[49]

Both parliamentary opposition and circles near the Bonn Government concluded that the Soviet Note was not clear on vital national questions which caused comments in the West German press to the effect that the Soviet Note had intentionally formulated a number of items vaguely in order to create the basis for endless debate over their meaning. For instance there was suspicion that after the conclusion of a German peace treaty the withdrawal of occupation troops would result in a vacuum in central Europe, which the Red Army only a few hundred kilometers east would be tempted to fill.

Chancellor Adenauer on 16 March 1952 in a speech in Siegen characterized the Soviet Note as a forward step (*gewissen Fortschritt*), but directed three precise questions to the Kremlin:

1) How does the Soviet Government conceive the construction of an all-German Government? According to the German interpretation such a government could only come about through free and secret elections.

2) How should the problem of German territory on the other side of the Oder-Neisse be settled? An answer to this question would be very enlightening.

3) How does Moscow interpret "national rearmament"? In view of the advancing techniques of wepons, national German rearmament proposed in the Soviet Note is impossible. Since 1945 such a great advance has been made in military science that Germany from its financial and material resources alone could not build up such a national armament.[50]

The SPD Parliamentary group had also taken a common stand with the Federal Government and the Government Coalition parties in the Bundestag that the way to construct an all-German Government was by way of free, all-German elections and that reunification would only come through free elections —not through an all-German constituted council with equal representation by East and West German delegates as Pankow (East German Zone regime) had demanded in a letter to Chancellor Adenauer on 30 November 1950. Moreover the Vice Chairman of the SPD, Erich Ollenhauer, stated in a radio address that "we do not recognize the Oder-Neisse Line as the legal East German boundary."[51] This united stand of government and opposition parties on such vital national issues as free elections and territorial questions underline the power of resurgent nationalism in postwar Europe, accentuated by the East-West Cold War and dramatized by the continuing deadlock over Germany, divided between East and West.

Ever since the Western Powers under the impact of the Korean War reversed the Potsdam policies of German demilitarization, various conferences between the Foreign Ministers of the Western Powers and the Soviet Union to find a mutually agreeable formula for German reunification have failed. The final result was to make German unification more remote than at any time since 1945. The continued stalemate makes reunification impossible on Western terms for obvious reasons: 1) Free elections in East Germany would result in an overwhelming defeat for Communism by a non-Communist majority of 80 or 90 per cent in favor of the Western constitutional democratic system. 2) It may be assumed that a united Germany would prefer membership in the Western alliance system of NATO to neutrality or affiliation with the Soviet dominated Warsaw Pact. 3) A non-Communist majority government would wipe out all social gains of the DDR—land reforms, nationalized industries (80%) and agricultural collectivization. 4) The USSR would loose its most advanced ally—the sixth industrial power in Europe. 5) The loss of Eastern Germany, moreover, would weaken, if not destroy the Soviet power position in Central and Eastern Europe, forcing Poland and Czechoslovakia into the German orbit.[52] The net result of the East-West stalemate is that German unification on Western terms is unobtainable.

V

Soviet Ultimatum on Berlin, 27 November 1958

Five or six years after the Soviet Note of 10 March 1952 the political discussion evoked by the Soviet Note was again revived. The occasion was Thanksgiving Day in November 1958 when Khrushchev presented his "Peace Treaty Proposal for Germany," in a comment in which he observed that Moscow had already specified "easy terms." This also recalled the turbulent midnight debate in the West German Parliament on 23 January 1958, when Bundestag deputies Dr. Thomas Dehler (FDP) and Dr. Gustav Heinemann (SPD) with strong passion expressed the opinion that in the spring of 1952 the opportunity had been lost for coming to an understanding with the Soviet Union and for reunification. In his note of November, 1958 requesting Allied withdrawal from West Berlin in return for his offer to make West Berlin a "Free City," Khrushchev tried to force a solution for the Berlin deadlock in his favor.

The Russians wanted two conditions: withdrawal of Western troops from Berlin and the recognition of the DDR Regime of the Soviet Zone by the West. In return for these concessions the USSR and the DDR might be induced to guarantee access to Berlin as indicated by Khrushchev in his plan for a "Free City." The main arguments contained in the Soviet Note of 27 November 1958 were: 1) Berlin had become a dangerous center of contradiction between the Great Powers, allied in the last war— a center of constant international tension. 2) The Potsdam Agreement generalized the historical experience of the struggle waged by the peoples to prevent aggression by German militarism. 3) The Western Powers violated the Potsdam Agreements by: their restoration of the military and economic potential of Western Germany—the very sources that forged the Nazi war machine. 4) The Western Powers tolerated and abetted German militarism by the notorious Munich policy of encouraging German military aggression against the Soviet Union. 5) When the Western Powers in violation of the Potsdam Agreement set up a separate state in West Germany occupied by troops of the three Western Powers, East Germany had no alternative but to create in its turn an independent state. Thus two states came into being in Germany.[53] Finally the Soviet Note concluded that:

1. The Western Powers had grossly violated the Potsdam Agreements.
2. The social structure of both German states was the concern of Germans themselves.
3. The people cannot, nor will they, let Germany be united in a militaristic-basis state.
4. There is a program for uniting Germany as a peace-loving and democratic state. There is but one way of carrying it out.
5. It is through agreements and contact between both German states and through setting up a German Confederation without affecting the social bases of the German Democratic Republic (GDR) and the Federal Republic of Germany (FRG).[54]

Protracted negotiations which followed the reception of the Soviet Note of 27 November 1958 only continued the stalemate and deadlock between the irreconcilable positions of East and West. "The constant din of publicity and propaganda forces a Western leader to be more concerned than ever with justifying his own position with his own nation, his political party and his allies and partners in the Alliance. It follows that he is daily less and less able to suggest proposals likely to be acceptable to the East—because of the Western propaganda."[55] During the heat of the discussions over the Soviet Note in the spring of 1959 Field Marshal Montgomery, Deputy Commander of NATO, 1949-1959, made a trip to Moscow to find out what the East thought about East-West relations. He found mutual mistrust and fear abroad in Europe with each side, East and West, frightened at what the other might do. With mutual suspicion, hate and fear, he found that the Russians greatly feared the Germans and therefore would never permit a united Germany until the whole European security problem was settled. "In the conflict between East and West the one factor is Germany. The problem of Europe is the problem of Germany." [56] Above all German unification, though desirable, was not practical politics because the Russians would not have it. The net result of the Foreign Ministers Conference in the spring and summer of 1959 was a continued stalemate, which only confirmed Montgomery's conclusions that unification of Germany on Western terms was unobtainable.

VI

Four Alternatives to the Problem of Reunification

A comparison of the positions taken by the four parties which won seats in the Bundestag in the parliamentary elections of 1957 reveals an overwhelming desire on the part of all German political parties for reunification and security. However, there was considerable difference between the coalition and opposition parties as to how to achieve these desired goals. Charts C, D, E and F in the Appendix reveal sharp differences as to methods, procedure and timing—that is the priority of German reunification *vis-à-vis* European security and disarmament.

49

The charts in the Appendix based on the four main alternatives for Germany's future focalize attention upon the vital importance of the German question to the European balance of power. They show graphically the impact of each major proposal upon the over-all balance of strategic resources—the foundations of national power—particularly the factors of population, electricity, coal and steel production. A comparison of the charts underlines the decisive importance of the German problem as a key to understanding the tremendous stakes of East-West diplomacy. The peace and security of Europe is closely linked to the solution of the German question.

The first alternative, i.e., a divided Germany means retaining the *status quo* as it developed since 1945, a condition which is strongly opposed by all German parties and politicians—except the German Communist Party (KPD), outlawed since 1956 by the German High Court in Karlsruhe—although they differ considerably in the means of ending the stalemate. Merely maintaining the *status quo* is no solution to the problem, but rather the evasion of a solution, in view of the East-West conflict.

Both the Federal Chancellor, Dr. Adenauer, and the leader of the opposition, Erich Ollenhauer, regretted the tragedy of a divided Germany. But whereas the parliamentary opposition called for numerous measures to overcome the stalemate, Adenauer warned Germans of the risks involved in excessive demands for reunification. Both statesmen were well aware of the dangers implicit in the continued division of Germany into opposing spheres of interest.

The second alternative, a reunified Germany allied with the West, is the solution aimed at by the Adenauer Administration at Bonn and also favored by the Western Powers in spite of some modifications. Here again the chart reveals how advantageous this solution would be to the West, not from the standpoint of population and resources, but rather the military advantages of strategy and area. In addition, there is the tremendous psychological value that would accrue from the union of the West with Germany, with the implication of economic aid to stimulate free enterprise and the so called market economy.

The third alternative, viz., the incorporation of the entire reunified Germany in the eastern system is the solution favored by both the Soviet Union and the Soviet Zone rulers. Here charts

D and E reveal that the Eastern Bloc would gain far more from an alliance with a reunified Germany than would the West, both in regard to population and the production of electricity, coal and steel. Moreover, the Communist influence would extend almost to the frontiers of Britain, France and Italy. The military and strategic implications of such a solution are clearly obvious —a solution which neither the West nor West Germany would ever accept, as the Kremlin is well aware. At a news parley in Moscow on 27 November 1958 Khrushchev urged the West to be "realistic." The Soviet Union is not engaged in the "fantasy" that West Germany can be persuaded to become Communist, he said. Therefore, he urged that the West not cling to "fantasies" about making East Germany a capitalist country. West Berlin rightfully belongs to East Germany, he said, but the Communist Bloc wants to be "realistic" and recognizes West Berliners' stakes in capitalism. So Khrushchev offered to let them keep capitalism if they accepted his plan for a free city.[58]

The fourth alternative—a reunified and non-committed Germany—could be regarded as the alternative solution which the Soviet Union would be glad to see in lieu of the third alternative, which Premier Khrushchev in his Berlin Note of 27 November 1958 admitted the West would never accept. Nevertheless, an uncommitted Germany need not be ruled out as a way worthy of consideration in view of the keen international rivalry over the status of *Mittel-Europa,* despite certain hazards. Chart F in the Appendix clearly indicates that one result of a Germany reunited and uncommitted would be a broad belt of neutral states in central Europe, including Sweden, Finland, Czechoslovakia, Austria and Yugoslavia. However, the West would stand to loose much more that the Soviet Bloc from such a solution, simply because the Soviet Zone of Germany is far inferior to Western Germany both in population and in strategic resources, particularly coal, iron and electricity. Moreover, military experts claim that this solution would greatly weaken NATO, whose radar network would be forced back of the French, Belgian and Dutch frontiers.[59] At the same time Soviet withdrawal from the East Zone of Germany would detract little from her vast land areas still available for military maneuvers.[60]

This fourth alternative—Germany reunited and uncommitted

51

—includes various proposals, some more radical than others. Yet this solution of the German problem is confronted with uncertainties growing out of the lack of internationally recognized definitions of neutrality in peace time. In fact, some authorities in international law contend that true neutrality can exist only in war time. Uncommitted means nothing more than the avoidance of military alliances, since this term also lacks an internationally recognized definition.[61]

Chancellor Adenauer has always emphatically rejected any proposals for a neutralized Germany between the powerful Eastern Bloc and the West European countries. For fourteen years Adenauer's foreign policy has been the main source of political controversy in Germany. Both parliamentary and local state elections in the *Länder* have been fought largely on issues of foreign policy rather than domestic issues. Fortunately for Dr. Adenauer, the four Foreign Ministers at the second Geneva "Summit" Conference in November, 1955 limited their discussions to three problems: first, reunification of Germany, second, European security and third, disarmament. On 6th of April 1956 the *U.S. News and World Report* published an interview with French Premier Guy Mollet, a member of the French Socialist Party. Mollet pointed out the belief of his Government that this was a wrong approach and cited the fact that as President of the Council of Europe at Strasbourg in 1955 he had sent to the Western Foreign Ministers then in Geneva a telegram stating: "it is by beginning with disarmament that you would best advance the other questions."[62]

The thesis of the French Premier was that if the first stage of disarmament resulted in a reduction for all countries in the size of armed forces and certain types of armaments, international negotiations could then lead to Russia accepting free elections in Germany—i.e., assuming that the Russians wanted the reunification of Germany, as seemed clear in the Soviet Note of 10 March 1952.[63] Following these negotiations, the status of Germany in relation to the security organizations might be changed.

The Foreign Office of the West German Federal Government made clear its disagreement with the priority of disarmament talks, which implied any tacit acceptance of the division of Germany and stood firm for the Geneva approach to the problem

52

in this order: German unity, European security and then disarmament. However, the West German Minister of Foreign Affairs, Dr. Heinrich von Brentano, in addressing the Council of the Assembly of Europe on 18th of April 1956, pointed out that M. Mollet had declined to say that disarmament should be given absolute priority of decision and even shared the opinion that the three problems were so intimately connected that all three might be approached simultaneously, thus eliminating any question of priority.[64] Emphasizing the deep concern of West Germany, he reminded the Council of Dr. Adenauer's statement to the Bundestag on 17th of May 1955 that "restricted and controlled disarmament is the only basis for an effective security system" was still as pertinent as ever.[65] In a note to the Soviet Ambassador in Bonn on the 28th of April 1957 Dr. Adenauer pointed out that he had clearly informed him that:

1. the Federal Government neither possessed nor had sought supplies of atomic weapons of any kind whatsoever;
2. that it could not welcome any evidence of other Powers' arming with nuclear weapons, since this course would render more difficult atomic disarmament;
3. that his Federal Government favored general controlled nuclear disarmament.[66]

Of all the issues of German foreign policy, the one that overshadows all the others is the struggle for German reunification. Ever since the Potsdam Conference in July/August 1945 each of the four Occupation Powers tried to mold its zone of Germany into its own image—from the organization of the police force to political institutions and cultural ideals. In the Soviet Zone the process was carried out most effectively, first through the forced merger of the German Social Democratic Party (SPD) and the German Communist Party (KPD) into the Socialist Unity Party (SED), then by making the Liberal and Christian Democratic Parties mere satellites. Today reunification means the integration of the Federal Republic, Berlin and the Soviet Zone. Yet according to international law, the Germany defeated in 1945 was divided into seven parts: 1) the Federal Republic, 2) the "German Democratic Republic" (DDR), 3) West Berlin,

4) East Berlin, 5) the Saar, 6) Oder-Neisse territories under Polish administration and 7) Northern East Prussia, annexed by the Soviet Union. This "Balkanization" of Germany, contrary to all trends of modern German history, is a continuous source of tension in Europe and of deep unrest in Germany.

Even more tragic, however, was the decision made early in the Korean War to rearm Germany, which thus became the advance post of both great military blocs, where the propaganda and intelligence services of both sides operate. Germans are confronted by the fact of two Germanies, each belonging to a military alliance hostile to the other and menacing the peace and security of both Germany and Europe. Naturally Germans will favor the side that does most to achieve unity, though this may involve a willingness to assume certain risks. If then the German people are to be persuaded that their unity is in better hands with the West than the Communists, we must avoid the mistakes of the past. If the Western democracies had been half as considerate of the Weimar Republic as they were of Hitler, there would have been no Hitler. And yet even today the Soviets are wishfully hoping for the revival of the unholy alliance of Communism and German nationalism, as it existed at Rapallo in 1922 and in the Nazi-Soviet Pact of 1939.

NOTES TO CHAPTER ONE

1. "New Talks Dispel the Mood of Crisis, Despite Shooting and the Wall," *The National Observer* (Washington, D.C., independent), 22 April, 1962, p. 15.
2. For details see Dwight Eisenhower, *Crusade in Europe* and Harry S. Truman, *Memoirs*.
3. Robert Murphy, "The Story of How Berlin Became the World's No. 1 Danger Spot," in *U.S. News & World Report* (Washington, D.C., independent), 9 April 1962, p. 73.
4. U.S. Dept. of State Bulletin, *Background Berlin—1961*, p. 5.
5. *Washington Post* (liberal), 5 October 1961.
6. *Ibid.*
7. *U.S. News & World Report* (Washington, D.C., independent), 9 April 1962, p. 74. See also James F. Byrnes, *Speaking Frankly*
8. The Potsdam Declaration, August 2, 1945, quoted from *New York Times* (3 August, 1945), by Louis Snyder in

Fifty Major Documents of the Twentieth Century (New York, Van Nostrand, 1955), pp. 113-114.

9. Dept. of State Bulletin, *Background Berlin—1961*, pp. 2-3.
10. Snyder, *Fifty Major Documents,* p. 115.
11. Robert Murphy, *U.S. News & World Report* (Washington, D.C., independent), 9 April, 1962, p. 74.
12. West German publicists consistently refer to the Soviet Zone as Middle Germany (Mitteldeutschland) in contrast to the lost territories, east of the Oder-Neisse Rivers, which they consider East Germany.
13. State Department Bulletin, *Background Berlin—1961,* p. 6.
14. Personal interview with Herr Sanders, Campaign Manager of the SPD in Bonn in September, 1961.
15. Dept. of State Bulletin, *Background Berlin—1961,* p. 12.
16. From James Reston's review of James F. Byrnes' *Speaking Frankly* in *New York Times Book Review* (19 October 1947), Sec. 7, p. 1 and 45.
17. William W. Wade, Fred W. Riggs and Howard C. Gary, *Problems of East-West Settlement,* Headline Series, No. 101, September-October 1955, pp. 11-12.
18. *Ibid.,* p. 15.
19. Dept. of State, *United States and Germany,* 1945-55, p. 23.
20. Department of State, *U.S. and Germany,* 1945-1955, p. 23.
21. Leo Lania, "Guns for Germans—But What Germans?" *United Nations World* (December, 1950), p. 13. Arold Wolfers, "West Germany—Protectorate or Ally?" in *Yale Review* XL, No. 2 (Winter, 1951), p. 224.
22. Editorial, "Germany: Cleavage on Rearmament," in *Newsweek* (20 Nov. 1950) p. 42.
23. *Ibid.*
24. Ernst Hans Fried, *Guilt of the German Army*
25. Editorial, "Germany: Cleavage on Rearmament," *Newsweek* (20 Nov. 1950), 42.
26. Editorial, "Schumacher on the Pleven Plan," *Guardian,* Vol. 64 (1 Feb. 1951) p. 3.
27. U.S. Dept. of State, *The U.S. and Germany,* 1945-1955, p. 23.
28. Editorial, "Germany," *Guardian* (Manchester, liberal), LXIII (23 Nov. 1950) p. 1.
29. Editorial, "Germany: Cleavage on Rearmament," *Newsweek* (20 Nov. 1950) 45.
30. Otto Kirchheimer and Arnold Price, "An Analysis of the

Effect of the West German Elections on the First Bundestag on 14 August 1949," *U.S. Department of State Bulletin,* Vol. XXI, No. 537 (17 Oct., 1949), p. 563.

31. *Ibid.*
32. Editorial, "German Anxieties," *London Times* (22 Nov. 1950), No. 51, 855, p. 7.
33. Editorial, "Germany: Cleavage on Rearmament," *Newsweek* (20 Nov. 1950) 45.
34. Heinrich Fraenkel, "Germans to the Front," *New Statesman and Nation,* (London), XL, (11 Nov., 1950), p. 420.
35. *Ibid.,* p. 420.
36. Special Dispatch, "West Germans Oppose Arms," *Toledo Blade* (30 Dec. 1950).
37. Editorial Summary: "From the Capitals of the World," *U.S. News and World Report* (29 December, 1950), Vol. XXIXX, No. 26, p. 27.
38. Special News Letter to the *New York Times* (27 January 1951).
39. World News Summary: "From the Capitals of the World," *U.S. News and World Report* (16 February 1951), Vol. XXX, No. 7, p. 32.
40. Quoted in *Foreign Policy Bulletin* (16 February 1951), Vol. XXX, No. 19, p. 4.
41. German Correspondent, "Schumacher on the Pleven Plan," *Guardian* (Manchester, liberal), Vol. 64, No. 5 (1 February 1951), p. 3.
42. Fred W. Riggs, "German Arms Issue Jeopardizes Western Unity," *Foreign Policy Bulletin,* Vol. III, No. 13 (5 January 1951), p. 3.
43. Editorial, "Eisenhower on Europe," *New York Times* (4 February 1951) , Sec. 4R, p. 1.
44. U.S. Dept. of State, *U.S. and Germany,* 1945-1955, p. 25.
45. G. A. Bürger, *Die Legende Von* 1952. p. 9.
46. G. A. Bürger, *Die Legende Von* 1952, pp. 15-17.
47. G. A. Bürger, *Die Legende Von* 1952, pp. 14-15.
48. *Ibid,* p. 15.
49. *Ibid.*
50. G. A. Bürger, *Die Legende Von* 1952, p. 17.
51. *Ibid.*
52. Karl Lowenstein, "Unity for Germany?" in *Current History,* Vol. 38 (January, 1960), No. 221, p. 39.

53. *Current History,* Vol. 36 (February, 1959), pp. 107-114.

54. *Ibid.,* page 109.

55. Field Marshal Montgomery, *An Approach to Sanity: A Study of East-West Relations.* New York: World Publishing Co., 1959. Pp. 84-85.

56. *Ibid.,* 85.

57. See Heinrich Siegler, *Reunification and Security of Germany* (Bonn, 1957), pp. 173-179. Compare James Warburg, *Germany: Key to Peace* (Harvard University Press, 1953), pp. 1-7. See also Harold and Margaret Sprout, *Foundations of National Power* (New York, Van Nostrand, 1951).

58. *New York Times* (independent), 28 November 1958.

59. Harold Stassen, Chairman of the American Delegation to the United Nations Disarmament Talks in London in 1957 set forth a plan involving mutual withdrawal of troops by the Soviet Union and the Western Powers from East and West Germany, but the Western Powers would be permitted to set up radar warning posts on the East German border and likewise the Soviets would be allowed radar warning installations on the Rhine. This plan would have afforded mutual protection for each side against surprise attack.

60. For a different view see George Kennan, "Disengagement Reconsidered," in *Foreign Affairs,* XXXI, (January, 1959), 199. Kennan states that "The ideal military posture is simply the enemy of every political detente or compromise and whoever is not prepared to make sacrifices and to accept risks in the military field should not lay claim to any serious desire to see world problems settled by any means short of war."

61. Siegler, *op. cit.,* 178.

62. *U.S. News & World Report* (Washington, independent), 6 April 1956.

63. Fritz Erler (SPD) representing West Germany in the Consulting Assembly of the Council of Europe (28 April 1956) stated that this Soviet Note was never given the consideration it deserved by the West.

64. Siegler, *op. cit.,* 155.

65. *Ibid.,* 156.

66. *Ibid.*

Chapter 2

THE CURRENT GERMAN POLITICAL SCENE

Background

The tragedy of Germany and Central Europe today is that there was for Germany no 1776, no 1789, no spirit comparable to what the French mean by *Liberté, Egalité, Fraternité*. German history is complex and frightfully difficult for many students because of the lack of any unifying force, until the late nineteenth century. By 1789, France, Spain, Austria and Russia were compact national states. Germany, in contrast, included over 300 independent, sovereign states, principalities and free imperial cities.

The Protestant Reformation and religious war that followed failed to unite Germany. Although most Germans withdrew in horror from the terrible French Revolution, the chief result of Napoleon's imperium was to reduce the number of independent German states from 314 to 38. The story of Germany's struggle for unification forms a vital part of any analysis, however brief, of the development of the German outlook on society and of Germany's emergence into the realm of world politics. In their efforts to achieve national unity, most German liberals gave a priority to nationalism *vis à vis* the general principles of liberalism. However, national unity was finally achieved not by liberals, but by Prussians who gloried in the use of military might (*Machtpolitik*).

Twice within the twentieth century the Western Powers have been drawn into a Herculean conflict with a united Germany bent on European hegemony or *Weltpolitik*. The implications of German military and economic power are already beginning to trouble many European statesmen. Whether or not a nuclear armed Reich may repeat past history, it seems certain that a resurgent Germany will again hold the key to European peace and security.[1]

The United States, because of her powerful position in world affairs since World War II, finds herself concerned with the contemporary German problem. In general, Americans, many of whom have only recently become cognizant of its complexities, find numerous aspects of German history and political development unintelligible. This is particularly true when these complexities are expressed in the various and often conflicting pronouncements of propagandists for the East and West Germans, the administration and opposition parties in West Germany, the Free Democrats and Social Democrats, the German party and Refugee Bloc, the internationalists, the neutralists and nationalists and the now outlawed Neo-Nazis and West German Communists.

The multi-party system, with its major and minor parties, splits and realignments, has also proved confusing to Americans. Notwithstanding the increasing evidence in contemporary Germany of a trend toward a two-party or two-plus party system, the roots of German political development lie deep in the past. Unlike American political parties, German parties are steeped in ideologies, past traditions and differences of class, religion and geography.

German Parties after World War II

The basic aims of the Potsdam program were: 1) disarmament and demilitarization to prevent German revival and reorganization; 2) denazification to destroy the National Socialist party and dissolve all Nazi institutions; 3) decentralization of Germany's political structure along with the development of local responsibility; and 4) democratization of German political life on the basis of peaceful cooperation in international life.

After the defeat of the Nazi regime there was no German state. A unique situation developed in which political parties were "founded, built up and approved by the Military Governments, not only in the absence of the state . . . but precisely for the purpose of organizing such a state, or at least aiding in its formation."[2] Yet the very object of a political party, according to Max Weber, was to control the state within which it existed.[3] Nevertheless, all four occupation powers proceeded to solve the problem of government by permitting four major political parties and even promoting their organization.

This unprecedented development resulted from the exclusive and tyrannic domination of the German state by the Nazi party, which eventually destroyed both German democracy and the German state in the holocaust of World War II. The supreme sacrifices made by Germans in concentration camps and in the underground against dictatorship are of profound significance for the political future of the German nation.

The Western Powers laid careful plans to reestablish German parties gradually on a local basis from the grass roots. Thus politically mature Germans had ample opportunity to prevent the growth of extremist parties of a neo-fascist or Communist nature. However, the Soviet armies had no military government apparatus comparable to that of the Western Powers. Depending on native German officials, they proceeded to capitalize on their lack of preparation and at the same time to gain the good will of Germans at the expense of the West.

Almost immediately after the cessation of hostilities, the Soviets imported exiled German Communists from Moscow, and licensed four parties in the Eastern Zone: the Communist party, the Social Democrats and then also two middle class parties, the Christian Democratic Union (C.D.U.) and the Liberal Democratic party (L.D.P.). This was a shrewd move; Germans vividly recalled the deterioration of the Weimar regime because of the confusion of too many parties. The idea of four major parties seemed also to guarantee against the tyranny of the one-party Nazi state.

Now the Western Powers were under strong pressure to follow Russia's lead. They too licensed four parties, including the Communists on the extreme Left, the Social Democrats Left of Center, the Christian Democrats in the Center and the Liberals, moderately Rightist.

New Forces in West Germany

In rejecting Nazism in the period after World War II, the West German electorate turned politically Left of Center. The miserable economic conditions of the years 1946 to 1948 induced even middle-class groups to favor various schemes for the nationalization of industry. All the *Land* (state) diets in Germany reflected the political mood of the times. Moderate and conservative elements opposed to this trend were politically and economically impotent prior to the currency reform of June, 1948. Social Democrats wanted the Minister-Presidents of the *Länder* replaced as spokesmen for the German people and as negotiators with the Allies, because they preferred a more efficient, a more centralized and a more German-minded leadership. The right wings of the Christian Democratic Union (C.D.U.) and Free Democratic Party (F.D.P.) also wanted this change, but for different reasons.

The formation of the West German Federal Republic at Bonn in September, 1949, introduced new forces in German politics and placed political influence in new hands. It shifted West Germany's center of political gravity to the Rhine-Ruhr area. Even more significant, it created a new set of policymakers and drew into the political arena groups which had heretofore been dormant. The currency reform and resulting economic improvements revived property interests. Relaxation of Military Government political controls encouraged passive and active supporters of Hitler's Reich to re-enter politics. Former Nazis and militarists now came forth with views hitherto prohibited under Military Government restrictions. They argued that Hitler's Germany had opposed the Bolshevization of the world and that the Allied victory over Germany had weakened the Western positions. Founding the *Deutsche Reichspartie* and other associations such as the *Brüderschaft,* they contended that Germany's role should be that of a "third force" to maneuver between East and West.[4] Thus by 1949 most Germans were aware that Germany was no longer a mere pawn in the hands of the occupation powers. Both these groups and the private property interests, revived by the currency reform, were hostile to the *Land* administrations as then constituted. Since the C.D.U. won the Bundestag elections of 1949, its Right-wing reaped the benefits of the change. Leaders of Dr. Adenauer's coalition cabinet were against all cooperation with the Social Democratic party (S.P.D.), which was now excluded from all participation in the formulation of foreign policy. Although Social Democrats had been outstanding in the work of reconstruction after the Nazi

61

holocaust in 1945, they were now relegated to the role of a national opposition party.

C.D.U.—Composition, Leaders and Tactics

The Christian Democratic Union (C.D.U.) was founded in 1945 and quickly developed into a genuine "people's party" on a very broad basis. For the first time in German history a party attracted strong Catholic and Protestant elements, without being clerical.[5] One significant result of the establishment of the Bonn Government was to accelerate the organization of the C.D.U., heretofore unable to agree on a uniform platform for either domestic or foreign affairs.

The C.D.U.-C.S.U. is essentially a coalition of non-Socialist politicians of various backgrounds: former Center leaders, representatives of the Protestant religious camp, old Liberals of various leanings—more to the Left than the Right, farmers and urban middle class and trade union elements. In domestic politics, the party represents a double compromise between Catholics and Protestants and between economic conservatism and trade union interests of co-determination and social welfare.

Since 1949, the C.D.U.-C.S.U. has been the mainstay of the Federal Government and is represented in the governments of seven of the ten *Länder*. In five Länder the Minister-President belonged to the C.D.U.: namely Schleswig-Holstein, the Saar, Hamburg and Baden-Württemberg. The Rhineland is represented by ex-Chancellor Konrad Adenauer and other high officials. "While South Germany retains formal political leadership, the Rhineland holds the administrative and bureaucratic controls." [6] Men from the Rhineland and South Germany occupy most key cabinet positions in the West German Government: Foreign Affairs, Economics, Finance and Defense. Baden-Württemberg deputies dominate the leadership in the Bundestag, holding important assignments on committees, particularly the Foreign Affairs Committee. By contrast North Germans participate relatively little in parliamentary or cabinet affairs.

Although the C.D.U. now derives more support from conservative forces and former Nazis than from trade unions, it is democratically elected and criticized constantly by the S.P.D. opposition, at times by the Free Democrats and even by members of its own coalition. At the Party Congress of the C.D.U. (April 27-29, 1956) Professor Ferdinand Ferdensberg (C.D.U. deputy) criticized Adenauer's foreign policy and called for more friendly relations with the Soviet Union. Moreover, the Chairman of the Bundestag Foreign Affairs Committee, Kurt Kiesinger, and the Bundestag President, Eugen Gerstenmaier (both C.D.U. deputies) have been continually pressing for a larger role in the formulation of West German foreign policy, but to no avail. In the main, the Chancellor has merely used them to advance policies already enunciated, insisting that in the first formative years of the Federal Republic, he must have full control of foreign policy.

For a time Heinrich von Brentano had the confidence of the press, the Foreign Affairs Committee and of the S.P.D. opposition with his frankness and conciliation toward the opposition. These characteristics were noted, however, when the Chancellor was either sick or on vacation. As Minister of Foreign Affairs, Brentano moved cautiously to avoid antagonizing the Chancellor and to improve the harmony and integration of the Foreign Office, with its 5,000 officials. No doubt professional diplomats were glad to see a career diplomat supervising the Foreign Office in the Cabinet and in the Government.

It is difficult to define the ideologies, groups and personalities which influenced Dr. Adenauer, who kept his own counsel. His role in policy determination is explained partly by his mastery of party politics and partly by his personality, at first artificially built up abroad and later by domestic public relations. Most important was his role as head of the government and head of the strongest party, the C.D.U. This meant control over personnel in the various ministries, the chiefs of which were in the C.D.U., were Catholic, and came from the Ruhr. For fourteen years German public opinion was trained to have such confidence in the Chancellor that it assumed that *der Alte* could do no wrong. Moreover, natives of the West German *Länder* were in full control of various government branches as well as the institutions which help frame public opinion.

Historic circumstances have largely determined the significant role of the Chancellor, who had not been plagued by the large Communist minorities nor by the extreme Right-wing nationalists, militarists and armed groups, who eventually ruined the Weimar Republic. Social Democratic opponents of his foreign policy are staunch supporters of German democratic institutions. Even their opposition to rearmament increased his bargaining power with the West. Another powerful factor contributing to the success of Adenauer's foreign policy was East-West cold war tensions, dominated by the conflict between the United States and the Soviet Union over the future of Germany. In the future German foreign policy may not be so dependent upon the United States.

S.P.D.—Composition, Leaders and Principles

The Social Democratic Party (S.P.D.) is the oldest of the existing German parties and the strongest opponent of the C.D.U., although it also played an important role in founding the Federal Republic and in drafting its constitution. The S.P.D., too, had to be refounded in 1945 after 12 years of Nazi rule. Although a minority party, it has a powerful political machine, with some 600,000 dues-paying members, as compared with 250,-000 in the C.D.U. Composed of white collar workers, manual laborers, civil servants, pensioners and some intellectuals, it has far less sociological range than the C.D.U. The S.P.D. is represented in six of the ten West German *Länder* (states). In four of them the Minister-President was or has been a Social Democrat, namely, North Rhine-Westphalia, Hesse, Bavaria and Bremen. In the West Berlin municipal elections of 1958, Mayor Brandt's Social Democratic Party won an absolute majority of seats in the lower house, despite Adenauer's urgent appeals for a C.D.U. majority.

As to campaign methods, the S.P.D. makes full use of films, slides, tape recordings and sound trucks as well as the spoken word. Stressing the importance of a well-considered platform, clarifying issues, as against mudslinging and wild political insinuations, the S.P.D. Press and Publicity Chief, Fritz Heine, stated that "we have been fighting Communists in the Federal Republic for over ten years as well as Communists in East Germany. As a result, in the Federal elections of 1957 only 2.2 per cent of the voters still voted Communist."[7] The dynamic, eloquent leader of the S.P.D. from 1945 to 1952 was Dr. Kurt Schumacher, who became a national figure, admired by his opponents for his intelligence and feared by his friends for his refusal to compromise.

Erich Ollenhauer succeeded Schumacher, who died in 1952, but Ollenhauer lacked his colorful personality and dynamic leadership, although he was more conciliatory. During the Hitler regime, he migrated to Prague, to Paris and finally to London, where he came under the influence of Clement Attlee and the British Labor Party. In the Bundestag debates, Ollenhauer often referred to his party as the loyal opposition.

Young Social Democrats in Berlin criticized the bureaucratic dogmatism of the party functionaries (paid secretaries) who constituted a ruling hierarchy in this highly centralized party. They wanted Ollenhauer to continue as chairman of the party secretariat, but preferred Professor Carlo Schmid (Bundestag Vice President) as chairman of the parliamentary fraction and Wilhelm Kaisen of Bremen or Willy Brandt of Berlin as chairman of the annual party congresses, which represent the party rank and file. However, Ollenhauer had the solid backing of the S.P.D. majority.

Inspired by C.D.U. defeats in Bavaria in 1954 and in North Rhine-Westphalia in 1956, the S.P.D. chairman prepared a trenchant critique of West German foreign policy for the Bulletin of the Asian Socialist Conference. His thesis was that the central issue of world disarmament linked together the interests of European Socialists, all desiring controlled disarmament. In the foreign policy debates in the Bundestag in June, 1956, the S.P.D. leadership called for a reorientation of foreign policy by the Adenauer Government, demanding: four-power negotiations for a European Security System; normal diplomatic and trade relations with Russia, China and the nations of Eastern Europe; and maximum relations between the populations of the Soviet Zone and West Germany.

This action by the Bundestag fraction of the S.P.D. was approved at the biennial Party Congress in Munich, July 4-14, 1956. Contending that the West German Federal Republic should be free from thinking in terms of bloc policy, a psychosis induced by the Adenauer Government, the Party Congress called for constructive cooperation among all political groups sincerely interested in international understanding, the rights of democracy and social justice. Recognizing the growing importance of Asia as a factor in international politics, the S.P.D. Congress reaffirmed its unqualified adherence to the right of self-determination.

In 1956 German public opinion polls ran in favor of the S.P.D. by 46 per cent as against 36 per cent for the C.D.U. The Hungarian uprising and the Suez Crisis in October, 1956, enabled the Social Democrats to argue that military strength in these two cases had failed to preserve peace and stability as claimed. However, the German press as a whole took no account of this switch in public opinion from the C.D.U. Consequently, there was no band wagon effect to aid the S.P.D. The ruthless suppression of the Hungarian revolt by Russian tanks and the Anglo-French retreat from Suez enabled Adenauer to claim that Germany was the number three World Power. Thereafter, public opinion polls showed a switch back to Adenauer, with the C.D.U. again polling 46 per cent and the S.P.D., 36 per cent. The turn of the year 1956 witnessed the turn of the tide, according to the *Institut für Democsopie*.

For a number of years the Social Democrats have been proposing a collective security system for Europe. The idea made its way gradually until now it can be found in various forms in Soviet and Western proposals. Among these various forms could be listed the Rapacki Plan, presented by the Polish Foreign Minister, Free Democratic proposals made in the Bundestag; and the Kennan Plan, presented over the British Broadcasting System in 1957. However, political parties in West Germany are allowed a small margin of choice, with major decisions of foreign policy still the prerogative of the Western Powers. In contrast, the Weimar Republic was able to determine economic policies, the system of government through the national constituent assembly, elected in 1919, and questions of foreign policy. "The as yet undigested past, the partial loss of political autonomy and the precariousness of the present European balance of power foster reserve and non-committal attitudes."[8]

F.D.P.—Composition, Leaders, Strategy

Founded in 1945 to attract both liberal and conservative forces, the Free Democratic Party (F.D.P.) has always been the third largest party, although the tide of world public opinion went against it after World War II.[9] The F.D.P. is the heir of the old German liberal parties; National Liberals, Progressives, Weimar Democrats and the People's Party of Stresemann. Standing for religious, political and economic freedom, it is also the heir of many splits and divisions among liberals. Free Democrats derive more sociological support from Protestant urban middle classes: professions, trades, small and medium-sized industries. They have no influence with manual workers and rural voters.

The strategy of the F.D.P. makes it stronger than its small percentage of votes would seem to indicate. It is a coalition partner in most *Land* governments: with the C.D.U. in Schleswig-Holstein, Lower Saxony and Rhineland-Palatinate; with the S.P.D. in Bavaria and North Rhine-Westphalia in 1956. A center party, it may align with either the Right or Left. From 1949 to 1953, the F.D.P. held the balance of power between the Government and the S.P.D. opposition; from 1949 it was a member of the Adenauer Government coalition. Because of the scathing attacks of the S.P.D. on his foreign policy, Dr. Adenauer made concessions to the F.D.P., aiding its moderate and extreme Right-wing in the *Länder* of Schleswig-Holstein, Lower Saxony and North Rhine-Westphalia to pursue a policy of economic conservatism and strong nationalism. Critics of the Right-wing extremists noted their efforts to attract ex-Nazis to expand the F.D.P. after the Neo-Nazi Socialist Reichs Party (S.R.P.) was outlawed in 1952. It was hoped that the F.D.P. would be unified by Dr. Thomas Dehler, Party Chairman and Minister of Justice in the Adenauer Cabinet from 1953 to 1956. Dehler combined legal acumen with vigorous intellectual and oratorical talents, liberal traditions and strong traits of nationalism. However, he seemed to lack the maturity and mellowness of a seasoned politician and was later dropped from the cabinet.

In September, 1954, the solid front of the Adenauer coalition on foreign policy was weakened when Dehler dissociated his party from Adenauer's tactics after the defeat of the European Defense Community (E.D.C.) in the French National Assembly. In a radio interview Dehler implied that in criticizing Mendès-France, the Chancellor was trying to rally the Popular Republicans in France against the French Premier, whom Adenauer claimed was not backed by a majority of the French people. Dehler emphasized that Free Democrats did not condone aggressive political tactics against the French, that Communist votes were not decisive and that the defeat of the treaty was due to national opposition, for which all those involved were responsible, including Germans. The F.D.P. chairman ranged the whole field of foreign affairs and showed that he was in almost complete disagreement with Dr. Adenauer. Dehler even criticized the Chancellor for not having invited the opposition leader, Erich Ollenhauer, to participate in the Buehler-Hohe Conference on foreign policy.[10]

In February, 1956, the Free Democratic Party took the major step of withdrawing from the Adenauer coalition and until 1961 it played an independent role, but in foreign policy it has moved closer to the position taken by the Social Democratic Party. Fear of an unduly powerful C.D.U. is stronger in the Rhine-Ruhr, where conservative financial interests are aware of elements in the C.D.U. fraction that after Adenauer's death might align with the S.P.D. The conservative wing of the F.D.P. in the Rhine-Ruhr, Lower Saxony and Schleswig-Holstein is balanced by a Left-wing group of old-style German liberals, led by Reinhold Maier, which is strong in Hamburg and southwest Germany. "Even though Maier was Chairman of the F.D.P., the official party position reflects the middle-of-the-road point of view."[11]

The views of German business are reflected in those F.D.P. deputies who mistrust Adenauer's pro-Western orientation and consider themselves the guardians of German national interests. They insist that those interests should not be forfeited by sacrificing to the West and burning bridges to the East. During the great parliamentary debate on foreign policy in April, 1957, the F.D.P. chairman, Reinhold Maier, and his deputy and military expert, Dr. Mende, argued long and hard for mutual withdrawal of troops by the Allies from West Germany and by the Soviet Union from its Zone. A year later, in January, 1958, Dr. Mende berated the Adenauer Government for its failure to give serious consideration to any of the various plans for disengagement, as proposed by Anthony Eden, the Polish Foreign Minister, Rapacki, and by George Kennan. He then pointed to the offer of Soviet Minister President Bulganin in a note of December, 1957, to reduce Russian troops in Germany or withdraw them completely in proportion to withdrawals by the NATO Powers —France, Great Britain and the United States. "It is the right and duty of American policy and strategy to think first of America . . . of British and French policy and strategy to think first of their countries. It is our duty, Mr. Chancellor, to think first of the unification of Germany."[12]

F.D.P. strategy in the parliamentary elections of 1957 was to make no commitments in order to be in position to align with either the C.D.U. or S.P.D. later. Immediately after these elections, F.D.P. Deputy Weyer told Adenauer "We are with the Social Democrats in the view that in Germany a three-party system is firmly established." Accusing the ruling majority of aiming to dominate foreign policy without consideration of the coalition parties, he also concluded that "We stand by our step in early 1956 in withdrawing from the Government Coalition."[13]

German Party—Composition, Leaders, Policies

The conservative German Party or Deutsche Partei (D.P.) has existed in Germany for over 80 years—founded in 1867 as a German-Hanoverian Party to protest Bismarck's *Machtpolitik* in his seizure of Schleswig-Holstein. Essentially a small federalist, states rights party, it polled only 4.5 per cent of the vote in the parliamentary elections of 1957 through the help of electoral alliances with the C.D.U. in Lower Saxony and Schleswig-Holstein. Under the leadership of Heinrich Hollwege, its chairman and Minister-President of Lower Saxony, it expanded in northern Germany.

The German Party proved to be the most loyal of all coalition parties in the Adenauer Government, following the line of the C.D.U. on the reunification of Germany in peace and freedom and at the same time advocating strong ties with the Western Powers. In contrast to the C.D.U., however, the D.P. opposes parochial schools, is less interested in large-scale social problems of modern industrial life and is suspicious of the collectivism of the C.D.U. and its trade union wing. Standing to the right of the C.D.U., the German Party emphasizes support for agriculture and middle class traditions.

Like the F.D.P., the German Party welcomes ex-Nazis and even protested the denazification procedure of the Allied Military Government. It flies the old imperial colors (red, white and black) and favors using all three verses of "Deutschland Uber Alles" as acceptable for the national anthem. This party, though small, is worth following. It could merge with the C.D.U. or, if events justify it, could form the nucleus of a new Right-Wing party. Prior to the parliamentary elections of 1961, the D.P. was absorbed by the C.D.U., although local remnants joined with the refugees to form the All-German Party (*Gesamtdeutsche Partei*) which failed to clear the 5-percent hurdle in 1961.

NOTE: Chapter 2 consists of an article published by the author in *Current History,* Vol. 38, No. 221 (January, 1960), 30-36 republished here by permission.

1. James P. Warburg, *Germany: Key to Peace* (Harvard Un. Press, 1953), pp. 1-7. Arguing that the world crisis following World War II began in Europe, this writer contends that "our misunderstanding and mishandling of the postwar crisis in Europe . . . were largely responsible . . . for failures to act in Asia, Africa, the Middle East and Latin America."
2. Dolf Sternberger, "Parties and Party Systems in Postwar Germany," in *Annals of American Academy of Political and Social Science* (Nov., 1948, Vol. 260, p. 10).
3. See Max Weber, *Wirtschaft und Gesellschaft,* pp. 167ff.
4. Samuel L. Wahrhaftig, "The Development of German Foreign Policy Institutions," in Hans Speier and W. Phillips Davidson, editors, *West German Leadership and Foreign Policy* (White Plains, N.Y., Row, Peterson and Co., 1957).
5. See Kassel Declaration of the Evangelical Labor Circle of C.D.U./C.S.U. (22 June, 1957). C.S.U. stands for Christian Social Union, the Bavarian counterpart of the C.D.U.
6. Samuel L. Wahrhaftig, *op. cit.,* p. 49.
7. *News from Germany* (April, 1957), Vol. 11, No. 4, pp. 3-4.
8. Otto Kircheimer, "The Political Scene in West Germany," in *World Politics: Quarterly Journal of International Relations* (April, 1957), Vol. IX, No. 3, pp. 433-444. See George Kennan, "Disengagement Revisited," in *Foreign Affairs* (January, 1959), Vol. 37, No. 2, pp. 187 ff.
9. In 1949, the F.D.P. polled about 12% of the votes, 10% in 1953 and 8% in 1957.
10. *New York Times* (7 September, 1954), Sec. C, p. 9.
11. Gabriel A. Almond, "The Politics of German Business," in Speier and Davidson, *op. cit.*
12. *Das Parlament* 8, 4 (29 January, 1958), p. 3.
13. "Wir sind mit des Sozialdemokraten der Auffassung, das sich in Deutschland und sie Duer ein Dreiparteiensystem festigen wird." *Das Parlament* 8 Jahrgang, No. 34 (1957), pp. 5-7.

Chapter 3

INTERNATIONAL OPINION ON THE BERLIN
PROBLEM IN EARLY AUGUST

In a TV address on Monday, 7 August 1961, beamed to both East and West, Premier Khrushchev proposed a Berlin Conference, yet offered nothing specific as a basis of negotiations to satisfy either President Kennedy or the Foreign Ministers of the Western Big Three—the U.S.A., Britain and France. Two days later, however, reaction of Congressmen in Washington was somewhat mixed—some finding the speech conciliatory, others threatening or ambiguously phrased to convey Soviet double talk. Whereas Senator Humphrey found the speech indicated an intensified Communist propaganda campaign, filled with warlike threats, Senator Fulbright found some of the statements conciliatory. The Chairman of the Senate Foreign Relations Committee, despite certain reservations, noted that the Soviet Premier did not intend to infringe upon Western rights in Berlin or rights of access and that he ruled out another Berlin Blockade. On the other hand, President Kennedy had previously indicated our difficult experience with Soviet double talk, which gave a special connotation to such terms as "freedom," "democracy" and "free elections"—terms which meant opposite things to the Kremlin and people in the United States. With prophetic vision, Senator Hickenlooper (Republican) of Iowa, stated: "They (Soviets) will interpret 'access' as meaning 'access' to West Berlin and not 'free access,' and so I am not encouraged at all by the statement which follows the consistent pattern of Russian double talk."[1]

71

A somewhat different approach to the Khrushchev speech was taken by the London papers, most of which, despite differences of interpretation, stressed the urgent need for negotiations to relieve the growing international tension. In this situation the *Guardian* (Manchester) found the failure of the West to propose negotiations as soon as possible lamentable.[2] The *Times* (London) which, though independent, often mirrors the views of the British Foreign Office, noted striking parallels between the speeches of President Kennedy on 25 July, 1961, and of Premier Khrushchev on 7 August in that both used language as hard as any heard since the end of the Second World War—but at the same time both stressed the possibility of negotiations.[3] Echoing Premier Khrushchev's warning against a "war psychosis," Lord Beaverbrook's *Daily Express* lamented the fact that the French and German Governments were far less ready to negotiate than were the U.S.A. and Britain. The conservative *Daily Mail,* however, advised against retreating from the demands of Moscow, lest this prove fatal, and reiterated the thesis of Dr. Adenauer of negotiation from a position of strength. In contrast, the *Daily Herald,* expressing the Labour viewpoint, believed that an agreement could be negotiated with Premier Khrushchev, despite his fresh military warnings, if only President Kennedy were prepared to overrule Chancellor Adenauer.[4]

Somewhat Machiavellian was the Khrushchev speech of 7 August, with its contrasting appeals for Big Power negotiations on the basis of reason and threats to call up additional army reserves to strengthen contingents on the Soviet Union's western frontiers.

Appealing to the neutral nations for calmness, reason and peaceful coexistence, the Soviet Premier warned against allowing Berlin to become another Sarajevo. The speech, which was broadcast all over the Soviet Union as well as to Britain and France, was Machiavellian in that it not only alerted the Soviet people but attempted to project the blame for the Berlin crisis upon the Western Powers should East-West negotiations fail. As if to beg the question, Khrushchev asserted that only a peace treaty such as he proposed with East Germany could checkmate "West German militarism and revanchism," which he accused Western capitalism of promoting. The Soviet Premier made light of the argument of self-determination for Germans, advanced by

72

countries involved in the shedding of blood in Algeria, Tunisia, Angola, the Congo and Suez. His charges were not limited to Britain, France, Belgium and Portugal. He charged the United States with responsibility for attacks on Cuba and Guatemala. Still Machiavellian was the Soviet Premier's tactic of listing alleged Western offenses, while at the same time suppressing the role played by the U.S.S.R. in creating crises not only in Berlin but in various parts of Central Europe, Africa and the Middle East.[5]

By 10 August, it was known that the East German *Volkskammer* (Parliament) was to meet to discuss a German peace treaty, and Walter Ulbricht, Chairman of the State Council of the so-called German Democratic Republic (DDR) of the East Zone, was to report on his recent conference in Moscow. According to information from Moscow and East Berlin, there were sharp differences between Khrushchev and Ulbricht over the date for a separate Moscow-East Berlin peace treaty, on which countries should attend the peace conference and over control of access routes to West Berlin after the conclusion of a separate peace treaty. Ulbricht won the last point, that only the East-bloc nations should take part in the peace conference. But Khrushchev's will prevailed on the more important points: that the date of the peace treaty would be moved to the end of the year 1961, instead of immediately after the German Bundestag elections, as Ulbricht preferred, and that even after the treaty, access routes to West Berlin would remain open.[6] Several German newspapers by 11 August predicted drastic action by the *Volkskammer* to check the mass exodus of refugees. The Soviet Zone news agency, ADN, reported that the *Volkskammer* was swamped with letters clamoring for strong measures against so-called "slave-traders and border-crossers."[7] Other reports from the Russian Zone, however, indicated that East Germans asking for elections on the issue of reunification, were being told that the West German elections of 17 September would be models of "terror elections," inspired by "NATO militarism," a clerical and fascist state organization, which permits neither democracy nor free elections."[8]

The number of refugees was increasing with every statement from Moscow. Following Khrushchev's speech of 10 August, the number of refugees reporting at Marienfelde in West Berlin was the largest in any 24-hour period since 1953 following the uprising of 17 June. The number at the time of the Khrushchev speech was 2,021 and only a few hours later it had risen to 2,605. Between 1 August and 8 August, inclusive, there were 10,979 refugees. Since over 60 per cent of the refugees were young and middle-aged men, the working force was so depleted that the exodus of another 200,000 workers from the DDR would have wrecked its entire economy.[9] Between 1949 and 1961, inclusive, a total of 2,600,000 refugees fled to 11 cities of the Federal Republic, namely, to Lübeck, Osnabrück, Dortmund, Aachen, Bonn, Darmstadt, Saarbrücken, Heidelberg, Karlsruhe, Nürnberg, and Augsburg. They came to the Federal Republic because they were in danger, body and soul, or because they objected to the lack of freedom. The Communist dictatorship of Ulbricht denies 16 million East Germans the right of self-determination, free, secret elections; while 10,000 political prisoners are confined to jails, penitentiaries or prison work camps. The state-security service, with 13,000 secret police, watches over all areas of public and private life in a regime which denies men the right to strike and mitigates against private ownership and free enterprise with industry and trade for the most part "nationalized" or "socialized." There have been no independent farmers since the spring of 1960; all have been forced to join so-called "agricultural production cooperatives" (LFP).[10]

Agriculture in the Soviet Zone has been broadly assimilated to the Soviet agricultural pattern. First came a so-called "land reform" in the fall of 1945, whereby farms of more than 247 acres were expropriated without compensation. These expropriated lands, comprising about 12,000 square miles (equal to the size of Belgium), were distributed to over 5,000,000 "land recipients" or given over to state ownership. In the summer of 1952, the collectivization of agriculture began on the model of the Soviet Russian *kolkhoze*, with the first "agricultural production cooperatives" (LFP). The three types of LFP differ mainly in the degree of collectivization; in Type III, the entire property (land, buildings, livestock and machinery) is collectivized, and the farmer-proprietor continues to work only as a paid farmhand.[11] Up to the turn of the year 1959/1960, about half the total of agriculturally-useful land was still privately owned by farmers. By the spring of 1960, however, the complete collectivization of the farmers was carried through with every possible means of propaganda, intimidation and terror, as well as a wide variety of economic reprisals.[12] Because of these structural changes and as a result of the Communist-controlled economy, agricultural production in the Soviet Zone has not yet reached the production peaks of pre-war years.

The Communist *Freie Deutsche Jugend* (Free German Youth) FDJ is the only youth organization, which makes totalitarian demands on all youth. Political science, natural science and art are all subordinated to the goals of Marxism-Leninism. Political science is not even offered at Humboldt University (formerly the University of Berlin); instead students are offered the Principles of Marxism and Leninism. The regime constantly pursues its atheistic and anti-church propaganda. Among many examples of this in the German press, the most outstanding incident in 1961 was the interference with the Evangelical Church Congress in Berlin and the refusal of the regime to permit the union of the Eastern and Western dioceses of the Protestant and Catholic Churches in Germany or even the travel of high dignitaries of the Catholic and Protestant Churches between East and West Berlin.[13]

East Germans expected that once a peace treaty was signed between the U.S.S.R. and the Zone Regime of East Germany, there would no longer be any chance of escaping westward. By June, 1961, Khrushchev had apparently decided to bring the matter to a head in the fall, come what might. It was obvious that once this decision was made and proclaimed the flood of refugees would increase until a peace treaty was signed. At his press conference on 10 August, President Kennedy answered a question on the explosive danger of the steady stream of refugees from the Soviet Regime by taking the stand that the United States would not encourage and not discourage the flow of refugees. As in the latter part of his radio address of 25 July, 1961, the President held forth every hope for negotiations both of disarmament issues and the Berlin question with the Soviets, despite increasing difficulties.[14] On the whole the President displayed a calm and composed attitude, which already reflected his desire to await clarification of Soviet plans before expressing his own ideas, to place more emphasis on diplomatic rather than military methods.[15]

Many German papers played up the foreign policy discussion of the Berlin Crisis in Caddnabbia, Italy, between Adenauer, Rusk, von Brentano and Ambassador Dowling. Afterwards Secretary Rusk told journalists that the Soviet Zone regime was primarily responsible for the current crisis. He added that Khrushchev was under pressure after the obvious failure of the Zone Government to retain the confidence of the people.[16] It was deplorable that the failure of the Soviet Zonal Government had become a problem for Khrushchev and for the West as well. Rusk indicated that Khrushchev should countermand his proposal for a peace treaty this year in order to allow time for preparations to discuss not only the Berlin and German problem, but the whole problem of peace in Central Europe.[17]

In conversations with the Italian Premier, Fanfani, and his Foreign Minister, according to reports of the *Frankfurter Allgemeine* (right-center), Dr. Adenauer learned that the first contacts for East-West negotiations should be made between the West German elections and the Moscow Communist Party Congress at the end of September. According to Fanfani, Khrushchev, whose primary interest seemed to be in a recognition of Germany's eastern border, had shown great interest in recent statements of Senators Mansfield and Fulbright.[18]

In general, the left-center German papers tended to react in a somewhat pessimistic manner to the international situation as of 10 August; whereas *Der Mittag* (right-center) indicated more satisfaction with the trend of events. The latter noted, with satisfaction, that both Kennedy and Khrushchev had indicated that the Berlin crisis must in no case lead to war. After two horrible world wars, followed by a more or less permanent cold war, none of the parties concerned wanted a hot war—not even in case of an uprising in the Zone.[19] On the other hand, the reporter of the pro-SPD *Neue Rhein Zeitung* indicated that the readiness of President Kennedy for negotiations in itself constituted a Western concession in that there was no reason for the West to talk with the Soviets on the continued presence of the West in Berlin.[20] The left-of-center *Frankfurter Rundschau* pointed out that, though intended for the defense of the Federal Republic, the *Bundeswehr* was in no position to defend Berlin from Soviet threats of massive destruction. Even from the standpoint of psychological defense, the *Bundeswehr,* according to this paper, was in no better position than the Communist officers of the People's Army, which were unable to check the flow of refugees out of Berlin. Arguing that the Federal Government had failed to initiate a constructive reunification policy, rearmament had rendered Germany no useful purpose.[21] *Der Mittag* echoed the warnings of the *New York Times* against a repetition of the 17 June uprising, which could only result in useless bloodshed. However, this right-center paper took courage from the fact that the U.S.S.R. would not be likely to repeat the incident of Hungary in 1956, lest it lose prestige with the neutral nations.[22]

With increasing threats of atomic annihilation against any attempts to interfere with his own plans for Germany and Berlin, Premier Khrushchev proceeded to test the will of the West and to force negotiations at a time unfavorable to the West. Thus, the Berlin Crisis came to affect more than just Germany. The fate of the world was at stake. Lenin always said that "for Communist purposes he who holds Berlin holds Germany, and he who holds Germany holds Europe."[23] As Lenin's successor, Khrushchev felt impelled to back the wretched East German regime with tanks and troops even more than Hungary in 1956, if only to gain some degree of recognition for the East German Regime.

A Practical Policy

In spite of Marxist-Leninist ideology, the Soviets have often demonstrated that in the struggle for power, they can be very realistic and pragmatic. So on 13 August, 1961, the Government of the U.S.S.R., with the full understanding and complete support of the States in the Warsaw Treaty Organization, proposed that the nations which took part in the war against Hitlerite Germany conclude a peace treaty with both German States.[24] It was proposed to settle the question of West Berlin by permitting it the status of a demilitarized "free city." "This proposal," it was claimed, "reflected the real situation, which had emerged in the post-war period in Germany and Europe. It was claimed that this was not directed against anyone's interests and had only one purpose, to remove the remains of World War II and to preserve world peace."[25] It was further stated that:

The Governments of the Western Powers heretofore had not been ready to come to an agreeable solution of this problem through negotiations of all interested countries; but had increased preparations for war, created a war hysteria and even resorted to threats of military force.[26]

Earlier in June, 1961, another proposal for a peace conference of all the fifty or more nations at war with Germany was frequently made by the Mayor of Berlin, Willy Brandt, who requested Senator Humphrey to carry his suggestion on to President Kennedy. Of course, Brandt's proposal was predicated on the assumption that such a conference would conclude peace with a united Germany. However, even this proposal of Brandt was rejected by Chancellor Adenauer as impractical.

Back of the timing and careful wording of the text of the Warsaw Declaration, which seems to have been completed early in August, was indicated the unique capacity of the Kremlin for the techniques of propaganda, hate and vituperation.

The Warsaw Declaration of 13 August continued:

> Official representatives of the NATO countries have announced an expansion of their armed forces and plans for military mobilization. In some NATO states, plans were even published for a military invasion of the territory of the DDR.
>
> The aggressive forces make the mistake of using a peace treaty in order to force the militarization of West Germany and to strengthen the increased tempo of the *Bundeswehr,* hereby to arm it with modern weapons. West German revanchists and militarists openly demand that nuclear and rocket weapons be placed at its disposal.
>
> Governments of the Western Powers which in every way encourage the armament of Western Germany have thus repudiated the most important international agreements—which aimed to prevent any revival of German militarism in any form.[27]

The Western Powers were said to have not only failed to encourage the normalization of the situation in West Berlin but made it a vital center for insidious agitation against the German Democratic Republic and other countries of the socialist community. There is no place on earth, it was claimed, where so many espionage and subversive centers of foreign nations were concentrated and where they could work so actively unhampered as in West Berlin. These numerous organizations hired agents in the DDR to undertake various diversions; they engaged spies and other hostile elements for the organization of unrest and sabotage in the U.S.S.R.

"Ruling circles of the Federal Republic and espionage organs of NATO countries," it was charged, "require the present means of intercourse on the borders of West Berlin in order to undermine the economy of the DDR." The Declaration continued:

> Through deceit, bribery, and blackmail, government agencies and military organizations of the West German Federal Republic influence certain unstable persons in the DDR to leave for West Germany. . . .
>
> These deceived persons are compelled to serve with the *Bundeswehr* or recruited into intelligence agencies of different countries to be sent back to the DDR as spies and saboteurs. Recently, this insidious activity proceeding from West Berlin has expanded, especially immediately after the Soviet Union, the DDR and other socialist countries had made proposals for an immediate peace settlement with Germany. . . .
>
> In view of these aggressive efforts by certain reactionary forces in the West German Federal Republic and its NATO allies, the Warsaw Treaty States, therefore, proposed to the East German Government that it should take measures to block the subversive activities in West Berlin in order to protect their security and above all the DDR in the interests of the German people as a whole.[28]

The Governments of the Warsaw Pact States, according to the

Declaration, turned to the *Volkskammer* (Parliament) and to the Government of the DDR with the proposal to establish on the sector border of Berlin effective control measures to check the nefarious activity against the countries of the socialist sphere. It was stated that these control measures must not affect existing provisions for traffic between West Berlin and West Germany. The Declaration recognized that the border measures would cause certain inconveniences for the population, for which the West German Republic was responsible. Heretofore, the West Berlin borders were held open in the hope that the Western Powers would not misuse the good will of the DDR.[29]

Despite the apparent suddenness of the Berlin measures, published Sunday, 13 August, by the Warsaw Pact States, they appear to have been drawn up at their Moscow Meeting of 3 August-5 August 1961. But the complexity of the measures put into effect on Black Sunday, 13 August, showed indications of a long period of preparation. The widespread assumption that they were taken only in response to the mass exodus of refugees—nearly 11,000 between 1 August and 8 August—appears to have little support. It is more likely that the same measures would have followed even if the flow of refugees had been only half as great. Nevertheless, the drain on East Germany's labor supply—half of the refugees were under 25—had become intolerable, to say nothing of political prestige. Thus, the Declaration of the Warsaw Pact States was a general resolution, whose immediate purpose was to stem the flow of refugees.

In summary, Khrushchev's pleas for calm reason and peaceful coexistence to world public opinion on both sides of the Iron Curtain and in neutral nations appeared at best as opportunistic and at the worst as pure chicanery. Moreover, his sharp tactics of alleged Western offenses, while at the same time suppressing the role of the U.S.S.R. in creating crises not only in Berlin, but throughout Central Europe, Africa and the Middle East were purely Machiavellian. Secretary of State Dean Rusk deplored the fact that the failure of the Soviet Zone Governmen had become a problem for both Khrushchev and for the West. Nevertheless, he emphasized the point that the Soviet Premier should not force the Berlin issue in 1961, but allow sufficient time for preparations to discuss not only Berlin and Germany, but the whole problem of peace and security in Central Europe.

The West German press focused on the complex tactics of the

Soviet Bloc in its careful wording of the Warsaw Declaration of 13 August in charging NATO and ruling circles in Bonn with espionage and subversion to undermine the economy of the Soviet Zone by methods of deceit, bribery and blackmail—that is, a propaganda campaign of hate, fear and vituperation. Anglo-American opinion, as exemplified in the United States Senate and the British press, was somewhat mixed. Several Senators had serious misgivings about the sincerity of the Soviet Premier in his proposals for negotiations, although Senator Fulbright, Chairman of the Senate Foreign Relations Committee, appeared to be less pessimistic.

Most of the British press, on the other hand, held forth hopes of negotiations. Whereas the conservative *Daily Mail* reiterated Dr. Adenauer's thesis of negotiations only from a position of strength, both Lord Beaverbrook's *Daily Express* and the pro-labor *Daily Herald* lamented the fact that the French and German Governments were far less ready to negotiate issues at stake between the East and West than were Great Britain and the United States. The *Times* of London, which usually mirrors the views of the British Foreign Office, viewed with alarm the severe language used by both Kennedy and Khrushchev, as hard as any since the end of World War II, although both men did hold forth hope for negotiations.

NOTES TO CHAPTER THREE

1. *Christian Science Monitor,* 9 August, 1961.
2. *Manchester Guardian,* 9 August, 1961.
3. *London Times,* 9 August, 1961.
4. See 9 August, 1961, issues of *Daily Express, Daily Mail,* and *Daily Herald.*
5. *Christian Science Monitor,* 9 August, 1961.
6. *Der Mittag* (Dusseldorf, right-center) 10 August, 1961.
7. *Neue Rhein Zeitung* (Cologne, pro SPD) 10 August, 1961.
8. *Neues Deutschland* (East German Communist) 10 August, 1961.
9. *Christian Science Monitor,* 10 August, 1961.
10. *The Soviet Zone of Germany: The Facts,* published by Federal Ministry for All-German Affairs. Bonn/Berlin. Druckhaus Deutz, November, 1960, page 30. From Sep-

tember, 1949, to September, 1958, over 2,000,000 refugees fled from the Soviet Zone into the Federal Republic and West Berlin, but there was no registration before September, 1949. Therefore, the total number of all refugees since 1945 could be placed at 3.2 millions. *Haupstadt Berlin:* Sonderheft der Zahlen bilder aus Politik, Wirtschaft, Kultur (Berlin, Erich Schmidt Verlag. 1959.) page 20.

11. In a personal interview with a staff member of the Humboldt University in East Berlin, the author was told that a farmer of Type III received a salary and in addition dividends from the land he had turned over to the Collective and also whatever he could realize from two hectares of land he was allowed to retain.

12. *The Soviet Zone of Germany: The Facts.* (1960) page 30.

13. *Hamburger Abendblatt,* 18 August, 1961. *Bild-Zeitung,* 23 August, 1961. *Stuttgarter Zeitung,* 24 August, 1961. The archdioceses of both Catholic and Protestant churches run across the border.

14. *Frankfurter Allgemeine.* 10 August, 1961.

15. *Die Welt,* 10 August, 1961.

16. *Frankfurter Allgemeine,* 10 August, 1961.

17. *Der Mittag* (Duesseldorf, right-center), 10 August, 1961.

18. *Frankfurter Allgemeine,* 10 August, 1961.

19. *Der Mittag,* 10 August, 1961.

20. *Neue Rhein Zeitung,* 10 August, 1961.

21. *Frankfurter Rundschau,* 10 August, 1961.

22. *Der Mittag,* 10 August, 1961.

23. *New York Times,* 15 August, 1961.

24. *Declaration of the Governments of the Warsaw Pact States,* published in *Neues Deutschland* (East Berlin, SED organ), 13 August, 1961.

25. *Ibid.*

26. *Ibid.*

27. *Ibid.*

28. *Ibid.* The rate of escape had doubled in five successive Augusts, making the total number of refugees about 2,700,-000. No country of that size can stand such a bloodletting, nor the failure which it advertises. *Daily Mail,* 14 August, 1961. The London paper pointed out that the way for the authorities to keep their people was not to plug the loopholes in the Iron Curtain but to make life worthwhile.

29. *Ibid.*

PART II.

THE BERLIN WALL, AUGUST 13-20, 1961

Chapter 4

BLACK SUNDAY—AUGUST 13, 1961

If the West expected Khrushchev would be naive enough to make the announcement of a separate treaty with the East German Zone Government and then remain passive while the flood of refugees mounted, the West underestimated its opponents. Khrushchev decided to act first and negotiate later. "By instructing Ulbricht to close the frontier before negotiations began, he turned a position of acute actual weakness into one of potenial diplomatic strength."[1]

Early Sunday morning, between 1:30 and 2 o'clock, the Soviet Zone Regime had a barbed-wire barrier installed along the entire dividing line between the East and West sectors of Berlin with the most decisive measures since the Berlin Blockade of 1948-49 and declared these borders, together with those along the Federal Republic, practically state frontiers. The expected measures of the East Berlin regime for the complete elimination of the stream of refugees into the West were taken at the request and with the entire approval of the Warsaw Pact Powers of the Eastern Bloc. From these measures, interzonal intercourse on land, in the air and on the water between the Federal Republic and West Berlin was explicitly exempted.[2]

Heavily armed units of the *Volksarmee* and *Volkspolizei* by early Sunday morning had enclosed the East Sector of Berlin in a giant concentration camp. No citizen of the Soviet Zone could any longer go to West Berlin. By these measures, the Zone Regime claimed it had put into effect a resolution of the Warsaw Pact States and boasted that "the insidious activity

85

against the countries of the socialist sphere was effectively removed until a 'German peace treaty' is in force."[3]

Western statesmen judged these measures as open violations of the Four-Power status of Berlin. The Lord Mayor of Berlin, Brandt, left his special train on the way from Nürnberg to North Germany, in order to fly back to Berlin, where the Senate, in a special Sunday morning session, advised him of the new situation.

At approximately 4 A.M., Sunday, 13 August, began the tight control of the Sector borders of Berlin by police and military forces of the SED-State. Officials of the State Security Service occupied the streets and house entrances, as police erected barbed-wire barriers on sector borders. Between 5 and 6 A.M. appeared masses of *Volkspolizei* (People's Police), the *Betriebs Kampfgruppen* (Factory Militia) and the para-military Society for Sport and Technology as well as student associations and associations representing industrial management and ownership. By 5:30 A.M., the first units of the East German *Volksarmee* (People's Army) with light panzers were sighted. Later, larger contingents of the *Volksarmee* with heavy weapons emerged from the Soviet Zone. Between 6 and 7 A.M., Red Cross Units of the Zone Regime interspersed themselves among the police. Between Potsdam Platz and the Brandenburg Gate, a stone wall was erected.[4]

When, in the morning, East Berliners awoke, the border control measures of the Soviet Sector were already completed. Also, the borders between West Berlin and the Soviet Zone were hermetically sealed. By the bridge, which led from West Berlin to Potsdam, stood heavily armed forces in addition to the East German patrol boats on the Havel River.

The Ulbricht regime resorted to methods of military force; everything was calculated and the regime took extensive precautions in order to be able to suppress any uprising. The step taken by the Pankow regime constituted a dangerous breach of international agreements, through which a territory with over a million inhabitants, which does not legally belong to the Soviet Bloc, but to the occupied part which was placed under the common administration of the Four Powers, a special zone of Berlin, although located within the Soviet Zone of Germany. Thus, for the first time since the Prague Putsch of 1948, the Soviet Union had practically annexed a piece of European

86

territory. The three Western Powers demanded that this insidious activity be ended, but the Bonn Government was also consulted on the plan because, on 29 December 1960, it entered into an agreement over German interzonal commerce, whose interruption by the Soviets could seriously threaten Berlin's economy.[5]

Drying Up of the Stream of Refugees

On the night of 12/13 August 1961, 16-million Germans in the Soviet Zone and in East Berlin vanished completely behind the Iron Curtain and were cast into the blackest tyranny. Also for Polish and Czechoslovakian citizens as for all other inhabitants of the East European satellite states of the Soviet Bloc, the door to freedom was closed. West Berlin, heretofore, on the basis of its Four-Power status, was for the inhabitants of Eastern Europe as easy to reach as the Western territory of the closely guarded borders of the Soviet Bloc. By the measures of the DDR, the frontier which has divided Europe in half has been completely closed. On Monday, a few more refugees came to Marienfelde; but no more mass exodus from the tyrannical regime of Walter Ulbricht. On the weekend, the refugee stream had swollen to its greatest proportions but now dwindled to a mere trickle.

A Declaration of the Governments of the Member States of the Warsaw Pact was published at the same time as the "Resolution" of the Council of Ministers of the DDR State, although this was described as a statement of the proposals of the Eastern Bloc States rather than the arbitrary action of Pankow. It is quite clear, however, that the decision for the inclusion of East Berlin within the Soviet System was made in Moscow and not in Pankow and that Khrushchev was directly responsible for the aggressive action.[6]

The Situation in Berlin

In the Declaration of the Warsaw Pact States, it was stated that the measures blocking traffic between East Berlin and West Germany were only temporary and that they would continue in force until a peace treaty with Germany was signed.[7] But this was belied by the unilateral action to incorporate East Berlin within the DDR State. This was part of the peace-treaty project of Moscow and now appeared as a partial anticipation of the so-called "free city" status of Berlin. Yet, the *fait accompli* of 13 August, despite the incorporation of East Berlin within the DDR, still did not remove the bone from Khrushchev's throat. The powerful broadcasting station in West Berlin (RIAS), deep within the Soviet Bloc, continued its psychological warfare, giving hope to all lovers of freedom, east of the Iron Curtain. At the same time, the city atoned for its vital function as a door to freedom. Every year nine million inhabitants of the DDR and the Soviet sector of Berlin had sought cultural relaxation from strain in the theatres, cinemas and other cultural institutions of West Berlin.

In political circles of West Berlin, it was feared that the crisis mood in East Germany could become acute. It was in consideration of this that inhabitants of the communities in the five-kilometer barricade zone of the Federal Republic could in no case attempt to force a breakthrough into West Germany. No doubt the Soviets were also aware of the danger of an explosion. The appointment of Marshal Konjev to the Command of the Red Army stationed in East Germany was a clearly-recognized warning to the population that any act of resistance against the Communist order would be useless. The appointment of Konjev and the concentration of the East Germany Army on the frontiers at such a critical time could scarcely be mistaken; they must have feared an uncontrollable situation in case Khrushchev should push the Berlin crisis to a head by an ill-considered policy in the question of the connections between West Berlin and West Germany used by the Western Powers.[8]

West German Press

On Monday, most West German papers focused on the Berlin Crisis with front-page pictures of East German troops and tanks near the new barbed-wire fences, sealing off West Berlin from East Berlin. Conservative, right center, independent and pro-Social Democratic papers carried Berlin headlines:

"All East Berlin a Military Camp."
"Escape Route of Refugees Blocked by Ulbricht's Tanks."
"Refugee Stream Halted by Use of Force."

"West Berlin Sealed Off: Arbitrary Action of Pankow."
"Tanks Before Brandenburg Gate."
"Explosive Situation Follows Ulbricht's Coup."[9]

To protect the barbed-wire fences along the Berlin borders near the Brandenburg Gate, Ulbricht ordered some 200 tanks—but some of the tanks directed their guns not against West Berlin but against the East. By Monday, the strength of military units in East Berlin was comparable to that used to suppress the East German and East Berlin uprisings of 17 June 1953.[10] In bold headlines, *Die Welt* proclaimed that the illegal barriers of the Zone Regime in Berlin had shocked public opinion—not only in Germany but in the Western World. It summarized the actions of the Soviet Zone authorities as follows:

1. Passes were required of all residents of East Berlin and the Soviet Zone to enter West Berlin,
2. 49,000 or more residents of East Berlin or the Soviet Zone who worked in West Berlin were forbidden to continue and ordered to seek employment in East Berlin.
3. Direct traffic on the S-Bahn (elevated train) between the two parts of the city was discontinued.
4. Trains of the Berlin City Railway, which cross Berlin in an East-West direction had to stop at the Friedrich-strasse station in East Berlin. These passengers had to pass through a checkpoint in order to continue their journey.[11]

All these restrictions on travel in Berlin aroused indignation throughout the Free World. Both Western and West German papers characterized the blockade measures as the most flagrant violations of the Four-Power status of Berlin since the Berlin Blockade of 1948-49. The European Advisory Council, created in October, 1943, by Great Britain, the United States and the Soviet Union, agreed upon the joint occupation of Greater Berlin by troops of the Big Three, represented by their Field Commanders. On 26 July 1945, the Big Three Powers and France confirmed an agreement, providing for:

1. Common administration of Berlin.

89

2. Unhampered intercourse of men and supplies in all four sectors of Berlin.
3. Right of Berliners to work in any part of the city.
4. Intercourse of persons and goods between the Soviet Zone and all four sectors.
5. Tolerance of no military action by Germany in any part of the city.

U.S.-Soviet conversations in New York in the spring of 1949 led to a Four-Power agreement for lifting the Berlin Blockade by removing all restrictions on trade and communications between Berlin and the Western zones of Germany and between the Eastern Zone and the Western Zone. This agreement was reaffirmed, strengthened and amplified later by the Council of Foreign Ministers in Paris.[12]

Yet the Soviet Union failed to adhere to its new pledges. The forcible and savage repudiation of the Four-Power Agreement of 1949 became the subject of editorial comment in virtually all Monday papers on 14 August 1961, in Western capitals and in West Germany. The German press stressed the complete bankruptcy of the Ulbricht regime, unable to maintain the loyalty of its own people. The action of the East German Communist, Ulbricht, taken with East Bloc approval was thought to endanger possible East-West negotiations. So highly charged was the Berlin atmosphere that many German papers warned both East and West Berliners against rash actions which could lead to an uprising like that of 17 June, 1953—so ruthlessly suppressed by Russian tanks.[13]

Papers close to the Adenauer Government or pro-CDU emphasized the political impact of the Communist Coup of 13 August upon the East-West power struggle. Opportunities for fair compromise through normal East-West negotiations were all but eliminated. The Soviets would simply consider any embarrassing items non-negotiable.[14] Hence, the only way to assist East Berliners, East Germans and all other enslaved nations was for the Federal German Republic to stand firm beside its Western Allies and prepare for real negotiations.[15] This was the Adenauer thesis of negotiation from a position of strength. Yet the events of 13 August in Berlin only confirmed a widespread belief in Germany that these words promised much more than they produced.

Apart from its primary objective in stemming the flow of refugees, the Eastern Bloc closed the Berlin border partly in an effort to force the West to negotiate a separate peace treaty with the wretched Zone Regime of Walter Ulbricht. Despite the Declaration of the Warsaw Pact States over the "Free City" status of Berlin, it would have been naive for the West to count on such a guarantee. Pretexts could always be found for issuing arbitrary decrees. Although war was not inevitable, there was still the danger of capitulation by degrees. It was certain that Western acceptance of a clear breach of contract by the Communist camp without serious resistance would only invite further threats and extortion.[16] In that case, the panzers would not stop at the Brandenburg Gate, nor at the Elbe, nor at the Rhine. Yet, despite the Soviet coup in Berlin supported by tanks and barbed wire, Ulbricht had to use force against his own people. Could he ignore the indignation of the inmates imprisoned in his vast concentration camp?

The right center and more independent West German papers repeatedly warned against any weakness or softness on the part of Western statesmen toward the East Bloc in the tough game of power politics. Joachim Schweilien of the influential *Frankfurter Allgemeine* argued that the intolerable acts of the bankrupt Ulbricht regime posed a serious challenge to the Western Allies. Were they to accept the illegal measures of 13 August, they would concede the claim to sovereignty of the so-called German Democratic Republic (DDR). Then the DDR could challenge both allied rights in Berlin and on its access routes. Therefore, it followed that the allies should protest the illegal Zonal measures not in Pankow but in Moscow. Paper protests alone would not suffice; the Western Powers must meet the Soviet Bloc challenge with economic and diplomatic weapons.[17]

The West German Press was all but unanimous in its criticism of the Mansfield Plan for a Free Berlin under the United Nations. Johannes Cross argued that statements of Senators Mansfield and Fulbright may have encouraged East Germans to seal off Berlin. He noted that Khrushchev had revealed to the

Italian Premier, Fanfani, that he considered Senators Mansfield and Fulbright (Chairman of the Senate Foreign Relations Committee) as legitimate spokesmen for the U.S. Government.[18] The latter had said in a TV interview that the Soviets could hardly be denied the right to stop flights of refugees through Berlin.

A calm but realistic appraisal of the cautious tactics of the Ulbricht regime led the conservative *Mittag* to regret the greater concern of the United Nations for the development of young nations in Africa and Asia than for the elementary rights of older nations in Europe. Adenauer's search for counter-measures was contrasted with what it termed the "meager" American protest to underline its expectation of stronger Allied counteractions.[19]

The independent papers called for prompt and effective action to prevent any further deterioration of the already critical situation in Berlin. Hans Zehrer, writing in the influential *Die Welt,* warned that the Western powers would have to make decisions to avert even tougher demands from Khrushchev, who "respects neither agreements nor his own timetable." [20] Hans Schwarze urged the West to recognize that the Four-Power Status of Berlin no longer existed. Out of respect for this status, the West had refused to make West Berlin a *de jure* land of the Federal Republic. But after West Berlin was isolated from East Berlin by Soviet action, the Bonn Government should ask the West to reverse its stand. Soviet violation of the Four-Power Agreements by supporting the incorporation of East Berlin into the so-called DDR State called for Western retaliation in kind in the view of the independent papers.[21]

The left-center and pro-SPD press matched the energy of the right-center and pro-CDU press in urging the West to meet the challenge put forth by the entire East Bloc. The *Hannoversche Presse* described the tension with which Western reaction was awaited as almost unbearable. "How will the West react? Is indignation sufficient to make Ulbricht revoke his measures? Or will the West tolerate them? Certainly, NATO must have countermeasures for all possible incidents, including the blocking of sectoral frontiers."[22] The *Süddeutsche Zeitung,* on the other hand, noted that the action in Berlin was intended to increase pressure on the Western Powers to negotiate on a basis and at a time most unfavorable to them. Nevertheless, Ulbricht's actions had greatly narrowed the field left for negotiations between the Kremlin and the Western Allies.[23]

Jens Feddersen, in the *Neue Rhein Zeitung,* cautioned East Berliners against an internal explosion such as the catastrophe of 17 June, 1953. With the bankruptcy of his regime, Ulbricht had risked a European Korea, trusting in the capacity of General Konyev to handle any uprisings. But Ulbricht's actions had challenged not only the three Western Powers, but all NATO countries. The entire East Bloc had challenged the entire West. Paper protests must be backed up by economic weapons or diplomatic action or both to prevent further depredations and brutalities.

In summary, Khrushchev, by instructing Ulbricht to close the frontier before negotiations began, turned a position of acute weakness into one of potential diplomatic strength. The decisive action of the Ulbricht regime, with full support of the nations signatory to the Warsaw Pact, was so sudden and unexpected to most West Germans that the West German press exhibited a muscular reaction. Only the *Süddeutsche Zeitung* saw in the events of 13 August evidence of an overwhelming desire of the Soviets to negotiate the Berlin issue, that is, to force the West to negotiate at a time most unfavorable to the West.

Ulbricht's illegal arbitrary action was a challenge not only to Berlin and Germany, but to the Big Three Western Powers and all NATO countries. The entire Eastern Bloc had challenged the entire West. The Berlin Crisis exhibited the drastic effects of power politics at its worst. The last door to freedom was closed to a million East Berliners and to sixteen million Germans in the Soviet Zone.

By its illegal measures of 13 August, the Zone Regime put into effect the Resolution of the Warsaw Pact States, which was a general resolution, whose primary purpose was to stem the flow of refugees. Prior to 13 August, the West, of course, expected some sort of barrier between East Berlin and the Soviet Zone to stop the mass exodus of its labor force. But barricading the dividing line between the two sectors of Berlin was tantamount to annexation. Blocking of any sort was nothing like the incorporation of East Berlin into the Soviet Zone of occupation. This arbitrary and illegal action was a flagrant violation of the Big Power Treaties of 1944 and 1949, which provided for the special status of Berlin. Not only were Soviet troops involved, but

40,000 troops of the East German *Volksarmee, Volkspolizei* and other military units of the Zone. This action of 13 August, therefore, was only the final step in a development that had continued ever since November, 1958, away from Four-Power Administration of Berlin. Every one of these illegal, unilateral steps was protested by the Western Powers, but to no avail.

NOTES TO CHAPTER FOUR

1. *Sunday Telegraph,* 20 August, 1961.
2. *Hannoverische Allgemeine Zeitung,* 13 August, 1961.
3. *Hannoverische Allgemeine Zeitung,* 13 August, 1961.
4. *Neue Züricher Zeitung,* 14 August, 1961.
5. *Neue Züricher Zeitung,* 14 August, 1961.
6. *Ibid.* Both the Declaration of the Warsaw Pact Countries and the so-called "Resolution" (or decree) of the Ministerial Council of the DDR became front-page news in the Communist papers of the East Zone, on Monday, 14 August. The *Berliner Zeitung,* in black and red headlines, exclaimed: "DEFENSE MEASURES FOR BERLIN: Clear, Decisive and Right." Both the Warsaw Declaration and the Decree of the DDR were printed in full on page 3; while the front-page featured photographs of East Berliners reading the Decree and of individuals and their comments on the subject of "Security for All of Us." On Tuesday, the *Tribune* (Organ of Executive Committee of the East German Trade Unions) featured a cartoon of a fist smashing the "Front City" of Hatred, Sabotage and Militarists. Articles dealt with "Clear Warning to Provcateurs," "Greater Political Activity in Socialist Factories and Obligations for Strengthening the Republic," and "Trade Union Functionaries Praise the Peace Program of the Government."
7. Generally regarded by Western officials as another case of Soviet blackmail. See *Times* (London, independent), 14 August, 1961.
8. *Neue Züricher Zeitung,* 14 August, 1961.
9. See Monday, 14 August, edition of: *Kölnische Rundschau* (CDU); *Deutsche Zeitung* (Cologne, right-center); *General Anzeiger* (Bonn, independent); *Neue Rhein Zeitung* (Cologne, pro-SPD).

10. *General Anzeiger* (Bonn, independent), 14 August, 1961.
11. *Die Welt* (Hamburg, independent), 14 August, 1961.
12. *West Deutsche Allgemeine* (14 August, 1961). See also Department of State publication, *Background: Berlin*—1961, page 12.
13. *West Deutsche Allgemeine,* 14 August, 1961. Cf. *London Daily Mail,* 14 August, 1961.
14. *Frankfurter Neue Presse* (pro-Government), 14 August, 1961.
15. *Kölnische Rundschau* (pro-CDU), 14 August, 1961.
16. *Rheinische Post* (Düsseldorf, pro-CDU), 14 August, 1961.
17. *Frankfurter Allgemeine Zeitung* (right-center), 14 August, 1961.
18. *Deutsche Zeitung* (Cologne, right-center), 14 August, 1961.
19. *Der Mittag* (Düsseldorf, right-center), 14 August, 1961.
20. *Die Welt* (Hamburg, independent), 14 August, 1961.
21. *Stuttgarter Nachrichten* (independent), 14 August, 1961.
22. *Hannoverische Presse* (pro-SPD), 14 August, 1961.
23. *Neue Rhein Zeitung* (Cologne, pro-SPD), 14 August, 1961.

Chapter 5

REACTION OF WEST GERMAN PARTIES TO THE BERLIN WALL

The reaction of German Party leaders to the crucial events of 13 August was prompt and decisive. On Sunday came various declarations of the CDU, SPD and FDP in Bonn, protesting against the Soviet Zone measures. Chancellor Adenauer, in a short radio address, asked Germans to have confidence in the forthcoming countermeasures of the West and to do nothing to worsen the international situation. He publicly accused the East Berlin authorities of having violated Four-Power agreements over Berlin simply because they were not prepared to handle internal difficulties within their own sphere of influence.[1] The West Berlin Senate, in a special session on Sunday morning, characterized the sealing off of the Soviet Zone and the Soviet Sector of Berlin as a shocking injustice. Counterproposals by the Berlin Senate, nevertheless, were not taken for several days.[2] The session was chiefly concerned with immediate problems of public order and communications, confronting West Berlin police.

Mayor Brandt, in a speech before the Berlin House of Representatives, urged the people of the Soviet Zone not to revolt regardless of how strong and justified was their provocation. Human beings could never be held permanently in slavery. The *Land* Committee of the Berlin SPD arranged for a Berlin rally for Monday evening at which Mayor Brandt and Bundestag Representatives Arndt and Mattick were to speak.[3] The Chairman of the Free Democratic Party (FDP), Erich Mende, was in Bremen at an FDP Federal Congress for Refugees on 13 August.

96

He declared that it was vitally important for all German parties as allies of the Federal Republic to form a united front against threats to Berlin to prevent it from becoming a "European Korea." The FDP Chairman refused to recognize the Oder-Neisse Line[4] as a *quid pro quo* for the settlement of the Berlin question. At the same time, he proposed special meetings of the parliamentary committees for All-German Affairs and Foreign Relations on Monday or Tuesday.

In spite of the West German parliamentary elections, there were no great differences in the immediate reactions of major German parties to the crucial events of 13 August. Von Brentano (CDU), Brandt (SPD) and Mende (FDP) all interrupted their electioneering journeys in order to deal promptly with the Berlin Crisis on Sunday. On Monday, Bundestag President Gerstenmaier, SPD Chairman Ollenhauer and FDP Chairman Mende flew to Berlin to gather first-hand information.

The Bonn Government's hand was strengthened in the world political situation in general and the Berlin Crisis in particular by Mende's call for a common stand of the parties.[5]

In their first comments on Sunday, both the Federal Government and the major political parties in the Federal Republic described the Soviet Zone barricade measures in Berlin as a breach of the Four-Power Status of Berlin and a crime against humanity. These events produced intense governmental activity on Sunday both in Berlin and Bonn. Chancellor Adenauer, who in Rhöndorf was informed of the events in Berlin, called Foreign Minister von Brentano and Chairman of the CDU/CSU Bundestag fraction, Dr. Krone, for a discussion of the situation.[6]

Von Brentano had already discussed the most recent Soviet Zone measures with SPD Chairman Ollenhauer and Vice-Chairman Wehner in Frankfurt-am-Main on Sunday forenoon. For the CDU/CSU, Representative Gradl (Vice-Chairman of All-German Affairs Committee) declared that the main objective of the "blockade" was the desire of the Eastern Bloc to sign a separate peace treaty with Pankow and to complete the isolation of West Berlin. Nevertheless, before negotiations had even begun, Pankow had tried to create a *fait accompli*. With this, it dangerously limited the area of negotiations between the Western Powers and the Soviet Union. Moreover, the drastic blockade proved, Gradl believed, that Ulbricht could with normal means no longer check the flow of refugees. Gradl termed the blockade measures playing with fire. Khrushchev and Ulbricht should have known that by cutting off the route of escape for Middle Germans through Berlin, they at the same time removed the safety valve through which, heretofore, the anger and indignation of the Zonal population could find an outlet. The West should, therefore, vigorously protest the violation of the basic rights of freedom of movement for Middle Germans.[7]

Franz Barsig, speaking for the SPD Executive Committee, declared that the blockade was no protective measure, as the East had maintained, but really an act of terror against its own people. Although the Zone authorities could travel on panzers, raise barricades and barbed-wire fences—all these things were only signs of weakness and impotence. The SPD speaker believed the Western Powers no longer held the initiative, but was sure that the Berlin people would accept the recent measures with their proverbial calmness and stability without losing their nerve.[8] FDP Chairman Mende characterized the Berlin measures as "a bitter psychological burden" on 17-million Zone inhabitants who must now live in "a great prison." Mende declared that these measures had unmasked the so-called "DDR" as the successor to the Hitler regime on German soil.[9]

The *Gesamtdeutsche Partei* (GDP), which represented a campaign combination of the former Refugee Bloc (BHE) and the former conservative *Deutsche Partei (DP)*, also sharply criticized the actions of the Zonal authorities. A speaker of the party declared that the illegal transformation of the Berlin borders into state frontiers showed a brutal disregard for treaties as well as the dependence of the Eastern Bloc upon barbed wire. Herbert Schneider (Bremerhaven), one of the two co-chairmen of the GDP, urgently demanded a special session of the Bundestag. It impressed the party as not only necessary, but self-evident that the Bundestag, as the freely-elected Parliament of the free part of Germany, should immediately commit itself to Berlin before world public opinion. It should take a stand for world peace and raise its voice for the whole German people.[10]

The Vice-Chairman of the weakened Refugee Bloc (BHV), Ludwig Rosenberg, described the Zonal measures as "the official concurrence" of a regime which runs counter to the interests of the people—a regime which now officially transforms its land into a huge "concentration camp." Rosenberg indicated that on Monday the GDP would occupy itself with the situation in Berlin.[11]

The first impact of the Berlin Crisis was to bring out the best qualities of prominent West German leaders of all political parties. Bundestag President Gerstenmaier and Dr. Krone, CDU floor leader, interrupted their election campaigns in order to fly to Berlin on Monday. Also, the opposition leaders, SPD Chairman Ollenhauer and FDP Chairman Mende, arrived in Berlin in order to obtain first-hand information.[12] Moreover, leading CDU circles on Sunday considered the possibility, in view of the serious situation in Berlin, of breaking off the election campaign if the other parties should agree. A CDU speaker stated that in the next few days and the following week the presence of all leading politicians in Bonn would be necessary. He concluded, therefore, that the electoral campaign should be limited to the minimum.[13]

Evidence of Social Democratic sympathy with this idea was given by SPD Chairman Ollenhauer, who was willing either to shorten the parliamentary campaign or even break it off entirely. The Social Democratic opposition offered to go even further and form a united front during the international crisis. As precedents for such action, Social Democrats pointed to the National Coalition Government of Ramsay MacDonald in England in 1931 and of efforts toward a bipartisan foreign policy in the United States during and after World War II. In any case, the SPD leadership urgently demanded a special session of the Bundestag and even went so far as to threaten to circulate a petition among the parliamentary deputies, one third of whom could force the call of a special session.

Erich Mende, Chairman of the Free Democratic Party, was just as insistent that a special session be called not only of the entire Bundestag, but also its key committees of Foreign Affairs and All-German Questions. Both in June, 1960, and again in June, 1961, the SPD fraction in parliament gave full support to the foreign policy of the Adenauer Government. Nevertheless, the Chancellor throughout the parliamentary campaign of 1961 repeatedly tried to disparage and discredit this gesture on the part of the SPD as well as its Bad-Godesberg and Hanoverian programs of 1959-60 as insincere.[14]

99

While affirming the need for national defense in a free democratic society, the SPD program called for adapting national defense to the political and geographical position of Germany and the need to ease international tensions and to create conditions for controlled disarmament and reunification of Germany. Yet time and again during the campaign, Adenauer ridiculed these programs of the opposition party as inconsistent with the 12-year record of the SPD, whose members had opposed his entire foreign policy—European Defense Community, West European Union, NATO, the *Bundeswehr* (army) and compulsory military service. However, the Social Democrats argued in defense of their past record and tactics that they were justified not only by the majority opinion of the German people, as indicated in numerous public opinion polls, but also by the terror of atomic weapons. Therefore, the SPD program stated that:

> The Social Democratic Party is striving for the inclusion of the whole of Germany in a European Zone of reduced tensions and of a controlled limitation of arms, a zone to be cleared of foreign troops in the process of German reunification in freedom and in which atomic weapons and other means of mass destruction are neither produced nor stored nor used.
>
> The armed forces must be under the political direction of the government and under the control of Parliament. A relationship of trust must exist between soldiers and democratic forces in the country. The soldier must retain his civic rights and duties. The armed forces must only be used for national defense.[15]

On the other hand, the tense international crisis after 13 August 1961 caused Adenauer and Strauss (CDU/SCU) and Brandt (SPD) to echo the warning of John J. McCloy not to overstress the natural right of self-determination as a means of propaganda to conjure up the danger of an uprising in the Soviet Zone.[16] McCloy was quoted in the West German press to the effect that Khrushchev was "very well aware of the great risk involved"[17] in Berlin. In fact, Western diplomats in Moscow were inclined to view the border measures of sealing off East Berlin as a "good rather than a bad sign" for the reason that it indicated that Premier Khrushchev had chosen the "less dangerous means" for curbing the exodus of refugees from the Soviet Zone.[18]

Although the dangerous Berlin Crisis of 13 August induced a high degree of parallel action by German parties and party leaders, it must be admitted that the Berlin issue was dragged into the political campaign. *Der Mittag* under the banner headline "Fresh Election Campaign Dispute, Adenauer-Brandt" led with Brandt's walking out of a meeting of West Berlin's Senate in protest against remarks about him made by the Federal Chancellor at an election rally in Regensburg.[19]

The Senate's CDU group showed understanding for Brandt's action. A report on Adenauer's Regensburg statement on Monday was handed to Brandt during the meeting, whereupon he left the hall. The meeting was suspended. Adenauer had referred to him as "Brandt alias Frahm."[20] *Die Welt* carried the heat of Adenauer's remarks and Brandt's bitter statement in reply:

> Dr. Adenauer's base attack came at a time of severe crisis for the German people almost three days after the East German authorities had sealed off Berlin's East-West border to westward traffic.
>
> "Chancellor Adenauer thought it right to attack me before a CDU rally in Regensburg in the lowest way, while I was performing my duty here in Berlin. Before the frightful events in Berlin last Sunday, I have expressed my scorn at such bad manners after such a personal attack by the CDU candidate for Chancellor. Today three days after the event, which has brought the German people to its most severe test, I can state my absolute incomprehension at the unworthiness of the attacks by the Federal Chancellor."[21]

Mayor Brandt said he could only leave the German people to judge Dr. Adenauer's behavior. "That Is All We Needed: Open Warfare Between Adenauer and Brandt" were the headlines of a story in *Abendpost*.[22] In the 1961 election campaign the CDU repeatedly referred to Brandt as "Brandt alias Frahm" when attacking him on his activities during his emigration. Until 14

August, Adenauer did not take part in these polemics, but this attack proved most shocking to members of his own CDU Party both in the Berlin Senate and the Bundestag. The incident became a lead story in *Der Mittag, Abendpost, Die Welt* and was reported in most other West German newspapers as well as the Western Press.[23]

On Tuesday, 15 August, virtually all West German papers urged the West to react drastically to the Soviet challenge in Berlin. Disappointment was frequently voiced at the West's failure to react immediately. Several papers criticized West Germany's policy in general and interpreted its present stand as indicating a readiness to put up with Ulbricht's action in Berlin.[24] It was also reported that West German Labor Union leaders had criticized Adenauer for not having considered it necessary to come to Berlin to inform himself of the situation on the spot.[25]

Several papers carried accounts of Adenauer's reason for not going to Berlin, which he revealed Wednesday in Bonn. Addressing a CDU election rally in Bonn on 16 August, Chancellor Adenauer said that what was happening in Berlin these days was merely a "preliminary crisis" and that the "real crisis" was yet to come. He strongly opposed the frequently-expressed view that the Western Allies had not reacted effectively enough to the latest Communist actions in Berlin. Adenauer argued that such views did not render justice to the attitude of the Western Powers, who were preparing themselves for the anticipated big crisis. Again the Chancellor emphasized that he did not believe that the crisis would lead to war.[26]

The independent Swiss paper, *Die Tat,* judged the hard words of Adenauer thus: "It is unfortunate how dull and colorless and lacking in personal contact the short radio declaration of the Federal Chancellor on Berlin sounded."[27]

The Presidium of the SPD at a Tuesday session in Bonn struck back at Adenauer's sharp attack on its chancellor candidate, Brandt. It was emphasized by the SPD that its party presidium had unlimited confidence in Brandt and that all its members called for stronger activity to give Brandt support. The party presidium discussed the Berlin situation for many hours. Finally, the party chairman, Ollenhauer, issued a declaration which characterized the arbitrary action of 13 August as nothing less than the annexation of East Berlin and its incorporation by the Soviet Bloc.[28]

The 16 August declaration of the SPD party presidium concluded:

> "The violent tactics of 13 August are a battle announcement (*Kampfansage*) to the whole German people in East and West. It puts the sincerity of the desire for freedom of the Western World to a severe test."[29]

The Social Democrats emphasized that the German people could only demand solidarity from others if it likewise practiced solidarity and achieved mastery over existing and threatening dangers as a task for the whole nation. "Therefore, it is a national obligation with political and moral responsibility to prove that Germans have the capacity to discuss frankly with one another internal questions and still stand side by side and fight shoulder to shoulder when vital questions of national interest are at stake. Distress and disaster in another part of Germany are distress and disaster for us all." [30]

The independent *New York Times* believed that the Berlin Crisis was only one phase of operations which concerned the fate of the world. "Lenin had for a long time declared that whoever controls Berlin also controls Germany and whoever controls Germany controls Europe."[31] Lenin's successor, therefore, felt himself obliged to support the weak East German regime with tanks and always believed he could do so without any penalty.

It was reported on Wednesday that Dr. Adenauer made his decision to visit Berlin two hours after Mayor Brandt had publicly appealed to Adenauer to set aside party strife and to visit Berlin immediately.[32] The Berlin visit of the Federal Chancellor was planned for the following Tuesday, 22 August, and received unfavorable comments from both opposition parties, especially the Free Democrats.[33] The Free Democrats represented the view that the Chancellor had not only refused to interrupt his election campaign to come to Berlin. They argued that the special session of the Federal Cabinet, which was held when the Ulbricht regime was closing the sector borders of Berlin, should have been held in the old capital rather than in Bonn.

This tactic might have given Adenauer a great psychological advantage and wider publicity for his cause.[34] The Free Democrats hoped that for the sake of democratic appearances, the Chancellor would make a convincing declaration to the Berlin people on why he came to the German capital two days after the American Vice President, Johnson, and over a week after the visit of Bundestag President Gerstenmaier and the floor leaders or fraction chairmen of the three parliamentary parties, Dr. Krone, Ollenhauer and Dr. Mende. Much shorter was the comment of the Social Democrat, Franz Barsig, who speaking for the Board of Directors (*Vorstand*) of the SPD merely said: "Earlier would have been better."[35]

On Sunday evening, 20 August, the Chancellor in a televised broadcast, affirmed that his total strength and effort were applied to the security of Berlin. He warned of a confidence crisis between the German people and the Western Allies. To this, one German paper replied, "There was no confidence crisis between the German people and the Allies, although for a time there was concern over the position of the Allies. But this is over. If there was any confidence crisis, and there still is, it is between the people and the Chancellor."[36]

In all fairness to Dr. Adenauer, it should be emphasized that he was perfectly willing to go to Berlin on the previous Friday to accompany Vice President Johnson, with whom he had had a four-hour conversation in Bonn. The Vice President explained, however, that he was going to Berlin as a representative of the United States Government, one of the Four Occupation Powers, and that the Chancellor's presence in Berlin would be termed a provocation by the Soviets.[37] The question still remains as to why Dr. Adenauer did not decide to go to Berlin earlier in the week. There are several explanations: namely, that the pressure of foreign relations kept him at his desk in Bonn, that his presence might have aroused East Berliners to revolt entailing mass slaughter; and, finally, that he could not choose the same tactics as Brandt, who did, of course, gain great political benefit from his role in the Berlin Crisis.[38]

In reacting to the events of 13 August, party leaders at first attempted to play the game of politics by ear. Moscow's tactic of acting first and offering to negotiate later set up a roadblock not only against fleeing refugees but also against the smoothly-engineered Adenauer election campaign just when it was reaching full flow.[39] Both CDU and opposition candidates had to adjust their strategy to the new situation. Mayor Brandt, the Social Democratic contender, was the quicker of the two. Dr. Adenauer's grievance was understandable. He had great electoral assets. After 1949, Adenauer had made the Chancellor's office what it was, for he was the first and only Chancellor of the Bonn Republic. So he and the West German Federal Republic were to most Germans identical. In contrast to the poverty and disillusionment of 1945, came wealth and comfort—what Germans called the *Wirtschaftswunder*. From a defeated, isolated outcast, the Bonn Democracy found itself firmly allied with the West, a key member of West European Communities (Coal and Steel Authority, Common Market and the Strassburg Assembly) and courted by underdeveloped countries in Africa, Asia and the Near East.

Such positive gains may have meant more to the nineteenth-century Rhineland European, Konrad Adenauer, than frustrating attempts to recover the territories of Brandenburg, Saxony or Silesia, epitomized by the old Prussian capital of Berlin. These gains made a deep impression on the average West German voter. Such a thesis is not untenable if it is recognized that powerful images of the German past mean far more than carefully constructed party programs.[40] The contrasting traditions between East and West Germany are geographical, religious and cultural. Thus, the southern and western parts of Germany, including the Rhineland, were far more influenced by Roman customs, manners and law than the colonial parts of Germany to the east and north. The tragedy of Germany and Central Europe is that there was no unifying force, until the late nineteenth century, to merge these conflicting trends. The Protestant Reformation failed to unite Germany. And contrasts in the sociological structure of the West German Federal Republic *vis-à-vis* the so-called "German Democratic Republic" of the Soviet Zone since 1949 have steadily increased.

Moreover, CDU/CSU politicians, whether Catholic or Protestant, are confronted by stark realities. They need the affiliation and backing of a strong Chancellor. The latter's role in policy determination is explained by his constitutional prerogatives under Article 65 of the Bonn Constitution. This provides that the Chancellor shall determine and be responsible for general policy; that is, set down the fundamental lines of policy. Thus, a strong Chancellor will make full use of his constitutional prerogatives. The ability of a strong Chancellor, like Adenauer, to play this role is determined partly by his personality and partly by his mastery of party politics. Most important was Dr. Adenauer's dual role as head of the government and head of the strongest party, the CDU. "This means control over personnel in the various ministries, the chiefs of which are in the CDU, are Catholic and come from the Ruhr."[41]

It was Dr. Adenauer's misfortune to be confronted with the cost of his achievements in foreign and domestic affairs. The bill, labeled "Berlin," was presented on 13 August just when the slogans of success and security were about to bring him his fourth electoral victory. Whereas in 1919 the Weimar Republic was immediately confronted with the political reality of the Versailles Treaty, the Second German Republic had delayed facing up to the stark political situation. Indeed, the Adenauer record of twelve years of internal and external achievements was put to a severe test. Not only Berlin and Germany were confronted by the Soviet challenge, but the Western Powers and the whole western world, as well as the neutral, uncommitted nations. Here was the most serious challenge of the postwar period. Dr. Adenauer wanted nothing more than to have the opportunity to continue the logic of his foreign policy even though it might mean preparing his people to accept the hard facts of historical events. Just before the elections of 17 September, Dr. Adenauer had been informed of the momentous questions his people would have to face with respect to the status of Berlin, the Oder-Neisse Line and finally a formula for relations with the so-called "German Democratic Republic" (GDP) of the Soviet Zone *(Mittel Deutschland)*.

And yet, despite the logic of events of the moment, despite the hard facts of the nuclear balance of terror between the East and West Blocs, perhaps Germans could take courage in the "logic of history." The dynamic forces and underlying currents of European history could not be altered by barbed wire, Chinese stone walls, panzers nor super bombs. In contrast to French logic and regard for pure reason, the German responds to organismic forces. He is always changing, always becoming something different. The German thesis is that no one political formula will fit the vast variety of political experiences and traditions. And so, German *Zeitgeist,* apart from logical reason, was apparent not only in the great romantic poets of the *Aufklärung* —Goethe, Schiller, and Herder, the finest Germans the world has known—but also in the allocation of increasing aid for the new under-developed nations of Africa, Asia and the Near East. Perhaps here the inexorable patience of Germans in scientific technology would find expression in an effort to help humanity. The dynamic forces of leadership in the Bonn Democracy, represented by Professor Theodore Heuss, First President of the Federal Republic, and by Dr. Adenauer and the very able chairmen of the opposition parties, Erich Ollenhauer and Dr. Erich Mende, could be compared to the leadership of a Frederick the Great or Otto von Bismarck and other eminent leaders of the nineteenth century. Under the inspiration of contemporary historians like Gerhard Ritter and Ludwig Dehio and the work of certain younger German historians, Germans may go through the long and difficult process of re-examination and re-evaluation of their recent, undigested past.

The Bonn Government's hand was strengthened in the world political situation in general and the Berlin crisis in particular by FDP Chairman Mende's call for a common stand of all political parties. In their first reaction to the Berlin Wall on Black Sunday, 13 August, all major political parties in West Germany described the Soviet Zone barricade as a breach of the Four-Power status of Berlin and a crime against humanity. These events produced intense governmental activity on Sunday both in Bonn and Berlin. Interparty harmony was shown by the willingness of Von Brentano to share vital information on the international situation with the opposition Social Democrats and by the offer of certain Christian Democrats (CDU) and Social Democrats (SPD) to shorten the electoral campaign or to call it off entirely and unite all forces to deal with the Berlin Crisis.

On Monday, 14 August, the leading politicians of all three major parties interrupted their electioneering plans in order to deal promptly with the crisis in Berlin: von Brentano (CDU), Brandt (SPD) and Mende (FDP). Moreover, Bundestag President Gerstenmaier (CDU), SPD Chairman Ollenhauer and Free Demo-

107

cratic Chairman Mende flew into Berlin to obtain firsthand, on-the-spot information. Although Chancellor Adenauer did not go to Berlin until over a week later, he had wanted to fly into the old German capital with Vice-President Johnson, but was informed that his presence there would be termed a provocation by the Soviets. Mayor Brandt did, of course, derive immense political advantage from his role in the Berlin Crisis. For instance, Brandt had over ten hours on television with Vice-President Johnson.

Despite many instances of interparty harmony and cooperation, inspired by the crucial events of 13 August in Berlin, the struggle for power between the major parties, CDU/CSU and SPD, involved one incident which most Germans, including prominent CDU leaders, considered unfortunate—the Chancellor's reference to his SPD opponent, Brandt, as "alias Frahm." This, plus his charge that Premier Khrushchev had created the Berlin Crisis in order to aid the Social Democrats (a charge belied by the heroic stand of Mayor Reuters during the Berlin Blockade of 1948) were widely regarded as decisive factors in the parliamentary campaign. Dr. Adenauer, nevertheless, had great electoral assets. As the first and only Chancellor of the Federal Republic, he had transformed a defeated, disillusioned outcast into the Bonn Democracy firmly allied with the West, a key member of the West European communities and courted by underdeveloped countries in Africa, Asia and the Near East. Throughout the electoral campaign, Adenauer had assured West German voters that they could have both peace and prosperity, security in NATO and reunification as well. But on 13 August it was Dr. Adenauer's misfortune to be presented with a bill labeled "Berlin" for the cost of his achievements in domestic and foreign affairs. This was Adenauer's most serious challenge in the postwar era.

NOTES TO CHAPTER FIVE

1. *National Zeitung* (Basel), 14 August, 1961.
2. *Die Welt* (Hamburg, independent) reported on Wednesday that the West Berlin Senate had proposed to the three Commandants prompt consideration of countermeasures:

(1) To deprive Zonal authorities of the right to supervise elevated train service (S-Bahn) in West Berlin;

(2) To ban SED activity in West Berlin;

(3) To determine whether recent Pankow action had destroyed the basis for existing legislation concerning West Berliners employed in East Berlin. *Die Welt*, 15 August, 1961.

3. *Die Welt*, 14 August, 1961.

4. *Die Welt*, 14 August, 1961. Dr. Mende told the author in a personal interview that the basic, historical reason why neither the FDP nor any other German party could recognize the Oder-Neisse Line as a German frontier was that to do so would only swell the ranks of the Refugee Bloc or *Gesamtdeutsche Partei*. The population of the West German Federal Republic includes nearly 20% refugees.*

5. *National Zeitung*, 14 August, 1961.

6. *Kieler Nachrichten*, 14 August, 1961.

7. *Deutsche Zeitung*, 13 August 1961.

8. *Abend*. See also *Kieler Nachrichten*, 14 August, 1961.

9. *Kieler Nachrichten*, 14 August, 1961.

10. *Kieler Nachrichten*, 14 August, 1961.

11. *Ibid.*

12. *Neue Rhein Zeitung* (Cologne, pro-SPD), 15 August, 1961.

13. *Frankfurter Neue Presse*, 14 August, 1961.

14. See *Basic Programme of the Social Democratic Party of Germany*, adopted by an Extraordinary Conference of the SPD, 13-15 November, 1959, at Bad-Godesberg, published by the SPD, Bonn, Friedrich-Ebert-Allee 170, printed by Bonn-Druck, Storbeck and Company, KG, Bonn, Burgstrasse 81.

15. *Basic Programme of the SPD* adopted 13-15 November, 1959, page 9.

16. *Deutsche Zeitung* (Cologne, right-center), 15 August, 1961.

17. *Frankfurter Neue Presse* (pro-Government), 15 August, 1961.

18. *Frankfurter Rundschau* (pro-SPD), 15 August, 1961.

*By 31 December, 1959, there were in the West German Federal Republic (exclusive of the Saar and Berlin), 9,550,000 refugees in a total population of 52,000,000. *Statistisch Jahrbuch Für Die Bundesrepublik Deutschland—1960*, Federal Statistical Office, Verlag: W. Kohhammer, GMBH, Stuttgart und Muteg, 1960, page 171.

19. *Der Mittag* (Düsseldorf, right-center), 16 August, 1961.

20. *Der Mittag* (Düsseldorf, right-center), 16 August, 1961.

21. *Die Welt* (Hamburg, independent), 16 August, 1961.

22. *Abendpost* (Frankfurt, independent), 16 August, 1961.

23. *Frankfurter Allgemeine* (right-center), 16 August, 1961, described as superfluous both the Chancellor's remark and Brandt's exaggerated reaction. See also *New York Times,* 16 August, 1961.

24. *Die Welt* (Hamburg, independent), 15 August, 1961. See Sebastian Haffner editorial, *Frankfurter Rundschau* (left-center), 15 August, 1961.

25. *Frankfurter Rundschau* (left-center), 16 August, 1961.

26. *Die Welt* (Hamburg, independent), 16 August, 1961.

27. *Die Tat* (Swiss, independent), 16 August, 1961.

28. *Die Welt,* 16 August, 1961.

29. *Die Welt* (Hamburg, independent), 16 August, 1961.

30. *Die Welt* (Hamburg, independent), 16 August, 1961.

31. *New York Times* (independent), 16 August, 1961.

32. *General Anzeiger* (Bonn, independent).

33. *Frankfurter Rundschau* (left-center), 22 August, 1961.

34. Both on the Friday prior to the elections of 17 September and on the Monday following, the author heard Dr. Adenauer chide the press for its treatment of his campaign at press conferences in the *Bundeshaus.*

35. *Frankfurter Rundschau* (left-center), 22 August, 1961.

36. *Bild Zeitung* (Hamburg, tabloid), 21 August, 1961. This mass tabloid has a circulation of 3,000,000, the largest in Germany. Owned by the publisher of *Die Welt* (Hamburg, independent), *Bild Zeitung* is independent, but very critical—at times even cheap. *Der Spiegel* (widely-read weekly magazine) has a somewhat higher political purpose in its criticism than *Bild Zeitung. Der Spiegel* is concerned with both truth and conjecture.

37. *Bild Zeitung* (Hamburg, tabloid), 21 August, 1961.

38. From a personal interview of the author with Count Gutenberg, CDU Bundestag representative, who was close to the Chancellor and was on the important Defense Committee of the Bundestag and who debated with Herbert Wehner (SPD) in the Bundestag session of 30 June, 1960, on issues of foreign policy. By far the most important reason for the

Chancellor's decision not to go to Berlin sooner is the fact that his presence there might have aroused Berliners to revolt on the scale of 17 June, 1953. This outweighed all other considerations—even the fact that he was poorly advised as to the political implications of such a journey.

39. *Daily Telegraph* (London Conservative), 22 August 1961.

40. Thus, the percentage of votes polled by the Social Democratic Party in 1912, in 1928, in 1949 and in 1961 varied only a few per cent because of past political patterns and traditions, notwithstanding the Bad-Godesberg program of the SPD in November, 1959. This program represented a turning point away from a working class party to a party of the people. In contrast to older Marxian tenets, the SPD definitely favors a free-market economy wherever free competition really exists, with as much competition as possible —as much planning as necessary. See *Basic Programme of the SPD*, page 10.

41. See John W. Keller, *"The Current German Political Scene,"* in *Current History*, XXXVIII (January, 1960), No. 221, page 33.

Chapter 6

MASS PROTEST RALLY IN WEST BERLIN
16 AUGUST 1961

The leading topic in the West German press Wednesday was Berlin and the German question. All organs of the Western press echoed a reaction to the barricade of East Berlin by the Soviet Zone Regime. All papers agreed that by these measures the Soviet regime showed its weakness and that it was well aware of the danger of an uprising with possible warlike results. In view of Soviet arbitrary acts of violence, a firm position by the West was demanded.[1] Nevertheless, there were various opinions as to how the West should react. Many papers gave primary emphasis to the protest note of the three West Berlin Commandants to their opposite number in East Berlin.[2] But as so often happened in all the years past, the protest ended in the wastebasket.[3]

By Tuesday night, the prevailing mood in Berlin was already gloomy and desperate. The largest, mass-circulation paper in West Germany, *Bild Zeitung,* used extraordinarily large type for its banner headline, "The West Does Nothing," and, alongside with pictures of statesmen concerned, said, "President Kennedy Is Silent," "Macmillan Goes Hunting" and "Adenauer Calls Brandt Names."[4]

West Germans had been conditioned to believe that the Atlantic Alliance was the best solution both for Germany and the West. Even after 13 August, the overwhelming majority of Germans were still of this opinion. This conviction, however, was not strengthened if at a time when the German cause was exposed to the gravest danger, some of the NATO partners said coolly: "Allied rights are not concerned. Berlin is no longer the gateway to freedom; the gate has been closed and nothing has happened apart from a paper protest by the Allied commandants. We are disappointed."[5]

The West was warned against causing a confidence crisis in the minds of West Germans. The feeling of being left in the lurch and doubts of Western loyalty to principles could have devastating consequences, such as a second "Munich" which was followed by war on 1 September 1939.[6] *Stadt Anzeiger* could not visualize that London, Paris and Washington would counter only with mild protests the violation of the rights of 16-million people in a giant concentration camp. "This would be equal to Munich (1938) plus Budapest (1956) with similar catastrophic consequences."[7]

The West took the position that one-sided arbitrary action on 13 August amounted to a declaration of political bankruptcy by the DDR,[8] which burdened Khrushchev and the entire Eastern Bloc. It would, nevertheless, have been disastrous if the Western Powers finding themselves unable to utilize this moral bankruptcy of the SED regime were to concede that they were now confronted with a *fait accompli*.[9] The danger of an explosion in the DDR was, nevertheless, not ruled out; but if the Western powers wished to avoid a future limitation of their basis for negotiations, they could not limit themselves to verbal protests. Large city dailies warned against hasty measures and inconsiderate actions mainly in the spheres of interzonal trade and trade with the East Bloc.[10] Leading British papers were even more emphatic with regard to an economic boycott.[11] The *Guardian* warned that closing the safety valve of West Berlin could only increase the danger of hostile demonstrations or an economic crisis in the Soviet Zone.[12]

With reports of the so-called People's Police (Volks Polizei) shooting at refugees, the prevailing mood in Berlin on Tuesday night was gloomy and desperate. Berliners kept asking the question as to if and when the West would finally do something in Berlin. The situation was marked by the following facts:

1. The Red Army was encircling West Berlin as Pankow ordered new harassments.

113

2. The Pankow regime announced a threat to blockade West Berlin if Bonn should unilaterally renounce the interzonal trade agreement.

3. Berlin was anticipating the complete closing of the sector borders.

4. Pankow had threatened persons violating new legislation on passes with severe punishment.

5. Despite all these measures, people continued to flee West.[13]

Nevertheless, it was pointed out in the British press that although the action of the East German Government was intolerable, it was no basis for panic because it was generally agreed that a government has the right to close its frontiers to its own citizens. Consequently, it was maintained that the just grievances of the Berlin populace could only be utilized at the conference table.[14] The West in general took the position that the one-sided, arbitrary action of 13 August amounted to a declaration of political bankruptcy by the DDR, which became a burden on Khrushchev and the entire Eastern Bloc. But if the Western Powers were unable to utilize this moral bankruptcy of the SED regime, they would find themselves confronted with a *fait accompli* by the DDR.[15]

If the Kremlin played only a secondary role in the whole affair, it still reaped a great profit. If the measure of closing the Berlin border had only a police or technical character, what could the Western Powers do? Protest? And then what? A maze of long diplomatic negotiations—but meanwhile the East German "People's Republic" confirmed by action its national sovereignty. The danger was that this meant the 17 million people of the Soviet Zone and the East Sector of the former German Capital, robbed of the hope of a way to freedom through Berlin, would come to the limit of their patience. Hence, the danger of a violent explosion, comparable to 17 June 1953.[16]

By Wednesday, 16 August, Berliners had reason to feel that they were betrayed by the West. French, Swiss and British papers interpreted the affair of 13 August as a *fait accompli*. A British Sunday paper came out with the headline: "No, No, No—Not For Berlin!" After Pankow gave Nehru its "explanation" of the situation, Indian newspapers showed understanding for Ul-

114

bricht. Radical French newspapers approved the actions of Ulbricht's SED[17] party because of mitigating circumstances.

The whole neutral world seemed unconcerned with the Berlin Crisis. It was reported in the West German press that even Washington believed it would accept what had happened. *The New York Times* announced that Washington had forbidden Bonn to break interzonal agreements. German industry opposed any possible barriers against interzonal trade. Professor Erhard warned against drastic measures. Meanwhile, the West German Cabinet conferred in Bonn and said it would confer again.

As if all this were not enough to try the patience of West Germans, the SED broadcaster from East Berlin repeatedly emphasized:

"England Deserts Berlin!"
"Adenauer Lets Willy Brandt Fall!"
"Cold War Stands There Alone!"
"London Bridles Willy Brandt!"[18]

"Willy Brandt fights on four fronts:

1. Against his own Berliners who are enraged, who clench their fists in revolt—and he must bridle them.
2. Against the West Berlin City Commandants, who even refused to rearrange S-Bahn Traffic in West Berlin and who refused to reinforce the West Berlin police in the rear.
3. Against the East—no words would be lost over it.
4. Against the West German Federal Government, from which he expected countermeasures, because he needed an outlet for his people, which, however, was not given to him." [19]

Editorial opinion in the West German press speculated over possible countermeasures. With few exceptions, a general feeling of dissatisfaction with the alleged inadequacy of Western action prevailed. Papers close to the CDU agreed that the Federal Republic was right in stating that Washington was primarily responsible for countermeasures. West Germany could only suggest minor restrictions on East-West trade and travel or discontinue the nonsense of joint cultural and sports events, which were always designed to enhance the prestige of the Soviet Zone regime (DDR). The stand taken by the Federal Republic and the U.S. Government was that of negotiations. Even Defense Minister Strauss, who was prone to issue bold statements, urged the West to do nothing to aggravate the present dispute which, he said, should be resolved at the conference table. Two questions, however, remained open:

1. Whether the failure of the foreign ministers to initiate East-West negotiations immediately was appropriate and,
2. Whether negotiations would merely delay an East-West rupture.[20]

The Western Allies faced the difficult problem of formulating a political reply which would be taken by the Soviets as a serious warning against further infringements without making it possible for the Kremlin to change the situation in West Berlin. Hans Hellwig, in *Deutsche Zeitung* defended the position of the Western Allies and the Federal Republic, pointing out that suspension of interzonal trade would imperil West Berlin rather than make things difficult for the Soviet Zone Administration.[21] Both independent and left-center papers contrasted the West's excessive caution with Ulbricht's shirtsleeve activity. People in West Germany were saying: "Dictatorship Acts—While Democracy Sleeps."[22] *Der Mittag* reviewed its praise of Kennedy's speech of 25 July 1961, in which he said:

West Berlin was "more than a link with the free world, a beacon of hope behind the Iron Curtain, an escape hatch for refugees." However, the President also said: "Today the endangered frontier of freedom runs through divided Berlin. We want it to remain a frontier of peace . . . The Soviet Government alone can convert Berlin's frontier of peace into a pretext for war." *Mittag* said this indicated that Kennedy had resigned himself to the idea that Berlin no longer had Four-Power Status and will form a part of the Soviet Zone.[23]

Most frustrating to West Germans was the feeling of helplessness and lethargy which marked Western policies. The prevailing attitude of the West German press was that the United States should not tolerate Ulbricht's unilateral action. Otherwise, the East might also take action against West Berlin, action that might lead to war.[24] In short, West Germans expected more rapid and resolute action. After all the Allied Conferences and endless planning by foreign ministers and experts, the feeling prevailed that Ulbricht had lost a battle but that Khrushchev had more than made up for it.[25] The situation was so critical that many people—not only West Berliners—felt themselves betrayed and sold down the river in a kind of second Munich. This lack of confidence in true Western principles could have devastating effects.[26]

Die Welt on Wednesday carried a detailed account of Chester Bowles' statement to the National Press Club in Washington, in which he had described the Communist threat against Berlin as the "most direct and most dangerous challenge" to the United States since the end of World War II.[27] The Under Secretary of State made the following points:

1. In the heart of Europe, the cockpit of two World Wars, there was a direct, total confrontation between the two greatest nuclear powers.

2. This is a challenge to which only one response is possible—we must adhere to our treaty rights and honor our commitments. Our word has been pledged to the free people of West Berlin. Unless we stand by that pledge, our word will not be trusted again by threatened people anywhere.

3. Mr. Khrushchev had thought competitive coexistence could be found in the two Germanies. The result was a free, prosperous and stable society in the West and failure, frustration and outspoken contempt for the Communist system in the East.

4. The refugees had been more than a daily irritant for Mr. Khrushchev; they represented in a most dramatic way a daily plebiscite which the Communists could never hope to win. Communism had failed.

5. To cover up this failure, Khrushchev wanted the West to agree to abandon the free people of West Berlin to the same system with all its misery.

6. Few Asians and Africans were impressed by America's

117

legal right to remain in Berlin. They had understood only when its role as a defender of right and freedom was stressed.[28]

Bowles emphasized that throughout the noncommunist world the tide of history was running full force for self-government, economic justice and social equality.

In West Germany, the feeling of dissatisfaction with the alleged inadequacy of Western reaction was expressed in all papers—pro-CDU, right-center, independent, and left-center papers—but was most articulate in the *Westfälische Rundschau* and *Neue Rhein Zeitung,* both pro-SPD. In the opinion of SPD leaders, the full meaning of the arbitrary action of Ulbricht and Khrushchev, on the night of 13 August was still not recognized by a large section of the people. The powerful presidium of the SPD issued on 15 August stressed the following items:

1. On 13 August, the Ulbricht regime completed the split of Berlin. Since that day, through Berlin runs the barbed wire of a concentration camp.
2. The arbitrary action of 13 August is actually an annexation of East Berlin by the Soviet Bloc, a crime against humanity and a flagrant violation of the UN Charter of Human Rights signed by the Soviet Union.
3. The arbitrary action of 13 August robs the people in the Zone and in East Berlin of the last possibility to choose in the other part of Germany the freedom denied them in their home territory.
4. The arbitrary action of 13 August is a battle cry to all Germans in East and West. It is a far-reaching challenge to the seriousness of the Western desire for freedom.
5. The arbitrary action of 13 August had far more than local significance—it increased tensions in the whole world and threatened peace.[29]

In the years from 1952 to 1955, the West German Government chose to follow a Western orientation in contrast to an Eastern orientation of the Weimar Regime in 1922, which culminated in the Rapallo Treaty with Russia. Germans pre-

118

ferred to go with the West, despite the fact that the Soviets offered them unity, whereas the West offered them only the hope of unity. For twelve years, Adenauer's foreign policy paralleled the Dulles Thesis of Negotiation from a position of strength. But on 15 August the influential *New York Times* wrote:

> If Soviet troops demonstrate an ability to control the East German population and to incorporate that country into Moscow's European domain without affecting Western rights in Berlin, officials believe that Premier Khrushchev may be able later this year to modify the whole arrangement of his promised East German peace treaty without further diplomatic conflict.[30]

By Wednesday, West Berliners were an angry people—angry with the Western Powers for yielding on Berlin, angry with the Bonn Government and angry with the Communists across the barricaded borders of Berlin. This anger and frustration, building up since Sunday, was directed at the West German Government in general and at the Chancellor in particular for unwarranted attacks on the Berlin *Bürgermeister*. Newspapers, officials, private citizens and student organizations in the West German Republic expressed strong sympathies for Berlin. Over a thousand inhabitants of Göttingen marched in protest against the blockading of Berlin and the General Student Committee of the University of Göttingen, supported by district associations of the CDU, SPD and FDP issued a call for a joint protest. Christian trade unions, Socialist Youth Organizations, the League of German student unions and teachers' organizations protested against the flagrant injustice in Berlin.[31]

Even the official Government Bulletin, in an unsigned article criticized the Western Allies for past delays. "The Four-Power Status of Berlin," it said, "has continually been breached in the past year, as far as the Eastern Sector is concerned, without the Western Allies doing anything about it. Now the Soviets have . . . undertaken a new annexation."[32] The great fear, which was so widely voiced in the German press, was that yielding power always tempts an opponent to intensify his pressures until further withdrawal is impossible and war becomes unavoidable.

119

Any policy of pacification involves this danger. A great power which sacrifices prestige and fails to perform its international role destroys the only basis which might guarantee peace by preventing a true balance of power from emerging out of pressure and counterpressure.[33]

The Lord Mayor of West Berlin, Willy Brandt, assured a mass rally of over 200,000 Berliners that Allied guarantees were as firm and binding as ever. But at the same time he warned that Berlin must not become a second Munich. Comparing the Ulbricht coup of 1961 with Hitler's annexation of the Rhine in 1936, he emphasized that the prestige of the Allies and the fate of the Western World were at stake.[34] Berliners, who answered the call of the West Berlin Senate, were in a quiet serious mood; but the banners they carried showed that they came to hear what was going to be done to counter the action of the Ulbricht regime. Homemade banners carried such slogans as:

"Betrayed by the West." "We Demand Countermeasures."
"Enough of Protests, Now Let Deeds Follow."
"Passivity Is Treachery to Berlin."
"Paper Protests Do Not Stop Tanks."
"Ninety Hours and No Action."
"Be Quiet, Many Are Still Asleep."
"Bundestag to Berlin."
"Where Is the Chancellor, On Vacation In Italy?"
"Kennedy to Berlin."
"Doesn't the West Know What to Do?"
"Munich, 1938—Berlin, 1961."[35]

Herr Brandt spoke for nearly an hour in a strained forced voice to a crowd that overflowed the square before the Town Hall and stretched down each of the nine streets. He said he wanted representatives of every nation in the free world to come to Berlin to see the barbed wire and the so-called Paradise of the Communist Regime. He even offered to put aside differences with Dr. Adenauer and said he would welcome the Chancellor to Berlin.[36]

The Bürgermeister said he had sent a frank letter to President Kennedy, putting before him the opinion of the people of Berlin over the present crisis. Amid great applause, he de-

clared: "Berlin expects more than words; Berlin expects political action."[37] He also called for the Berlin question and inhuman
acts of the Communist Regime to be brought before the United
Nations. "The Russians were aiming at a decisive defeat
of the West; coexistence meant for them only another word
for trial and strength, which could be avoided by capitulation."[38]
When Herr Brandt declared that the Allied Commandants' protest was "good but not enough," he had exactly expressed the
crowd's uneasy questioning mood.

Finally, the Lord Mayor appealed to all officials, officers and
members of the People's Army, People's Police and Factory
Militia in East Berlin and East Germany not to shoot their own
people. He said West Berlin would never desert East Berlin or
the people of East Germany and called for stronger ties between
West Germany and West Berlin.[39] Herr Amrehn, the CDU
Vice-Mayor of West Berlin, spoke before Brandt and warned
Berliners not to let themselves be carried away with actions
which could harm them. Alluding to the Hitler tactics of Ulbricht, he declared the Germans would never, never be Communist but would remain one people. He concluded with an appeal
to the UN and the peoples of the Free World to consider the
problem of East Germany. Berlin by itself was not a suitable
subject for negotiations—but only as a part of the All-German
Question.[40]

The leading topic in the West German press on 17 August
(Thursday) was Berlin and the German question. Brandt's
speech at a mass protest rally in which he called on President
Kennedy for political action was the main item, reported in
many papers under the following headlines:

"Berlin Protest of 500,000."
"Berlin Expects More Than Words."
"One Cannot Stop Tanks with Paper."
"250,000 Berliners Demonstrate: 'We Request
    Toughness—Kennedy to Berlin.' "
"Powerful Protest of Free Berlin."[41]

Bild Zeitung emphasized Brandt's statement: "We expect
more than words," and *Die Welt* stressed Brandt's pledge: "We
do not surrender." *Die Welt* and *Frankfurter Allgemeine Zeitung*

referred to protest demonstrations in Darmstadt and Braunschweig.

On the same day that Bürgermeisters Brandt and Amrehn were giving grains of comfort to anxious Berliners at a mass protest rally, Chancellor Adenauer addressed a CDU rally in Bonn. Referring to the events of the last few days in Berlin as merely a "preliminary crisis," he said that the real crisis was still to come.[42] The Chancellor was firmly convinced that the crisis would not lead to war but used strong words against widely expressed views that the Western Allies had not reacted effectively against recent Communist actions in Berlin. Such views, the Chancellor insisted, did not render justice to the attitude of Western Powers, who were making careful preparations for the anticipated big crisis.[43]

Commenting on his meeting with the Russian Ambassador, Smirnov, Dr. Adenauer said that questions raised on behalf of Khrushchev deserved serious consideration in the interests of general world peace. The Adenauer-Smirnov meeting on Wednesday was the lead story in pro-government papers and reported in many others on Thursday.[44] The German Press Office announced that the Soviet Ambassador in Bonn had informed the Chancellor of Khrushchev's plans in foreign policy and of possible developments in German-Soviet relations. Adenauer had assured Smirnov that he would carefully study his statements and do nothing to worsen Bonn-Moscow relations nor aggravate the international situation. Adenauer and Smirnov also exchanged views on Berlin.[45]

Frankfurter Allgemeine, under the heading, "Utmost Self-Control," described the nearly enigmatic attitude of the Chancellor in his talks with Smirnov. During the crucial days after 13 August when most Germans were waiting impatiently for a decisive Western reaction to the measures of Moscow and Pankow, the spokesman of the nation most deeply affected replied with assurances of his unshakable good will.[46] The only logical explanation was that the Chancellor saw a close link between the German and the international cause and realized that his discussion partner in Moscow was also aware of this.

A joint meeting of the Bundestag Committees for Foreign Affairs and All-German Questions was interrupted Wednesday because von Brentano had to leave to attend the Adenauer-

Smirnov meeting, initiated by Khrushchev. This caused the *Frankfurter Rundschau* to conclude that this illustrated the fact that political initiative rested with the Soviets and the West played only a secondary role.[47]

Notwithstanding Dr. Adenauer's impatience with German press criticism of the Western Allies, Western reaction to events in Berlin was still the main editorial subject. Criticism of alleged Western passivity continued to dominate the West German Press, whether right-center, independent or left-center.[48] Several papers pointed out that the Federal Republic should have prepared Germans for the fact that, without risking war, the West could not counter Eastern action in Berlin. On the other hand, papers close to the CDU and several independent ones objected to nationalist and neutralist criticism of the Western Allies, explained Washington's attitude and expressed confidence in President Kennedy.[49]

Pro-CDU/CSU papers in their support of the Western Allies stressed the following items:

1. Regardless of public opinion in West Berlin and West Germany, any Western counteraction would be carefully calculated by the political general staffs of the West.
2. The West would withhold economic weapons for the real Berlin Crisis expected in the fall of 1961.
3. The real test of Germans would be to resist efforts of demagogues and a sensational press to weaken confidence among Allies and promote neutralist or nationalist conceit among Germans.[50]

In contrast to the above, the right-center press voiced strong criticism of the Western Powers, emphasizing the following points:

1. German disappointment at Western reaction was understandable because no one knows the limit of Western tolerance.
2. The West should not underestimate the unrest in West Berlin and West Germany resulting from Western "indifference."

3. Khrushchev might not have violated the Four-Power Status of Berlin if the Paris Foreign Ministers' Conference had set a date for negotiations.
4. 13 August in Berlin was tantamount to taking over Czechoslovakia in 1948. It represents a new phase of German postwar history.[51]

Disappointment over the weak reaction of the West dominated discussion in the independent press, which stressed the following items:

1. Care should be taken to prevent the Soviets from misinterpreting the weak reaction of the West.
2. The only countermeasures Germans considered effective —economic weapons—as Adenauer had once suggested, were later rejected by the West and the Federal Republic as impractical.
3. Western politicians were perplexed to find Germans so deeply disappointed over the events of 13 August —although time and again it was asserted that any move by the East would be effectively countered.
4. The damage caused by the omissions of the Western politicians would be difficult to repair—as indicated by the frank posters displayed in front of the West Berlin City Hall.[52]

Although several independent papers showed understanding for Western moderation lest Moscow shut off Berlin's power and water supply,[53] the left-center press was far more critical. Even greater than disappointment in Bonn was the shock caused by Western Powers giving the cold shoulder to their faithful ally, Dr. Adenauer. Moreover, Bonn's political activities could hardly conceal prevailing helplessness. Without risking a war, the West would have to tolerate the *fait accompli* in Berlin just as it did the brutal suppression of the uprisings in the Soviet Zone on 17 June, 1953, and later in Hungary.[54] Even greater than criticism of the West was that directed against West German politicians for deliberately concealing facts from their people. If the Foreign Ministers in Paris were unable to prevent the isolation of East Berlin, then the German people should

124

have been prepared for this. When the West tried to play down Ulbricht's actions in East Berlin, it left the Germans isolated with their most serious problem—reunification.[55]

NOTES TO CHAPTER SIX

1. *Süddeutsche Zeitung* (left-center), 16 August, 1961.
2. See *Kölnische Rundschau, Deutsche Zeitung* and *Stadt Anzeiger* for 16 August, 1961.
3. *Neue Rhein Zeitung* (Cologne, pro-SPD), 16 August, 1961.
4. *Bild Zeitung* (Hamburg, independent, tabloid), 16 August, 1961.
5. *Ibid.*
6. *Neue Rhein Zeitung* (Cologne, pro-SPD), 16 August, 1961.
7. *Stadt Anzeiger* (independent), 16 August, 1961.
8. So-called "Deutsche Demokratische Republick" of Soviet Zone.
9. *Neue Züricher Zeitung* (conservative), 16 August, 1961.
10. *Kölnische Rundschau* (CDU, Catholic), *Frankfurter Neue Presse* and *Frankfurter Rundschau* (pro-SPD), 16 August, 1961.
11. *Daily Telegraph* (British, conservative), 16 August, 1961.
12. *Guardian* (Manchester, liberal), 16 August, 1961.
13. *Allgemeine Zeitung* (Mainz, independent), 16 August, 1961. *Frankfurter Allgemeine* (right-center), 16 August, 1961. *General Anzeiger* (Bonn, independent), 16 August, 1961. *Wiesbadener Kurier* (pro-CDU), headlined "Volks Now Harassing Also West Berliners." 16 August, 1961.
14. *Daily Herald* (British, ultra-conservative), 16 August, 1961.
15. *Neue Züricher Zeitung* (conservative), 16 August, 1961. Although this paper is considered conservative in Switzerland, it is more liberal in its analysis of international events. It is highly regarded not only by Germans but by Europeans in general as most objective and fair in its analysis of international questions.
16. *Combat* (French—conservative), 16 August, 1961; *Le Figaro* (French—conservative), 16 August, 1961.
17. For the Berlin elections of October, 1946, the Communists tried to force a merger of the non-Communist Social Dem-

ocratic Party (SPD) with the Communist Party (KPD) into the Socialist Unity Party (SED). The result of these elections —the first and last free elections for all Berlin were:

Social Democratic Party (SPD) 48.7 percent.
Christian Democratic Party (CDU) 22.2 percent.
Socialist Unity Party (SED) 19.8 percent.
Liberal Democratic Party (LDP) 9.3 percent.

(See *Background Berlin—1961*, U.S. Department of State, 18 August, 1961, page 5.)

18. *Neue Rhein Zeitung* (pro-SPD), 16 August, 1961.
19. *Ibid.*
20. *Frankfurter Neue Presse* (pro-Government), 16 August, 1961. *Deutsche Zeitung*, 16 August, 1961.
21. *Die Welt* (Hamburg, independent), 16 August, 1961; *Deutsche Zeitung* (Cologne, right-center), 16 August, 1961.
22. *Der Mittag* (Düsseldorf, right-center), 16 August, 1961. *Neue Rhein Zeitung* (Cologne, pro-SPD), 16 August, 1961.
23. *Der Mittag* (Düsseldorf, right-center), 16 August, 1961.
24. *General Anzeiger* (Bonn, independent), 16 August, 1961; *Der Mittag* (Düsseldorf, right-center), 16 August, 1961.
25. *Die Welt* (Hamburg, independent), 16 August, 1961; *General Anzeiger* (Bonn, independent), 16 August, 1961.
26. *Neue Rhein Zeitung* (Cologne, pro-SPD), 16 August, 1961.
27. *Die Welt* (Hamburg, independent), 16 May, 1961.
28. *Die Welt* (Hamburg, independent), 16 August, 1961; *New York Times* (independent), 16 August, 1961.
29. *Hamburger Echo* (pro-SPD), 16 August, 1961. See also *Stuttgarter Zeitung*, 16 August, 1961.
30. *New York Times* (independent), 15 August, 1961, quoted by *London Times*, 16 August, 1961.
31. *Die Welt* (Hamburg, independent), 16 August, 1961.
32. Bulletin der Bundesregierung, 16 August, 1961.
33. *Die Welt* (Hamburg, independent), 15 August, 1961; See also "The Balance of Power System" in Walter Dorn's *Competition for Empire*, 1740-1763 (New York, Harpers, 1939), pp. 1-13.
34. *Guardian* (Manchester, liberal), 17 August, 1961.
35. *Ibid.; Köln Stadt Anzeiger* (Independent), 17 August, 1961.
36. *General Anzeiger* (Bonn, independent), 17 August, 1961, said Adenauer made his decision to visit Berlin two hours after

Mayor Brandt had publicly appealed to Adenauer to set aside party strife and to visit Berlin now. It was announced that the Chancellor and his party would make the trip on the following Tuesday or Wednesday.

37. *London Times* (independent), 17 August, 1961.
38. *Ibid.*
39. *Guardian* (Manchester, liberal), 17 August, 1961.
40. *Die Welt,* 17 August, 1961.
41. See *Die Welt* (Hamburg, independent); *Deutsche Zeitung* (Cologne, right-center); *Der Mittag* (Düsseldorf, right-center); *Allgemeine Zeitung* (Mainz, independent); *Neue Rhein Zeitung* (Cologne, pro-SPD); *Bild Zeitung* (Hamburg, independent, tabloid), 17 August, 1961.
42. *Die Welt* (Hamburg, independent), 17 August, 1961. *General Anzeiger* (Bonn, independent), 17 August, 1961.
43. *Frankfurter Neue Presse* (pro-Government), 17 August, 1961, criticized the slogans displayed at the West Berlin protest rally and the general impact of Brandt's speech.
44. See *Frankfurter Allgemeine* (right-center); *Kölnische Rundschau* (CDU); *Frankfurter Neue Presse* (pro-Government); and *Abendpost* (Frankfurt, tabloid) for 17 August, 1961.
45. *Frankfurter Neue Presse* (pro-Government), 17 August, 1961.
46. *Frankfurter Allgemeine Zeitung* (right-center), 17 August, 1961.
47. *Frankfurter Rundschau* (left-center), 17 August, 1961.
48. See *Der Mittag, Die Zeit, General Anzeiger* and *Frankfurter Rundschau* of 17 August, 1961.
49. See especially *Frankfurter Neue Presse* (CDU), *Stuttgarter Nachrichten* (independent), *Frankfurter Allgemeine Zeitung* (independent) and *Rheinische Post* (pro-CDU).
50. *Rheinische Post* (Düsseldorf, pro-CDU), 17 August, 1961; *Münchner Merkur* (pro-CSU), 17 August, 1961; *Frankfurter Neue Presse* (pro-Government), Friedrich Herzug, 17 August, 1961.
51. *Der Mittag* (Düsseldorf, right-center), 17 August, 1961, *Die Zeit* (Hamburg, weekly, right-center), Countess Marion Doenhoff, 17 August, 1961.
52. *Die Welt* (Hamburg, independent), 17 August, 1961. *General Anzeiger* (Bonn, independent), 17 August, 1961.
53. *Allgemeine Zeitung* (Mainz, independent), 17 August, 1961.

Stuttgarter Nachrichten (independent), 17 August, 1961. The latter praised Kennedy's caution, coupled with his reinforcement of conventional forces as well as nuclear.

54. *Frankfurter Rundschau* (left-center), 17 August, 1961. *Süddeutsche Zeitung* (Munich, left-center), 17 August, 1961.

55. *Welt Der Arbeit* (Cologne, DGB weekly); *Abendpost* (Frankfurt, tabloid), 17 August, 1961.

Chapter 7

SPECIAL SESSION OF WEST GERMAN PARLIAMENT
18 AUGUST, 1961

By Friday the reaction of West German public opinion to
Allied Berlin Policy had reached the stage of a "confidence
crisis." Uneasiness in Berlin and West Germany was spreading
to Bonn and even into CDU quarters. People were asking what
would the Americans do in case of a serious showdown over
Berlin. The independent press held the Federal Government
partly responsible for public disappointment because Adenauer
and the Cabinet had announced Western countermeasures in
statements made the previous Sunday and Tuesday. Later the
Allies and Bonn had agreed to take no action that might aggravate the international situation. This created the impression in
Bonn that the East could act as it pleased. The U.S. Embassy
near Bonn feared a possible confidence crisis between the Federal
Republic, the United States and NATO.[1] Berlin demonstrations
at the mass rally in West Berlin, Wednesday, further intensified
concern about future German-U.S. relations. Hereafter, the
United States Information Agency (USIA), headed by Edward
R. Murrow, focused attention mainly on Berlin, with daily
reports of American Embassies, Consuls and USIA Bureaus in
90 nations.[2]

The reaction of German public opinion now became more
understandable and found some sympathy in foreign countries.
Politicians, however, could not expect a general pardon. It would
have been much more desirable if they had frankly admitted
that the Western Powers could not take really effective countermeasures, without the danger of overthrowing the neat balance

129

between war and peace. With the present nuclear balance of terror, only a fool could advocate war as "a continuation of policy by other means."[3]

Nevertheless, Germans found themselves in the first stage of a war of nerves over Berlin, whose dangerous climax was expected in October or November. For East-West negotiations then the *sine qua non* would be cool blood and confidence in the Western alliance. All this became increasingly difficult in the election campaign and led to sincere appeals for a party truce, which, for various reasons were rejected. The election campaign was already dominated by the Berlin question. As campaign propaganda for 17 September, the cry of Munich by the Berlin Bürgermeister was just as useful as his "inexpedient letter" to President Kennedy in the view of papers close to the Government.[4]

Hitherto existing errors had caused a negative echo in the British and American press. Large newspapers eagerly carried the symptoms of unrest in Germany and their analyses were based on concepts which recalled the critical period of the early post-war years. For months already Khrushchev's propaganda—hitherto vain—had tried to defame the Germans as war instigators and to revitalize the anti-Nazi Coalition. "What was read in a whole series of Western newspapers as an echo of various demonstrations and also of Willy Brandt's speech before the Schönberg City Hall recalled to mind the risky Moscow propaganda slogans of recent months."[5] A confidence crisis between the Federal Republic and its Western Allies, however, might have ruined even modest hopes of mastering the international crisis.

In view of the tense international situation and the growing mistrust of West Germans toward their Western Allies, so widely discussed in the German press, the special session of the Bundestag on Friday, 18 August, had to be regarded with considerable apprehension. Despite the effort of Bundestag President Gerstenmaier to make this the hour for all parties to unite in a common declaration of all fractions, this was subordinated to election campaign tactics, as the Government Party wrote: "the impression of a political—especially foreign policy United Front must be avoided, since otherwise there would be no check on the SPD and their foreign policy scapegoats."[6]

130

The answer to the violent tactics, used against Berlin on 13 August, came with the Bundestag Declarations of the Federal Chancellor, of the Lord Mayor of Berlin and of the Political Parties on 18 August 1961. Ulbricht's arbitrary action of 13 August, the virtual annexation of East Berlin through the barricade of the Sector borders with barbed wire and tanks, caused the Bundestag to break into its vacation and meet together for a special session in Bonn. The 18th of August, 1961, saw a fully occupied hall in the presence of almost the entire federal cabinet and numerous members of the Federal Council. What should be the official position of the Federal Government of Germany before world public opinion with regard to the aggression of the Eastern Bloc in Berlin? This was the important question, to which the Federal Government, the Berlin Burgermeister and the political parties gave their answer. All parties united in an indignant protest against the aggressions of the SED and the attitude of the Soviet Union and manifested the will to overcome the untenable situation through discussions over the Berlin and German question and to guarantee their determination to keep faith with the oppressed people in the SED sphere and to fight for the right of self-determination for the German people.[7]

Dr. Adenauer opened the session with the presentation of the Government Declaration. This was a ringing appeal to the governments of all nations in the world, who accept the charter of the United Nations to recognize:

1. The barricade of Berlin on 13 August by the Soviet Zone authorities as a clear and unmitigated declaration of political bankruptcy by the Ulbricht regime after 16 years of misrule.
2. The flagrant violation of the Four-Power Agreements was a brutal denial to East Berliners of their freedom of movement.[8]
3. The Soviet Government had given repeated assurances since November 1958 that the freedom of West Berlin would be guaranteed. The tanks of the People's Army, People's Police and Factory Militia in order to give military support to an illegal attack against the status of the City of Berlin was a preview of how the Soviet

131

guarantee of a so-called "Free City" would be carried out.

4. The illegal action of the Zonal authorities demonstrated once and for all to world public opinion in which part of Germany militarism and aggression were practiced. Nevertheless on 3 August, the Soviet Union had renewed its demand for a so-called peace treaty and the transformation of the Four-Power Status of Berlin into a so-called "Free City" based on the claim that this was necessary in order to resist militarism and revanchism in the Federal Republic.[9]

Real Reasons for Aggression of 13 August

The Federal Government maintained, before world public opinion that the real reason for the aggressive action of 13 August in Berlin was not the militaristic and revanchist policy of the Federal Republic, but rather the refusal of the Ulbricht regime to provide living standards, which the Germans living in that Zone desire. Hence, it was grotesque for representatives of the Ulbricht regime to declare that the Germans in the Zone had already exercised the right of self-determination on 13 August. The continued stream of refugees of the past weeks and years spoke another language, the language of reality. The great increase of refugees came with Premier Khrushchev's decision to conclude a separate peace treaty with the Soviet Zone regime because East Germans lost all hope of living in freedom, except by fleeing from the Zone. Nothing else remained for them except to "vote with their feet"—to borrow a phrase used by Lenin.[10] After 16 years of tyranny and terror under Communist functionaries, 90% of the Germans living in the Zone, desire nothing more than union with Germans living in freedom. Denying repeated Soviet claims that the current status of the city of Berlin was one of the causes for existing world tension, Dr. Adenauer concluded that a solution of the German problem on the basis of self-determination was the best, indeed, the only way to end world tensions and to preserve world peace.[11] Having completed a devastating attack on the illegal arbitrary measures of the Marionette regime of the Soviet Zone and having refuted with Aristotelian logic the arguments and

132

claims of the East, and having made a penetrating analysis, exposing the real reasons for the violent tactics in Berlin, the Federal Chancellor used the middle part of his address to clarify Bonn's close relations with the Western Powers in the NATO alliance. Confirming again the complete harmony between the Federal Republic and its Western Allies in view of the dangers threatening the free world, he expressed confidence in the deliberations of the Foreign Ministers of the Four Western Powers in Paris, because they were amplified and confirmed by further consultation between the Big Four Western Powers and all the other NATO Partners.[12] This resulted in the determination of all NATO states to preserve the freedom of Berlin. At the same time the NATO Council repeated its firm conviction that a fair and peaceful solution of the German-Berlin question could only be reached on the basis of the right of self-determination of the whole German nation.[13]

The critical international situation, caused by the illegal action of the Soviet Zone authorities necessitated stronger defense measures by the Western Powers in NATO and especially by the free part of Germany representing the Federal Government. Therefore, in response to President Kennedy's request for greater defense contributions by all NATO partners in his televised address to the American people on 25 July, 1961, the Federal Government had offered to strengthen its striking forces. "We know and the Soviet Union knows that the total military potential of the West is superior to that of the Soviet Union."[14] Therefore, the threats which the Soviet Union from time to time makes against one or the other NATO partner would result in the destruction of its own territory by atomic bombs. "In this hour, when the destiny of Berlin is our destiny, self-preservation compels us to join with our Western Allies and with them to exert common efforts, which are required to meet the common danger.[15]

Nevertheless, the Federal Government was not convinced that the Soviet Premier would resort to war, which would also destroy his country. The Chancellor continued to believe that a way out of the present impasse could be found through negotiations. Despite the aggressive tactics of the Ulbricht regime, with the full support of the Soviet Union, the Chancellor would not give up hope that negotiations would soon be undertaken and lead to a solution of German problems and also the Berlin question on the basis of the right of self-determination of peoples. "This principle that nations must be given the right to determine their political future has won support throughout the whole world." The Federal Government was confident, therefore, that it could also be established in the heart of Europe, where this right is still denied to 16 million Germans.[15]

The Federal Government had declared many times and again repeated that it was prepared to cooperate in plans, which in the event of German Reunification, would give to the Soviet Union security guarantees. "Finally," the Chancellor said, "I even confirmed this offer again in this Bundeshaus on 17th June of this year. In this respect nothing has changed. The re-establishment of German unity would not only promote world peace, but also the legitimate security interests of the Soviet Union and of all other nations."[16]

Appeal to the Soviet Union

The three Western Allies, who by the Four-Power Agreements, have undertaken a special obligation for Berlin and for Germany, have lodged a strong protest with the Soviet Union. They have denounced the measures of 13 August as illegal and characterized them as an irresponsible unilateral breach of existing agreements. They have rightly condemned the presumptuous assertion, which is contained in the so-called recommendation of the Warsaw Pact States, namely, that these measures of 13 August were in the interest of the German people; that they have emphasized this assertion means nothing less than an interference in the internal affairs of the German nation.[17]

The Chancellor concluded his appeal to the Soviet Union by stressing the following items:

1. The Russian Government and people should not assume that a part of a great nation should be transformed against the will of its inhabitants into a concentration camp.
2. People in Moscow should realize that all people in the world who accept the charter of the United Nations recognize the right of self-determination of peoples.

3. A new era of relations between the Russian people and the German people is unthinkable in terms of recognition of the authorities of the Soviet Zone.
4. Closing of the Sector borders of Berlin was tantamount to a declaration of bankruptcy; it showed that the people who are forced to live in this part of Germany, could only be prevented by physical force from leaving this paradise of workers and peasants.
5. There is only one way to place the relations between the Russian and German people on a new foundation: the right must be restored to the German people, which is denied to no nation in the world, to form a government of their own choice, which has the legal authority, to speak, to act and to decide for the entire nation.[18]

Dr. Adenauer then concluded the Government Declaration with a statement on the responsibility which the Federal Government felt for three and a half million refugees[19] which had fled from the Soviet Zone, causing great suffering and the division of families. The Chancellor closed with a final word of comfort to Germans in the Soviet Zone and in the Soviet Sector of Berlin not to give up hope for a better future for themselves and their children. "We do not stand alone in the world; justice is on our side and all nations of the world who love freedom stand on our side."[20]

Following the Chancellor, the speaker called for the Declaration of the Lord Mayor of Berlin, Brandt, also a member of the Bundestag, who simply refused to recognize the actions of 13 August in the Zone as a *fait accompli*. He characterized the use of barbed wire, stone walls, tanks and armed soldiers as nothing more than a "Second Hungary." This brutal attack trampled even the primitive right of human beings to flee from one land to another or even to flee within a country or within a single city. Therefore, it was not only a question of Berlin, but a problem for the world forum of the United Nations.[21]

The Mayor then discussed the question whether Western Germany could afford to have no business relations with the people of the Zone. Naturally the people whom Ulbricht held in the Soviet Zone with panzers and those in barricaded East Berlin felt deserted. They must restrain their indignation. For this

135

reason it was well that the German Bundestag had assembled in order to demonstrate signs of unity and solidarity. Berlin citizens urged West Germans not to do business with the Ulbricht people.

Above all a new situation existed in Berlin. No longer could sixty thousand citizens of Berlin live in the east sector and work in the west sector. In one year nine million tickets were sold to East Berliners for cultural events in the Western sector. Many men who might be able to cross over the barbed wire barrier, could not abandon their wives, children and relatives on the other side.[22]

The Berlin Bürgermeister drew applause from the whole house when he declared: "My fellow citizens, have confidence that freedom for the people of West Berlin will be guaranteed by the presence of Allied Troops in West Berlin. I am not only convinced, I know—and I have said it to my fellow citizens at a great rally—that crossing over the barbed wire line would be more than a risk. These guarantees are now the guarantees of peace. They are the basis of our very existence in Berlin. However, this also applies to West Germany and the West itself. For more than twelve years, Germans have proved that they would rather endure privations than bend their necks under the yoke of a new dictatorship. Today more than ever, in spite of bitter disappointment, we are firm and determined to stand on the side of our friends.[23]

Next the Lord Mayor of Berlin refuted the thesis, expressed in sections of the Western press, that the action of the Communists on 13 August in their own Zone was not an action against freedom in the Western sphere. Herr Brandt insisted that the interests of free Berlin were immediately affected and that the life of the divided nation was deeply affected. Not only were innumerable individual destinies affected, but they in turn were connected with the whole people and both parts of Germany. The Bürgermeister maintained it was false to believe that the people in the Federal Republic would not understand the meaning of the events since 13 August in Berlin and in the Zone. "Our nation has not fallen a victim to a cold materialistic-ideology. Our people have preserved a common sense of responsibility. And that is important for our people over in the Zone to realize."[24]

136

Herr Brandt characterized the action of the so-called People's Army and other military groups on 13 August as tantamount to annexation of East Berlin. Soviet panzers had destroyed the Four-Power Status of Berlin. The Zone regime had expanded its quasi-sovereignty over all of East Berlin. It had annexed East Berlin and it had used this sovereignty above all in order to be able to take over East Berlin. Brandt emphasized that these actions simply could not be accepted. Recognition of conditions brought about by armed force is a form of recognition of a political organization. "Whoever has read recent issues of *Neues Deutschland,* knows with what a tone of triumph, satisfaction and pride it expresses its scorn of the West. After the actions of the Zonal authorities, the sector border of Berlin —characterized as the 'border of the German Democratic Republic'—extended even to the Potsdamer Platz and the Brandenburg Gate.[26] Nevertheless, the Soviet Ambassador had declared that Premier Khrushchev did not wish to increase tensions in Berlin. It is clear, therefore, that relations between the West German Government and the Soviet Union are bound to be influenced by the events of 13 August.[27] Naturally both the Federal Government and the Berlin Senate bear a responsibility to do nothing to worsen the international situation. And certainly a secure peace is desired by no one more than Berlin and the German people. However, the Government of the Soviet Union must not believe that it can slap us in the face and we will continue to smile." [28]

The Berlin Bürgermeister emphasized that the illegal actions of 13 August also infringed the rights of the Western Powers, who on Thursday had lodged a strong protest in Moscow. They had held the Soviet Union entirely responsible for the illegal measures of 13 August, which should be revoked. This coincided with the views of the Berlin Senate and the Berlin people. Moreover, the Western Powers in their protest notes had stated that the "unilateral abandonment of the Four-Power Status of Berlin could increase tensions to a point of danger."[29] The guilt of the Soviet Union lay in its support of the brutality and incapacity of the Ulbricht regime. Therefore, the Soviet Union must be made to realize how dangerous was its breach of the Four-Power agreements over Berlin. The bonds between the Federal Republic and West Berlin must not be broken—

they must be strengthened. Therefore, the Federal Republic, which had undertaken the legal representation of the Land of Berlin, must make no international treaty without guaranteeing the interests of Berlin.[30]

The Berlin Senate would be most grateful for a clear sign of Allied presence and of Allied rights which would follow if all possible political initiative were grasped. Moreover, the Senate expected a world-wide advertisement of these new injustices would be undertaken. The Senate of Berlin in behalf of the house of representatives and the Berlin people memorialized the Federal Government to take non-military measures. No criticism of the Western Allies was intended. It only wanted to avoid weak countermeasures which would cause a roar of laughter from Potsdamer Platz to Vladivostok.[31]

The Bürgermeister concluded his address by warning the Bundestag against the tactics of 13 August as only one act of a drama, whose second act was already announced—the much discussed "Free City of Berlin." The Soviet Premier had already taken half of what he had first demanded. Such results could only increase the appetite of any dictator. The basic law (constitution) obligates the Federal Republic to be concerned with the people in the Soviet Zone of occupation. Therefore, the Federal Republic can not and dare not recognize a partial dictatorship without violating its constitution. We are united with our Allies, who have made reunification the goal of their policy. We are one people—as the Berliners have shown in view of the threatening dangers of these days—a people that has its own self-respect. Justice and morality obligate us to support this viewpoint. This position also results from our democratic convictions; for without this deep and unshaken conviction, we would out of weakness or opportunism even become pioneers of a new nationalism. And no man, who values peace whether in East or West could wish this.[32]

Following the Berlin Bürgermeister, came the Declaration of the ruling majority party of the West German Parliament, by its floor leader, Dr. Krone, Chairman of the CDU/CSU fraction. In his introductory remarks, Dr. Krone expressed words of comfort for the numerous German families on both sides of the barbed wire and for leaders of both Catholic and Protestant churches, whose activities were hindered by recent measures. He

138

explained the decision against a joint government declaration of all parties as a way to avoid a foreign policy debate at such a critical time. What influenced us most, he declared, was that: "Here at the critical hour of the German people, the German Bundestag, with the authority which it enjoys as the freely elected spokesman of the whole German nation, would take a position for the whole German nation. We wish to speak for the Germans of the Federal Republic, but also and especially for those Germans who must now remain silent but who, behind the barbed wire, expect that we here in freedom will speak for them. And this statement must emphasize, as did the great freedom rally in Berlin: Away with the barbed wire! Now, finally, after 12 years of slavery, give our German brothers freedom." [33]

The CDU fraction chairman devoted the rest of his time to developing a case in support of the foreign policy of the ruling majority party of the past twelve years. This carefully constructed case included the following items:

1. If, in view of the events of 13 August, it could be said that this day was the result of a false policy, it would be the basis for a new orientation of German defense policy. On the contrary, Dr. Krone maintained that the policy followed, of a close military alliance with the West, was the only right policy and expressed his thanks to the Federal Chancellor for carrying out this policy against strong opposition.

2. In this connection, he did not believe it wise to question the Four-Power Status of Berlin, as proposed in the press that day, to substitute a Three-Power Status for the former capital city, despite the events of 13 August.

3. The CDU/CSU fraction maintained that the real cause of the mass flights of refugees was the bankruptcy of the Ulbricht regime, which was demonstrated to the world by the barbed wire enclosing a giant concentration camp. The stream of refugees swelled because the Zone population feared the announcement of a separate peace treaty would close the last door of escape.

4. The Communists were able to stop the mass "plebiscite with the feet" only by the most brutal measures,

139

including the annexation of East Berlin in violation of International Law.

5. Under free democracy, in contrast to totalitarian dictatorship, the political cooperation of free states can not be commanded. But it was not constructive criticism to make a crisis, which in truth was a crisis of Communism on German soil, into a crisis of German confidence in the Western Powers. Many critics had gone so far that they were more critical of the Western powers than of the Soviet Union and its stooges.

6. Only because of NATO had Ulbricht's tanks not rolled through Brandenburg Gate toward West Berlin. Nevertheless, peace can only be preserved through negotiations.

7. Good relations with Russia are predicated on the rights of 17 million Germans in the Zone to unity, freedom and self-determination.[34]

Next came the Declaration of the largest opposition party, the SPD, given by its fraction chairman, Erich Ollenhauer. It was a brief but powerful polemic against the tactics of military force used by the Zone authorities on 13 August—a violation of international agreements, and a brutal attack upon human rights. The speech was constantly interrupted by lively applause from all parties, SPD, CDU/CSU and FDP—an indication of its strongly patriotic and not too partisan sentiments.

The Social Democratic Declaration contained the following items:

1. The hermetical sealing off of East Berlin was a forced annexation and an introduction to the final partition of Germany. The aggressions of the Soviet Zone Communist authorities threatened the existence and freedom of West Berlin as well as the peace and freedom of the entire world. The Soviet Union is responsible for this dangerous action, without whose consent the violent tactics of 13 August would not have been possible.

2. We understand the sorrow and suffering, which those who must accept the barbed wire and tanks of a giant

concentration camp bear for all of us. They should have the assurance that no amount of force can separate us and that we remain one nation and that we here will not rest until we can again live together in one Germany in freedom.[35]

3. We regard ourselves as one with the people of Berlin. We thank you in Berlin for your brave fortitude during these severe trials. The preservation of the way of life and freedom of Berlin is the task of the whole German nation. We stand together with you.

4. The SPD appeals to all West Germans to unite in protest against the violence of 13 August. The need of our people in East Berlin and the Zone is a national need, vital to all Germans. Our destiny and our hopes for a peaceful and prosperous future are bound up with the struggle for freedom and for existence of the East Berliners and our people in the Zone.

5. Our solidarity must first find its practical expression in material and humanitarian aid for the refugees. The way we here, as individuals and as a people, meet this challenge must prove to the entire world the sincerity of our all-German consciousness.

6. The answer of the Federal Government and our Allies to the violence of 13 August must not be exhausted in protests in Berlin, Karlsruhe and in Moscow. The objective must be to cancel the violence of 13 August and bring about the removal of the barbed wire and stone piles in East Berlin.[36]

7. The crisis of the hour and the difficulties of the problems forbid a detailed analysis of possible and effective countermeasures. In any case the people of Berlin rightly expect action and we also expect further information from the Federal Government over the results of its efforts.

8. We appeal to all to be aware of the deeper significance of the events of 13 August. The violent tactics of 13 August were a decisive step toward Soviet concepts of cementing the division of Germany and the incorporation of all Berlin into the Communist power sphere. Toleration of this step would create no satisfaction,

but would only cause new tensions and conflicts. It will not relieve the position of the free world, but only aggravate it and increase the danger of war.

9. Above all the violence of 13 August was a brutal attack on elementary human rights. The basic rights of the charter of the United Nations, which the Soviet Union has also signed, were violated. Charges should be brought before this body. The people of East Berlin and Soviet Zone live in fear and their only hope is the free world. We dare not disappoint them.

10. Men in both East and West live in fear of war. Since the 13th of August this fear has increased. We expect the Federal Government to urge our Allies, without further delay, to make the effort in negotiations with the Soviet Union, to cancel the actions of 13 August and seek a solution to international tensions and German problems on the basis of self-determination.

11. We are confronted with the danger of a confidence crisis in the Western world. How the Federal Government and our Allies in the next few days react to the violence of 13 August will be decisive for the question whether the West will meet the challenge.[37]

Dr. Erich Mende made a declaration in behalf of the Free Democratic Party, the third largest fraction in the Bundestag. In his opening remarks the FDP Chairman commented favorably on the close harmony among the three parties in their approach to the Berlin and German questions. Nevertheless, both the form and content of the Bundestag election campaign were bound to be influenced by the events of 13 August. Parties are not ends in themselves, but only means to an end. Above parties stands the common fatherland. Therefore, the important question to decide on 17 September was not whether the CDU, SPD or FDP won the greatest success, but whether all three fractions could work together as responsible democratic parties for the destiny of Germany in dealing with the Berlin and German questions and in close harmony with our Allies to counter the threat to Berlin and Germany in order to preserve Europe and Germany from becoming a second Korea.[38]

142

In the remainder of his address, the FDP Chairman stressed the following items:

1. The occupation of East Berlin by the so-called "People's Army" and the declaration of the sector borders as state borders was an act of aggression and annexation. Depriving East Berliners and East Germans of their freedom of movement violated a basic right guaranteed by the constitutions of both the Federal Republic and even the DDR of the Soviet Zone, an unrestricted right of every people.

2. The Soviet Union should realize that all nations in the world who have recognized the absolute value of freedom of individuals and of nations are deeply concerned if freedom is threatened anywhere in the world. At a time when the young nations of Asia and Africa proclaim the rights of self-determination and national freedom, the violation of these rights in Germany must mean a fallback into Colonialism. The behavior of the Soviet Union in the Berlin and German question must cause world public opinion to question the honesty of Russia's claims to the young nations of Asia and Africa.

3. Our thoughts at this hour are with the Germans on the other side of the Brandenburg Gate and on the other side of the Iron Curtain. Barbed wire can not disrupt the community of interest of the German people, based on a deep feeling of belonging together, for which, after the most painful experiences freedom and humanity were regarded as the most highly valued possessions of the nation.[39]

4. Germans on the other side of the Iron Curtain bear the burden of the German partition. Their fate must therefore be the measure of our actions. Our Constitution (Basic Law) obligates this freely elected Parliament of Germans to act for our people in the Zone to whom participation in our political life is denied.

5. The policy, which has been pursued since 1945, will some day be judged on the basis of what will have been achieved for the whole German nation. The goal

143

and objective is, therefore, the definite reestablishment of German unity in freedom. This is the political mandate of our generation in whose fulfillment the success or failure of our policy will be judged.

6. The rebuilding of the free part of Germany was only possible because the men in the Soviet Zone resisted Communism and have made an enormous sacrifice for us all. If we, through an overestimation of material welfare, destroy the willingness to sacrifice in the Federal Republic, to help Germans on the other side of the Iron Curtain withstand Communist rule at a daily sacrifice, how could we expect them to have confidence in all German national solidarity? No one of us and in the world should believe that a part (of Germany) "can also live in prosperity tomorrow."[40] The attitude of the Free World in the next weeks and months will prove whether this sacrifice was worthwhile.

7. The Four Powers as signatories of the Potsdam Agreement undertook the political responsibility for the political unification of Germany. Article 7 of the German-Treaty confirms the obligation of our Western Allies to work for the common objective of a reunited Germany with peaceful means. Our treaty partners would not be justified in the letter and spirit of the treaties should they consider the Berlin question alone under the item of their rights in Berlin. The barricade in Berlin is not an internal affair of the Soviet Zone. The obligation undertaken by the Allies to make the cause of German unification its own also obligates them to hold to the last clamps between the divided parts of Germany.

8. The right of freedom of movement between the two parts of Germany, that has been so completely suppressed in these days, was the most important and effective clamp. A recognition of the Soviet Zonal measures for the removal of these in one way or another would mean a breach of the treaties. The right of freedom of movement for all Germans, guaranteed in the Basic Law, prevents any German Gov-

ernment from accepting the measures of the Soviet Zonal authorities.[41]

9. The German people desire good relations with the peoples of the Soviet Union. But the Government of the USSR must recognize that the illegal measures, which it consented to, violated the deepest feelings of the German people. So long as the right of self-determination is denied the German people as a whole, so long as our country is illegally divided, so long will peace in Europe denied by the Soviet Union remain endangered. The Berlin question can only be settled within the framework of the German question in the sense of the reestablishment of political unification.

10. The Government of the Soviet Union will recall the sentence, which it included in its *aide mémoire* of 19 March, 1958, which I cite: "In order to prevent further false rumors, the Soviet Union considers it necessary to firmly declare that it favors a single peace treaty with Germany as a whole."[42]

Dr. Mende concluded with a Declaration for Peace Negotiations: "Aware of the responsibility to our people and for the peace of the world, we Free Democrats demand that we Germans now take a stronger hand in the cause of German unification. Our task is to show the Allied nations and their governments the common objective of the re-establishment of political unity of Germany, for which we expect their aid. I repeat the words spoken by the Bundestag president on June 30 this year before this house with the applause of all parties in the German Bundestag: "I believe, however that it is the command of the hour to urge negotiations for a peace treaty with Germany by agreement between the Western Powers and the Soviet Union. The peace negotiations should clarify:

1 The military and political status of the future Germany as a whole.

2. It is obvious that a peace treaty must bring about a definite settlement of material and legal questions, which emerged from the Second World War. In this

category falls the question of the frontiers of the country.

3. It is indispensable the possibility be guaranteed to make use of the "principle of equal rights and self-determination of peoples," as it is stipulated in Article I of the Charter of the United Nations.[43]

Next came the Declaration of Representative Schneider, Chairman of the DP Fraction (German Party) until its dissolution in July 1960, who spoke as a fractionless deputy, although he also participated in the Bundestag election campaign of 1961, as the candidate for the All-German Party (GDP).[44] Herr Schneider began his address with the observation that the Declaration of the Federal Chancellor, the Bürgermeister of Berlin and all the party chairmen had emphasized the brutal attack of 13 August of Bolshevism against the most elementary human rights. He then spoke of the feelings of helpless impotence and painful disappointment of the most widely distributed class in the population—the refugees, comprising over a fifth of the population of West Germany.

Herr Schneider commented on the widely expressed view that 13 August was a keystone in the postwar history of Germany and of Europe. He would compare it with the Prague Coup of March, 1948, as a new part of the ring around Europe. Schneider predicted that future historians would not focus on 13 August, but on the last days of endless debate, unfulfilled announcements and manifest perplexity of the free world.

Since the November, 1958, ultimatum of Khrushchev, we knew and the world knew the Berlin Plans and the German Plans of Moscow. Since the Vienna meeting between President Kennedy and the Soviet Chief of State, the world was dying with thirst. After the Paris Conference of Foreign Ministers in early August, it was announced that the West was prepared for any possible eventuality. Now with the 13th of August past, the reaction of the West was entirely otherwise than the great majority of Germans had expected. At this moment the West German press confirmed the wide disappointment of Germans with the lack of effective Western countermeasures.[45]

Schneider concluded that the greatest danger to world peace lay in the conviction of a totalitarian regime that it had only to deal with weak opponents who had prepared no effective defense. A political task of the greatest significance was to win the sympathy of the greatest part of the world for the cause of the oppressed, and to mobilize them against their oppressors. Hence the forum of the UN was the place to attack the ideology of Bolshevism.[46]

Bundestag president, Dr. Gerstenmaier, closed the special session of the Bundestag with a brief summary of the points on which all political parties were agreed:

1. All speakers were united in their will to resist the terror and inhumanity which prevailed in the Soviet Occupation Zone of Germany since 12 August, 1961. We also resist the violation of treaties and of international agreements on human rights, consented to by the Warsaw-Pact States.
2. We are also united in this hour, as we have always been for years in solidarity with the oppressed and terrorized, with those who for years were humiliated and insulted behind the Zone and sector borders. In this solidarity is shown the determination of Germans, even in divided Germany, to be one nation and the hope to remain one nation. We are united in solidarity with the free world and its defense organizations, of whose value and meaning we are well aware.
3. This Bundestag is, I hope, just as completely united in loyalty to freedom and today this means: united with all the German people in the firm determination to realize self-determination for all of Germany. Great emphasis was placed on words of comfort and courage to those who suffer behind the sector and Zone frontiers.

Dr. Gerstenmaier concluded the special session of the Bundestag with this final statement:

"I believe there is a real cause, on the basis of which we can appeal to those over there: the Bundestag recognizes the charter of the United Nations and its proclaimed human rights.[47] —They are for us no empty words—particularly Article I with its recognition of the right of self-determination of peoples. The

147

Bundestag in this hour acts according to the meaning and spirit of the Constitution (Basic Law), which commands it to speak for all Germans. We remain loyal and obedient, now and for all time, to the demand of the Constitution, expressed in the last sentence of its Preamble: "The whole German people is called upon to complete the unity and freedom of Germany in free self-determination." We work for this goal, in which we believe.

Press Reaction to Special Bundestag Session

The Bundestag session was the leading story in virtually all West German papers on the weekend. Headlines included the following:

"Bonn Accuses Pankow Before All the World"
"Bundestag Unanimously Denounces Pankow's Breach of Law"
"Adenauer Calling for Negotiations on Germany"
"Chancellor Says, 'Barbed Wire Must Disappear'"
"Berlin and Bonn"
"Resignation in Bonner Bundestag"[48]

Press reaction to the Bundestag session was somewhat mixed. With its special session over the most serious crisis of German postwar history, the Bundestag had fulfilled its obligations in a worthy manner in the view of *Süddeutsche Zeitung*.[49] There was no doubt that 13 August, the day of the Communist *coup de force* in Berlin, had changed the political climate of the Federal Republic. The Bundestag had reflected the will of the German people to resist Communism; but unfortunately grief over the fate of the people in East Berlin and the Soviet Zone had shifted much press criticism over to the Western Allies. This was, of course, more true of the right-center and independent press than of papers close to the government or CDU. On the other hand, reason had prompted both Adenauer and Brandt to stress solidarity with the Western Allies as the only means for maintaining West Berlin's freedom. Unfortunately, however, emotionalism prompted many Germans to call for countermeasures.[50]

As for its contents, right-center, independent and left-center papers generally regarded the special parliamentary session a master performance, with the declarations of all parties more or less parallel to that of the government. Speakers from all political parties were in essential agreement in their judgment of the events of 13 August, with differences limited to ways of removing the Berlin Crisis.[51] Words like Allied Western Powers, NATO Strength or Protest, Freedom or Self-Determination were all familiar words—correct words about sacred rights and high goals —but no word about what the Government will finally do in order to realize its goals in the acute danger.[52]

This seeming inconsistency between political aims and objectives of parties and the lack of Government policy to realize them, as pointed out by *Neue Züricher Zeitung* and *Süddeutsche Zeitung* may be accounted for by the severe limitations upon the freedom of Bonn to act with Germany divided and the question of a future Germany's frontiers, political and military status still to be decided by the Big Four Powers, who were victors in World War II.

The opposition parties found themselves so obligated to the need for national solidarity that no word of criticism fell upon the government. That this declaration of bankruptcy by the Ulbricht Regime might at the same time be a defeat of Bonn foreign policy, no one dared to suggest. The SPD had, indeed, shortly before been converted to this policy. And so it remained to give the Zone people, barricaded over there, confidence and to admonish them again to educate their children as Christians. "One day you will, if you believe as I do, be united with us in freedom!"[53]

In the government declaration there was a starting point for the political action which Brandt demanded. In it the right of self-determination for Germans was demanded and at the same time a security guarantee for the Soviet Union was sought in the event of German unification. To the Chancellor it had become clear that such guarantees could not come from the mere signing of agreements, but had to emerge from political reality.[54]

If it were possible in the West to put forth a plan for the political order of Europe, which would guarantee Soviet Security needs in the eyes of the world, which guards the interests of

East European peoples and which, therefore would demand the right of self-determination for Europe, Moscow would not find it so easy to push her propaganda for a separate peace treaty with the East German Zone Government.

NOTES TO CHAPTER SEVEN

1. See *Die Welt* (Hamburg, ind.), *Westdeutsche Allgemeine* (Essen, ind.), *Neue Rhein Zeitung* (Cologne, ind.), for 18 August, 1961.
2. *Die Welt* (Hamburg, ind.), 19 August, 1961.
3. Classic definition of war by von Clausewitz.
4. *Frankfurter Neue Presse* (pro-Government), 18 August, 1961. Brandt's letter to President Kennedy evoked bitter resentment in CDU quarters.
5. *Ibid.*
6. *Neue Züricher Zeitung* (right-center), 19 August, 1961. *Der Kurier (West Berlin)*, 19 August, 1961.
7. *Das Parlament: Die Woche Im Bundeshaus* (Bonn, Heraus gegeben von der Bundeszentral Für Heimatdienst) Bonn, 23 August, 1961.
8. *Frankfurter Neue Presse* (pro-Government), 19 August, 1961; *Frankfurter Rundschau* (left-center), 19 August, 1961.
9. *Das Parlament,* 23 August, 1961, pp. 1-2.
10. *Ibid.*
11. *Das Parlament,* 23 August, 1961, pp. 1-2.
12. *Ibid.* This was significant in view of the strong criticism of this Four-Power Working group expressed in much of the West German press, particularly, *Mittag* (Düsseldorf, right-center) and *Die Zeit* (Hamburg, weekly, right-center), 17 August, 1961.
13. Applause from all sides of the Bundeshaus.
14. This pre-election statement of the Chancellor would not increase his popularity with young voters, confronted with longer military service.
15. *Das Parlament* (Bonn, pro-Government), 23 August, 1961, p. 2.
16. *Das Parlament* (Bonn, pro-Government), 23 August, 1961, p. 2. (Applause from the benches of the CDU/CSU and from representatives of the SPD and FDP opposition parties).

17. *Ibid.* (Applause by CDU/CSU and deputies of SPD and FDP).
18. *Das Parlament* (Bonn, pro-Government), 23 August, 1961, p. 2. (Applause from the CDU/CSU and deputies of the SPD and FDP).
19. The Federal Office of Statistics in Frankfurt on 5 October, released figures of 3.3 million between 1950 and 1960.
20. (Long applause from the CDU/CSU and from SPD and FDP deputies of the opposition).
21. *Das Parlament,* Nr35/August, 1961, p. 3.
22. *Das Parlament,* NR35/August, 1961, p. 3.
23. *Ibid.* (Applause from the entire house).
24. *Das Parlament,* Nr.35/August, 1961, p. 3.
25. *Ibid.*
26. *Ibid.*
27. *Ibid.* (Applause from the SPD and center benches).
28. *Das Parlament,* Nr 35/23 August, 1961, p. 3. (Lively applause from the SPD, FDP and deputies of the CDU/CSU).
29. *Ibid.* (Applause by the SPD, FDP and deputies of the CDU/CSU).
30. *Ibid.*
31. *Ibid.*
32. *Das Parlament,* Nr 35/23 August, 1961, p. 4. (Continued lively applause from the SPD and from the CDU/CSU benches and the right).
33. *Ibid.,* p. 4. (Applause from all sides of the house).
34. *Das Parlament,* Nr 35/23 August, 1961, p. 4.
35. *Das Parlament,* Nr. 35/ 23 August, 1961, p. 4. (applause from all sides of the house by all parties.)
36. *Das Parlament,* Nr. 35/ 23 August, 1961, p. 4. (applause from the SPD and CDU/CSU and FDP benches.)
37. *Ibid.,* p. 4.
38. *Das Parlament,* Nr. 35/ 23 August, 1961, p. 5.
39. *Ibid.*
40. Implied criticism of CDU election slogan.
41. *Das Parlament,* Nr. 35/ 23 August, 1961, p. 5.
42. *Ibid.*
43. *Ibid.*
44. *Gesamtdeutsche Partei* (GDP) resulted from a merger of the German Party and Refugee Bloc, but only polled 2% of the total vote on 17 September, 1961.

45. *Das Parlament,* Nr. 35/ 23 August, 1961, p. 6.
46. *Ibid.*
47. *Das Parlament,* Nr. 35/ 23 August, 1961, p. y. (Strong applause from all sides of the House.)
48. See *Kölnische Rundschau* (CDU); *Frankfurter Neue Presse* pro-CDU); *Deutsche Zeitung* (right-center); *Frankfurter Rundschau* (left-center), 19 August, 1961.
49. *Süddeutsche Zeitung* (left-center), 19 August, 1961.
50. *Die Welt* (Hamburg, independent), 19 August, 1961.
51. *Süddeutsche Zeitung* (left-center), 19 August, 1961; *Industrie Kurier* (Düsseldorf, independent), 19 August, 1961.
52. *Neue Züricher Zeitung* (independent), 19 August, 1961; *Süddeutsche Zeitung* (left-center), 19 August, 1961.
53. Closing statement of Declaration of the Chancellor, *Süddeutsche Zeitung* (left-center), 19 August, 1961.
54. *Stuttgarter Nachrichten* (independent), 19 August, 1961.

Chapter 8

JOHNSON-CLAY VISIT TO BERLIN
19/20 AUGUST 1961

Vast Importance of Johnson-Clay Visit

Amid the lively applause of the Berlin people, Vice President Johnson, acting as the personal representative of President Kennedy, reaffirmed Allied guarantees of the freedom of West Berlin. Thereby, he also assured inhabitants of East Berlin and the Soviet Zone that the United States had not forgotten them either. At the same time some 1500 United States troop reinforcements came from the Federal Republic to strengthen the American garrison in West Berlin. With a parade of additional units of American troops down the *Kurfürstendamm* and other main streets of the Western Sector, the Johnson visit, on Saturday evening, reached a high point. Expressing gratitude to the Americans, but also to the Berliners and to their Bürgermeister, Zehrer, in a lead article in *Die Welt,* concluded by saying that it is now up to the people of the Federal Republic to show whether they are also prepared to make sacrifices.[1]

The Germans were full of gratitude to the American Government for its welcome gesture, the mission of Johnson to Berlin. Not since the days of the Berlin Blockade had any statesman aroused such a stream of sympathetic feelings as the Man from Texas. The thanks expressed by the ordinary people was even more convincing than that coming from the politicians. This was due to Johnson, his entourage and above all to General Clay whose courageous efforts in the Berlin Blockade were not forgotten. Thanks were particularly due to Kennedy's quick decision. Washington understood that it was not sufficient to call for calmness and patience—however much they were needed during the crucial week in Berlin—but that the psychological imponderables of the people concerned also had to be considered.[2]

After the shock of the events of 13 August, Americans reacted quickly and efficiently. The moral effect of Johnson's visit and the sending of 1500 men into Berlin was to make Berliners feel that they were not written off and that "Kennedy had not left them in the lurch."[3] Along the streets from Tempelhof Airport to the *Rathaus* at Schönberg Platz some 500,000 Berliners gave an enthusiastic reception to the highest representatives of the U.S.A. At the beginning of the parade Johnson called the troop units to their task, "to help fulfill the promise of America to continue vigilance over the fate of Berlin as the crisis develops."[4]

All West German papers on Monday led with reports on Vice President Johnson's Berlin visit and the arrival of 1500 U.S. troops in Berlin. Among the leading headlines were the following:

> "Hundreds of Thousands Cheered Vice President Johnson in Berlin."
> "Storm of Enthusiasm in Berlin over New U.S. Troops."
> "Johnson Welcomes U.S. Troops in Berlin."
> "Johnson Renews Pledge of Protection to West Berlin."
> "All Berlin Turned Out—Cheers and Flowers for Vice President Johnson."
> "Berliners Cheer U.S. Soldiers—Vice President Johnson Endorses Guarantees."
> "U.S. Combat Troops Enthusiastically Welcomed in West Berlin."
> "U.S. Stands by Berlin."[5]

Johnson's Message to Berlin

In the name of the President, Johnson, on Sunday morning, delivered the answer of Kennedy to the letter, which the governing Bürgermeister on the previous Wednesday had sent to Washington. In this letter Brandt had described in detail the serious situation of Berlin after the blocking of the Eastern Sector, and made suggestions for necessary countermeasures. With the delivery of the reply to this letter at the house of the American Ambassador Dowling, in Dahlem, there was a long political discussion. Participating in this discussion, besides Johnson and Brandt, were Ambassador Dowling and Bohlen along with other high officials of the American State Department and of the Berlin Senate.[6]

On Saturday evening, before a special session of the Berlin Senate and House of Representatives, Vice President Johnson again confirmed the binding political and moral obligation of the U.S.A. to guarantee the freedom of West Berlin and free access to the city. *Die Welt* printed long excerpts from Johnson's address, which is worth quoting here:

"I come here at a moment of tensions and danger in your lives, the lives of my countrymen and the common life of the free world. To the survival and to the creative future of this city we Americans have pledged in effect, what our ancestors pledged in forming the U.S.: 'our lives, our fortunes and our sacred honor.'[7] A barrier of barbed wire has been thrown across your city. It has broken for you, more important, for your brethren to the East, vital human and communal ties—ties that reach back into the lives of families and friends and into the long life of this city. I understand the pain and outrage you feel. I understand the anger you feel as the Communist authorities and their hirelings congratulate themselves on having throttled the flow of men, women and children who could stand it no longer and have come to the West, even at the cost of abandoning their homes for unfamiliar places, and all that they have created. 'What a victory' they claim. *What a failure* they prove. I tell you the Communists congratulate themselves too soon. Stop for a moment and consider what this crisis is about. This crisis has arisen because of a massive fact of history. The free men of Germany—both here and in West Germany—have succeeded in the years since the end of the war beyond our most optimistic hopes. I am referring not only to their

155

economic success, which all the world knows and admires. They succeeded in far more important ways. They have built a vital democratic life. They have accepted with remarkable self-discipline, restraints on their military establishment. They have played a great constructive role in building a unified Europe. They are now coming to face a world scene—from India to Bolivia. Make no mistake. This fact of history is well understood in the Kremlin. What they are trying to do now is to interpose barbed wire, bayonets and tanks against the forces of history. In the short run the barbed wire is there, and it will not go away by a wave of the hand. But in the long run, this unwise effort will fail. Lift your eyes from the barricades and ask yourselves: Who can really believe that history will deny Germany and Berlin their natural unity? Who can really believe that the German people will choose Communism after what they have seen on their own soil? This is a time then, for confidence, for poise, for faith— faith in yourselves. It is also a time for faith in your allies, everywhere in the world. This island does not stand alone. You are a vital part of the whole free community of free men. Your lives are linked not merely with those in Hamburg, Bonn and Frankfurt. They are also linked in every town of Western Europe, Canada and the United States and with those on every continent who live in freedom and are prepared to fight for it."[8]

Johnson made it absolutely clear that the West would fight for Berlin, if it were clear that the Soviet Union wished to destroy the freedom of West Berlin or block off access to the city. With increasing warmth the Berliners on Saturday evening greeted General Clay, one of the creators of the Airlift in 1948. Amid long and loud applause Brandt called him the "Rescuer of Berlin." Moreover, in the evening of the same day, Berliners stood for six hours before the *Rathaus Platz* (City Hall Square) and asked the U.S. President for Clay's recall to active duty and be given a special command in Berlin.[9]

West Berlin police estimated that around 500,000 people watched the arrival of Johnson and the motorcade of Johnson and Brandt through the streets.[10] With a large group of American politicians and diplomats, Vice President Johnson, on Sunday afternoon, visited the refugees stationed at Marienfelde. Over 1700 refugees were still quartered there. They belonged to the 12,158 persons, who only from the 14th to the 18th of August were transported to the Federal Republic and West Berlin. The great majority there, of course, had left the Russian Zone before the barricade of the sector boundaries. Johnson had to shake hands with hundreds before he could be freed from the deep throngs of refugees. He spoke with the refugees for a quarter of an hour many times repeating the sentence: "I marvel at the way you have voted for freedom."[11]

Brandt's Gratitude to Johnson and Kennedy

"After the address of Vice President Johnson before the Berlin House of Representatives," the Berlin Bürgermeister declared, "the weight of German-American friendship has endured." Brandt insisted that he had no doubt that the Allied guarantees were valid for Berlin. But it is also good to hear an oral confirmation from the American Vice President in person. Brandt firmly believed that Berlin stands for freedom as no other city, but the people of this city could not look to only one side. "They have shouted a protest against those who barricade men in concentration camps and who build a Chinese Wall through the city." Brandt believed that it went far beyond a mere defense of Berlin and involved everything that was done to hold the people in the Soviet Zone of occupation, above all, with the accusation of the entire world. The German question must not be isolated from the agenda of international affairs.[12]

Brandt cited in particular an apt sentence of Johnson: "We in America are united across all party lines in our sympathy for the German people in its present trial."[13] These words echo all over Germany. "We find ourselves in the midst of a crisis," said Brandt. "We will come through this crisis if the spirit continues which animates this session of the Representative House in Berlin. I know that justice and freedom will not perish."[14]

Brandt's previous anxiety was expressed in a personal letter which he had directed to President Kennedy on Wednesday, 16 August, on the occasion of the mass protest rally before the *Rathaus* in Schönberg, which read as follows:

157

Dear Mr. President:

After the developments of the last three days in my city, may I in this personal letter convey to you only the ideas and historical points which confront me. The measures of the Ulbricht Regime, supported by the Soviet Union and the Eastern Bloc, have completely destroyed what remained of the Four-Power Status [of Berlin].

. . . I consider this the most serious incident in the postwar history of this city since the Blockade (1948). This development has not weakened the will of the West Berlin people to resist, but rather united them, to raise a doubt over the capacity to resist and the resoluteness of the Three Powers to act . . . .

I know very well that the guarantees for the freedom of the population, the presence of troops and free access only for West Berlin are valid. Nevertheless, it is a question of a deep incision into the life of the German people and of outward pressures, the common responsibility of Berlin and Germany as a whole, through which the total western prestige is affected.

I see a political psychological danger in double hindsight: 1) Inactivity and pure defense could lead to a confidence crisis for the Western Powers. 2) Inactivity and pure defense could lead to the over-expanded self-confidence of the East Berlin Regime, that today already boasts in its press of the success of its demonstrations of military power.[15]

The Soviet Union has now achieved half of its Free City proposals through the use of the *Volksarmee* (German People's Army). The second act is only a question of time. After the second act, there would be a Berlin like a Ghetto, that had not only lost its function as a refuge of freedom and a symbol of hope for reunification—but that would be cut off from the free part of Germany. Then could we experience instead of a refugee movement to Berlin, the beginning of a flight out of Berlin.

I would consider it adequate in the situation if the Western Powers desire the reestablishment of Four-Power responsibility, but at the same time would proclaim a Three-Power Status for West Berlin. The Three Powers

158

should repeat a guarantee of their presence in West Berlin until German reunification and in case of a plebiscite of the people in West Berlin and of the Federal Republic. It must also be made clear that the German question permits no unilateral solution by the Western Powers, but rather that the emphasis should be placed on a peace settlement which corresponds to the right of self-determination for the German people and the security interests of all parties concerned.

Moreover, I would consider it fortunate if the West on its own initiative brought the Berlin question before the United Nations, to present the argument that the Soviet Union has in a most flagrant manner violated the declaration of human rights . . . In such a situation, it is so much more expedient to attempt to seize the political initiative, if there is still a possibility of taking the initiative.

After tolerating a Soviet step which is illegal (since it has been so characterized) and considering the many tragedies, which take place in East Berlin and in the Soviet Union, we can ill afford to take the risk involved in a late solution. It would be most welcome, if the American garrison could demonstrate a show of strength. I estimate the situation serious enough, Mr. President, to write to you with great frankness, as is possible only among friends, who have complete trust in one another.[16]

Controversy Over Brandt Letter

Giving as its source "SPD quarters," *Frankfurter Allgemeine* in its Saturday edition, published the letter from Brandt to Kennedy under the heading, "Social Democratic Crisis."[17] In reply to this, the SPD Presidium (Parteivorstand) in Bonn informed the reporter of *Die Welt* that no member of the presidium of the SPD had ever had access to the Brandt letter.[18] Washington officials attributed German criticism of the inactivity of the Western Powers to the election campaign situation in the West German Federal Republic. This applied in particular to Brandt's letter to Kennedy. The White House took the position that a letter to a Head of State by a person who was not at least a Chief of Government was contrary to diplomatic protocol. The United States had reason to resent Brandt's remark that what was needed was deeds, not words.[19] Brandt's letter met with strong criticism in political circles in Bonn. Reproaches were made to Brandt by members of his own party in a meeting of the SPD Bundestag fraction on Friday. They criticized both the style of the letter and passages regarding the responsibilities of the city of Berlin.[20] This is partly explained by the two wings of the SPD: the moderate revisionist wing of the majority, which includes Brandt, Party Chairman Ollenhauer, Fraction Chairman Mommer and Professor Carlo Schmid in contrast to the more traditional, Marxian wing, including the die-hards and older party functionaries, who were, outvoted at the Bad-Godesberg and Hannoverian conferences in 1959 and 1960.[21]

Die Welt under "Inactivity Leads to Crisis of Confidence" carried the text of Brandt's letter to Kennedy and, together with other Monday papers referred to the suit filed by Western Berlin's Senate against persons unknown in connection with the release of the text in the Saturday edition of *Frankfurter Allgemeine*. *Die Welt* commented that Kennedy's letter to Brandt would not be published, just as Brandt's letter to Kennedy should not have been released." [22]

A few hours before the arrival of Chancellor Adenauer in West Berlin on Tuesday, 22 August, 1961, a heavy press feud broke out over the question whether Adenauer or Brandt was right and which of them gained more political advantage by the visiting American Vice-President Johnson and the strengthening of the American garrison. The press close to Adenauer, and in West Berlin, that is practically only *Der Tag,* attempted to remove the Anti-Adenauer-Attitude by a leading article. Its chief editor defended Adenauer against the reproach that "he lacked any feeling for the importance of national demonstrations."[23] He argued that Adenauer could not come to Berlin sooner because of political responsibility and his duty as a statesman and maintained that, it was, nevertheless, the Chancellor who had caused the quick action of the Americans and the sending of Vice-President Johnson.

In contrast to this the *Telegraf* wrote: "Both the visit of Johnson and also the dispatch of a battalion from West Germany to West Berlin were in the first place due to the earnest and apprehensive letter of Mayor Brandt to Kennedy." The

160

Telegraf denied the statement of the Chairman of the CDU/CSU Fraction, Dr. Krone, who had referred to the visit of Johnson as the direct result of the Chancellor's action and thought that some kind of public alibi could be created for Adenauer's Berlin journey and the deep confidence crisis be overcome, which "his lack of activity in the Berlin Crisis had caused." The *Telegraf* [24] said very definitely that Johnson had declared here in Berlin that it had been the letter of Brandt that had deeply influenced Kennedy and his decision to send Johnson, Clay and Bohlen to Berlin.[25]

The reaction of the independent press to Brandt was somewhat mixed: part of it deploring the fact that this election maneuver had extended beyond Berlin and the other opinion that it would have been well if the question could have been discussed freely and calmly.[26] *Der Mittag* dealt with the controversy between CDU and SPD over who prompted Johnson's visit and criticized both parties for exploiting the visit for the sake of the election campaign.[27]

Ahlers, writing in *Frankfurter Rundschau*, used unusually strong language in the most severe criticism of the Federal Chancellor. Reviewing the situation in the light of Johnson's visit, he said Dr. Adenauer had given fresh evidence that he was no statesman. He argued that what benevolent people praised as a special achievement, his silently putting up with the unavoidable, his justification of Western inactivity was basically only a proof of the fact that he had no solution.[28] This writer considered a big coalition the only reasonable countermeasure against Soviet intentions in Berlin which could correct the policy hitherto pursued.

Vice-President Johnson himself related that the President had called him on receipt of Brandt's letter and had urged him to fly to Berlin. Johnson related that at first he would have really preferred that the initiative come from Congress, but that the tone of the letter had convinced both Kennedy and himself that his journey had to be made immediately.[29] Thus the assertion of the Fraction Chairman of the CDU/CSU, Dr. Krone, who tried to trace Johnson's Berlin visit back to the direct influence of the Chancellor was misleading the public, in spite of irrefutable evidence to the contrary. Even before Brandt's letter was published in *Frankfurter Allgemeine* against his will, it was described by the Chancellor himself in a party caucus of the CDU/CSU as "arrogant and presumptuous."[30]

There seems to be no doubt that the letter was published in the paper through the indiscretion of the Bonn Government. At the same time it was through this indiscretion of Bonn that the communication was opened and that the letter was not answered, but was merely placed at the disposal of the Four-Power working group in Washington. SPD Chairman Ollenhauer expressed the view that the Federal Government had tried to stop the American Government from replying to Brandt's letter.[31]

Mayor Brandt, both in his address before the lower house and in a personal conversation with Berlin journalists stated that in questions of foreign policy the Federal Government did not represent Berlin diplomatically. Rather Berlin had a special status and consequently a special relationship with the Western Allies. That fact did not permit him any delay; he had to write his letter immediately, when he realized that Berliners expected positive political action from the Western Powers.[32]

Adenauer, Johnson and Berlin

Several West German papers on Monday carried front-page headlines of Dr. Adenauer's plans to fly to Berlin on Tuesday. Reports indicated the Chancellor wanted to visit the sector border and the refugee camp in Marienfelde. Papers emphasized that at the "polite, but definite request of the Americans," Adenauer dropped his plan to accompany Vice President Johnson to Berlin. The explanation was that the Americans could not afford to give the impression of trying to influence the German parliamentary elections.[33] *Neue Rhein Zeitung* mentioned the bitter disappointment of Adenauer over Johnson. Despite the Chancellor's tacit expectation, Johnson did not invite him to accompany him to Berlin. Such a trip would have been the last chance for Adenauer to carry out a long overdue visit to Berlin with real effect.[34] Whereas the Eisenhower-Dulles Policy was to give definite encouragement to Dr. Adenauer's CDU/CSU party both in 1953 and 1957,[35] the Kennedy Administration was careful to avoid the slightest appearance of interference in the German parliamentary campaign.

According to the *Allgemeine Zeitung*, the CDU felt that

Brandt's joint activities with Johnson in Berlin gave the impression that the Kennedy Administration favored the SPD. The CDU leadership felt particularly bad about Brandt's taking advantage of Johnson's remark that the Americans stood by Berlin irrespective of party affiliations.[36]

Frankfurter Allgemeine on Tuesday described the plans for the Chancellor's short visit to Berlin, which included the following items:

1. Greeting of the Chancellor and his party by Mayor Brandt at the airport at 11:00 a.m.
2. A journey along the sector border to see the blockade measures of the Soviet Zone Regime.
3. A visit to the refugee center at Marienfelde.
4. A special session of the Berlin Senate with the Chancellor as its guest.
5. A press conference in the Berlin City Hall and
6. The Chancellor's return flight at 6:45 p.m.—allowing the Chancellor only eight hours in Berlin.[37]

After Adenauer and his party were greeted at the airport by the Federal Minister of All-German Affairs, Ernst Lemmer, Mayor Brandt said: "Herr Chancellor, you will see the Berliners calm and full of confidence that the future means freedom." The comments of the Chancellor at the airport, which already suggested the theme of his deliberations with the Senate, stressed the following points:

1. Inhabitants of the Soviet Zone and East Berlin must be assured that "they have not been written off by us."
2. The measures of 13 August change nothing in the conviction of the Chancellor that Germany will be reunited in peace and freedom and that Berlin will again become the capital of Germany.
3. The "shameful wall" on the sector boundaries is a reminder for all Germans not to forget reunification.
4. All Berliners and all Germans on the weekend have experienced with great satisfaction, how the leading power of the West, the United States, and all NATO Powers stand behind the German people.[38]

163

At his press conference Adenauer showed that he was very deeply impressed by the "extraordinary fortitude" of the Berlin people. "I am not of the opinion," Adenauer said in reply to a question, "that these barricade measures have anything to do with communications between the Federal Republic and West Berlin."[39] In the Chancellor's opinion the conclusion of a separate peace treaty between Moscow and East Berlin would not change anything. "Russia has guaranteed the security of the means of access and without evidence to the contrary, I believe that Soviet Russia upholds what it has guaranteed."[40]

In Adenauer's opinion, the special obligations for Berlin, undertaken by the U.S.A., Great Britain and France were of far greater significance than a closer political connection with the Federal Republic. Therefore, Dr. Adenauer spoke against a protest to the Warsaw Pact States against their support of the Soviet Zone barricade measures. Notwithstanding the seriousness of the situation he had experienced, the Chancellor pleaded for a carrying forward of the electoral campaign. To the rumors of prior information of the Western Powers over the Soviet Zonal barricade measures through the Soviets, Adenauer replied that he did not believe that the Western Powers had known anything about these measures beforehand.

Chancellor Adesauer was accompanied by representatives of the German economy, German Trade Union Associations and German medicine, CDU Fraction Chief, Dr. Krone and the Federal Refugee Minister von Merkatz. They were greeted by Federal Minister Lemmer, head of the Federal Ministry for All-German Affairs—an agency which has carried on a very lively propaganda campaign for the last ten years, publishing hundreds of pamphlets on the problems of refugees from the Eastern territories, shortcomings of the Ulbricht regime and many related subjects. It maintains large offices both in Bonn and Berlin and wields a large influence on world public opinion.[41]

The Chancellor's visit to Berlin inspired editorials in seven West German papers. *Kölnische Rundschau* and *Deutsche Zeitung* both defended Adenauer's decision not to go to Berlin immediately after the closing of the sector boundaries. *Die Welt* maintained that Dr. Adenauer's attitude created a vacuum within public opinion which the Chancellor should never have permitted. Hence his visit to Berlin on Tuesday, ten days after the crisis of 13 August could not remove this impression. *Der*

Mittag pointed out that this delayed trip had the features of awkward embarrassment. Statements by the distinguished guest contained nothing that could have inspired the right mood. Hence, the strongest and noisiest reaction to the Chancellor's visit came from the propaganda machinery of East Berlin functionaries.[42]

General Anzeiger focused attention on the angry reaction on the part of the West Berliners and criticized both the Chancellor for his late visit to the divided city and Brandt for having taken shelter in the "sulking corner" of the Schöneberg city hall instead of accompanying the Chancellor when he toured Berlin. The voter was disgusted at seeing the destiny of Berlin linked with the election campaign. *Neue Rhein Zeitung* said respect was paid the Federal Chancellor, but that it was demonstrated to campaigner Adenauer that the yardstick wih which a politician is measured is in Berlin and not on the Rhine.[43]

Arno Scholz in *Der Telegraf* said Adenauer would learn that Berliners, who on Monday of the previous week had seen together with Bundestag President Gerstenmaier, party Chairmen: Dr. Krone (CDU/CSU), Dr. Mende (FDP) and Erich Ollenhauer (SPD), would not receive him with the same enthusiasm with which they had greeted the American Vice President.[44] Preparations for the late visit to Berlin were not well planned.

Reaction of West German Press to Johnson Visit

At a press conference in Berlin before a hundred German and foreign journalists, Dr. Adenauer finally admitted that he regretted the lack of more effective countermeasures against the barricades on the Berlin border. Although he reproached the West for not criticizing more severely the one-sided breach of the Four-Power agreements, the important thing was to make Berlin the subject of Big-Power negotiations. Deeply impressed by the enclosure of the East Berlin people within the sector boundaries and a "Zone of Silence and Death," Adenauer considered the strengthening of American troops in Berlin an act of great political significance. Also this step would make a deep impression on the Soviet Union.[45] Schroeder, discussing new election campaign tactics of German political parties, wrote in *Die Welt* that the SPD wants to underline its solidarity with

Berlin while the CDU will put stress on the prevention of war.[46]

Editorial comment in the West German Press on Monday was extremely favorable to the Johnson-Clay visit. Practically all papers—pro-government, right-center, independent, left-center and pro-SPD—expressed deep appreciation of Kennedy's decision to send Vice President Johnson to Berlin. *Frankfurter Neue Presse* called it "more than a non-committal gesture aimed merely at soothing temporary doubts of the attitude of the Western Powers."[47] If Washington seemed too hesitant and worried over Germans and West Berliners, the prompt and well-considered decision of Kennedy had restored confidence. *Frankfurter Allgemeine* also noted the warm sympathy of Berliners for Johnson and Clay, whose heroic stand in the Berlin Blockade of 1948 was not forgotten. Above all Washington had realized that caution and patience alone were not enough to satisfy the psychological imponderables of the population in a crisis. Moreover, the violent reaction of Moscow confirmed the political importance of Johnson's trip and the solemn reaffirmation of American aid even though existing facts had not yet been changed.[48]

Deutsche Zeitung stressed the enthusiastic welcome Berliners accorded General Clay, who personifies the very quality Berliners expect in a crisis from their protecting powers—calm determination.[49] *Die Welt* noted with great satisfaction that for the first time in its history the United States had concluded a declaration of guarantee for a friend by quoting from the Declaration of Independence as Johnson did before the Berlin City Parliament.[50]

Stuttgarter Nachrichten noted that Berlin's claim to be the German capital was not included in the American statement. Johnson had said the U.S.A. would protect West Berlin, but failed to announce action that might force Ulbricht to revoke his measures. Thus Johnson showed that the U.S. would tolerate Ulbricht's action and respect the Soviet Union's sphere of influence even where it exceeded its lawful limits. Nevertheless, the paper concluded that in this crisis one reassuring result of the "American Sunday" following the "Black Sunday" of 13 August was the mutual respect of the two world powers for each other's spheres of influence.[51]

Süddeutsche Zeitung complimented Kennedy's keen psychological insight and the symbolic reinforcement of allied troops in Berlin. However, the situation in Berlin and the basic

166

line of U.S. policies remained unchanged. Visits and troop reinforcements were no countermoves to Ulbricht's stone wall barricades.[52] Despite the blunt facts of the barbed wire and concentration camp, *Neue Rhein Zeitung* found Johnson's visit significant in that it ended creeping fear and gave confidence to West Berlin, to East Berliners and Germans in the Soviet Zone. Mayor Brandt and Berliners took over the leadership in foreign policy in "days of trial" in a "powerful, dynamic and rousing manner."[53]

Westfälische Rundschau, also pro-SPD, hoped that both the West and the Adenauer Government would be better prepared for negotiations than they were for the erection of the barricade in Berlin on 13 August.[54] *Der Spiegel* carried an editorial by Jens Daniels lamenting the "lack of a genuine parliamentary opposition" in Bonn and reproaching Franz Joseph Strauss, Federal Minister of Defense, for contributing to the Berlin crisis by calling for nuclear weapons for the West German army.[55] *Der Spiegel* focused on the deep concern of Premier Khrushchev over the mass exodus of refugees from the Soviet Zone—a concern shared by Senator Fulbright, Chairman of the Senate Foreign Relations Committee, and by the Western Powers, for whom Soviet action in checking the flow of refugees came as a welcome relief.[56]

West Berlin papers expressed complete confidence in the West after initiative was finally seized. *Der Tag* interpreted Johnson's rush flight to Berlin as an indication that "Americans themselves had a feeling of not having reacted as satisfactorily as the world expected them to do." [57] The Berlin *Morgen Post* expressed deep gratitude to President Kennedy, his Vice President, General Clay and all members of the American delegation for coming to Berlin at a time of deep mourning.[58] *Der Tagespiegel* focused on the gratitude Berliners owed to President Kennedy for his prompt reaction to Mayor Brandt's urgent message on ending the confidence-crisis. Since the Khrushchev ultimatum of November, 1958, both the Western Powers and NATO countries stressed the defense of the freedom of West Berliners in all their propaganda. This was in order to prepare the people of the democratic countries to meet an extreme case of Communist aggression.[59] Both independent papers in West Berlin were moderate and reasonable in their expectations of Western aid, considering the seriousness of the Berlin Crisis of 1961.

1. *Die Welt,* (Hamburg, independent), 21 August, 1961.
2. *Frankfurter Allgemeine Zeitung* (right-center), 21 August, 1961.
3. *Der Mittag* (Düsseldorf, right-center), 21 August, 1961.
4. *Die Welt* (Hamburg, independent), 21 August, 1961.
5. *Kölnische Rundschau* (pro-CDU), 20 August, 1961, and 21 August, 1961; *Deutsche Zeitung* (Cologne, right-center), 21 August, 1961; *Frankfurter Allgemeine Zeitung* (right-center), 21 August, 1961; *Der Mittag* (Düsseldorf, right-center), 21 August, 1961; Die Welt (Hamburg, independent), 21 August, 1961; *General Anzeiger* (Bonn, independent), 21 August, 1961; *Frankfurter Rundschau* (left-center), 21 August, 1961.
6. *Die Welt* (Hamburg, independent), 21 August, 1961.
7. This may well have been the first time in the history of the U.S.A. that the final sentence of the "Declaration of Independence" has been used in a declaration to stand by a friend in the world. Zehrer in *Die Welt,* 21 August, 1961.
8. *New York Times* (independent), 21 August; *Die Welt,* 21 August, 1961.
9. *Die Welt* (Hamburg, independent), 21 August, 1961.
10. Altogether Brandt received between 10 and 12 hours of free television time with Johnson, a fact noted with great regret in CDU headquarters in Bonn.
11. *Die Welt,* 21 August, 1961; *"Ich bewunder mich euch, wie ihr die Freiheit gewählt habt."*
12. *Die Welt* (Hamburg, independent), 21 August, 1961.
13. "Wir in Amerika sind uns über alle Parteigrenzen hinaus einig in unserer Sorge für das deutsche Volk in seinen gegenwärtigen Prüfung. Diese, Worter geht alle in Deutschland an."
14. *Die Welt* (Hamburg, independent), 21 August, 1961.
15. See *Neues Deutschland* (East Berlin, pro-SED), 14-19 August, 1961. It is weighted with none too subtle East German Communist propaganda and disparaged by most West Germans as unreliable.
16. *Die Welt* (Hamburg, independent), 21 August, 1961.
17. *Frankfurter Allgemeine Zeitung* (right-center), 19 August, 1961.

18. *Die Welt* (Hamburg, independent), 21 August, 1961.
19. E. Walter in an ex-Washington special to *Süddeutsche Zeitung* (Munich, left-center), 19 August, 1961.
20. *Die Welt* (Hamburg, independent), 21 August, 1961.
21. See *Basic Programme of the Social Democratic Party of Germany* adopted by an Extraordinary Conference of the SPD, 13-15 November at Bad-Godesberg, published by SPD, Bonn, pp. 5-12.
22. *Die Welt* (Hamburg, independent), 21 August, 1961. On the controversy over the Brandt letter, see also the Monday editions of: *Der Mittag* (Düsseldorf, right-center); *Kölnische Rundschau am Sonntag* (pro-CDU); *Frankfurter Allgemeine Zeitung* (right-center); *Deutsche Zeitung* (independent).
23. *Der Tag* (West Berlin, pro-CDU), 22 August, 1961; *National Zeitung* (right-center), 22 August, 1961.
24. *Telegraf* (West Berlin, pro-SPD), 22 August, 1961.
25. *Ibid.*
26. *National Zeitung* (Basel, independent), 22 August, 1961.
27. *Der Mittag* (Düsseldorf, independent), 22 August, 1961.
28. *Frankfurter Rundschau* (independent), 22 August, 1961.
29. Arno Schulz, "Ein Brief hatte Erfolg." in *Telegraf* (West Berlin, pro-SPD), 22 August, 1961. For the sake of the record, it must be stated, as Johnson himself related, an important factor was a direct cable to President Kennedy on Sunday, 13 August, from the Chief of the U.S. Information Agency, Edward R. Murrow, who had flown into Berlin on "Black Sunday" and was deeply impressed by the reaction of Berliners to the wall.
30. *Ibid.*
31. *Kölnische Rundschau* (CDU, Catholic), 23 August, 1961, *Neue Rhein Zeitung* (pro-SPD), 23 August, 1961; *Deutsche Zeitung* (independent), 23 August, 1961.
32. *Telegraf* (West Berlin, pro-SPD), 22 August, 1961.
33. *Frankfurter Allgemeine* (right-center), 21 August, 1961.
34. *Neue Rhein Zeitung* (Cologne, pro-SPD), 21 August, 1961.
35. See Hans Speier and W. Phillips Davidson, editors, *West German Leadership and Foreign Policy* (White Plains, N.Y.), p. 49.
36. *Allgemeine Zeitung* (Mainz, independent), 21 August, 1961.
37. *Frankfurter Allgemeine* (right-center), 22 August, 1961. The

169

Chancellor's last previous visit, earlier in the summer, was 25 hours, according to Arno Shulz in *Telegraph*, 22 August, 1961.

39. *Ibid.*

40. *Ibid.*

41. Write to the Ministry *Für Gesamtdeutsche Fragen* for a list of the many publications.

42. *Kölnische Rundschau* (CDU-Catholic), 23 August, 1961.

43. *General Anzeiger* (Bonn, independent), 23 August, 1961; *Neue Rhein Zeitung* (Cologne, pro-SPD), 23 August, 1961.

44. Arno Schulz, "Ein Brief Hatte Erfolg" in *Telegraf* (West Berlin, pro-SPD), 22 August, 1961.

45. *Frankfurter Allgemeine Zeitung* (right-center), 23 August, 1961. The reaction of the Soviets and East Germans to these events will be covered in the next chapter.

46. *Die Welt* (Hamburg, independent), 23 August, 1961.

47. *Frankfurter Neue Presse* (pro-government), 21 August, 1961.

48. *Frankfurter Allgemeine Zeitung* (right-center), 21 August, 1961.

49. *Deutsche Zeitung* (Cologne, right-center), 21 August, 1961.

50. *Die Welt* (Hamburg, independent), 21 August, 1961.

51. *Stuttgarter Nachrichten* (independent), 21 August, 1961.

52. *Süddeutsche Zeitung* (Munich, left-center), 21 August, 1961.

53. Jens Fedderson in *Neue Rhein Zeitung* (Cologne, pro-SPD), 21 August, 1961.

54. *Westfälische Rundschau* (Dortmund, pro-SPD), 21 August, 1961.

55. *Der Spiegel* (Hamburg weekly, independent), 21 August, 1961.

56. *Ibid.* Only sympathy for their West German ally prevented the Western Powers from expressing this gratitude openly.

57. *Der Tag* (West Berlin, pro-CDU), 21 August, 1961.

58. *Berliner Morgenpost* (independent), 21 August, 1961.

59. *Der Tagespiegel* (independent), 21 August, 1961.

PART III.

REACTION TO EVENTS OF 13 AUGUST 1961

Chapter 9

SOVIET AND EAST GERMAN REACTION TO BERLIN CRISIS

Soviet Reaction—Hard Facts Hidden by Soviet Press

Within 24 hours after receiving the Western protest notes against the barricade measures in Berlin, Russia in three identical notes delivered on 18 August, to Britain, the United States and France, "categorically rejected" Western protests against the Communist sealing of the East Berlin frontier. The Soviet notes continued the verbal war over Berlin along expected lines. They seemed to be designed more for Afro-Asian opinion rather than for the Western Powers. It was argued that in closing the border East Germany was merely using the ordinary rights of every sovereign state to protect its interests. *Die Welt* printed an abbreviated excerpt of the essential parts of the note to the U.S.A. verbatim:

In connection with the note of the U.S.A. Government of August 17, 1961, the Government of the U.S.S.R. deems it essential to clarify the following points:

1. The Soviet Government understands and supports without reservations the steps of the Government of the East German Democratic Republic (DDR), which has established an effective control over its boundaries with West Berlin, in order to remove insidious agitation of West Berlin against the DDR and other states of the Socialist community. By its border actions the DDR

only exercised the universal right of every sovereign state for the protection of its interests.

. . . The control of state boundaries belongs to the internal questions of every state and its exercise requires neither the recognition nor approval of other governments. The attempts of the U.S. Government to interfere in the internal affairs of the DDR are, therefore, entirely unfounded.[1]

The West was accused of responsibility for this step which had been caused by its political and economic provocations against the East Germans. The note seemed to contain only one significant addition to a similar rejection made by the Soviet Commandant in Berlin, Colonel Soloviev, and published 48 hours previously. This was the statement that the new border measures were only "temporary." It was hinted that the conclusion of a separate Peace Treaty with East Germany would help matters in this respect.

The Soviet note of 18 August continued:

2. The Government of the U.S. is no doubt aware of the reasons which rendered the establishment of controls over the border crossings between the DDR and West Berlin necessary and even mandatory. It played no small part in creating these conditions. West Berlin has been transformed into a center of subversive activity, of diversion and espionage—a center of political and economic provocation against the DDR, the Soviet Union and other socialist countries.

Formerly and recently leading West Berlin authorities described West Berlin cynically as an arrow in the flesh of the DDR, as a Front City, as a sore spot, as the cheapest Atom Bomb in the center of a socialist state. The doors of West Berlin were wide open for international violators and provocateurs of all shades. Only thus could international tensions be sharpened and subversive activities against the countries of the socialist community be widened.

Ruling officials of West Germany, assisted by the occupation authorities, had converted West Berlin into

174

the main base of incessant economic sabotage against the DDR. Following their aggressive militarist line, hostile to the cause of peace, they turned West Berlin into an arena of overt revanchist gatherings and program manifestations directed against the neighboring peaceloving Socialist states. An incendiary slanderous propaganda hostile to Russia, East Germany and other Socialist States has been and was systematically conducted by radio and television from West Berlin.[2]

The note emphasized that this was due to the connivance and direct encouragement by Western occupation authorities. These had long since bartered away their commitments under Four-Power Agreements "for the advantages they got from West Germany as a member of the NATO aggressive military bloc." [3] East Germany had tolerated an absolutely revolting and impermissible situation for many years. But the subversive activity from West Berlin against East Germany and other socialist countries had recently been conducted on a still wider scale, particularly since the Communist proposals for a German peace treaty.

The Soviet note of 18 August continued:

3. It is well known that in West Berlin more than 80 subversive divisions, agitation and espionage organizations have established themselves in West Berlin and are carrying out their agitation against the DDR, the USSR and other socialist states. Documents were transmitted to the Western Powers with exact addresses and a register and names of persons who were engaged in carrying out the hostile plans of West Berlin, the Federal Republic and NATO to undermine the economy of the DDR. And yet the West Berlin authorities and occupation agencies of the USA, Great Britain and France had done absolutely nothing to end the misuse of the territory of West Berlin for such inadmissible international provocations. The facts are quite obvious that West Berlin has become an espionage center for the paid agents of American, British and French Intelligence and for subversive espionage agencies of the West German Federal Republic with its branch offices.

This raises the question whether such operations have even a remote connection with the reality of the Four-Power Status of Berlin, which was set up immediately after the destruction of Hitlerite Germany and to which the note of the U.S. Government refers.[4]

The joint Four-Power program for renewing the life of Germany on a democratic, peaceful basis had been implemented only on East German territory, it was claimed. West Germany had developed along the path of the revival of militarism, and now chauvinist and revanchist forces, dangerous to the cause of peace, which had been the inspirers and organizers of Nazi aggression, were again in the saddle. Much had changed in the past 16 years: two independent states had emerged on German territory and no one had the right to interfere in the affairs of these two German States as long as their actions fell under their internal jurisdiction. In conclusion the note said the Berlin border measures were provisional. Conclusion of a German peace treaty and normalization of the situation in West Berlin on the basis of such a treaty would not infringe the true interests of either side, but rather would benefit the peace and security of all peoples.

In the extensive coverage on Berlin given to the Russian people by the Soviet press and radio, no mention was made of the two main factors in the situation. The Soviet people were not told either about the westward flight of refugees or the economic plight of East Germany. Closing of the Berlin borders was explained to Soviet readers as a means of safeguarding the eastern sector of Berlin against "spies and slave traders," and only one sentence in the Warsaw Pact Communique could have given any hint that the barbed wire, People's Police and stone walls were to prevent a mass exodus westward, rather than infiltration eastward.

According to Pravda, "The government organs and military agencies of the Federal Republic are by deceit, bribery and blackmail inducing a certain unstable portion of the inhabitants of the DDR to leave for West Germany." [5] Pravda added that the Federal Republic was being turned into the mainspring of NATO's aggressive policy.

Moscow's general estimate of the border ban of East Berlin was that East Germans were grateful. The main impression con-

176

veyed by the Moscow Radio and press to Soviet citizens was that "nothing remarkable has happened in Berlin and nothing is going to happen." [6] However, Soviet reports on the events in Berlin were unsensational to the point of distorting the true picure of events in Berlin immediately after 13 August. Pravda claimed that the people of East Germany approved of their government's decision and thanked it for protecting their peaceful labor.[7]

East German Reaction to Berlin Barricades

On Tuesday the situation in the Soviet sector of Berlin had scarcely changed since Sunday. Government quarters behind Potsdamer Platz and east of the Brandenburg Gate were guarded by military and police forces of the SED-State.[8] The occupation of East Berlin by the troops of the East German Regime, which was a flagrant violation of Four-Power Agreements against the setting up of military bands in all Berlin, was regarded by the Communists as an execution of a Resolution of the Member-States of the Warsaw-Pact Organization.

The SED press emphasized the character of the DDR as a member state of the Eastern Military Organization. The action of Ulbricht was taken as the expression of a pretended strength of the SED-State and as evidence of the claim that East Berlin was the capital of the DDR.[9]

The Central Organ of the SED, *Neues Deutschland* wrote:

With the strengthening of the DDR, with the security of peace and order in Berlin, we are prepared to conclude a Peace Treaty which definitely blocks the designs of the militarists. Thus and only thus will the way be free for the rebirth of Germany as a peaceloving, anti-imperialistic and neutral state. We have preserved: humanity from inhumanity, order from disorder and labor from labor crushers and speculators.[10]

Another propaganda technique used was to print statements praising the border closing measures as given by representative East Berlin citizens: locomotive repairman, university professors, factory foremen and managers of East German Farm Cooperatives, as follows:

177

LPG Manager Helmut Fieburg:
"We farmers still have confidence in our government. Everything it has done benefits us and the cause of peace."
Shop foreman Günter Kurz:
"August 13 was a black day for war instigators."
Locomotive repairman, Friedrich Otto:
"Naturally we must tolerate many small inconveniences in connection with the border closing; but these are a small sacrifice in contrast to the great sacrifice for war."
Prof. Dr. Walter Meyer, Director of the Institute of West German and Foreign Civil Law at Humboldt University in East Berlin:

"The recently proclaimed declaration and measures are for the protection of our Republic and could be greeted by every rational man as absolutely necessary. West Berliners must also be grateful that their true interests could only be secured by the transformation of the Front City into a peaceful free city." [11]

The Tuesday issue of *Neues Deutschland* carried the headline: "West German Peace Fighters: That is a Blow Against War." Citizens of the Federal Republic regard the measures of our Government as a protection of peace. Trade Union Secretary Arthur Böpple declared Sunday before a Labor Conference of the German Peace Union (DFU) in Bremen:

The border measures were a necessary step towards peace in view of the revanche demands repeatedly put forth by the Federal Government. The Federal Government has failed to render a united contribution to peace and the normalization of relations. It is astonishing with what patience the DDR has tolerated the intrigues of the West Berlin Espionage Center. The Western Powers, through the misuse of their power, have lost the right of existence in West Berlin.[12]

Dr. Gustav Heinemann, former Interior Minister in the Adenauer Cabinet and SPD deputy in the Bundestag declared: "With the measures of the DDR Government on Sunday, the Federal Government has an answer to its 12-year false German policy. The foundation of the West German Policy is shattered and the discharge of the federal Chancellor is urgent."[13]

Psychologist Dr. Xylander of Munich found no grounds for panic, "The West has no grounds for panic. For it is, indeed, necessary to discuss with one another and, of course, as rapidly as possible."[14] The Munich scientist emphasized that the basis for the measures of the DDR Government was the policy put forth by the West German Government.

Metal worker Ernst Völkner of Essen attributed the measures of the DDR Government to the cold war, pushed by the West. Finally, the Foreign Minister of the DDR, Dr. Lothar Bolz, before the East German Parliament (Volkskammer) emphasized the readiness of the DDR Government to negotiate with Bonn over the question of a peace treaty."[15]

Harry Czepuck in an article on "The Bankrupt Policy" heaped strong criticism on Mayor Brandt, SPD candidate for Chancellor, for supporting a strong anti-Communist program. "Nürnberg, a city famous for Nazi party Congresses, again heard on the previous weekend (12 August, 1961) emphasis on anti-Communism, as it was last heard there in 1938 and 1939."[16] Had it come from the same revanchist or military organizations or from the CDU or CSU Party members: Strauss, Giöbke or Lemmer, the result would have been the same.[17] *Neues Deutschland* characterized the political conception of the Brandt-Wehner group in the SPD as bankrupt for making common cause with the CDU in its effort to replace the East German DDR Government by counter-revolutionary adventurers. This Brandt policy, shattered by the events of 13 August, was compared to the policy of Goebbels, which was destroyed in the halocaust of the Nazi Reich.

Allowing for the anxiety within the SPD over the Brandt-Wehner policy, the *Neues Deutschland* correspondent noted that the SPD Chairman, Erich Ollenhauer, "whom the party had suppressed for a long time, came to the platform in Nürnberg and emphasized that the Left must come into power in the Federal Republic because only in this way could the peace be saved."[18] This indicated under what pressure the SPD leadership stands. Also the personal attacks against Strauss as one who was power conscious and whose rise to power could only have disastrous results for democracy, was, in the view of *Neues Deutschland,* a concession to the mood of the West German people and above all to the SPD membership.

Neues Deutschland further declared that:

The ruling party (CDU/CSU) has the right-wing SPD leaders and the right-ging German Trade Union leaders only until they have accomplished their traditional task—the task they have always performed when the ruling class in Germany was in difficulty or involved in a war—of hitching Labor to their cart. This happened in 1914 when the right-wing SPD leaders—with the breakup of the Second International—voted for war credits and thus made possible the war of the German Imperialists. This was also true on May 1, 1933 when the German Trade Union Leadership (ADGB) was called upon to demonstrate under the Nazi colors and thus the German labor class bowed to the brown mob. And the same is true today when Brandt and Wehner support Herr Strauss, his NATO Policy, his psychological warfare, his power politics and even declare openly: "We have no alternative to the present foreign policy of the West German Government." [19]

Following the great protest rally before the West Berlin City Hall on 16 August, the East Berlin SED paper continued its diatribes against Mayor Brandt and the SPD, stressing the following items:

1. Since 6 September, 1948, the bankrupt policy of Brandt and the SPD had produced no results.
2. Since the Berlin election of 1946, the SPD had commanded a majority of the West Berlin House of Representatives, enabling it to determine policy at the Schöneberg City Hall.
3. Therefore, the SPD might have followed a policy of friendship and understanding. The fifth party Congress of the SED had appealed to the SPD to make Berlin a city of peace.
4. Not only had the SPD missed the chance to promote peace and a relaxation of international tensions in West Berlin, but instead the Brandt program had poisoned the atmosphere in Berlin. Death and sabotage were conducted and the slogan was "Berlin—the Cheapest Atom Bomb!"
5. As often as Friedrich Ebert, ruling Bürgermeister of

East Berlin, the capital of the DDR, offered proposals, they were rejected and derided.

6. The most important task remained for Brandt to sow discord. He travelled to the U.S.A. and shocked American citizens before television with his unholy plans. He flew to foreign countries from whom he hoped to win support for his plans.

7. Brandt staked everything on one trump card—a card whose value had already fallen and was finally worthless. Brandt and the SPD floundered in the dreams of a policy, which for 13 years had no vision and produced no success, but only injury and derision.

8. Adenauer, hitherto the true representative of the "Front City" had already abandoned the sinking ship; whereas Brandt more recently acted to shift the guilt for the shattered policy to the Chancellor.

9. Certainly this was for Brandt not the last lesson— although nothing more remained for him after this bankruptcy. But for the honest members of the SPD this should have been the last lesson.[20]

Herr Kuhn, SPD deputy in the Bundestag, told the author in a personal interview in June, 1961, that a Soviet delegate to the Congress of the Inter-Parliamentary Union in Geneva, Switzerland, early in 1961 stated that Khrushchev preferred an Adenauer victory in the Bundestag elections to that of the SPD. In its propaganda for the Satellite States in central Europe, the Soviet Union could then equate Adenauer with militarist and revanchist policies.

East German Attack on West German Foreign Policy

On Thursday, the SED organ concentrated its propaganda attack against West German foreign policy and attempted to justify the Berlin border stakes as a necessary protection for the DDR population against:

"West German Militarists"
"Atomic War Makers"
"NATO-Dictatorship Over the DDR"

"War provocateurs against the DDR"—in order to prevent the danger of a Third World War and to guarantee a peaceful and democratic reunification of Germany.[21]

The factory militia at the Brandenburg Gate, the preparedness of the tank troops and the disciplined control of the people of the DDR were thanked for demonstrating to the Bonn "Blitz Kriegers" the unquestioned power of the first German Workers and Farmers State. The strategy of the SED regime was to heap criticism upon the Adenauer Government for its continued tolerations in the post war years of militaristic and imperialistic forces as symbolized by Strauss. It was claimed that this was contrary to the desires expressed by sizeable majorities of all West Germans in free elections and popular plebiscites for a Germany without increased armaments and militaristic Junkers. *Neues Deutschland* argued that the Berlin border stakes turned attention away from Strauss war-makers to negotiations over a German peace treaty. Thus the real power relationship in Germany was understood: it was clear that the interests of the DDR and Berlin could not be discussed without representatives of the DDR.[22]

It was claimed that the DDR was the only German state which for years had represented the true national interests of the German people—that is, the peaceful and democratic reunification of Germany. For years, it was said, the Bonn Potentates had abandoned the idea of a German national state and had tried to veil their treason to the nation with phrases such as "the West" and "European Integration." Adenauer had boasted to a Federal diplomat that he was the "best American in Europe" and "the only Chancellor, who placed the interests of Europe above the interests of his own country." Atomic War Minister Strauss declared that the time of national states had passed and his follower, Brandt, affirmed at the Bonn Campaign Congress of the SPD: "the time has passed when the national state had the highest political value."[23] In view of these confessions of national treason, it was argued, the complaints of these people against the security measures of the DDR sounded hypocritical. Out of fear for this united, manifestly democratic popular will, they have systematically split our land into two ruined parts of Germany and have sold the split-off western part to NATO. Already in 1948, by means of a separate currency reform, the Western Powers established the frontiers through Germany and through Berlin, over whose stakes they are today so indignant.[24]

The SED propaganda attack against West German foreign policies continued:

> Immediately after the split currency reform in 1948, came the establishment of the separate West German state, the unilateral and illegal remilitarization of West Germany, the outlawing of the German Communist Party (1956) and the establishment of compulsory military service under Hitler Generals and the chaining of our West German people to the policies of NATO. Finally came the split over atomic weapons which, because of the aggressive policies of NATO were directed against the cities of the German Democratic Republic.[25]

The article concluded that the Atom Bomb Ultras in Bonn, who dreamed of overthrowing the DDR must be suppressed. Therefore, in the interests of world peace and of our nation, we must unite all forces—border guards, battle groups and panzer units in order to destroy all aggression and attempted attacks against the DDR. Therefore, a peace treaty was imperative as was the German peace plan of a Confederation of both German states. Such was the distorted argument of the SED organ, combined with deceit, treachery and half-truths—all to confuse and control the ranks of West German labor. The technique was to focus on historical conflicts of the past, even pre-1914, to turn attention away from the new Soviet type of imperialism practiced not only in central and Eastern Europe since World War II, but in Asia, Africa and Latin America—all part of the cold war of nerves and Soviet propaganda of hate, fear, mistrust and vituperation.

1. "Die Antwortnote Moskaus an den Westen," in *Die Welt* (Hamburg, independent), 21 August, 1961.
2. *Die Welt* (Hamburg, independent), 21 August, 1961.
3. *Ibid.*
4. *Die Welt* (Hamburg, independent), 21 August, 1961. See also the unofficial translation of the Soviet note of 18 August by Reuters, which was published in the *New York Times,* 19 August, 1961.
5. "Hard Facts Hidden by Soviet Press," *London Times* (independent), 21 August, 1961.
6. *Guardian* (Manchester, independent), 16 August, 1961.
7. *Ibid.*
8. Sozialische Einheits-Partei Deutschlands (SED) or Socialist Unity Party of the Soviet Zone resulted from the forced merger of the German Social Democratic Party and the German Communist Party in 1946.
9. *Neue Züricher Zeitung* (right-center), 15 August, 1961.
10. *Neues Deutschland* (East Berlin, pro-SED), 15 August, 1961.
11. *Neues Deutschland* (East Berlin, pro-SED), 14 August, 1961.
12. *Ibid.* The German Peace Union (DFU) was the only political party in the West German parliamentary elections which was favored by the East Germans and Soviets. This party, despite the support of Albert Schweitzer, polled less than 2 per cent of the total vote on 17 September, 1961.
13. *Ibid.* Speech at an SPD electoral rally in Neustadt. In quoting the statements of a West German Social Democrat and former Minister of the Interior in the Adenauer Cabinet, *Neues Deutschland* was obviously appealing to certain segments of West German public opinion, which was most critical of Bonn foreign policy.
14. *Neues Deutschland* (East Berlin, pro-SED), 15 August, 1961.
15. *Ibid.*
16. *Ibid.* The author was there to hear Mayor Brandt, Party Chairman Ollenhauer and Professor Carlo Schmid, all condemn Communism for the mass exodus of refugees, but also condemn Adenauer's 12-Year Policy for its failure to solve the All-German Problems.
17. Strauss, West German Defense Minister, criticized in *Der*

Spiegel and by much of the West German press for his aggressive policy; Dr. Hans Globke, one of the Chancellor's most trusted assistants, despite his prominent Nazi record; Ernst Lemmer, active Head of Ministry of All-German Affairs.

18. Harry Czepuck, "Der Bankrott einer Politik," in *Neues Deutschland* (East Berlin, pro-SED), 15 August, 1961.

19. *Ibid.* Here obviously the tactic of the SED paper was to split the Social Democratic Party as it was split in 1919, and thus perpetuate the tragic division of European Labor which contributed to the fall of the Weimar Republic and finally to the current East-West tension in Europe and the world.

20. *Neues Deutschland* (East Berlin, pro-SED), Thursday, 17 August, 1961. SPD deputy, Herr Kuhn, a journalist from Cologne.

21. *Neues Deutschland* (East Berlin, SED organ), 17 August, 1961.

22. *Ibid.*

23. *Neues Deutschland* (East Berlin, pro-SPD), 17 August, 1961.

24. *Ibid.*

25. *Ibid.*

Chapter 10

POSITION OF THE EAST GERMAN COMMUNISTS ON THE BERLIN AND GERMAN QUESTIONS

Communist Objectives in the German Federal Republic

East Berlin is the main center of agitation and sedition for attacks on the constitutional order and stability of the German Federal Republic. East Berlin serves as the base of operations for the Eastern Intelligence services. Ever since the abortive revolutionary attempt to take over Berlin in January, 1919, the Communists have tried to control Germany, an industrial country in the center of Europe. For years they have indulged in various subversive activities and violent revolutionary actions. Ever since the collapse of the Hitler regime in 1945, Germany has remained a key target in the Soviet policy of aggressive imperialistic expansion. Tactics may vary, but the ultimate Soviet objective remains. In 1952, and 1953, the Soviet Zone's Communist Party, the SED, and other Communist organizations in both parts of Germany aimed at the overthrow of the Federal Republic. More recently SED leaders have pretended that they wish to set up only a "parliamentary democratic system." Thus, Walter Ulbricht, First Secretary of the SED, in a speech before the so called "People's Chamber" in East Berlin on 6 July, 1961, explained his reasons for the "German Peace Plan," as follows: "It is . . . not our intention to intervene in West Germany's social system." The Communists wish to attain this "parliamentary system not, however, as a result of democratic elections but through "mass efforts." This so-called "parliamentary demo-

186

cratic system" postulated by the Communists is merely a short-range objective containing "the germ of socialist revolution." Despite all assertions based on tactics the real intentions of the Communists were made clear by Walter Ulbricht in an address before the 11th meeting of the SED's Central Committee on 17 December, 1960:

> "Socialism is the final solution of the German problem . . . For this reason we do not in the least pass over in silence the fact that the triumph of socialism in the twentieth century will take place in West Germany too."[2]

The proposal to bring about German reunification by way of a confederation is also directed towards extending the Communist system to the free part of Germany. Moreover, Communist leaders both in East Germany and in Moscow make no secret of their intentions to use force, if necessary to obtain their objectives.[3] This was confirmed by the "Declaration of the Conference of Representatives of the Communist and Workers' Parties" made in November 1960, in Moscow:

> In the event that the sweater classes use force against the people, another possibility must be kept in view: that of the non-peaceful transition to socialism. Leninism teaches, and the experience of history confirms, that the ruling classes do not surrender power voluntarily . . . Under these conditions the forms taken by class warfare . . . will depend on the strength of the resistance with which the reactionary circles oppose the will of the people . . .[4]

Methods of Attack and Operations

Since only about 2 per cent of the West German population are willing to assist the SED in its aims, the Communists are striving for a broad general basis as a beginning for the realization of their objectives. Their battle cry is "unity of action by the working-class," whereby they hope to win over the workers, trade unions and Social Democratic Party for joint political action. In addition, they appeal to the middle-classes, particularly young people and intellectuals, to join forces with labor in a

187

"broad democratic rising." Yet this Communist policy of alliance is only a means to an end.

More recently Communist efforts were mainly directed toward the building up of a popular front (from the forces of the Center and Left) against alleged threats of war on the part of the "Western Militarists." The Communists are simultaneously soliciting support for the Soviet peace treaty proposals and the Soviet plans for Berlin. Finally the SED and their auxiliary organizations are also working to undermine popular feeling for the worthiness of the State in order to alienate people from their readiness to defend it. Daily practices indulged in by the Communists include slanderous statements, vehement agitation and spreading of lies, according to the principles of Lenin, who justified any kind of action to overthrow the old society as right and proper.[5] At the third Congress of the "National Front of Democratic Germany," in September, 1958, Walter Ulbricht, First Secretary of the SED, stated:

"It is the duty of every peaceloving citizen in West Germany to take advantage of every opportunity to support the DDR's struggle against the Bonn Government's waging of psychological warfare and against the arming that is going on in West Germany. There must be no production of armaments, no aerodromes, no rocket bases not recognized by leaders of the forces for peace in Germany, which are directed from Berlin."[6]

Attacks against the constitutional system of the Federal Republic are directed by the Central Committee of the SED in East Berlin. It directs and controls both the activity of the German Communist Party (KPD), which is banned in the Federal Republic as of 1956, by the Supreme Court in Karlsruhe, and the entire "Western Operations" of the mass organizations of the "State" apparatus of the Soviet Zone. In operations against the Federal Republic, the SED's Central Committee and Politburo direct the activities of "Instructors," who enter the Federal Republic clandestinely, and nearly 15,000 functionaries. For carrying on this subversive activity, special "Departments West" have been established. With the aid of "Deparments West," new Communist auxiliary organizations are continually being established in the Federal Republic. Whereas outwardly non-Communists head these auxiliary organizations as representatives, direction is actually in the hands of trained Communist functionaries.

The detail of agitation against the Federal Republic that is carried on by the press and radio in the Soviet Zone is determined on the lines of general principles of the Politburo by an Agitation Commission within the SED's Central Committee. This Commission meets regularly and makes known to the Soviet Zone's newspapers and radio the points to emphasize in attacks on the Federal Republic and the kind of language to be used. The SED's Central Committee also trains the editorial staffs of the Communist Party newspapers that are published illegally in the Federal Republic.

The Politburo and Central Committee of the Federal Republic's illegal Communist Party (KPD) have their headquarters in the Soviet Sector of Berlin and direct operations of the KPD in the Federal Republic according to instructions of the SED's Central Committee. The illegal KPD operates under-cover names, uses forged identity papers, secret identification cards and passwords. Its henchmen cross over from the Soviet Zone in a clandestine fashion and bring into Federal territory the money required for party operations. The KPD maintains its own school at Oderburg-on-the-Oder, where some 1,000 members of the illegal KPD have been trained for political activity since 1958.

Since only a small percentage of West Germans belong to Communist organizations, the SED's Central Committee tries to influence the mass of people by large-scale agitation. Therefore, it uses the Soviet Zonal Press, the entire Soviet Zonal Radio and T.V. networks, especially the so-called "Freedom Station 904."[7] In addition, over 10 million propaganda items per month are printed in the Soviet Zone by numerous political organizations under instructions from the SED's Central Committee, secretly channelled into the Federal Republic and distributed there. With assistance from Soviet Zone headquarters, a further two million propaganda items are produced every month in the Federal Republic. Communist agitation and seditious activity against the Bundeswehr (West German Armed Forces) and the Federal Government's defense policy are carried out mainly by "Independent Departments" of the "Political Administrations" of the Soviet Zone's "Ministry of National Defense" and its "Ministry of State Security."[8]

Communists have initiated a campaign of defamation against the Federal Republic in all Eastern Bloc countries, in Scandinavia, Western Europe, Asia and Africa. Asserting that Nazism and Militarism have been revived in the Federal Republic, with key positions in the military and political fields in the hands of National Socialists and Militarists, seeking to unite Germany by military means and to regain the Oder-Neisse territories by force of arms ("revanchism"), they then allege that an acute danger may undermine European security and lead to a third World War. The main propaganda theme charges the existence of a "well-advanced process of reviving fascism," with accusations against so-called "Nazi" politicians, diplomats, economists and "Nazi officers." Here again the SED's Central Committee influences the international propaganda in favor of Soviet policy *vis-à-vis* Germany. This agitation is carried on by political organizations such as the "National Council of the National Front" and the "Committee for German Unity" under the control of Albert Norden, a member of the SED's Politburo. The latter often uses national Press conferences for initiating measures of agitation. The Soviet Zone's radio and T.V. network is constantly expanding its overseas broadcasts. For instance, a program, "Democratic Germany Speaking to You" is broadcast for 60 minutes daily to listeners in Britain. With other programs the Communists appeal in many languages to the peoples of the Free World. Nearly all the large conferences of Communist parties denigrate the Federal Republic, as do the international Communist organizations—the World Federations of Trade Unions, World Peace Council, World Federation of Democratic Youth and the *Fédération Internationale des Résistant*. They constantly participate in the campaign of defamation against the Federal Republic.

Communist Attacks Against the German SPD Party and Trade Unions

The entire agitation and seditious activity of the East German Communists against the German Social Democratic Party (SPD) is in charge of a special section of the SED's Central Committee in East Berlin. By means of a network of go-betweens, the SED and KPD make use of several left-wing Socialist associations and reading clubs legally active in West Germany. They acquaint the SPD members with Communist ideas. Among these associations are the "Karl Marx Society" in Munich and other "Marxist working-groups" in the Rhine-Ruhr area and West Berlin, as well as *Die Andere Zeitung,* a journalistic organ published in Hamburg, along with other similar organizations.[9]

The Communist National Trade Union Federation in the Soviet Zone, the FDGB, with its 15 branch trade unions, is charged with the task of promoting the "Unity of Action of the Working-Class" in the Federal Republic and thus preparing the conditions for a "new democratic popular movement" to help in undermining the "constitutional free system in the Federal Republic." By means of trade union contacts, the FDGB, a mass organization of the SED with 6 million members, is striving for trade union solidarity on a broad mass basis in the Federal Republic demanding unity among all German trade Unions. According to reliable information, which is confirmed by Soviet Press reports, in 1958, the FDGB was able to persuade some 50,000 West German workers and trade union members to visit the Soviet Zone.

Within the ranks of its executive committee, the FDGB has established the "Office for National Trade Union Activity" for the central guidance of the seditious operations directed against factory workers, the trade unions and the Social Democratic Party (SPD). This Committee receives its instructions from the "Section Trade Union Policy" of the SED's Central Committee. On 17 August, 1961, Hans Kiefert, Assistant Secretary to the District Leader of East Berlin in an obvious effort to counteract the powerful appeal of Mayor Brandt at the giant protest rally before the Schöneberg City Hall on the previous day, Wednesday, 16 August, three days after the erection of the Berlin Wall. Describing himself as an Old Berlin Worker who had fought the battle of the Berlin laboring class for four decades, he denounced Brandt's speech as a war speech against us. "As the Chairman of the SPD in Berlin, he accomplished nothing more than to call for help by the imperialistic governments of the U.S.A., England, France and West Germany to take action against the worker and peasant power in the German Democratic Re-

191

public (DDR)."[10] Condemning the SPD Chief Candidate and Chairman of the West Berlin SPD for "calling the capitalists to military action against us Berlin workers," the speaker called this war hatred. More specifically, Kiefert criticized Mayor Brandt for:

> Going completely over to the position of German militarism, for risking the lives of all the Berlin people, for encouraging revanchist steps from which a war against the East might emerge and for seeking aid from the tanks of the old Hitler generals; for demanding American military action against the DDR, for being the house-servant of the capitalists and for failure to act the part of a true representative of a labor party.[11]

The same article, published in *Neues Deutschland*, maintained that Brandt was more dangerous than Strauss because more successful than the latter in calling for American military support against the DDR. "Brandt was furious" it declared, "because East Berliners love their worker and peasant state and, therefore, will defend it, since tanks have come to the aid of the East Germans." For years Brandt had boasted that he had made West Berlin a "Front City" against the DDR, that he wanted to roll up the DDR and show the national people's army, people's police and other battle groups that they could not make anything of a Labor-Farmer State.[12]

The East Berlin Communist functionary concluded his T.V. address with an appeal to West German workers to recognize that the common enemy was German militarism, revanchism and German monopoly capital. The conclusion of a peace treaty, however, would lead to the conquest of German militarism and was the urgent command of the hour. Posing as an old Berlin worker, Hans Kiefert (East German Communist functionary) concluded his address by advising West Berliners:

> Forget not the revolutionary traditions of our common struggle against German militarism and fascism. Do not make yourselves servants of those men who have destroyed our nation in two senseless wars. Brandt has already led you too far his way unfortunately. It is time that you

reconsider your course and begin to work toward a labor policy.[13]

SED Summary of Soviet Note of 18 August, 1961

On 20 August, 1961, *Neues Deutschland* carried a brief summary of the main points of the Soviet Note of 18 August, which was a categorical rejection of the Western Protest Notes to the Soviet Government on the previous day, 17 August. Not only did the USSR gladly support the security measures of the DDR, but reprimanded the U.S. Government for interference in the affairs of the DDR. The Soviet Government called on the Western Powers to replace the unsound and absurd Four-Power Agreements because the security of all peoples requires a peace treaty and the normalization of the situation in West Berlin. The main arguments used in support of this thesis were as follows:

1. The DDR, like any sovereign state, has the unquestioned right to establish necessary control measures over its border with West Berlin. West Berlin is a center for agents, adventurers, terrorists and other lawbreakers.
2. Those who appeal to the former Four-Power Statute have never answered the protest lodged against espionage tunnels of old Bliekdecke. Bonn makes West Berlin the main base for economic diversion against the DDR. West Berlin lives a hectic life at the expense of the people of the DDR.
3. Bonn led a whole army of defenders out of West Berlin. West Berlin became an arena for revanchist clubs and agitation movements against the Socialist States. The radio and television in West Berlin try to create unrest and to transmit the coded instructions of Western espionage agencies. The illegal actions of Bonn authorities in West Berlin is beyond the jurisdiction of the Federal Republic.
4. The Western Powers violated their obligations under the Four-Power Agreements, which forbade military service in West Germany. After the Soviet Union's

193

proposal of a peace treaty, its enemies stopped at nothing to complicate the situation in the Federal Republic.

5. The common program of the Anti-Hitler Coalition in the DDR is aware of the rebirth of militarism in West Germany. No one has the right to interfere in the internal affairs of the two German States. Certainly the Occupation Powers and the Bonn Government alone are to blame for the inconveniences on the Sector Borders of Berlin.[14]

Radio Address of Walter Ulbricht on the Position of the East German Communists on the Berlin and German Question

On Saturday, 19 August, 1961, Walter Ulbricht, First Secretary of the SED and Chairman of the State Council of the DDR, in a radio and televised address, presented a complete summary of the position of the so-called German Democratic Republic (DDR), on the entire Berlin and German question. Ulbricht immediately stated:

Thanks to all who took part in the battle for the security of the capital of the DDR, the State Organization proved its capacity. The plan of the Bonn Government was to create a situation for civil war and for breaking the peace by 1961. Our measures have saved peace in Europe and in the world. We have defeated the Ultras at the Brandenburg Gate; the West Germans must defeat the Ultras on the Rhine and in the Ruhr.

The division of the German nation can only be overcome by a great popular struggle for subduing militarism. The first order for mankind is to secure peace. Hence, the most important task is preparation for a peace treaty by strengthening the DDR.[15]

According to Ulbricht, the major error of the militarists was that they had mininterpreted East German patience for weakness. "The dangerous plans of Bonn, however, were recognized; they included pushing agitation to a head in order

194

to create such conditions that after the West German elections, they could openly attack the DDR, could begin civil war and open military preparations."[16] Ulbricht claimed that the measures of the DDR on 13 August in closing the Berlin border, had helped to preserve peace in Europe and the world, threatened in the early fall of 1961 by West German militarists and revanchist policies. Citizens of West Germany and West Berlin would also realize that by these barricade measures their lives may have been saved. Otherwise the German House would have been set on fire by a second Sarajevo.

Nevertheless, the DDR State was arranging new conditions for negotiations between the Soviet Union and the Western Powers on the basis of discussions with the Government of the Fedtral Republic. The Chairman of the Council of Ministers of the DDR tried to justify the use of force by stating:

> It seems to me especially important that leading politicians and the people of West Germany are not aware of the real power relations in Germany and the world. Our barricade measures show how determined we are to complete preparations for a peace treaty and to transform West Berlin into a demilitarized Free City.

> Peaceful construction was effectively protected. Were tanks necessary? Indeed! The working class is no longer defenseless. It was necessary that reactionaries, militarists and monopolists from Globke to Brandt be made to recognize that in the First German Workers and Farmers State there are no such fools and weaklings who bow to the threats of the militarists. Our tanks and our soldiers have done their duty. Our security measures enabled peace-loving forces in Western Germany and also part of the bourgeoisie, which desires no military conflict, to subdue the Ultras around Strauss and Brandt . . . Since the atmosphere has cleared, many now see clearly.[17]

In the German Revolution of January, 1919, the extreme left wing Social Democrats (Spartacists), like Karl Liebknecht and Rosa Luxemburg, tried to appeal to reason at a great mass meeting in Berlin and, therefore, rejected use of military force. As a result they were shot down in cold blood by young officers of the *Reichswehr* (Army) sent to arrest them.

As if to underline the bankruptcy of the rightist SPD leaders, Ulbricht cited the example of a former bourgeois politician who was recently converted to the SPD, Dr. Heinemann, who declared: "In these days at the Brandenburg Gate the 12-year policy of strength of Dr. Adenauer was finally shattered." While admitting this, the DDR Chief said that Dr. Heinemann forgot that his SPD Party "bears a considerable part of the blame that things had come to a climax on August 13." Therefore, the policies of both Dr. Adenauer and the right-wing SPD leaders were shattered at the Brandenburg Gate, as were all revanchist policies and all plans of West German militarists and monopolists to push eastward.[18]

During the 12 years that the SPD had governed in West Berlin, Ulbricht continued, it had a unique opportunity to make West Berlin an example of peaceful cooperation between both German States, despite their different social orders. Unfortunately, however, according to Ulbricht, SPD leadership, by its Anti-Communist orientation and ignominious submission to West German militarists and imperialists, had forfeited its great chance at Berlin as well as its great political chance. There had been in Berlin in 1945, after the defeat of Hitlerite Germany, a good basis for a peaceful development. Berlin could today be a united, peaceful city, of which people throughout the world would speak of in no other way than, for instance, of Zürich or Stockholm. If the principles laid down by the Anti-Hitler Coalition had been carried out in all Berlin, there would be no West Berlin question.[19]

After May, 1945, the active population of Berlin revived economic life and in the course of time created a unified, antifascist administration, as united political parties existed in all Berlin and also united trade unions were developed in Berlin along normal, democratic lines. All that was changed, when the French, British and American Occupation Zones were combined in West Berlin and were aided and abetted by the Rightist SPD leadership, instead of the SPD working with an anti-Hitler Coalition against fascism.[20]

In developing his case in support of the border security

measures of 13 August, Ulbricht argued that Berlin was systematically split by the Allies and thus emerged the "Front City" in West Berlin—a city which soon became a bastion in which the ideology of the Hitler Reich was conserved. The Chairman of the Council of Ministers of the DDR charged the Social Democratic Senate in West Berlin with part of the responsibility for transforming the "Front City" into a center for warmongers and war interests—a paradise for slave traders, espionage and diversion.

Ulbricht chided Brandt for begging his foreign protectors in God's name to protect him in order to preserve this system. The way to reunification leads over the conquest of the militarists. Hence, the first task of humanity is to secure peace, to prevent war and to use all means to achieve its goals. Hitler and Goebbels also misused the concept of humanity, without any scruples, in order to prepare for aggression. The forceful occupation of Czechoslovakia, the march into Austria and the attack on Poland —all were loudly proclaimed as humanitarian measures. Hitler called Czechs and Poles "inferior peoples."[21]

Ulbricht concluded his radio address of 19 August, 1961, by denouncing the insidious propaganda from West Berlin. Western entrepreneurs, bankers and militarists, he said, had a neat propaganda system. Adenauer and the West German militarists lamented over barbed wire and wished to forget that they, together with the Western imperialists had split Germany, split Berlin, split the German currency and split West Germany away from the structure of the German nation and made it an American satellite state. It was because of them, Ulbricht continued, that the barbed wire was stretched through Germany. We have gone to great trouble to prevent this development. "In organizing border provocations and border demonstrations on the frontiers of the German Democratic Republic (DDR), the Bonn Government had already encouraged civil war. Our security measures served to prevent civil war and provocations."[22]

All Berlin Elections of 20 October, 1946

The answer to the above arguments of Ulbricht, deriding the SPD leadership and defaming the Federal Republic is that in the last and only free elections in all Berlin in 1946, the Soviets

197

tried to force a merger of the non-Communist SPD with the German Communist Party (KPD) into the Socialist Unity Party (SED). They succeeded in the Eastern Zone of Germany where they had full control, but failed in Berlin, which was under joint Allied control. No doubt the Soviets were confident the Communists to make a good showing in the city-wide elections. Before 1914, Berlin was a Social Democratic stronghold and under the Weimar Republic several Berlin districts had been Communist strongholds. Nevertheless, the results of the all-Berlin elections of 20 October, 1946, were as follows:

Social Democratic Party (SPD)	48.7 per cent
Christian Democratic Party (CDU)	22.2 per cent
Socialist Unity Party (SED)	19.8 per cent
Liberal Democratic Party (LDP)	9.3 per cent

Therefore, the Communists won less than one fifth of the vote and the City Parliament elected a Social Democrat as Mayor.

In April, 1947, he was repudiated by the parliament because he had signed a promise to cooperate with the SED. He resigned and on 24 June, 1947, parliament elected Social Democrat Ernst Reuter as Mayor. The Soviets "vetoed" Reuter's election. Until December, 1948, a Deputy Mayor conducted the city's affairs.[23]

East German Assessment of the Meaning of the Berlin Wall

On Monday, 21 August, 1961, *Neues Deutschland* printed a long article by its Bonn Correspondent. Harry Czepuck, entitled: "Taking Stock of Broken Fragments of a House." The writer argued the thesis that the greatest danger in West Germany comes from the Right. In support of this contention, he claimed the Moscow Declaration of the Warsaw Pact States, the security measures of the DDR for protecting its borders and the position of the Western Powers—the overwhelming events after 13 August —prevented the West German Ultras from West Berlin from provoking a third World War. He pointed out that Adenauer before the Bundestag and at various election rallies, in speaking of the Berlin problem, of a peace treaty and other questions

198

had toned down his customary threats and had come to recognize the limitations of his sphere of power. Not only Adenauer, but more recently Strauss, had spoken of the need for negotiations, whereas before they had preferred to impress people by rattling atomic rockets. That they had suddenly advised calmness and discretion and placed less reliance on war-cries called for an explanation. The reason was Bonn officials had clearly understood the Moscow Declaration of the Warsaw Pact States because equally concrete measures for the security of the DDR State followed on 13 August, 1961.[24]

The Bonn correspondent of *Neues Deutschland* maintained that peace was preserved in Berlin, in Germany and Europe by two factors: the decision of the DDR State to protect its frontiers and because West German Ultras were forced to accept the decision of Secretary of State Dean Rusk, who in Candenabbia, Italy, had stated very firmly and clearly that the Western Powers would welcome and accept any regulation which would preserve security in the Berlin area.[25] Chancellor Adenauer in particular had obviously understood that the Western Powers undertook nothing in the way of countermeasures as had been predicted. Hence, Czepuck concluded that the policy of strength, which was predicated on the idea of Western military support, had been shattered by the events of 13 August and after.

The West German Press, after a week of intensive hatred, began to reflect on the reasons for the seeming defeat of this policy. For instance, *Frankfurter Rundschau* wrote:

Adenauer not only lived to see the defeat of his own policy, that has endured because there was nothing else to expect. Still worse is the fact that with his defeat the danger is that the faith of the German people in the West is shattered. Actually there is a genuine confidence crisis against the West, caused by false government propaganda.

The propaganda world of the Adenauer Government is completely shattered and if it is not rebuilt, it is obvious that the ruling Mayor of Berlin, Willy Brandt, will attempt to fill the breach with his speeches . . . What now remains? Negotiations and nothing but negotiations. Thus we find ourselves in complete harmony with all Western Governments of those nations who never want to become involved in a war over Berlin.[26]

Voicing its agreement with this analysis, *Neues Deutschland* added that the tragedy for West German labor lay in the fact that since the Bad-Godesberg Congress of the Social Democratic Party in 1960, adventurers and representatives of this policy of strength at the head of the SPD became a source of chauvinistic hatred, of anti-Communism and also Pan-Germanism, directed against the West just like that experienced only in the Nazi period. *Neues Deutschland* alleged that the right-wing command of the Presidium of the SPD, Brandt and Wehner, find themselves—and here lay the tragedy and at the same time the danger—right beside the extreme right, the fascist politicians of West Germany.

Bild Zeitung, mass tabloid paper with a circulation of three million, considered by *Neues Deutschland* to be the most vitriolic organ of West German chauvinism, even attacked Chancellor Adenauer and maintained that in the special Bundestag session of 18 August, 1961, (five days after the Berlin Wall) only two speakers had seized the core of the problem and had desired military measures, such as the occupation of access routes to West Berlin by NATO: the Fascist Schneider of the so-called *"Gesamtdeutsche Partei"* (All-Germany Party) and Willy Brandt, Mayor of West Berlin. Both had declared: "Not words—but actions. In other words: not negotiations—but shooting. So far it is Schneider and Brandt—hand in hand. Right and right associate together."[27]

Neues Deutschland tried to warn West German Social Democrats of the danger of such tactics, arguing that the conduct of the right-wing SPD leaders in 1933 made possible the rise to power of the Hitler-Fascists. Nevertheless, today these rightist adventurers, at the head of the party of August Bebel, strive to come into power on the wave of chauvinism and anti-Communism. *Neues Deutschland* concluded:

> Brandt and Wehner want to make your party, which was once socialist, into a National Socialist Party. These people both in the *Bundestag* (West German Parliament) and at election rallies hope for support from all Chauvinists. Poison and gall against all seemed the only way out of the present impasse without war and counter-revolution to cause hatred of the Soviet Union, of the DDR State and

all socialist lands. They even criticize Adenauer from the standpoint of chauvinism only because he, directly under the pressure of realities, advised calmness and because he had spoken directly with the Soviet Ambassador. They even abuse the Western Powers because they do not do what the adventurers wish, because they do not shout.[28]

Finally the official paper of the Communist Zone Party (SED) concluded by stating that the Western Powers should reread all the notes and documents of the Soviet Union and the DDR State, in which the dangers of the developments in West Germany are pointed out. The echo, that certain circles emphasized since 13 August toward the West, confirmed all this. Therefore, the Western Powers should understand what it means that there is a DDR State to checkmate Ultras and Adventurers.[29]

Conclusions

By way of summary, we have noted that the long-range goal of East German Communists is to take over control of Germany, notwithstanding various switches and detours in party tactics. Among the latter are such devices as a "parliamentary democratic system," the "German Peace Plan" and the proposal to reunite Germany by way of a Confederation. Since only about 2 per cent of West Germans are willing to support the aims of East German Communists, the latter raised the battle cry of "unity of action of the working class," to win over workers, trade unions and the SPD Party. In addition, young people and intellectuals were urged to join forces with labor in a "broad democratic movement." More recently Communist efforts were directed toward building a popular front of forces from the Center and Left against alleged threats of war, revanchism and irredentism on the part of "Western militarists" and Bonn "neo-Nazi fascists." Meanwhile Communists solicit support for Soviet treaty proposals and Soviet plans for Berlin. To undermine loyalty to the State and respect for the constitutional order in Bonn, East German Communists resort to daily use of slander, lies, violent agitation and subversion according to the principles of Lenin.

To carry out these nefarious activities, the East German

SED's Central Committee and Politburo employ thousands of "Instructors," spies, saboteurs and nearly 15,000 functionaries to work with special "Departments West" in the Federal German Republic. Constant use is made of the Soviet Zone Press, radio and T.V. network, in addition to 10 million propaganda items per month, which are printed, smuggled into West Germany and distributed, plus two thousand more items per month, which are printed illegally in West Germany. Moreover, Communists have initiated a campaign of defamation against the Federal Republic in all Eastern Bloc countries, in Scandinavia, Western Europe, Asia and Africa. The main propaganda theme alleges the existence of a "well-advanced process of reviving fascism," with accusations against so-called "Nazi" politicians, "Nazi" diplomats, "Nazi" economists and "Nazi" officers. Strong attacks were mounted against the German SPD Party and trade unions by both the SED Party and the German Communist Party (KPD), outlawed in West Germany in 1956, with headquarters in East Berlin.

The Berlin Crisis of 13 August, 1961, resulting in the Berlin Wall, was created by Khrushchev, made to order for the East German Communist subversive apparatus. All the above devices were then used to confuse and control German, European and world public opinion. Particularly significant in the crucial days after 13 August, 1961, were: the appeal to Social Democratic workers in West Berlin by Hans Kiefert, SED party functionary; the address of Walter Ulbricht on the position of the East German Communists on the Berlin and German Question; and the article by the Bonn Correspondent of *Neues Deutschland*, Harry Czepuck, assessing the results of the crucial week in Berlin from 13 August to 20 August, 1961. *Neues Deutschland*, the official organ of the SED, delights in reprinting statements from various West German, European, British and some American newspapers, which it interprets as favorable to its cause—despite the fact that most West Germans regard Neues Deutschland as notoriously inaccurate in everything except the date. In the light of its militant agitation and large-scale subversive activities to undermine the constitutional order of the Bonn Republic, is it any wonder that Konrad Adenauer has consistently refused to have any formal diplomatic relations with the so-called "East German Democratic Republic" (DDR) or with any

European or Afro-Asian State which recognizes the Pankow regime of Walter Ulbricht?

Despite his advanced age, Dr. Adenauer stands as a tower of strength in the ideological conflict between East and West, symbolized by the struggle for Germany and for the kind of Germany that coincides with the democratic principles of self-determination. Neither the Chancellor nor any party or leader in the Bundestag can afford to run the risk of favoring any recognition of the so-called "German Democratic Republic" or of the Oder-Neisse line or any limitation upon the freedom of West Berlin. In the formulation of a country's foreign policy, attention must always be given to historic traditions, patterns of the past, to geographic and strategic considerations. These factors are permanent considerations, despite ideological or political differences.

NOTES TO CHAPTER TEN

1. *Neues Deutschland* (East Berlin, SED), 7 July, 1961. This is the official paper of the Communist Party of the Soviet Zone, SED, which resulted from a forced merger of the German Social Democratic Party (SPD) and the German Communist Party (KPD) to form the Socialist Unity Party (SED).
2. *Neues Deutschland* (East Berlin, SED), 18 December, 1960.
3. Albert Norden, of SED's Politburo in *Neues Deutschland,* 10 Sept., 1959.
4. *Neues Deutschland* (East Berlin, SED), 6 December, 1960.
5. Lenin/Stalin on "Youth" (Berlin, 1950), p. 86.
6. *Neues Deutschland* (East Berlin, SED), 24 September, 1950.
7. *EAST BERLIN: Main Center of Agitation and Sedition for the Attack on the Stability and Constitutional System of the Federal Republic of Germany and Base of Operations of the Eastern Intelligence Services* 327.88 (430.2) (430-2.1-11) a2/-600-2-1 (West Berlin, 1961), pp. 7-10.
8. *EAST BERLIN: Main Center of Agitation and Sedition,* pp. 10-11.
9. *EAST BERLIN: Main Center of Agitation and Sedition,* pp. 12-13.
10. *Neues Deutschland* (East Berlin, SED), 18 August, 1961.
11. *Ibid.*

12. *Neues Deutschland* (East Berlin, SED), 18 August, 1961.
13. *Ibid.*
14. *Neues Deutschland* (East Berlin, SED), 20 August, 1961.
15. *Neues Deutschland* (East Berlin, SED), 19 August, 1961. Since East Berlin has only three newspapers and *Neues Deutschland* is the official organ of the Executive Committee of the SED, this paper is indispensable.
16. *Ibid.*
17. *Neues Deutschland* (East Berlin, SED), 19 August, 1961.
18. *Ibid.*
19. *Neues Deutschland* (East Berlin, SED), 19 August, 1961.
20. *Ibid.*
21. *Neues Deutschland* (East Berlin, SED), 19 August, 1961.
22. *Ibid.*
23. *Ibid.*
24. *Neues Deutschland* (East Berlin, SED), 21 August, 1961.
25. *Neues Deutschland* (East Berlin, SED), 21 August, 1961.
26. *Frankfurter Rundschau* (pro-SPD), quoted by *Neues Deutschland,* 21 August, 1961.
27. *Neues Deutschland* (East Berlin, SED), 21 August, 1961.
29. *Neues Deutschland* (East Berlin, SED), 21 August, 1961.

Chapter 11

REACTION OF WORLD PRESS TO THE BERLIN WALL

Complexities of Berlin—German Crisis

Two months before the erection of the Berlin Wall, on 15 June, 1961, five outstanding young journalists in West Germany were asked to participate in a panel discussion before a packed audience at Bonn University, which climaxed "Freedom Week." The subject for discussion was "Is German reunification still possible?" Manfred Klein, Berlin deputy, in a final summary of the conclusions of the five journalists, declared: "Everything was still not lost!" But they also agreed that "the West must abandon its purely defensive approach." [1] The panel consisted of: the young writer from the east, Gerhard Zwerenz, author of the much discussed book, "Vexations between Mars and Memel," Kurt Wessel of the *Deutsche Zeitung* (discussion leader), Paul Wilhelm Wenger of the *Rheinische Merkur*, Stefan Thomas, Chairman of the Eastern Bureau of the SPD, and the Berliner, Manfred Klein. Zwerenz recognized five possibilities of unification:

1. War, the first possibility, was rejected.
2. Revolution or underground resistance was offered as the second possibility with the words: "It is not possible for us to advance against dictators."
3. Publicity—agitation to rally efforts for reunification appeared to Zwerenz as unacceptable: "That is cheaper than the (East) German mark!"

4. The desperate hope in the possibility of good fortune, such as negotiations with Poland over trade boundaries. It was often said that Poland is still not lost!
5. Finally, a reasonable compromise was listed as the fifth and last possibility.[2]

The Berliner, Manfred Klein, again supported the thesis that propaganda had already gone far enough. Stefan Thomas considered the five possibilities of Gerhard Zwerenz as no alternatives. A clever policy must combine several of these. The SPD politician meant that good fortune comes to those who do something. He characterized a skeptic as one who does nothing. P. W. Wenger demanded that the West should finally abandon its defensive posture and take the initiative. He argued that the two years which had elapsed during the Berlin Crisis offered the West ample opportunity to demand all of Berlin as a Free City. Western leaders might still urge as a basis for discussion making all Berlin a Free City and seat of the United Nations. However, Stefan Thomas and the Berliner, Manfred Klein, again opposed this idea.

But all were in agreement that negotiations must begin as soon as possible and without long, frustrating delays. "Next week begins the great contest over Berlin," said Wenger. "We must negotiate in order to gain time and moral advantage. Negotiations with Poland must be put in motion with regard to proposals for trade and the lost territories."[3]

The strong trend of West German public opinion toward faith in negotiating the issues at stake, as shown by this panel of key West German and Berlin journalists, stood in sharp contrast to the more rigid and inflexible position of Adenauer during most of the 12 years in which he dominated West German foreign policy. This policy was long criticized by the opposition Social Democrats, the Free Democrats and by the independent and opposition press in West Germany. In spite of the Social Democratic switch in tactics in 1960 away from the intransigeant opposition to "bipartisan" support of Bonn's foreign policy, there was still a strong undercurrent of feeling in the SPD rank and file as well as in the SPD and independent West German Press that the 12-year boycott of the East German regime had produced no kind of political or diplomatic result. The positive gains of the Adenauer Administration included:

1. attainment of West German political sovereignty and military independence;
2. Western orientation and alignment with NATO and West European Union for defense;
3. international cooperation through the coal and steel authority, Euratom, the West European Council and Assembly and the Common Market;
4. good relations with France, as shown in the solution of the Saar problem and diplomatic cooperation between Adenauer and De Gaulle.

Nevertheless, the opposition politicians and press, as well as the independent West German press, placed increasing emphasis on the problems of Berlin, the Oder-Neisse territories and relations with *Mittel-Deutschland* (Soviet Zone) and its 17 million victims of Soviet tyranny. Perhaps these difficult problems connected with reunification might have been negotiated during the years 1950 to 1954 on terms favorable to the Soviet Union. For instance, at the Berlin foreign ministers conference of January-February 1954, called to discuss the future of Germany, Soviet Foreign Minister Molotov suggested to the French Foreign Minister, Georges Bidault, that the Soviet Union would help arrange an armistice in Indo-China in exchange for French abandonment of the European Defense Community (EDC) then being debated in the French National Assembly. "Molotov's efforts were in fact instrumental in obtaining the Geneva settlement, which ended the war in Indo-China and the French National Assembly defeated EDC."[4] Apart from its European interests, the USSR had other reasons for halting the Indochina war. Secretary of State John Foster Dulles had announced the doctrine of massive retaliation in January 1954. He was striving to persuade our European allies to join in a "united action" military intervention.

But after 1955, it became increasingly clear that German Soviet negotiations had accomplished nothing—except the release of German war prisoners and the restoration of diplomatic relations. After paying such a high price for such small gains, Chancellor Adenauer enunciated the doctrine of negotiation only from a position of military strength. At their conference in April 1961, Kennedy and Adenauer reaffirmed their standard Allied pledge for "the reunification of Germany in peace and

207

freedom and the restoration of Berlin as the capital of a reunited Germany."[5] At the Vienna Conference with Premier Khrushchev on 4 June, 1961, Kennedy failed to convince the Soviet Premier of his firm determination to fight for Berlin. The realities of events in the summer of 1961 publicly demonstrated that the prospects for reunification were as remote as diplomats had privately recognized for years. Diplomats in Washington and London were convinced that the tensions over Berlin would be removed in one way or another at the conference table and not on the battlefield.

Pankow Regime No Longer Taboo

After the erection of the barbed wire barricade on the sector borders of Berlin on 13 August, 1961, the Berlin Crisis became the principal theme in the Western capitals, as well as in the old German capital. The *Times* of London observed that the establishment of controls on the borders of the East German Democratic Republic (DDR) with West Berlin had relieved much of the Berlin problem.[6] It refuted the contention that the DDR measures had destroyed the Four-Power Status of Berlin with the statement that this status had been destroyed for a long time and reminded its readers of the separate currency reform in the Western Zone in 1948. Conservative papers in both America and Great Britain as well as West Germany were well aware that no cheap and sweeping victory over the West in Berlin was possible.[7] The reunification of Germany, recognition of the existence of two German States and the demand for negotiations were subjects frequently featured in the editorials of leading British and European papers.[8] The London paper, *Observer* wrote:

The Western Powers have again made nothing of the greatest part of their success in the Federal Republic, in that they have refused recognition of the Soviet Zone Republic. They not only insisted that Germany must be reunited through free elections—which is fair and reasonable—but argued that a reunited German people has the right of self-determination as every other people.

However, the international status and foreign policy

of Germany are not only the affair of Germany herself; they are also the concern of Czechoslovakia, Poland and Russia, just as much as Great Britain, France and Belgium.[9]

Also, the British weekly paper, *Economist,* advocated a changed German policy on the part of the Western Powers: For better or worse, the West cannot avoid negotiating with East Germany. The boycott of the DDR, during the last 12 years, is itself a form of communication, but it produced no political or diplomatic result.[10]

As for the connection between the recognition and reunification questions, the *Guardian* wrote, "If the West has the desire to postpone recognition of the Pankow regime without the risk of war, then the best way to do this is to propose German reunification on terms which the Soviet Union can accept."[11] A policy of disengagement, neutralization and withdrawal of the Federal Republic from NATO would, in the view of the Guardian, "be the only policy, which could give the Soviet Zone freedom in some form which is acceptable to Moscow."[12]

The influential *Daily Telegraph* published a selection of letters from readers on this same subject, which without exception favored negotiations and recognition of the Pankow regime in East Germany. But here again the reproach was made that the West bowed to the wishes of Adenauer in this question and thus lost all perspective.[13]

Also the Swedish press was concerned with the question of German reunification. The *Arbeiterbladet (Labor News)* believed that a genuine desire for German reunification could be found neither with the Western Powers nor the Soviets. Therefore, the realistic thing would be to accept the partition of Germany and agree to a status which would end the latent war danger, which constitutes the German question.[14] A recognition, even if only *de facto,* could, in the view of the Stockholm *Tidningen,* perhaps create a situation that would reduce the depopulation of the Zone if the Berlin Gate should again be opened.[15] In Canada the widely read and influential political periodical, *Maclean's Magazine* was fully aware that Canada and the NATO Allies were only obligated to fight if West Berlin were attacked. "German national heritage means nothing to us and also German reunification is not a primary consideration." The Federal Republic, therefore, has no other alternative than recognition and negotiation with the East German marionette regime.[16]

With complete understanding of the situation in Berlin, most newspapers warned against precipitate measures. "The Western Allies should not allow themselves to be led to an explosive situation by emotions," as the *Daily Herald* wrote.[17] Above all influential voices warned against cutting off trade with East Germany "because the Interzonal Commercial Agreement is connected with an East German obligation to respect ways of access to West Berlin."[18] The *Guardian* emphasized the idea expressed by other American and British papers that if the Western Powers pressed economic sanctions against the Soviet Union, then, unfortunately, it would cause great hardships for the German inhabitants of the Soviet Zone.[19]

The French paper, *Le Figaro,* stated that it would be false to assume that people in the West were thinking of appeasement when they spoke of negotiations—this was the opinion of most Western newspapers.[20] "Negotiations must come," wrote the *Daily Herald*. "Closing of the means of escape is no reason for the postponement of negotiations over Berlin. Rather it makes much more imperative the acceleration of preparations for a conference."[21]

Finally the Swiss paper, *National Zeitung,* saw a moral basis for negotiations in the speech of Kennedy. Even if Khrushchev persisted in his own viewpoint, there was . . . enough room for negotiations if carried on in secret and if the Western Powers insisted on answering force with force.[22]

Cautious Reaction of American, Swiss, and British Press

Powerful forces in the American, British, West European and also in part of the West German press, after the crucial week of 13-21 August, were united in urging negotiations as the only way out of the impasse over Berlin. Adventurers' policies connected with the use of military force in power politics were widely criticized as unnecessary and dangerous. This trend was most pronounced in the independent, right-center and conservatives press. Despite a few notable exceptions,[23] the left-center and pro-socialist papers tended to give strong support to the more aggressive and dynamic tactics of Brandt with strong undertones of German nationalism and irredentism.

The *Washington Post* declared that the United States would not allow itself to be pressured by German politicians to interfere in the West German electoral campaign.[24] The *New York Daily News* declared the visit of Vice President Johnson to West Berlin was a great political maneuver. On the other hand, the *New York Times* interpreted Johnson's visit, and the dispatch of 1500 U.S. troops to West Berlin, as a symbol to make clear to Khrushchev that: "the West is under obligation to prevent with all necessary means any further encroachments on the frontiers of freedom."[25] The *Washington Post* considered the Johnson-Clay visit to West Berlin as no answer to the Communists, but rather as a means to strengthen the morale of the population of West Berlin.[26]

Like the *Washington Post,* the Swiss paper, *Die Tat,* believed that the military and political measures of the Allies in Berlin would hardly impress the Russians and declared:

> The Western Powers have been finally called upon, through obvious demonstrations, of course, not to retreat before the Soviets and their followers from their occupation rights and to compel a settlement of Berlin—but at last to act decisively against the loss of confidence, which was emerging in the Berlin population through the inactivity of the allied protecting powers.

Another Swiss paper, *Tagesanzeiger,* stressed the hard realities of the Berlin Crisis, which were:

1. That the interests of the Allies were not in all respects identical with the interests of the West Germans, despite many beautiful words and
2. That the Western Powers were not apparently ready to grant priority to West German interests at the risk of a third World War.[28]

Various British papers were just as cautious as the American and Swiss journals cited above. The conservative *Daily Mail* considered the wall through Berlin an admission of instability and insecurity by the Zonal regime and wrote:

> History overcomes such walls, whether they were built by the Romans, the Chinese or modern peoples and were named after Maginot, Siegfried or Mannerheim. History will likewise find no greater hindrance in the Berlin Wall than in some of its forerunners.[29]

The London *Daily Herald* considered Kennedy's decision to defend the freedom of West Berlin reasonable and necessary to end the confidence crisis in West Germany, but sounded this warning:

> The tension and alarm in both halves of Germany must convince us as before of the deep apprehension. We must all wait a long time until the Soviets and West begin the task of positive statesmanship, which consists in removing the powder keg over the struggle for Berlin in the heart of Europe.[30]

Likewise, the London *Daily Express* complained that both Adenauer and Willy Brandt were allowed to threaten with the use of force. What can Great Britain do to prevent this? Our role should be to use the force of moral conviction—in the sense that it comes to discussions and not to war.[31] The influential *Daily Telegraph* urged calm nerves and cool blood in West Germany and West Berlin as the best guarantees against an encounter, which could conjure up an unwanted conflict.[32]

The Scottish newspaper, *Scotsman,* even raised the question whether it was wise on Kennedy's part to calm West Berlin in such a dramatic manner. "Johnson's visit as also the arrival of 1500 American soldiers," it declared, "could raise hopes which could not be completely fulfilled."[33]

The London *Observer* found it alarming that the great Powers were no longer complete masters of the situation and therefore, advised:

> The international status and the foreign policy of

Germany are not only the affair of Germany herself; but also the concern of Czechoslovakia, Poland and Russia, just as much as of Great Britain, France and Belgium. No one can maintain that after the experience of the last fifty years these nations have no voice in the matter. In the long run neither the Russian nor the German policy will be of any use. It can be maintained that the policy of both sides will lead to war.[34]

The *Observer* concluded that any solution, therefore, was bound to be temporary, leaving the way open for later changes. Among these it listed two: a new status for Berlin and some kind of recognition of East Germany.

Critical Reaction of Belgian, Italian and French Press

The same opinion was expressed by the President of the Belgian Senate, Struyel (Christian Social Party), namely, that direct contacts between the West and Pankow were unavoidable. He wrote in the Brussels paper as follows:

East and West are in essential agreement on the basis of: recognition of the uncontested rights of two million West Berliners to independence and security. A peace treaty between Moscow and Pankow would merely normalize the already existing situation. Actual relations already exist. Western firms take their commodities into the Zone and carry on intercourse.

On the sector boundaries control functions were already actually taken over by the East German police. At stake now is only the question of guaranteeing the freedom of West Berliners. Everything else merely showed additional modalities. Negotiations over this are not possible, but in the highest degree desirable.[35]

Seldom mirrored in the events of 13-21 August in Berlin was an article entitled, "Oil on the Flames," featured in the Belgian weekly, *Pourquoi Pas?* The writer asked whether Khrushchev could have done otherwise after they (Bonn at the head) had done everything to turn him to such action, which is typical for dictators who hear the thunder rumbling. "The Berlin island, as it was created at the end of the war, by the participants of the Potsdam Conference in their stupidity, permitted, as everyone knows, every East German to come into the Western World."[36] Three million people have made use of this freedom and no one can deny that this mass exodus spotlights the preachers of the Soviet Paradise. The principle of self-determination, which Adenauer used to advantage, is incontestable. But, this article concluded:

> One would not dare go too far with this, through his use or misuse of an incredible arrogance in order to justify extreme forms of national irredentism . . . What one must reproach the West Germans for is that they have not understood or do not wish to understand, because they feel so mighty and powerful, that Berlin is an extraordinarily delicate point of friction . . . The fact is that they have missed no opportunity to bring things to a boiling point and to throw tons of oil into the fire.[37]

In the opinion of the Italian newspaper, *Corriere D'Informazione,* strengthening the Allied garrison in Berlin had a purely symbolic meaning. Although Allied troops might have been able to repel a border aggression of the Zone army, they could do little in a general widening of the conflict. Hence the primary task of the Berlin garrison was of a moral nature.[38] In Rome, *Il Tempo* stressed the same theme: There are circumstances in which a demonstration of strength can avoid other actions, which are less demonstrative and, therefore, more dangerous. Sending a contingent of American troops to West Berlin was a clear demonstration of firmness and strength. The Soviets placed no hindrances in the way and the East Germans vanished from the scene, which lies in their territory and over which the Pankow Regime claims sovereignty.[39] Also in Moscow they seemed to have understood the meaning of the visit, as was shown by the angry reaction of *Pravda:*

> In connection with the visit of the American Vice President Johnson, the West Berlin authorities have organized a warlike hell-cat sabbath. They have needed his encouragement as a stimulant to increase still further the

military psychosis of the city. What the personal representative of Kennedy himself is concerned with, is to recall the actions and speeches in the pattern of a John Foster Dulles, with his policy of going to the brink of war, which has sunk into oblivion.[40]

Under the title, "The Most Renounced and Decisive Warning," the nationalist paper, *L'Aurore,* wrote of troop reinforcements in Berlin:

> The protection of West Berlin, the island of Western freedom within a Communist world, has certainly only a symbolic value. But why the symbol! It is a question of respect of treaties. It is again a symbol of resistance against those, who should presume at any time to destroy the peace.[41]

The French newspaper, *Humanité,* took a much more extreme stand on the Berlin crisis than other French or Italian newspapers. It argued that the Soviet Union and other Socialist countries are aware of the lessons of history and that if De Gaulle had forgotten the speeches which he delivered over the London radio against German militarism, the French nation has no such short memory. It would not march to the call of "self-determination" and of "free elections" under the *Klang* of *"Deutschland über Alles."* [42]

Reaction of Eastern Bloc, Belgrade and Nehru

In diplomatic circles of the Eastern Bloc States in Berlin, the opinion was expressed that negotiations between the Great Powers would be facilitated by the action of the DDR State in sealing off the Berlin border. Heretofore, the question of negotiations had been complicated by the refugee problem. The Eastern Bloc diplomats also discussed the agent theory of the deceased American Secretary of State. Just prior to his death, John Foster Dulles had indicated that the U.S.A. might allow East German officials to act as agents for the USSR at the check points for American vehicles entering Berlin. The case of the Eastern Bloc was based on the following factors:

1. Annexation of East Berlin by the DDR was described as a "fixation of the *status quo*."
2. This would constitute no change in the balance of power.
3. The DDR had respected the rights of the Western Powers to be in Berlin.[43]

On August 21st, *Die Welt* reprinted an article in the Berlin paper, *Tagespiegel,* thanking Kennedy and Brandt for protecting Berlin. The writer asked why the western Powers had sent their notes of protest only to Moscow and did not at the same time protest to Warsaw and Prague, along with all the governments in the Eastern Bloc, with whom they had diplomatic relations.[44] The Berlin paper argued that every member of the Warsaw Pact was responsible for threats to peace through an act of violence, which every one of these governments had recommended to Ulbricht. "Why should one leave it to Moscow to intimidate every individual member of NATO, as has happened for years with rocket threats?" [45]

By 22 August, 1961, the United States had recalled its diplomatic representatives to the neutral, non-aligned States in order to explain to the governments of their host countries the Western policy on Berlin and to inform them that Moscow had manufactured this crisis. In a television interview, Secretary of State Dean Rusk, said that the reaction of the uncommitted states to the Soviet-American-Berlin struggle might strengthen peace. This confidence above all was based on the report of Under Secretary Bowles, who had recently returned from a long journey through 18 Asiatic and African countries. The opinion of Bowles was that the right of self-determination for Germans and the American decision to support this right would have found complete support in the lands visited.[46]

"The German problem in all its aspects had already become complicated and difficult," wrote the chief editor of the Belgrade paper, *Borba* (standing near the Communist Party) with respect to the Berlin problem. "On the initiative of the Soviet Union, to find a solution for the Berlin problem in attack, the other side has reacted with a demonstration of force, which in turn has led to alarming demonstrations of force on both sides." [47] Without mentioning the thesis of two German states (the cardinal thesis of the Belgrade Government) this paper merely argued that "the solution of the German question rests directly on all nations of the earth, because with this the indivisible peace of the world is threatened and the pressing desires of the small nations, including those peoples of Asia and Africa still struggling for their independence, would be pushed into the background."[48]

Although *Frankfurter Allgemeine* did not accept this interpretation completely, it did look forward to the approaching Belgrade Conference for a solution to the Berlin-German Problem. Not only was Secretary of State Rusk concerned to inform the non-committed nations of the U.S. position, but also Adenauer, Brandt and Khrushchev all proceeded to instruct the uncommitted neutral nations as to their respective positions. Mayor Brandt received numerous delegations from the Afro-Asian Bloc Countries, while both Adenauer and Khrushchev wrote a series of letters expounding their respective positions to the Free-Bloc States, participating in the Belgrade Summit Conference.

Several days before the Conference opened, on 1 September, 1961, it was known that only 18 or 20 states would actually participate. Therefore, to give this conference a truly representative character and to make it effective, Nehru's participation was essential.[49] Nehru's authority and also his position on the German question had to be taken into consideration by Belgrade to prevent an open break in the conference. Belgrade itself prepared to exercise a free hand in order to deal with eventualities of the conference. This called for a certain degree of flexibility in the acute crisis over Berlin.

In his speech for the opening of the foreign policy debate in the Indian House of Representatives, in late August, Nehru placed Germany and Berlin at the beginning of his statement. German press correspondents noted the relation of this to the forthcoming Summit Conference of neutrals in Belgrade, where Nehru, as the most prominent neutral, would play a decisive role. Nehru opened his speech before the lower house with a reference to the sharpening of the international situation which has been made more dangerous by:

the failure of the Disarmament Conference,

the conflict over Berlin and particularly by
the recent events in Berlin. The Indian Premier then
emphasized three crucial points:

1. Whether one likes it or not, there is the geographical fact of two German states.
2. Both German states can only be reunited either by war or by agreement of the Super-Powers.
3. Such an agreement can come about only if existing tensions were overcome.

"In spite of the fact," Nehru declared, "that West and *Mitteldeutschland* (Middle Germany) are in opposition and members of fighting organizations, contacts between them existed as great numbers of workers went from one part of Germany to their work in the other. Nevertheless, that has been the case until very recently.[50] "On the other hand," Nehru observed, "there is a constant fear in the minds of many people of a revival of German militarism in West Germany." A second fear emerges from the unique position of Berlin in the heart of Mitteldeutschland.[51] Nevertheless, the Indian premier insisted that we could solve these problems born of fear. The only way to overcome this fear was by immediate disarmament. Nehru mentioned in his speech neither the favorite idea of Khrushchev, a "Free City of West Berlin" nor his threat to conclude a separate peace treaty with the Zone Republic.

The *New Delhi Link* viewed with increasing alarm what was being organized in Bonn and West Berlin as "a diversion maneuver at a time when a strong current of public opinion flows toward East-West negotiations over Berlin and other related questions."[52]

Conclusion

The impact of British newspapers, like the London *Times*, *Daily Telegraph*, *Observer* and *Manchester Guardian* on the formulation of British foreign policy is much greater than German press influence upon foreign policy. German foreign policy is made by the Chancellor and his close advisers, guided only by public opinion polls, a few very trusted advisers and private intelligence. Even the powerful government and opposition parties of the Bundestag could only influence foreign policy —not control it. So in many questions of foreign policy—specifically rearmament, decisions on placement of nuclear weapons and compulsory military service—Chancellor Adenauer was able to proceed contrary to the wishes of the majority of German citizens. Moreover, public opinion later accepted the decisions, while the parliamentary opposition gradually withered away and finally joined the government in support of its foreign policy.

Thus the West German Government approached the Berlin crisis of the summer of 1961 in close accord with the French on the futility of negotiation.[53] In fact West German officials became convinced that American and British exploratory talks with the Soviet Union in search of a Berlin solution might result in a Big Power agreeement at the expense of West Germany's future development. As a counterbalance, therefore, the West Germans laid down terms which must be met in any Berlin settlement. Meanwhile, confronted with increasing criticism from the opposition parties, West German officials pushed for closer ties with Berlin than they had prior to the events of 13 August, 1961, in Berlin.[54]

After the erection of the barbed wire barricade, the Berlin crisis became the principal theme in the Western capitals as well as in the old German capital. Frequently featured in the editorials of leading British and European papers were: German reunification, recognition of the existence of two German states and the demand for negotiations. The international status and foreign policy of Germany were not only the affair of Germany herself; they were also the concern of Czechoslovakia, Poland and Russia, just as much as Great Britain, France and Belgium.

Powerful elements in the British, West European and much of the West German press after 13 August were united in urging negotiations as the only way out of the impasse over Berlin. Much of the press criticized the use of military force in power politics as unnecessary and dangerous. This trend was even more pronounced in the independent, right-center and conservative press than in the left-center and pro-socialist papers. The latter in general tended to give strong support to the more aggressive and dynamic tactics of Mayor Brandt, with strong overtures of German nationalism and irredentism. This enabled the East German Communist press and the Soviets to mount a campaign of vituperation against the conservative, right-wing leadership of the German Social Democratic Party (SPD), as noted in the previous chapter.

The cautious and critical attitude of certain Belgian, French and Italian papers was shown in the emphasis placed on negotiations between the West and Pankow and the avoidance of any precipitate action in Berlin which might overturn the neat balance of power between East and West. Although the principle of self-determination was incontestable, Germans were warned against its misuse and arrogance to justify extreme forms of national irredentism. Conservative papers urged that in the long run the extreme demands of neither the West Germans nor the Soviets would prove workable. Some papers even suggested that it would be next to impossible to evolve a formula for German reunification which could prove acceptable to both East and West Germans and satisfy the legitimate security needs of Soviet Russia and Germany's neighbors: Britain, Belgium, France, Poland and Czechoslovakia.

Not only Kennedy and Adenauer, but Brandt and Khrushchev were all concerned that their positions on the Berlin and German questions be clearly understood by the uncommitted so-called neutral nations—18 of which finally attended the Belgrade Conference, which began 1 September, 1961, to discuss the dangerous threats to world peace and the *status quo*. Prime Minister Nehru showed a remarkable understanding of the crucial issues at stake in Berlin and exerted a strong influence for moderation in the final Communique, which avoided mention of two German states.

Although the United States and Britain were effectively blocked in July and early August, 1961, from their partially formulated ideas for taking a diplomatic initiative in the Berlin crisis by French and West German intransigence, the reaction of the world press to the Berlin Wall was far from insignificant. Senator Hubert H. Humphrey, in a personal interview with Chancellor Adenauer, nearly a month after his party's loss of its absolute majority in the parliamentary elections of 17 September, 1961, was told that "the position of the West German Federal Government was always and still is diametrically opposed to any system of military disengagement limited to Central Europe." [55]

Today the West German newspapers are among the freest in the world. It was this freedom of the press in Germany that forced West German parties and public opinion to reassess past policies and to re-examine the assumptions on which German foreign policies were based. This painful process caused 28 per cent of Germans to remain undecided only two weeks prior to the parliamentary elections of 17 September, 1961. This large undecided vote worked to the advantage of the opposition parties —Free Democrats and Social Democrats—at the expense of Dr. Adenauer's Christian Democrats. Whereas before the Berlin Wall, Chancellor Adenauer was influenced very little by either the German press or the powerful opposition parties, the period since the election of 17 September, 1961, was marked by three new developments: 1) the 7-week interregnum between the parliamentary elections and the selection of a Chancellor; 2) instead of an absolute No to Soviet proposals of October, 1961, Chancellor Adenauer gave a qualified No; 3) before going to Washington to meet with President Kennedy in November, 1961, Chancellor Adenauer not only conferred with key members of his own party, but met with his coalition partners, the Free Democrats, and members of the Social Democratic opposition and SPD Mayor Willy Brandt.

Finally the *Spiegel Affair* in November, 1962, caused criticism of Dr. Adenauer to reach new heights. After the resignation of all five Free Democratic Ministers from the Cabinet, the Chancellor was forced to remove high officials to save his Government. Certainly his prestige suffered. Many Germans considered the police action taken against four editors of *Der Spiegel* too much like Hitler's Gestapo for comfort. Despite the Chancellor's brilliant defense of his Government before the National Press Club on 17 November, 1962, young Germans, in particular, accused Adenauer of scuttling a free press and democracy. Not in years had the German public and politicians been so aroused.

1. Five Journalists, "Ist Wiedervereinigung noch moglich?" in *General Anzeiger* (Bonn, independent), 15 June, 1961.
2. *Ibid.*
3. *General Anzeiger* (Bonn, independent), 15 June, 1961.
4. Oliver E. Clubb, Jr., *The United States and the Sino-Soviet Bloc in Southeast Asia* (Washington, D. C., Brookings Institute, 1962) quoted by *The National Observer* (Washington, D. C., right-center), p. 18 (15 October, 1962).
5. *Washington Post* (liberal), 19 November, 1961.
6. *Times* (London, close to British Foreign Office), 19 August, 1962.
7. *Times* (London, conservative), 19 August, 1961.
8. Besides the London *Times, Observer, Economist* and *Daily Telegraph* for 19 August, 1961, see also *Der Mittag* (right-center), *Industrial Kurier* (independent organ for politics, economics and technology), *General Anzeiger* (Bonn, independent), *Frankfurter Allgemeine Zeitung* (right-center), *Die Welt* (Hamburg, independent), *Hamburger Echo* (independent) for 19 August, 1961. *Die Zeit* (Hamburg weekly, right-center) was most critical of the Foreign Ministers Conference in Paris, which had even failed to set a date for negotiations. Had it done so, the Berlin Wall might not even have been erected on 13 August, 1961.
9. *Observer* (London, liberal), 22 August, 1961.
10. *Economist* (London, liberal weekly), 22 August, 1961.
11. *The Guardian* (Manchester, liberal), 21 August, 1961.
12. *Ibid.*
13. *Daily Telegraph* (London, conservative), 21 August, 1961.
14. *Arbeiterbladet* (Stockholm, pro-SPD), quoted by *Hamburger Echo,* 22 August, 1961.
15. Stockholm *Tidningen* (pro-Government), quoted by *Hamburger Echo,* 22 August, 1961.
16. *Maclean's Magazine* (Ottawa, liberal), quoted by *Hamburger Echo,* 22 August, 1961.
17. *Daily Herald* (London, pro-Labor Party), 21 August, 1961.
18. *Times* (London, Conservative), 21 August, 1961.
19. *Guardian* (Manchester, liberal), 21 August, 1961.

20. *Le Figaro* (Paris, Conservative), 21 August, 1961.

21. *Daily Herald* (London, pro-Labor), 21 August, 1961.

22. *National Zeitung* (Basle, right-center), 21 August, 1961.

23. *Süddeutsche Zeitung* (Munich, left-center), 19 August, 1961, criticized the propriety of Brandt's letter to President Kennedy as contrary to protocol.

24. *Washington Post* (Liberal), 21 August, 1961.

25. *New York Times* (Independent), 21 August, 1961.

26. *Washington Post* (Liberal), 21 August, 1961.

27. *Die Tat,* quoted by *Die Welt* (Hamburg, independent), 22 August, 1961.

28. *Tagesanzeiger* (Zurich, independent), 21 August, 1961.

29. *Daily Mail* (London, conservative), 21 August, 1961.

30. *Daily Herald* (London, socialist), 21 August, 1961.

31. *Daily Express* (London, independent), 21 August, 1961.

32. *Daily Telegraph* (London, conservative), 21 August, 1961.

33. *Scotsman* (Glasgow, independent), 21 August, 1961.

34. *The Observer* (London, liberal), 20 August, 1961.

35. Struyel, "Kontakte Westen" in *La Libre Belgique* (Brussels, liberal), 21 August, 1961.

36. *Pourquoi Pas?* (Brussels, liberal), quoted in *Frankfurter Allgemeine Zeitung* (right-center), 22 August, 1961.

37. *Ibid.*

38. *Corriere D'Informazione* (Rome, independent), quoted in *Die Welt* (Hamburg, independent), 22 August, 1961.

39. Il Tempo (Rome, independent), quoted in *Frankfurter Allgemeine Zeitung* (right-center), 22 August, 1961.

40. Quoted from *Pravda* by *Frankfurter Allgemeine Zeitung* (right-center), 22 August, 1961.

41. Quoted from *L'Aurore* by *Die Welt* (Hamburg, independent), 22 August, 1961.

42. *Humanité* (Paris, Communist), 21 August, 1961.

43. *Frankfurter Rundschau* (pro-SPD), 22 August, 1961.

44. *Tagespiegel* (West Berlin, pro-SPD), quoted by *Die Welt* (Hamburg, independent), 21 August, 1961.

45. *Ibid.*

46. *Ibid.*

47. *Borba* (Belgrade, close to Communist Party), quoted by *Frankfurter Allgemeine* (right-center), 22 August, 1961.

48. *Ibid.*
49. *Frankfurter Allgemeine Zeitung* (right-center), 22 August, 1961.
50. *Frankfurter Allgemeine Zeitung* (right-center), 22 August, 1961.
51. *Ibid.*
52. "Demand for Negotiations," *Link* (New Delhi, independent), 21 August, 1961.
53. *New York Times* (independent), 18 November, 1961.
54. *Washington Post* (liberal), 19 November, 1961.

PART IV.

GERMAN PARLIAMENTARY ELECTIONS OF
17 SEPTEMBER 1961

Chapter 12

CHANGES IN PARTY TACTICS AFTER
THE WALL, 1961

The parliamentary election of 17 September, 1961, proved to be the most remarkable election which the West German Federal Republic had experienced in its entire existence. The campaign went through a complete transformation—out of its own grave on the battle lines of the Berlin Wall it had risen, like a Phoenix out of the ashes. That which was considered dead became more alive than ever.[1]

The waves of this electoral campaign flooded Bonn on Tuesday (22 August, 1961) with placards of Brandt and Adenauer. The presence of the parliamentary representatives in Bonn for a short special session of the Bundestag was used by all parties for discussion of the question: how should the electoral campaign be adapted to the changed climate caused by the events of 13 August?[2] Only with this electoral fever was it said that whoever suggested the journey of Vice President Johnson and the transfer of American reinforcements to West Berlin would gain an astounding amount of publicity. The Free Democrats gleefully declared that "the quarrel between the CDU and SPD over the real origin of the idea had no relation to the interests of the German people."[3] Harry Gilroy of the New York *Times* reported from Bonn that partisans of Brandt and Adenauer were each claiming credit for the successful mission of Vice President Johnson to Berlin. Rarely had Chancellor Adenauer come under such unanimous attacks by the press.[4] He complained of this at his press conference in the Bundeshaus immediately before and immediately after the elections on 17 September, 1961.

This campaign, which should really not have affected vital national interests during a dangerous international crisis (an area which was essentially "off-limits"), developed unforeseen into a most tense federal German election. Interest continued right up to the last day, as evidenced by record attendance at campaign rallies. The bloc of undecided voters, which normally falls off sharply five weeks before the election, remained at 28 per cent in the Emnid Survey of 3 September.[5] To win over this group, the election was fought over again and, of course, within the theme of Berlin. Whereas before 13 August the desire for security of business and increase of profits might have been decisive, these considerations were subordinated to the fear of war and desires for peace. Before 13 August the lack of evident alternatives in the program offered by parties and their parallel concurrence in welfare promises allowed the number of undecided to increase to 31 per cent. So out of a politically colored propaganda campaign for higher living standards came competition between business and fear of war.[6]

New Tactics of CDU/CSU

Consequently almost overnight a new campaign was planned and executed for the party of the Chancellor. Konrad Adenauer had developed such an amazing degree of skill which made his party victorious in so many elections that many Christian Democrats expected the CDU/CSU would win an absolute majority in the Bundestag with 52, 55, 58 or even 60 per cent. Some even hoped for a two-thirds majority. However, Dr. Adenauer's failure to go to Berlin until ten days after the crisis of 13 August caused many West Germans to lose confidence and develop a fatal impression of their Chancellor. When he finally did go to Berlin, the Federal Chancellor, in company with his Minister of All-German Affairs, Ernst Lemmer, visited Marienfeld, refugee reception camp in West Berlin. Here he was asked by German refugees from East Berlin why he had delayed his trip to Berlin so long. Dr. Adenauer explained that he was occupied in Bonn with upholding the threatened freedom of West Berlin and the support of Western efforts to restore the violated status of the city as a whole. Above all, he explained, it was a problem for negotiations between the Four Occupation Powers.*

Campaign manager Bach gave three main reasons for the "considerable losses of the CDU in the sympathy of voters after Black Sunday in Berlin:"

1. The shock over the delay of Western countermeasures, disappointment over the fact that the Chancellor, regardless of his reasons, waited more than a week to visit Berlin.
2. Brandt's total of 12 hours appearance on television, above all with Vice President Johnson.
3. Adenauer's unfair tactics immediately after 13 August in a talk in Regensburg: "Brandt alias Frahm," and in Hagen: "The Berlin crisis is merely help for the SPD." [7]

On the point of election aid for the SPD, the Chancellor regarded himself, after the last attack of Khrushchev against his person and his government, as clearly confirmed. Khrushchev said: "Germans who vote for Adenauer and the supporters of his policy in West Germany have agreed on the same slogans with which Hitler came to power with the second World War resulting." [8] *Der Mittag* described the CDU fraction as apprehensive that the Berlin crisis would entail a gain in prestige and votes for Brandt at the expense of Adenauer.[9] Berliners generally welcomed Brandt's initiative in writing a letter directly to Kennedy. Brandt appeared to be the man of action who enlightened Washington about the real feelings of Berlin and Germany.[10]

Editorial opinion in the West German Press of Dr. Adenauer's Berlin visit was most unfavorable. Pro-CDU, right-center and independent papers criticized the visit on the following grounds:

1. Adenauer was ill-advised and did not properly analyze the psychological mood of the German people when delaying his trip to Berlin for ten days.
2. An immediate visit of the Chancellor to Berlin might not have helped Berlin's cause, but would have deprived the SPD of an effective campaign slogan.

3. Adenauer's Berlin visit was marked by "agonizing embarrassment," meagerness and "poor psychology."[11]
4. Adenauer's delayed Berlin visit did not remove the vacuum which resulted from the days when Berliners' expectations of their political leaders were not fulfilled.
5. Adenauer and Brandt should both be criticized for continuing their feud and trying to exploit the Johnson visit for campaign purposes.[12]
6. Voices of "victory" from East Berlin derided Adenauer, but East Berlin citizens cheered him as their Chancellor. West Berliners reminded him that he had come too late.[13]

Fears of a negative result of crucial events in Berlin on the electoral chances of the Christian Democrats led Adenauer to call the Federal Executive Committee of the CDU to Bonn for Friday. The Chancellor was disturbed, when, after the echo of the Hagen SPD help remark, the experienced mediator, and the CDU floor leader, Dr. Krone, had to reject two parts of the 6-Point Declaration of the Hagen Speech because of the changed circumstances of the campaign. Propaganda of the past, over which was clearly stamped welfare at Campaign Headquarters at 48 Koblenz Street, would no longer work with the new tactics. Earlier slogans such as "no experiments," "To continue to enjoy freedom" and the Brandenburg Gate could remain, but most of the expensive television film went into the waste paper basket. Instead of this, CDU leaders gave prominence to seeing the actual conversation before the cameras.

But all this was no problem. The real problem was the new direction of the campaign toward the new anxieties of the electorate, toward saving the community and toward national solidarity. And this problem remained unsolved. Calculated on this "only now no quarrel," on this still evident stamp of the formerly manipulated diabolical fate, "Mass forces" of the electorate, the CDU had not reacted fast enough. Above all, however, campaign strategists could not produce the "image" of a leading picture of a Matador by several rapid costume changes. They wanted the Chancellor in this situation to run exclusively as "the Great." [14]

Near the end of August, Moritz Pfeil, writing in *Der Spiegel*, criticized Adenauer: for treating the SPD as the common enemy; for being incapable of objective discussion; for playing off pressure groups against his cabinet ministers; for calling down minister presidents as if they were lackeys; for degrading the office of Federal President; and for publicly criticizing the Constitutional Court for having passed a "wrong" judgment.[15] Emnid Research Service published a Public Opinion poll, showing that of the votes sampled: 46% favored the CDU/CSU, 38% the SPD, 9% the FDP and 5% the All-German Party, with 1% favoring the DFU.[16]

SPD Tactics: Solidarity with Berlin

Not only did the editor of *Der Spiegel* criticize the Chancellor for treating the SPD as a common enemy, he came out in support of the SPD, contending that it represented the alternative to Adenauer because the maltreated FDP would not resist him. In giving its support to the SPD, *Der Spiegel* stressed the following arguments:

1. Brandt's foreign policy could not be worse than Adenauer's.
2. Brandt would promote democracy because he knows how to discuss, respects institutions and is never vindictive.
3. He would respect his opponents.
4. Under his chancellorship, elections would become a real political struggle because neither the clergy nor industry would aid him.
5. If Brandt were unable to neutralize the bad effects of Adenauer's German policy, democracy would have a chance under an SPD government.[17]

Chancellor candidate Brandt at a press conference following an SPD Congress and rally in Nürnberg on 12 August, 1961, told the author that heretofore 90% of his campaign was devoted to domestic issues—living standards, welfare benefits, income and taxes. In a televised radio interview on 6 August, the SPD campaign manager, Sanger, stated that his party would use:

231

1. posters, advertisements in newspapers and periodicals;
2. giant public rallies with expert campaign orators like Willy Brandt and Professor Carlo Schmid;
3. party functionaries (district secretaries) and special speakers in command of various languages and local German dialects;
4. short, televised radio speeches of Chancellor candidate Willy Brandt, Chairman Ollenhauer, Carlo Schmid, Fraction leader Mommer and Dr. Helmut Schmidt, SPD expert on defense policy.[18]

Above all Herr Sanger stressed the idea that German political and economic progress was not the result of government policy, as so often claimed by the CDU, but was the result of the common efforts of all Germans—but unfortunately only a part of the population (never a majority) enjoyed prosperity. It was most important, therefore, to give all the people a feeling of social security, which would in turn create a strong feeling of loyalty to the land which must be defended under all circumstances, not only with weapons, but with ideals and ideology. This was the best answer to Communism.[19] Therefore, voters were urged to strive for a fair division of the common product of labor and then for a common political solidarity as we are able to improve the position of our country in world affairs.[20]

After the momentous events of Black Sunday (13 August) the election propaganda of the Social Democrats gave priority to conditions in Berlin. Party Chairman Ollenhauer coined the new campaign slogan of the Social Democrats: "Get out the vote—Help Berlin and Willy Brandt." In contrast the Christian Democrats centered their campaign propaganda around the "Prevention of War." "Our policy has preserved for the Germans in West Berlin and the Federal Republic, Peace and Freedom."[21] The CDU Campaign was aimed at the preservation of peace and the *status quo*—continued support of NATO, with an eventual goal of disarmament, that is, reduction of armaments, but controlled in all spheres. Speaking before 20,000 people in Mannheim, Adenauer reproached the SPD, contending that their late recognition of NATO was not sincere. "That is clear from the "Appeal 'weapons for all in NATO—only Germans not in the center of the defense sphere.' "[22]

232

In contrast to the CDU emphasis on peace, the status quo, NATO and controlled disarmament, SPD tactics stressed solidarity with Berlin and national unity. Brandt questioned the logical consistency of Adenauer in attempting negotiations after 13 August, when, heretofore, he had continually refused them. The Berlin Bürgermeister deplored the fact that the last conversations of the Chancellor with the Soviet Ambassador, Smirnov, had not prevented the aggravation of the situation in Berlin. Brandt stated that until 17 September, he would spend every day at the City Hall in West Berlin and limit his campaign speeches to the evening hours.[23] Before nearly 20,000 people in Offenbach, Brandt declared: "on the basis of the new aggravation one must accept the fact that the Berlin crisis moves steadily to a climax."[24] In view of the serious international situation, he considered it impossible to carry on the electoral campaign in the hitherto customary form. He called for national unity and demanded abstinence from personal insinuation.

Brandt on Sunday in campaign speeches in Hagen, Hamm and Osnabrück criticized the utter "confusion" of the Government in the two weeks after 13 August. "I must say that in the last 14 days it seems as if there is no German Government at all and that was the case above all at the most critical time. The present Federal Government seems to be paralyzed, surprised, incapable and completely confused."[25] The SPD candidate continued:

> Before the crisis the present Federal Government represented the viewpoint one could not negotiate under pressure. After the event in Berlin it is prepared to negotiate on a condition of voluntary expression ... Before the crisis it spoke of the legal violations of the Soviet Union and said the Soviet Union was not trustworthy at all . . . After the crisis, on the contrary, Dr. Adenauer declared in Berlin that until there was evidence to the contrary, he would believe that the Soviet Union respects what it has guaranteed in treaties.[26]

Speaking over the South German radio on 23 August, Fritz Erler (SPD Bundestag deputy) declared that after the events in Berlin, the election campaign could not go on as if nothing had happened. The cold annexation of East Berlin by the Soviet Bloc and its separation from West Berlin affected everyone. He continued:

> We are one people and belong together. Ulbricht's next goal is West Berlin. If the lights go out there, all Germany will be in darkness. We will only defend ourselves from further aggressions and re-establish law and order, if we Germans stand together in vital questions affecting the nation. We must learn to dispute internal affairs with each other and still be able to join forces in foreign affairs. Self-righteousness and arrogance do not help. It would be better for Berlin if the CDU had accepted the overtures of the Social Democrats to work together instead of at cross-purposes.[27]

The SPD deputy contended that whoever treats upright citizens as enemies and personally attacks them places party politics above the welfare of the state and nation. We Social Democrats as the Government of tomorrow have definitely decided to treat the opposition of tomorrow better than we were treated. The events in Berlin were a hard lesson for our whole nation. The Government can, nevertheless, not very well evade responsibility for the resulting policy. The problem of the year 1961 can not be resolved with the concepts of 1952. The Union Party will also have to learn this. Today self-determination has priority.[28] The SPD would have welcomed this, if only, before the decision for the rearmament of the Federal Republic and its entrance into NATO, an earnest effort had been undertaken to reach other security solutions in central Europe with the reunification of Germany.

The above radio comments of Fritz Erler are basic to an understanding of the Social Democraic opposition to Adenauer's foreign policy during the ten years from 1949 to November, 1959. Then the Bad-Godesberg program of the SPD marked a definite shift from the revolutionary Marxian position to the idea of a middle class people's party.[29] Later in June, 1960, came the Bundestag debate on foreign policy, in which Herbert Wehner speaking for the SPD, made a complete switch over to the side of the Adenauer Government.[30] This was followed on

30 June, 1961, by the Bundestag Declaartion, which represented a united stand of all the parties on the Berlin-German question.

Before the era of Soviet long distance rockets much was possible, which is no longer true today. Nevertheless, only the affairs of today count. The West must maintain its military strength and not allow laxity here. A Social Democratic Government will also render its contribution here. "Whoever demands of Kennedy and Khrushchev the continuation of Eisenhower's and Stalin's policies must also expect that Willy Brandt will continue the political obligations of Adenauer." [31] To doubt this—and thereby the desire of the German worker for freedom—means to encourage Khrushchev toward adventures. That is to say, Fritz Erler concluded, that the role of the SPD is to recognize frankly the need for common defense efforts and confidence in Germany's Western Allies. A reasonable division of labor not only lightens the defense burden, but prevents the possession of atomic weapons by every individual state. Atomic weapons for everybody would end all security.[32] Therefore, the military preparedness of the West was a *sine qua non* to checkmate Soviet adventures. This, however, would have been useless in order to prevent the events in Berlin. There are dangers which even military means can not resolve. Hence the need not only for close cooperation between Germany and the West, but for a Western initiative instead of always reacting to Soviet offensives.

Speaking for the SPD on the same radio program—Parties before the Election—Heinz Kuhn stressed the following items:

1. News of elaborate plans of the Federal Ministries for making Bonn the most beautiful capital in Europe is an admission that Dr. Adenauer's promises of the results of his policy for strength was for Germany a terrible self-deception. At the Brandenburg Gate Adenauer's predictions were wrecked on the shameful wall of Ulbricht.

2. Misery is now even more widespread among our educated since we dared to discuss the mistakes and shortcomings of the past—than perhaps in the 1950's when the Soviets had neither atomic and hydrogen bombs nor long distance rockets and astronauts. If reunification in freedom and security were then attain-

235

able with a different government policy, the first need will be to investigate the evidence if and when the government archives in East and West are opened.

3. It is no longer necessary that we all belong to a certain party in order to find a way to secure and preserve freedom for our people and in order to win back those behind the barbed wire of the Soviet Zone.

4. Differences between parties are unavoidable and necessary. But there are times in the life of a nation in which the internal political opposition is entirely agreeable to a partnership in foreign policy. We must, therefore, raise the question whether one dare—as Adenauer's Deputy, Professor Erhard, did—describe the social requirements of Willy Brandt's government program as *Husten*—bonbons (cough drops)—or, if not, in the otherwise still self-praised *Wirtschaftswunder* system (economic miracle) as a minimum standard of social security.[33] Certainly for our ten thousand millionaires, 225 marks would be "cough-drops"; for many millions, however, it is vitally important.

5. We must, therefore, raise the question whether we can at the same time still agree upon measures which are urgent for the guarantee of freedom in Western Berlin. We must, therefore, question whether it is proper for Chancellor candidate, Dr. Adenauer, to charter a military plane for his electioneering journey, and to use public tax revenues uncontrolled by parliament to promote the partisan aims of a government party.

6. Above all it must be questioned whether one can still agree upon measures which are necessary to make our just cause of freedom and reunification intelligible and convincing to all nations, who represent a majority in the United Nations.

Heinz Kuhn concluded his radio appeal in behalf of the SPD by emphasizing the urgent need for the German people to grasp the methods the Chancellor used heretofore against his competitors for the office of Chief of State—methods of cheapening and degrading the office, which even the Bundestag president, his own party friend, characterized as "unseemly" and which, moreover, completely ignored the demand of the Federal President, Dr. Lubke, for a fair election campaign. We can not in our threatened position use the quarrelsome nature of a man who, in this parliamentary session, will reach the age of ninety, whether or not he is re-elected to the office of Chancellor—an office which demands not only the power of vitality, but also readiness for harmony and concord. Moreover, in our threatened position we can not use in the office of Chancellor such an irresponsible and unrestrained man as Strauss, who in the shadow of Adenauer waits his time like a genuine crown prince. The Chancellor's office must in the future no longer be an office of discord and internal division of our people.

FDP—Ideology, Policies and Tactics

On 6 August the RIAS radio station in West Berlin broadcast a program in which four party campaign managers explained their activities in the campaign for seats in the Bundestag. Dr. Erich Mende, spoke for the Free Democratic Party (FDP), not only as campaign manager but also as party chairman and fraction chairman in the Bundestag. Mende recalled that in 1949, ten different parties were represented in the Bundestag, ranging from the Communists on the extreme left to the Socialist Reichs Party (neo-Nazi) on the right. In the twelve years since 1949, the number of parties in the Bundestag had declined from ten to only three. The main objective of Dr. Mende was to have this three-party-trend preserved and confirmed by the German electorate on 17 September. "We believe that it is necessary, in the postwar German democracy, that beside the CDU as a definitely controlled confessional party, and beside the SPD, as a traditional socialist party, a third way must be possible."[34] That is the way of political liberalism. The FDP Chairman pointed out that Dr. Adenauer himself, in the Chancellor's office in the presence of Ollenhauer, (SPD Party Chairman) had thus characterized this third way:

Herr Mende, there are now millions of voters, who will not vote for me and my party because to them it is black. But neither will they vote for Herr Ollenhauer and his party, because to them it is red. For these millions of our

237

citizens there must be a third political choice. And if there were no Free Democratic Party, they would have to create one.

Then Adenauer concluded: "I, therefore, consider the Free Democrats a political necessity in Germany." Mende replied: "May I make use of this?" "That you may," he said. "That's my opinion."[35]

The Free Democrats appealed to the employees in commerce —handiwork, business, the free professions and agriculture—in short to the middle classes, and also to the laboring classes. They realized, however, that they only reached a certain part of the workers, the qualified and skilled workers, who might gladly take over employee relations. In the main, however, they focused attention on the middle classes which were directly represented by neither the German Trade Union Federation nor by the Bundesverband (National Association of Business). The structure of the FDP Party could be compared to neither the SPD, which is a party of functionaries (paid secretaries), nor to that of the CDU. There were no electoral agreements of the FDP with either the CDU or the SPD. The Free Democratic Party directed its campaign independent of both with sharp competition, but without personal vituperation.

In order to mobilize the voters to support its policies, the Free Democrats issued millions of copies of a pamphlet, "A Call of the Free Democratic Party." In an objective manner they pointed out that certain questions in reunification policy, in the economy, in social policy, cultural policy and in the defense in the past years were not handled as they would have desired. The middle classes are especially concerned with the purely material aspect of finance and legislation. But the Free Democrats also emphasized the spiritual responsibility of the German people. In contrast to both other parties, CDU and SPD, the Free Democrats refrained from promises of more welfare benefits and directed their campaign along spiritual lines.[36] To illustrate this aspect, the FDP Chairman quoted from the Preamble of the pamphlet, "Call of the Free Democratic Party,":

Our Fatherland is divided. The East-West Conflict can lead to catastrophe any day. Prosperity in the Federal Republic veiled the threat to our national existence. Our nation is not prepared to taste a serious deficit. It is worthwhile to recognize these dangers; only a free, modern and sound nation can conquer them. And then we explain specifically what we understand by a free nation in the broadest sents of the word, by a sound nation, materially, morally and spiritually sound, and what we understand by a modern nation in the new industrial society and what direction we might give our political development in the Federal Republic.[37]

Dr. Mende concluded the broadcast by explaining the elaborate organization of his Free Democratic Party with its 650 organizations on the state, district and community levels and 10,000 voluntary campaign workers. As to methods of publicity, he listed television, radio, then films, then illustrated materials and above all public rallies, followed by press reports and newspaper advertisements. He divided the FDP campaign into three phases:

1. Confidence publicity with a poster of Theodore Heuss, our first chairman and former Federal President, under whom the motto ran: In his spirit, with new force! emerging from the National party congress in Frankfurt in March, 1961.
2. Then came the second phase, with branch congresses. From the Health Congress in Mainz to the Middle Class Congress in Nürnberg, to the meetings of the German Young Democrats at Hermanns-Denkmal in Detmold.
3. From the middle of August ran the last phase, the hard campaign phase of public rallies, which we contest through hundreds of meetings of all our speakers and also through modern demonstrations, which, however, it would be too early to announce publicly.[38]

The momentous events in Berlin after 13 August—the Berlin wall, Protest Rally in West Berlin, Special Bundestag session, Johnson-Clay visit to Berlin and continued agitation of the Berlin crisis in the press inspired the opposition parties to intensify their efforts in the election campaign. The Free Democrats focused attention on three items: 1) role of the FDP as the representative of political liberalism in Germany, 2) danger of misuse by the governing CDU-Party of its absolute majority and 3) conditions of a future coalition of the FDP and CDU. By Liberalism the FDP Chairman meant not licentious freedom, but the disciplined freedom of modern Liberalism. "We submit to the Ten Commandments, to the categorical imperative of Emmanuel Kant and the moral principle: What you would not have others do to you, that also do not to others!" The freedom of man is closely bound to moral responsibility and to obligations to the community.

Looking forward to the election of 17 September, the Free Democrats concentrated all efforts to break the absolute majority of the CDU and thus remove the strong temptation to abuse this power. They asserted that the past years proved that fear of the misuse of this absolute majority was not groundless. The FDP, therefore, proposed to reverse the trend toward one-party rule by a mutual partnership of two parties in which both are considered and neither can make decisions for itself alone.[39]

On the question of a coalition, the former fraction chairman of the FDP and Minister of Justice in a Coalition Cabinet with Adenauer, 1949-1953, Dr. Thomas Dehler, declared that this question could only be decided after the election and only then by the elected representatives of the party, not by party cliques or other groups. If another coalition between the FDP and CDU parties were desired, Dehler insisted that "there must be a clear agreement over a common program. Above all there must be in this program a common line on foreign policy."[40] Although the FDP deputy cautioned that all speculations over a coalition were premature, he did suggest that the declaration of Bundestag President, Dr. Gerstenmaier, on 30 June 1961, was a possible basis for an understanding between the CDU and FDP over foreign policy in case of a coalition government.[41]

Against the person of the present Federal Chancellor, Dehler offered a relatively new consideration and declared that in his view a politician, who at the end of the next legislative period would reach the age of 90, was not suited to determine the fate of the nation. The same point was raised the following day by Dr. Mende, who merely stated that one must ask the question whether the responsibility of government could still be placed on a man 85 years old. Outside the circles of the Federal

Executive Committee of the Free Democratic Party, reservations against Adenauer were even stronger.[42]

At the beginning of its campaign Congress, with which the Free Democrats wished to direct the final phase of their campaign, the Executive Committee offered a Resolution in which the FDP declared:

1. That it would never give its vote to human rights treaties which emerge from the split of Berlin of 13 August.
2. The Western Allies of Bonn could not consider the Berlin question alone from the standpoint of their own rights in Berlin.
3. The barricade of East Berlin violated the Four-Power Status of all Berlin. By the obligation undertaken by the Allies, they made the cause of German unity their own cause.
4. A settlement of the Berlin and German crisis could in the view of the Free Democrats, only be achieved by a Summit Conference of the Big "Four" Powers. In case of failure here, the FDP proposed to bring the Berlin-German question before the United Nations.[43]

Party Chairman Mende repeated before the Executive Committee his proposal to consider the possibility of a Great Coalition of all parties, in case of any further sharpening of the Berlin Crisis. The Executive Committee of the FDP gave unanimous consent to both this proposal and to a resolution to discuss no details of any eventual coalition prior to the parliamentary elections.[44] Dr. Mende gave full support to a previous proposal from the former Chairman, Dr. Dehler, that the basis of any potential coalition of Free Democrats with the CDU/CSU would be the Berlin-Declaration of Bundestag President Gerstenmaier, delivered before the Bundestag on 30 June, 1961, without opposition and with the applause of all parties.[45]

At the FDP Election Congress in Hannover (24/25 August) representative Doring repeated a suggestion, which FDP Chairman Mende had already made in the Bundestag on 18 August: that West Berlin be taken into the Federal Republic as a state (*land*) with all the consequences, in case the Soviets consider the Four-Power Status of Berlin as nothing more than a worthless piece of paper. This proposal advanced by Doring in the name of the Free Democratic Party before over a thousand delegates, among whom were all the FDP Bundestag candidates, evoked loud applause.[46] This would require formal treaties between both the old German capital and Bonn.

As a further demand of his party, Doring named the settlement of the Berlin and German problem with universal controlled disarmament. This goal, in the view of the Free Democrats would be achieved, if there were disarmament in regional spheres.[47] For such an experimental area, the European area above all was sought. From the next Federal Government the Free Democrats expected, as Doring said, negotiations with the western Allies in order to clarify with the Soviet Union, the political and military status of a reunited Germany. This was predicated on the assumption of the conclusion of a peace treaty on the basis of the right of self-determination. In his foreign policy report Doring had previously reproached the Adenauer Government, which had shown little initiative in German foreign policy and had even paralyzed the negotiations of the western allies.[48]

The FDP deputy concluded by pointing out that the Free Democrats had loyally supported the alliance policy of the Federal Government from complete conviction and still supported the alliance treaties with NATO. In contrast to the CDU, however, the FDP considered these treaties not as "Dogmas of Eternity," but rather as factors which should secure for the Federal Republic a basis for political operations for the achievement of further objectives.[49]

Before the delegates in the Hannoverian Hall in Lower Saxony, FDP Chairman Mende also criticized the fact that within the Federal Government as also with the Western Powers, there had been a woeful neglect to use the postwar years as a point of departure for future Berlin and German negotiations. "We can not today spare the Federal Government and the CDU from the reproach that with all their speeches about 'no experiments' and 'security and welfare for all' they have gone far toward paralyzing the will for negotiations."[50] Mende concluded his speech with a firm rejection of any potential coalition with the Social Democratic Party, whose government program was a contradiction of the most important principles of the FDP, which related to economic and social policies. The FDP will

242

give to 37 million German voters on 17 September the possibility of choosing a third way.[51]

Gesamtdeutsche Partei (GDP)—
All-German Party—Campaign Tactics

On 20 August, 1961, the North German Radio invited Frank Seiboth of the All-German Party to a Press Conference, with four journalists: Johannes Gross from the CDU, Konrad Ahlers from the SPD, Hans Bursig from the FDP and Karl Pfeiffer of the GDP.

Herr Gross, correspondent of *Deutsche Zeitung,* pointed out that the GDP was a new party, although it represented a combination of two previous parties: the *Deutsche Partei* (German Party) and the Refugee Bloc (BHE). He then posed the question how this new party could hope to command enough voter support to pass two hurdles: to win 5 per cent of the total electoral vote or three electoral districts. The German Party (DP) in 1957 only polled 4.5 per cent, but won three electoral districts, simply because the CDU Party withdrew its own candidates in these districts and formed an electoral alliance with the DP.

Herr Seiboth, speaking for the All-German Party, pointed out that his party had already elected 80 deputies in seven *Landtage* (state parliaments) and held four ministries in four state governments. Moreover, he emphasized the fact that although Chancellor Adenauer had heretofore (20 August) not had time to fly to Berlin, he had campaigned in every electoral district of Lower Saxony where the All-German Party had hoped to win its three or more district mandates.[52] In 1957, the Refugee Bloc (BHE) and German Party (DP) together polled 2.4 million votes. Therefore, the All-German Party could theoretically loose 800,000 votes and still get 5% of the total vote of 37 million German votes. In any case, Herr Seiboth believed his party would have no great difficulty in obtaining 4 or 5 direct mandates in Lower Saxony.[53]

Herr Ahlers, speaking for the SPD, asked Herr Seiboth if he did not think that the impact of the Berlin crisis of 13 August against West German foreign policy called for a common foreign policy of all West German parties, as proposed by Social Democrats, particularly the Vice-Chairman of the SPD fraction Herbert Wehner. Although Herr Seiboth welcomed general agreement on questions of foreign policy, he took the view that the

243

basic ideas of the Adenauer Government were generally correct, especially in the military and political aspect. Nevertheless, he would prefer within the Western Alliance more clarification as to the possible solutions of the German question.[54]

Hans Bursig, Chief Editor of the *Freies Wort* (pro-FDP) asked why, on the previous Sunday only one week after the walling off of East Berlin, his All-German Party had issued a party declaration rejecting negotiations with the Soviet Union—despite probable negotiations by the Western Powers. "Can your party logically reject such negotiations, when it is the only peaceful alternative to the partition of Germany?" Herr Seiboth replied that instead of negotiations with the Soviet Union, his party desired Western agreement on specific steps to counter the illegal measures of the Soviet Union. That was the meaning of the Declaration of the GDP. Herr Schneider, the Chancellor candidate of the All-German Party had clarified his position in the special session of the Bundestag on 18 August. Schneider spoke frankly in Parliament of the lack of definite Western countermeasures against the events of 13 August. This dynamic Eastern policy demanded by the All-German Party with its undertones of extreme nationalism failed miserably on 17 September and polled only 2.8% of the total vote.[55]

NOTES TO CHAPTER TWELVE

1. *Stuttgarter Zeitung* (independent) 9 September, 1961.
2. *Die Welt* (Hamburg, independent), 23 August, 1961.
3. *Ibid.*
4. The Chancellor's visit to Berlin was top news in all West German papers except *Der Mittag* (right-center), on 22 August, 1961.
5. *Stuttgarter Zeitung* (independent), 9 September, 1961.
6. *Ibid.*
   * See the *Bulletin:* A weekly survey of German affairs, issued by the Press and Information Office in Bonn, 29 August, 1961.
7. *Stuttgarter Zeitung* (independent), 9 September, 1961.
8. *Ibid.*
9. "Adenauer Criticized in CDU Bundestag Group," in *Der Mittag* (Düsseldorf, right-center), 22 August, 1961.

10. *Neue Züricher Zeitung* (independent), 22 August, 1961.
11. *Rheinische Post* (Düsseldorf, pro-CDU), 22 August, 1961; *Deutsche Zeitung* (Cologne, right-center), 22 August, 1961; *Der Mittag* (Düsseldorf, right-center), 22 August, 1961.
12. *Die Welt* (Hamburg, independent), 22 August, 1961; *General Anzeiger* (Bonn, independent), 22 August, 1961.
13. *Neue Rhein Zeitung* (Cologne, pro-SPD), 22 August, 1961. For the sake of the record, it must be emphasized that neither of the above analyses takes account of the decisive factors in Adenauer's delay in going to Berlin. Campaign manager Bach failed to admit his own mistake and that of Adenauer's advisers. None of the West German papers gave sufficient emphasis to the fear of another Berlin uprising on the model of 17 June, 1953, if the Chancellor had risked a trip to Berlin immediately after the crucial events of 13 August.
14. *Stuttgarter Zeitung* (independent), 9 September, 1961.
15. *Der Spiegel* (Hamburg, weekly, independent), 27 August, 1961.
16. *Emnid Institute* Nr. 34, 28 August, 1961.
17. *Der Spiegel* (Hamburg, weekly, independent), 27 August, 1961.
18. Party Campaign Managers Explain Their Tactics, RIAS II (West Berlin Radio), 6 August, 1961, ANHANG II.
19. *Ibid.*
20. *Ibid.*
21. *Die Welt* (Hamburg, independent), 23 August, 1961.
22. *Frankfurter Allgemeine Zeitung* (right-center), 24 August, 1961.
23. *Ibid.*
24. *Frankfurter Allgemeine Zeitung* (right-center), 24 August, 1961.
25. *Ibid.,* 28 August, 1961.
26. *Ibid.*
27. *Süddeutscher Rundfunk,* 23 August, 1961. *Anhang* 5.
28. *Ibid.*
29. See *The Bulletin:* A weekly survey of German affairs for 17 November, 1959, for the Bad-Godesberg Program.
30. Nevertheless, the sincerity of this new stand was seriously questioned by Chancellor Adenauer and by the CDU deputy, Count Gutenberg who debated with Wehner. The

author interviewed the former regarding his position on foreign policy, as well as Fritz Erler.

31. *Für die SPD;* MdB Fritz Erler, "Parteien zur Wahl," *Süddeutscher Rundfunk*/23 August, 1961, 12.40/Mei *Anhang* 5.
32. *Ibid.* Fritz Erler told the author that the classic example of this was the Suez Crisis of 1956. If Nasser had had the bomb would he not have used it against the Israeli?
33. About $56 monthly.
34. See John W. Keller, "The Current German Political Scene," in *Current History* (January 1960), XXXVIII, pp. 30-36. Dr. Mende again confirmed his belief in the three party system for postwar German democracy in a personal interview with the author in the *Bundeshaus* in June 1961.
36. Dr. Erich Mende, "Party Campaign Managers explain their activity," RIAS II, 6 August, 1961/12.00/Ge/Mei *Anhang* II.
36. *Ibid.*
37. *Ibid.*
38. *Ibid.*
39. Dr. Erich Mende, for the FDP: "Parties before the Election: in Hers. Rf./23 August, 1961—18.40/Ro. Mende pointed out that the partnership of the CDU and FDP in the first Adenauer Government from 1949-1953, had proved advantageous to both parties. In the first four years the votes of the Free Democrats were cast in support of basic decisions for Euratom, Coal and Steel Authority (Schuman Plan), a free market economy, the basic social security law and the laws for equalization of the burdens of war victims, for the protection of federal frontiers, for the creation of the Bundeswehr (Army) and membership in NATO and West European Defense Union.
40. *Frankfurter Allgemeine Zeitung* (right-center), 24 August, 1961. Considered a non-conformist in foreign policy, Dr. Dehler argued that the Adenauer foreign policy for the past 12 years was no small factor in the deterioration of Russo-German relations and the erection of the Berlin wall on 13 August.
41. *Ibid.* See also *Die Welt* (Hamburg, independent), 25 August, 1961.
42. *Die Welt* (Hamburg, independent), 25 August, 1961.

43. Declaration of the Free Democrats on the opening of their Campaign Congress in Hanover on 24 August in *Die Welt* (Hamburg, independent), 24 August, 1961.

44. *Ibid.*

45. *Ibid.*

46. *Die Welt* (Hamburg, independent), 26 August, 1961.

47. This was a revival of the Disengagement Theory put forth by Dr. Erich Mende (Military expert of the FDP) and Reinhold Maier, former fraction Chairman of the FDP, in the great foreign policy debate in the Bundestag in 1957. See John W. Keller, "Current German Political Scene," in *Current History* (January, 1960), XXXVIII, 32.

48. *Die Welt* (Hamburg, independent), 26 August, 1961.

49. *Die Welt* (Hamburg, independent), 26 August, 1961.

50. *Ibid.* In the Bundestag session of June, 1961, the FDP deputies demonstrated their conservative economic convictions by voting against two welfare laws, supported by both the CDU/CSU and SPD fractions: Unemployment Insurance and Sickness Insurance (Krankengeld), which they regarded as quasi-socialist ideas. Because of the scathing attacks of the SPD on his foreign policy, Dr. Adenauer made concessions to the FDP, aiding its moderate and extreme right-wing in the *Länder* of Schleswig-Holstein, Lower Saxony and North Rhine-Westphalia to pursue a policy of economic conservatism and strong nationalism. During the parliamentary campaign of 1961, however, Adenauer campaigned hard in Schleswig-Holstein and Lower Saxony not for the FDP, but against the All-German Party, formed by a coalition of the former Conservative Party (DP) and the refugee bloc.

51. *Die Welt* (Hamburg, independent), 26 August, 1961. See also *"Fur die FDP:* Dr. Erich Mende, "Parteien Zur Wahl," Hers. Rf./23 August, 1961/18.40 ro. *Anhang* 8.

52. Press Konferenz der Gesamtdeutschen Partei mit Frank Seiboth (Parteien geben Auskunft), NDR/WDR, 20 August, 1961/19.30/Mei Ho *Anhang* A. p. 1.

53. *Ibid.*

54. Frank Seiboth, at Press Conference of the All-German Party, NDR/WDR, 20 August, 1961. *Anhang* A, p. 2.

55. *Ibid.*

247

Chapter 13

RESULTS OF BUNDESTAG ELECTIONS OF 17 SEPTEMBER, 1961

Triumph of the Major Parties

An analysis of the results of the West German parliamentary elections of the 17th of September, 1961, reveals the following factors:

1. The CDU/CSU fraction, with 45.3 per cent of the vote and 241 seats, retained its position as the strongest fraction in the Bundestag, in contrast to the other parties—the SPD, with 36.3 per cent and 190 seats, the FDP, with 12.7 per cent and 66 seats. The CDU/CSU, however, no longer commanded an absolute majority as in the third Bundestag and this called for the formation of a coalition government.

2. The change in relative party strength in comparison with 1957, meant that the CDU/CSU had lost 25 seats, whereas the SPD had gained 21 and the FDP 25.

3. All other parties, apart from the CDU/CSU, SPD and FDP, could win neither the minimum 5 per cent of the total vote nor three direct mandates and thus fell under the so-called prohibitive clause of the electoral law: which excludes splinter parties from representation in the Bundestag. Hence the fourth Bundestag must include only three parties.

4. In contrast to the previous Bundestag election law,

248

which designated 494 elected deputies—besides 22 non-voting representatives from Berlin—the fourth Bundestag contains a total of 521 members—five more than foreseen. This was due to the success achieved by the CDU which elected five more candidates by direct mandate—four in Schleswig-Holstein and one in the Saarland. With 155 direct election victories, the CDU/CSU carried the most districts and thus obtained 155 deputies for the fourth Bundestag, whereas the SPD only seated 90 candidates by direct election and the FDP elected no candidates apart from the *Land* lists.[1]

5. The different origins of the new representatives and an analysis of the number of votes in individual electoral districts show regional centers of strength of the two major parties, whereas the FDP obtained its quota in a more or less equally distributed increase through all electoral districts.[2]

6. Consideration of the question from where the FDP and SPD had obtained their percentage increases in votes, leads to far-reaching speculations. The primary factors to explain this switch would certainly include the following: 3.7 million new voters, the flux of German Party (*Deutsche Partei*) votes of the Third Reichstag, which could not accept the heterogeneous alliance with the Refugee Bloc (BHE) and finally the switch of voters away from the CDU, whether achieved by propaganda or by declarations regarding later coalitions. Expert decisions and personal sympathies exerted a confusing influence on voters in this election.[3] One expert analyst complained that the West German press as a whole did not do enough to clarify issues for the voters.[4]

7. The image of the Bundestag has been transformed; but the solid organization of a stable democracy has remained. The radicals could again win no converts; the splinter parties made no headway in overcoming the limitations of the 5 per cent clause. The lively interest of citizens was expressed when over 85% of the qualified voters went to the polls. In the Soviet Zone of Germany, where on the same day Communist represen-

tatives were "elected" on a single list, the percentage of voter participation was even higher. But would they have been as high had East German voters not been subject to all the pressures of a totalitarian state?

Leading Candidates and Issues

Those who heard the Bundestag speeches of Chancellor Adenauer and Mayor Brandt of Berlin have ¡involuntarily compared:
1. the speeches and the men themselves;
2. their views of the violent tactics of the Soviet Zone Regime and
3. their political proposals.

Both politicians were noted for the location and skill of their political commandos. Willy Brandt, the Berlin Burgermeister, spoke to the people immediately concerned with the actions of Ulbricht, eye witnesses of the barbed wire and stone barricades, and directed his attack toward those in Moscow responsible for the unfree part of the old German capital. As a front commander of a dangerously exposed sector, he urged a dangerously localized attack with a higher staff and aid, which the higher echelons found untenable. Therefore, Brandt appealed to the Federal Government and Western Allies to take firm countermeasures. He was most embittered to find the officials of both the West German Government and Allied Governments were again on vacation.[5]

Konrad Adenauer argued as a more composed chief of state neither as an eye witness nor one directly concerned with events in Berlin, but rather as one responsible for the welfare of the whole Federal Republic and, therefore, concerned that the Western alliance first be put to the test whether free soil should be given a price.[6] Whereas Brandt criticized the Allies for their inactivity and also indirectly criticized the Chancellor's conversations with the Soviet ambassador, Smirnov, Adenauer stressed unity with the Western Allies. Whereas Brandt appealed to the national pride of Germans, Adenauer was concerned with German security needs.

There was also a contrast between Adenauer and Brandt in

the judgment expressed of the barricades of East Berlin. Mayor Brandt above all saw how Ulbricht and Khrushchev had destroyed the basis of Four-Power control, on which rested the justification for their presence in Berlin. He considered the advance of the Soviet Zone Volksarmee to the Brandenburg Gate as the "annexation" of East Berlin and saw further attacks coming. No doubt, Brandt was justified in the view that West Berlin was no longer the same as before the Black Sunday of August 13th. The violent tactics of Khrushchev were attempts to achieve the existence of the so-called "Free City." This was also recognized by the Federal Government and the Allies.

The Chancellor, nevertheless, saw above all the despair of the Pankow regime, a government which could hold back the stream of refugees with no other means than barbed wire and stone walls. He regarded the barricade as an admission by Khrushchev that Moscow's sphere of influence could only be held by the use of armed force. Adenauer utilized the Soviet advances in order to win support for the right of self-determination for Germans. His restraint tended to preserve Western unity for still more serious trials and to remove as far as possible the danger of war. He apparently estimated correctly the attitude of foreign nations, if he did not demand immediate countermeasures. Above all Adenauer reserved to himself the hour when German and Allied interests would completely coincide.

In the Government Declaration of 18 August, before a special session of the Bundestag, a starting point was finally found for the political action which Brandt demanded. In it the right of self-determination for Germans was demanded and at the same time a security guarantee for the Soviet Union was sought in case of German reunification. To the Chancellor it became clear that such a guarantee could not come from the mere signing of agreements, but rather that it must emerge out of political reality.

If it were possible for the West to put forth a plan for the political order of Europe, which considers Soviet security needs sufficient in the eyes of the world, which guards the interests of Germany's East European neighbors and which, therefore, demands the right of self-determination for Europe, Moscow certainly would not find it so easy to push her propaganda for a separate peace treaty with the East German Zone regime. If then the Federal Government, in cooperation with its Allies should seek to establish a peaceful order in Europe, Bonn and the West together might produce a relaxation of East-West tensions and eventually create an atmosphere of mutual respect and freedom to extend to Berlin.

Unique Features of 1961 Bundestag Elections

On the 17th of September, 1961, not only was a new Bundestag elected, but also an epoch of German post-war history came to an end. What had become obvious during the preceding weeks in the realm of foreign policy was also confirmed in domestic politics: the period of recent history heretofore, of truckling condescension and political stagnation was past. The following months and years would see many illusions destroyed and strong claims of the German people put forth. It was predicted that the stream of political life in the free part of Germany would flow faster and that German policy would certainly be more alert and more capable of reaction.

The German voter had demonstrated a maturity and foresight in the elections of the fourth German Bundestag, which must have exceeded the expectations of even the most optimistic. Not only did the extraordinary high percentage of votes for the democratic state and the clear rejection of all Left or Right extremist groups show strong faith in democracy in the German people; but the fact that millions have understood at this moment that the hegemony of any one party is in no way related to continental democracy was actually more than could be expected after such a short period of parliamentary democracy in Germany.

The Free Democrats proved to be the only party, which not only achieved its electoral goal, but exceeded it. For besides breaking the absolute majority of the CDU/CSU, on which the party had concentrated, the Free Democrats had exceeded the electoral results of both 1953 and 1957. That the FDP on 17th of September would let itself lag far behind its hitherto greatest electoral gain of 1949, was more or less assumed by the party members.[7] The FDP had to work very hard to achieve this result. After its electoral defeat of 1957, (7.7%) it had a psychological handicap, having lost votes from election to election, and came dangerously near the 5 per cent limit. The number of those who no longer gave the Free Democrats a real chance to still overcome this hurdle was in the years 1957/58 considerable. The thesis of the pretended unhalting trend to the two-party system was, in these years, found in almost all German and foreign newspapers.

It speaks well for the internal strength of the party of German liberalism, that in this almost hopeless situation it did not falter, but on the contrary coordinated all its forces in order to overcome the fact, which seemed unavoidable. An energetic leadership a clear program and belief in the justness of its cause were powerful factors in causing the political community to make the impossible possible: that is, not only to check the trend toward defeat, but even to achieve the greatest victory in its history. Other factors present were: the Berlin Wall, the large percentage of undecided voters and the Chancellor's tactics.

The FDP was fully aware of its responsibility to the German people, arising from its victory on 17 September. When over 4 million voted for the FDP, certain negative phenomena in German domestic politics were removed and for the next four years a government could be formed, which would reexamine and reevaluate foreign policy aims and objectives. The Free Democrats also realized what a heavy burden those will bear, who in the coming years undertake responsibility in the Federal Republic.[8]

The leadership and personality of Dr. Erich Mende, a 44-year-old Silesian-born refugee and a shrewdly chosen program not only doubled the vote of the FDP, but proved that today's strong trend toward two mass parties in a democracy could be broken. The Free Democrats drew most of their support from the German middle classes—professional people and small businessmen, largely Protestant, and refugees from Germany's lost Oder-Neisse territories, dissatisfied with the long years of Christian Democrat rule. Dr. Mende's assets to the Free Democratic Party include:

1) unusual personal appeal and intelligence,
2) skillful diplomacy in ending internal party quarrels,
3) his decoration for military service in World War II, and
4) his moderate tone in foreign affairs, showing a con-

ciliatory position between government and opposition in foreign policy questions, for instance, diplomatic relations with Poland and other East Bloc states, despite the Hallstein doctrine.[9]

Decisive Factors in the Campaign

a. Impact of Berlin crisis on relative strength of German parties

The charts on page 272, note 10, show the relative strength of the parties from April to August, 1961, as determined by the Emnid Institutes Monthly surveys of voter preference. Between the end of July and the end of August, 1961, the percentage of voters over 21 preferring the CDU/CSU decreased from 50 to 46 per cent; whereas those indicating a preference for the SPD increased from 34 to 38 per cent. How much of this double switch was influenced by the Berlin crisis is difficult to say because two thirds of the interviews were conducted prior to 13 August.[10] But events since then seemed to have led voters to the opposition Social Democrats and Free Democrats. That was the opinion of the SPD itself, as well as the CDU/CSU. By the end of August many in Bonn believed the chance to obtain an absolute majority no longer remained with the CDU/CSU.[11]

In prior elections for parliament, Dr. Adenauer had repeatedly outclassed all rivals in his grasp of political tactics. But after 13 August, the Federal Chancellor committed three strategic errors:

1. His ill-considered reference to Mayor Brandt as *alias Frahm* in Regensburg on Monday, 14 August, boomeranged.
2. His failure to go to Berlin until ten days after the tragic events of 13 August proved to be an irreparable strategic error on the part of Adenauer and his advisers.
3. His ill-chosen statement at Hagen that the events of 13 August in Berlin were the deliberate design of Khrushchev to aid the Social Democrats was too much for Germans, who recalled the heroic resistance of the

Social Democratic Mayor, Ernst Reuters, during the
Berlin Blockade of 1948.

Disavowed by his own CDU party followers, Dr. Krone and
Bundestag President Gerstenmaier, Dr. Adenauer later qualified
his statement. The events of 13 August in Berlin were favorable
to Social Democratic prospects; but Khrushchev, with his direct
attack against Adenauer and the Federal Government, again put
wind in the sails of the Christian Democrats. The formation of
a new CDU/CSU (Plus FDP) Government seemed, after the
crucial events of August, to have been very questionable together
with a previous trend away from the CDU/CSU. From that time
on, people scarcely expected the governing CDU Party to recover the ground it had lost to the opposition parties by 27
August, 1961.

Naturally, CDU/CSU Campaign Managers took advantage
of the Soviet Premier's unjustified interference in a German
parliamentary election when he stated on 31 August, 1961, in
Moscow:

> Adenauer and those elements who support him are
> responsible for turning West Germany into a military
> state, armed to the teeth. The chief aims of West German
> foreign policy are revenge and revision of European
> boundaries drawn after the Second World War. Un-
> fortunately far too many West Germans let themselves be
> confused by the revanchist spirit and led along the war-
> path by new leaders.
> How can it be denied that the people of the West
> German Federal Republic who always vote for Chancellor
> Adenauer and his political henchmen drive the Germans
> to new acts of aggression? Germans who vote for Adenauer
> must know that Adenauer and the supporters of his policy
> in West Germany are using the same slogans of Anti-
> Communism and revenge under which Hitler rose to
> power and then the Second World War followed.[12]

Naturally, CDU/CSU campaign managers replied that: "In
this hour of overt threat the German people stood firmly behind
Konrad Adenauer. He has always led us out of trouble and he

will preserve peace and freedom. The German people will give Khrushchev the right answer on 17 September."[13] In Bonn there was always vigorous discussion if and to what degree the Adenauer Government and Western Allies were guilty of gross neglect after 13 August. If it had been too slow to react, the West would have lost a psychological battle, it was generally contended. Dr. Erich Mende in an FDP political advertisement stated:

> Millions of voters have decided that whoever reacts too late whether in Berlin or in the election campaign will find himself holding a receipt for failure. Millions of voters know what they want because what they all say is the old receipt no longer works. The election campaign has opened all eyes. Even the followers of old Adenauer say: This will not do—since the CDU/CSU and SPD have called each other names. How disappointed the voters were. Therefore, the general conviction was expressed: "This time I will vote FDP." Millions again want a strong government as in the years 1949 to 1953 when the Free Democrats had a real voice in the government.
>
> Ask all of your friends and every conversation will confirm that whoever no longer approves the policy of Adenauer and whoever believes that with Willy Brandt the old (die-hard) Socialists will return, will support the Free Democrats. Whoever loves freedom and believes in Germany—whoever thinks twice will vote FDP.[14]

Social Democratic advertisements emphasized that "now was no time for discord. Germany can exist in these times only if all good elements work together in common. Only by working together and not against each other can we preserve peace for ourselves and our children." [15] Consequently, Willy Brandt called for a strong government broadly based on the support of all major parties to meet the national emergency created by the Berlin crisis. Social Democratic strategists used the Soviet threat of Super atomic bombs to call for an end to petty party quarrels and a united stand of all the German people with their Western Allies, in order to give support to Berlin and Willy Brandt.[16]

After 13 August, all major parties had to adjust their tactics to the new situation. Although both opposition leaders were quicker to adjust than Dr. Adenauer, the latter had strong electoral assets:

1. Germans identified Dr. Adenauer with the German Federal Republic, its first and only Chancellor.
2. The big assets of the Federal Chancellor were West Germany's prosperity and Germany's vital role in NATO.
3. Franco-German *rapprochement* underlined the role of the Federal Republic in the Coal and Steel Authority, Euratom, Common Market and other agencies of European economic cooperation.

On 10 September, 1961, the London Sunday Times wrote:

> All those gains mean far more to the nineteenth-century Rhineland European, Dr. Adenauer, than does the pull of the Eastern regions—Brandenburg, Pomerania, Saxony, Silesia—they are symbolized by the dethroned Prussian and Imperial capital, Berlin. It is a tenable thesis that they also mean more to the average West German voter . . .
>
> Prosperous and successful as West Germans are, they have been left with a price to pay for the last war. It has been Dr. Adenauer's bad luck that the bill for a stiff installment, headed "Berlin," should be presented just when the slogans of security and success were about to bring him his fourth electoral victory.[17]

For twelve long years the Chancellor had been able to assure Germans they might have both their comfortable prosperity, NATO, peace and freedom and eventual reunification, that is, after the international situation changed. The problem Adenauer faced after 13 August was that the number of German voters still able to believe this would fall below 50 per cent—not enough to give power to the SPD, but sufficient to prevent another CDU/CSU absolute majority.[18]

b. Reactions to Soviet Superbombs

Moscow's announcement of its resumption of atomic tests and and worldwide reaction to it dominated the news in virtually all West German papers on 1 September. Addressing an election rally in Göttingen, Adenauer called for more sacrifices from Germans to meet the Soviet threat which demonstrated the need to equip the Bundeswehr with nuclear weapons. Another statement of the Chancellor stressed the seriousness of the situation, but also the nuclear capability of the United States. A CDU/CSU parliamentary representative urged the West to counter Soviet aggressiveness with intensified defense efforts. Similar statements came from Social Democrats and some Free Democrats. FDP Chairman Mende, however, argued that negotiations should not be abandoned just because the international crisis was intensified in the nuclear sphere.[19]

In the face of Western opposition to his Berlin and German plans, Khrushchev, threatened the world with war and annihilation. Therefore, he touched off another armament race and practically admitted he used the Geneva negotiations as a maneuver of delay.[20] The Soviet Premier did not want war, but hoped to win Berlin without it. His resumption of nuclear testing was designed to show the West that Berlin was not worth an atomic war. Khrushchev would go to the very brink of atomic war to have his way in Berlin.[21] The so-called Berlin Crisis was designed by the Soviet dictator in order to threaten the United States with nuclear war and thus destroy its position in world affairs. Clearly he wanted to make Asians and Africans afraid to oppose his demands.[22]

Western mistakes culminated in the attitude of European and overseas countries toward France as a fourth nuclear power, an issue highlighted in the Soviet declaration on the resumption of nuclear testing. Khrushchev apparently wanted to intimidate German voters. But his clumsy attempt to promote the cause of some pro-Moscow "friends of peace" in West Germany underlined the propaganda purposes behind the Soviet announcement. This, in the view of the *Stuttgarter Nachrichten* was no reason for alarm.[23] The *Stuttgarter Zeitung* believed Khrushchev may have feared that the world had not taken Soviet threats seriously even after Soviet Astronaut Titov had encircled the globe seventeen times. So he felt impelled to issue a mega-threat.[24]

Although Moscow did intensify the crisis over Berlin, this is not to say the West had done enough to achieve control of nuclear weapons. Acting under pressure from U.S. military and political quarters, the United States was seeking a "watertight" control agreement at Geneva. The Soviets were not ready for this. Nevertheless, if the United States had signed an agreement even though not "water-tight," it would have offered no absolute security against possible nuclear tests to be made by the Soviets. The existence of some agreement, however, would have made Moscow appear as a trespasser. In this case the West had shown a lack of political courage in the view of West Germans.[25] In addition, French nuclear tests had furnished the Soviets a pretext for ending the tacit test ban.

The West Berlin press reported that Chancellor Adenauer had urged western counter-measures in a letter to President Kennedy in case Soviets and East Germans continued unilateral actions in Berlin even though they did not directly interfere with routes of access. Many in Bonn believed the Western powers should have taken strong countermeasures immediately after 13 August. However, the West German Government tactfully refrained from revealing that on 13 August it had urged concrete counteraction which the Western powers rejected.[26]

East Berlin papers for the most part focused on the exploits of Soviet Astronaut Titov. *Neues Deutschland,* however, printed a statement of the East German Democratic Republic (GDR) Council of Ministers regarding the so-called "protective measures of the USSR." Under the headline, "USSR Also Protects Our People—Now Tame the Bonn Militarists," the SED paper argued that the USSR planned measures to strengthen peace forces in the fight for the prevention of nuclear war.[27]

With their resumption of new atomic testing the Soviets clearly demonstrated that they wanted Berlin to be considered not as a local subject for negotiations between East and West, but as a point of departure for a world crisis. On the basis of these developments, experts offered very plausible explanations. The Soviet aim, as the Western powers have long recognized, was a global consideration of the subject of disarmament in the

UN General Assembly in contrast to negotiations between the U.S., Great Britain and Soviet Russia at Geneva; with no limitation upon atomic weapons, but handling disarmament under the category of all weapons.[28] The United Nations had for some time recommended the discussion of complex disarmament questions, including the Geneva negotiations, whereby the cessation of atomic testing should be handled under the subject of atomic disarmament. Moreover, since the Red Chinese would obviously soon be in a position to build their own atomic bomb, they were able to convince the Soviet of this, that is, the Geneva negotiations without Red China would be useless and for her would not be binding.[29] As for the resumption of atomic testing by the Soviet Union, there was another reason—namely the defection of the Soviet Scientist, who several weeks before had attended a Congress in Canada. This Scientist was said to have betrayed the secrets of the sources of propulsion of Soviet rockets.[30]

c. Reactions to Belgrade Conference—Hallstein Doctrine

For the Federal Republic it was very important to consider what the free and still neutral world, including the new nations of Asia and Africa had declared with regard to the true conditions in Germany. In case the German problem would come before the UN much would depend on whether free Germany had understood this neutral world in order to make clear its desires and aspirations to other peoples. If the entire world wanted peace and no war over Berlin, this meant that Germans would be more dependent on their Western Allies and might even be inclined to reconsider a neutralist foreign policy.[31]

That Moscow decided to resume its testing of atomic weapons on the first day of the Belgrade Conference of so-called neutral states, was no accident. From the Soviet viewpoint: the heads of the free-bloc states assembled in Belgrade had such a fear of war that they considered Berlin only from this viewpoint and, therefore, were only concerned with it in order to discuss disarmament as soon as possible before the UN, in a forum adapted to Soviet propaganda tactics and in which the interest of Asiatic and African States in European problems was very questionable. The Soviets also speculated on the fact that world understanding of German interests had deteriorated. The fear of war over Berlin drove many neutrals, who were more fearful of the consequences of nuclear war than of the loss of Berlin, to accept the arguments of the Eastern Bloc.

It was these considerations which allowed the West to delay the submission of the problem to the UN. But it appeared as if it was still more probable that the Soviet claims *re* use of air corridors would produce a situation which could immediately threaten world peace and consequently could convene the UN Security Council. Thus one should certainly not expect that the maintenance of the *status quo* in Berlin appealed to neutrals. On the contrary, they seemed inevitably nearer to recognizing that Germany must be considered as the nation which lost the war.[32]

In view of the national emergency Mayor Brandt called for a Government formed on a broad basis of all parties (*Stark Regierrung*).[33] On the week-end of 2/3 September, 1961, many West German papers carried headlines to the effect that the "neutral" countries had accepted the existence of two German states.[34] Among the Saturday headlines of West German papers were:

> "Neutrals Want East-West Negotiations"
> "Neutrals Want Influence on World Affairs"
> "Free-Bloc Nations Fear Danger of War"
> "Berlin Main Topic in Belgrade" and
> "Neutrals Criticize Soviet Decision on Atomic Test."

"Bonn's Disappointment about Neutrals," was highlighted in *Allgemeine Zeitung*.[35] A closer analysis of the attitudes of the "Neutral States represented at Belgrade reveals that they were least concerned with objective truth and most concerned with preventing a war over Germany and the Berlin problem. Peter Grube made the following points in *Die Welt:*

1. The only reason that most neutrals did not open diplomatic relations with Pankow (East German regime) was their interest in West German money.
2. The Oder-Neisse line is the definitive border of Germany.

3. The neutrals would prefer to see Germany neutralized. Neutrals see no difference between the presence of Western troops in West Germany and Soviet troops in East Germany.

4. Neutrals in Belgrade made no critical evaluation and distinction between the Bonn and Pankow Governments as to legitimacy from a democratic standpoint. For them Adenauer and Ulbricht were equal.[36] *Die Welt's* correspondent was repeatedly told by delegates that German reunification was possible if all Germans really desired it for its own sake and would ignore the defense measures ordered by the East and West Blocs.[37]

The pro-CDU Press argued that the reason neutrals refused to support the German demand for self-determination was the refusal of the Bonn Government to keep free from alliances and that it had joined the western camp because it formed a correct judgment of the international situation.[38] But from the standpoint of the neutrals, Bonn's affiliation with NATO weakened its argument for self-determination because in this case the problem was connected with the international balance of power. Although Belgrade Conferees strongly urged Germany to become neutral, this advice was even rejected by the Social Democrats. Soviet expansionism in Berlin made neutralization even less acceptable in the view of the *Rheinische Post* which criticized the Social Democratic opposition for trying to exploit the Belgrade Conference for attacking the Federal Government.[39] *Die Welt* wrote that the Belgrade Conference had clearly demonstrated the complete failure of the information campaign of the Federal Republic in neutral countries. Practically all the Belgrade Conferees voiced ideas on Germany and Berlin which came very close to Moscow's thesis. So the German opposition exploited the diplomatic defeat sustained by the Bonn Foreign Ministry, Press and Information Office. For weeks prior to the Belgrade Conference *Die Welt* had emphasized the need of information activities in uncommitted countries.[40]

Under the headline "Belgrade—End of Hallstein Doctrine," the *Hannoverische Presse* called the recognition of the division of Germany into two states by most neutrals in Belgrade the "funeral oration of the Hallstein Doctrine"—that is no West

German diplomatic relations with states recognizing the Soviet Zone regime (DDR).[41] The SPD paper also criticized the Federal Republic for poor publicity work in neutral states and called the "favorable reaction to Adenauer's letters" claimed by the German Foreign Office as mere wishful thinking. It would be most difficult to compensate for such losses, suffered in those crucial days of struggle for the sympathies of neutrals. The *Westfälische Rundschau* discussed an SPD report on "The Tragedy of the German Information Policy" under the headline: "Belgrade Events Reveal Mistakes Made by the Federal Republic." [42]

"Bonn Upholds Hallstein Doctrine" became headlines in many West German papers. The Federal Republic was planning to warn neutral states that it would consider diplomatic relations with Pankow an unfriendly act which would entail counteraction from Bonn—i.e. severance of diplomatic relations. The FDP on the other hand favored dropping the Hallstein Doctrine.[43] The viewpoint of the German opposition was neatly summarized by Conrad Ahlers who wrote: "It is tragic to see the neutral bloc discuss Germany and Berlin in Belgrade, that city where the Federal Republic is not represented by an ambassador because Bonn severed relations with Yugoslavia on account of that very Soviet Zone which is accepted as a sovereign state by Tito and by leaders from the newly developing countries."[44] Although Nehru, and Nasser did not want to increase international tensions nor lose West German development aid, the Hallstein doctrine in the view of the German opposition was still doomed. "Why should the neutrals continue to support Bonn's policy which has proved to be a failure and which, to quote Nehru, has never sought reunification on neutral terms? What has happened in Belgrade should have been anticipated."[45]

The independent press in West Germany found the result of the Belgrade Conference most discouraging for the West because: 1) Pressure from Khrushchev on the delegates prevented any reference to the German right of self-determination; 2) Freedom for East Germans was no longer discussed; 3) Fear of war pervaded the neutrals and focused attention on prevention of an armed conflict between the two blocs; 4) Tito's attitude toward the German problem was rigid after Bonn broke off diplomatic relations with Belgrade in 1957.[46]

Although Sokarno yielded to Nehru and Nasser, he did not change his mind. The crisis for the Hallstein doctrine would come inevitably.[47] Even the pro-government press warned the Federal Government to be prepared that countries like Ghana, Burma, Ceylon and Indonesia would continue their plans to recognize the Pankow regime in East Berlin.[48] Correspondents of various West German and other papers in reviewing the Belgrade Conference, made it clear that the moderating influence of Nehru on the radical leaders to refrain from recognition of two German states in the final communiqué did not mean the end of efforts in favor of Pankow by some of the neutrals. They, therefore, suggested that the Bonn Government would do well to reconsider the Hallstein doctrine. Erich Mende, FDP Chairman and candidate for Chancellor, consistently favored diplomatic relations with Eastern Bloc States, despite the Hallstein doctrine.

d. East-West relations

The worsening of the world political situation fostered in most cases not entirely unexpected aggressions. The tensions over Berlin, which on 13 August emerged as the Berlin Crisis, had already become more or less latent in previous weeks. A steadily increasing percentage of people in the Federal Republic saw a sudden worsening of the prospects of European peace. The proportion of pessimists, in view of the future political outlook for the next half year increased from 21 per cent to 34 per cent. Moreover, the proportion of those who regarded the European peace situation as "unchanged" sharply declined from 65 to 53 per cent; whereas the proportion of optimists decreased by one third, from 9 to only 6 per cent.[49]

These statistics clearly underlined the impact of the sharpening East-West conflict. A previous low-point had been reached in the previous year from May to September, 1960, just prior to the American presidential election. In the months following September, 1960, a clear trend toward a more positive outlook was observed. This trend apparently was connected with the clear statements of President Kennedy on Germany, making the Berlin-problem his cause. From March to April, 1961, there was then for the first time a slight turn to the negative side. This negative trend did not continue from April to May because there was a slight improvement in the over-all situation. The June result had probably been very strongly influenced by the meeting of Kennedy and Khrushchev in Vienna at the beginning of June and the utterances connected with this by both sides.[50]

Just how did increasing East-West tensions affect the relative strength of German political parties in the parliamentary elections of 1961? The strategy of the governing CDU/CSU Party was to stress the importance of East-West negotiations and strong bonds between Bonn and its Western Allies. "Bonn and the Allies" was the headline of an article in *Allgemeine Zeitung,* which analyzed relations between the Federal Republic and the West emphasizing the following items:

1. American prestige in Berlin precluded any withdrawal from this city;
2. Bonn believed U.S. surrender on Berlin would reduce the United States to the status of a second-rate power for decades to come;
3. The Federal Republic noted with satisfaction the growth of parallel thinking in the United States.
4. The Bonn Government did everything to avoid the role of trouble-maker.
5. Bonn officials, after careful study concluded that Johnson's veto of Adenauer's request to accompany him to Berlin did not constitute interference with the German parliamentary campaign in favor of Brandt;
6. Rather Washington's foreign policy and military plans were predicated on a personal and factual continuity in the leading position in Bonn.
7. Adenauer, therefore, continued to stress the importance of East-West negotiations.[51]

Alarm over the intransigent positions of Khrushchev and Kennedy and German excitement forced Vice President Johnson to go to Berlin and commit American prestige to this isolated city. Then came the Soviet announcement on 1 September, 1961, to resume nuclear testing. This seemed to indicate the Soviet Union had abandoned the diplomatic phase of the East-West

265

conflict for the military one. In any case the Soviets would retract none of their basic demands for Germany. They also saw the U.S.A. committing herself to a forward position. With mega-threats the Soviets then tried to dislodge the United States from its position.[52]

Moscow reasoned as follows:

1. Washington knew that the USSR surpassed the USA in conventional weapons.
2. Soviet super-rockets enabled the USSR to risk nuclear war—but the U.S. could not do so without risking suicide. Therefore, Khrushchev was playing an even more risky game. The more acute the crisis, the more the role of reason diminished according to the independent *Stuttgarter Zeitung* which cited three instances to support its views:
   1) What logic was there in sending U.S. Troops to Berlin—from a position of strength into a trap?
   2) Where was reason when Bonn de-emphasized its all-German obligations despite the possibility for some roll-back policy in Germany?
   3) How could Bonn emphasize Berlin's all-German role in 1961, when even the most primitive voter must have realized it would be utopian to believe in German reunification?

Therefore, this paper argued that the real meaning of Khruschev's mega threat was not for the West to equate reason with surrender. Rather the West should reconcile reason with existing possibilities.[53] The *Stuttgarter Zeitung* concluded its argument for the role of reason as follows:

It is irresponsible to reply to Soviet demands with an uncompromising "No" if their demands are based on actual superiority . . . The USSR has not yet launched an all-out attack on the Federal Republic . . . It is aiming its thrust against German unity, which we lost in 1945, and, again, in the period 1952 to 1959, when we gave preference to pro-Western policy over one of reconciliation with the Soviet Union . . . After the Federal Government had

266

missed those opportunities, its assertion that Berlin was the symbol of future reunification was no longer valid. Berlin was merely an outpost that could be defended so long as the international position of the U.S. was stronger than that of the Soviet Union. Now the balance of power has changed because we all—U.S., Britain, France and the Germans—had slept and cherished illusions while the Communists built their military machinery. The Soviet announcement of nuclear tests with super-bombs had destroyed these illusions.[54]

This sharp criticism of Bonn's over-all foreign policy by the independent *Stuttgarter Zeitung* was confirmed by Conrad Ahlers in an article on Bonn-Moscow Relations in *Frankfurter Rundschau* (left-center). This writer emphasized the following points:

1. To justify new nuclear tests, Khrushchev accused Germans of revanchism for re-electing Adenauer. This represented foreign interference in a German parliamentary election.
2. Nevertheless, Germans should recall that the Soviet Union on 15 August, 1953, had warned that West Germany's integration in a European army and in NATO would prevent reunification.
3. Similar warnings came from Moscow against the revival of German militarism and plans to equip the *Bundeswehr* with nuclear weapons.
4. Whatever the criticism of the Kremlin, it could not be charged with failure to warn Bonn of the consequences of its foreign policy. This also applied to the Berlin problem.
5. Obviously the Soviet Union tried and failed to bring about a shift in German policy.
6. Germans could not be surprised if Moscow drew certain conclusions from Bonn's refusal to come to terms with the USSR. For instance Moscow inferred from Bonn's policy that certain West German leaders wanted war with the Soviet Union.
7. Germans know this is not true. However, the Federal Government has repeatedly passed measures bound to

267

create this very wrong impression in Moscow and has failed to convince the East of German peaceableness.

8. This is not to say an agreement with Moscow on reunification would have been possible, but simply that the Federal Government has failed to bring about a reconciliation and has made light of all Soviet feelers.[55]

Frankfurter Rundschau, therefore, concluded that as a result of Bonn's policy and Soviet action in the Soviet Zone and Berlin, Germany and the Soviet Union were agin at swords points. Therefore, the Federal Chancellor could not deny his responsibility. Regarding his complaints of the lack of any will by the West Germans to make sacrifices, the opposition press contended that this was largely the result of such CDU slogans as "No Experiments." Moreover, the opposition argued that armament alone was no substitute for an effective policy toward the East. And despite the sudden caution and reserve of Adenauer and Strauss in September, 1961, Germans could not forget that for years they had been making aggressive statements and advocating a policy of strength, which turned out to be a policy of weakness.[56]

On 8 September, 1961, the Washington correspondent of *Die Zeit,* observed bitterly that the "softs" among President Kennedy's advisers had gained influence at the expense of the "hards." The former were reported to favor: 1) de facto recognition of the Soviet Zone regime; 2) avoidance of war (nuclear war)—except that U.S. prestige was geared to the defense of West Berlin in any case; 3) negotiations as the only alternative to war—i.e. for new guarantees on Berlin the West must be prepared to pay a price: not merely recognition of the Oder-Neisse line, but recognition of the East Zone regime; and even, 4) acceptance of the east and west boundaries of the Ulbricht regime as state boundaries for right of access to West Berlin and direct contact with East Berlin; and finally, 5) discussion of the question of military security—an atom-free Zone in Central Europe.[57]

Representatives of the other group of advisers, recommending a hard course, also had the ear of the President and warned that the above concessions could only satisfy Soviet ambitions for one or two years. Then security would again be threatened in the next great crisis. Although the "softs" seemed to have the advantage over the "hards" they clearly understood the President was a cool, calculating, unsentimental and pragmatic statesman.[58]

The German opposition press heaped criticism on Von Brentano for going to the U.S. immediately before the West German elections without consulting important groups in the Federal Republic. *Hannoverische Presse* contended he had slavishly submitted to the directives of Adenauer, who did not want the West to hear the voice of the entire German nation. Consequently neither representatives of the German parties nor the *Bundestag* foreign affairs committee, nor the Mayor of Berlin were invited to state their views on German foreign policy prior to discussions in Washington. This paper observed that President Kennedy was consulting non-partisan experts and representatives of the German opposition prior to any East-West negotiations.[59]

Westfälische Rundschau emphasized the growing complaints that Adenauer's rigid attitude left the West no room for negotiations. Brentano was expected to indicate to the foreign ministers what issues were negotiable, which Bonn heretofore had failed to do.[60] On 15 September, 1961, the *New York Times* and *Washington Post* printed a Reuters dispatch from London to the effect Khrushchev had said on Wednesday that the USSR was ready to discuss a peaceful German settlement anytime if the negotiations were not used to delay a German peace treaty. Walter Lippman in discussing the enormous difficulties in negotiating over Berlin, emphasized the following items:

1. If Berlin is to have a real vital function—not just the right to exist—there will have to be a new attempt to negotiate a wide settlement in Germany and Central Europe.
2. The West might not have lost the initiative to Khrushchev in June, 1961, if Americans and West Europeans had been prepared by their leaders for a diplomatic attempt at a wide settlement.
3. East and West should not close the door to eventual reunion of East and West Germany—despite Soviet

opposition as expressed by the partition of Berlin and despite strong Western opposition to German reunification though less openly expressed.

4. In both NATO and the Common Market there is a basic assumption that in fact Germany will remain divided.

5. All of Europe—France, Poland and Czechoslavakia— are committed to the division of Germany.

6. Although Bonn does not condone German partition, Adenauer's foreign policy for 12 years was not predicated on German reunification, but on West European Union and NATO.[61]

7. An all-European consensus to accept the partition of Germany explains why there is no crusading spirit in Europe to reunify Germany.

8. The key to policy in France and Germany is not that there is objection to the fact of partition—but rather that they fear the effect of acknowledging it.

9. If partition were recognized in treaties to satisfy Khrushchev then the loyalty of West Germans to the Atlantic Alliance would be greatly weakened. Germans might again look toward the East in the shadows of Rapallo.[62]

The cautious policy of Bonn in not counteracting German partition, but learning to live without German reunification was severely criticized by the independent West German paper, *Stuttgarter Zeitung* as follows:

1. East-West negotiations should not confirm irreconcilable views.

2. The USA, while ready to fight for access to Berlin, its political freedom and presence of U.S. troops there, is not prepared to wage war for German wishful thinking. It is ready to discuss the legal basis for its presence in Berlin and an adjustment of the issues of security in Central Europe.

3. The time has come for Bonn also to recognize facts and to formulate new policy aims. Heretofore, the

Federal Republic adhered to the thesis of reunification in peace and freedom—that was predicated on bringing overwhelming pressure on the East.

4. 13 August demonstrated the weakness of this policy, confirmed by the Confidence Crisis of German public opinion. Therefore, German reunification was ruled out as an immediate policy aim.

5. Only close cooperation with Western Europe and NATO could create a bulwark against Communist expansion.

6. Only thus could Bonn hope for a Central European settlement without German reunification, but rather "peaceful co-existence" between two Germanies, despite contrasting ideologies.

7. Berlin can no longer be a symbol of the will to reunification. Rather it is a place where the United States defends its world prestige, but not German interests.

8. Berlin could, however, be a bridge between two co-existing Germanies of the future—a means for free exchange of ideas and free communication between Germans who respect human rights and their common past.

9. Our immediate policy aim should be improvement of conditions in the Soviet Zone instead of reunification. This would serve to intensify Bonn-East Berlin contact.[63]

NOTES TO CHAPTER THIRTEEN

1. *Das Parlament: Die Woche im Bundeshaus,* (Bonn), 20 September, 1961. Every German voter has two votes, one direct vote for a candidate and one indirect vote for the party list.

2. For instance, the FDP polled 12 per cent or more of the total vote in all the *Länder* except in Bavaria. The percentages of FDP votes for the various *Länder* were as follows: 9 per cent in Catholic Bavaria; 12 per cent in Rhineland Westphalia; 13 per cent in Lower Saxony, Saar and Palatinate; 14 per cent in Schleswig-Holstein; 15 per cent in

Bremen and Hesse; 16 per cent in Hamburg and 17 per cent in Baden-Württemberg.

3. *Das Parlament* (Bonn), 20 September, 1961.
4. Professor Charles Foster, professor of Political Science at Cornell College, Iowa, in a public address at the Amerika-haus in Frankfurt in early September, 1961, stated: 1) In all election rallies, more youth are present than formerly; 2) A definite trend away from *Weltanschaung* speeches, which formerly were more in the foreground; formulation of policy by means of compromise, rather than through ideal principles. 3) The German press was less active than the American press in clarifying the claims of politicians by a sharp presentation of political questions. "Public opinion in Germany and also other European countries is formed by the parties, not by newspapers." This observer finds it hard to accept this statement at face value. The German voter has a distinct advantage over the American voter during the last months of a parliamentary campaign in that German newspapers whether pro-government, right-center, independent, left-center, or tabloid, do a good job of presenting various interpretations of complex foreign and domestic issues. In contrast to West German, Swiss and London papers, American newspapers tend to oversimplify complex national issues. Too often the American voters are spoon-fed by newspapers or entertained in great television debates. In general, German and European voters show a more vital interest in comparing different shades of political opinion found in German daily and weekly papers, particularly during a parliamentary campaign.
5. *Stuttgarter Nachrichten* (independent), 19 August, 1961.
6. *Ibid.*
7. The FDP Chairman, Dr. Erich Mende, told the author in a personal interview in the *Bundeshaus*, in June, 1961, that he hoped to elect 60 Free Democrats to the Bundestag. The FDP elected 66. *Frei Demokratische Korrespondenz: Presse Digest der Frei Demokratische Partei* (FDK), Jahrgang 12/76 Bonn, 18 September, 1961.
8. *Frei Demokratische Korrespondenz*, 18 September, 1961.
9. *London Times* (independent), 19 September, 1961.

10. *Party Preferences of German Voters over* 21 *in* 1961.

	April	May	June	July	August
CDU/CSU	49	46	50	50	46
SPD	34	36	35	34	38
FDP	10	11	8	10	9
GP (BHE & DP)	5	3	5	4	5
DFU	—	—	0	1	1
Other Parties	2	4	2	1	1

Emnid—Informationen: Heraus geber K. V. von Stackelberg. *Emnid Institute,* Nr. 34/28 August, 1961, 13 Jahrgarg, p. 2.

11. *London Times* (independent), 19 September, 1961.
12. *Emnid Institute,* 3 September, 1961, Nr. 35 Jahrgang 13, p. 10.
13. *Die Welt* (Hamburg, independent), 5 September, 1961, p. 11. Translation of a CDU/CSU political advertisement.
14. Political advertisement of the Free Democratic Party in *Die Welt* (Hamburg, independent), 15 September, 1961. My own translation.
15. *Neue Rhein Zeitung* (Dortmund, pro-SPD), 16 September, 1961.
16. *General Anzeiger* (Bonn, independent), 6 September, 1961.
17. *London Sunday Times* (independent), 10 September, 1961.
18. See Public Opinion analysis of Emnid (27 August, 1961), Nr. 34.
19. Top headlines included:
"Worldwide Indignation about New Soviet Atomic Test Plans," *General Anzeiger* (Bonn, independent); "World Horrified about Moscow," *Der Mittag* (right-center); "Atomic Blackmail, Kennedy Declares," *Rheinische Post* (pro-CDU); "Moscow Again Testing Atomic Bombs," *Süddeutsche Zeitung* (Munich, left-center); "Moscow Again Increasing Tension," *Hannoverische Presse* pro-SPD); *Frankfurter Allgemeine Zeitung* (right-center), 1 September, 1961.
20. *Die Welt* (Hamburg, independent), 1 September, 1961.
21. *General Anzeiger* (Bonn, independent), 1 September, 1961.
22. *Stuttgarter Zeitung* (independent), 1 September, 1961. See also *Die Welt* (Hamburg, independent) and *General Anzeiger* (Bonn, independent), 1 September, 1961.

23. *Stuttgarter Nachrichten* (independent), 1 September, 1961.

24. *Süddeutsche Zeitung* (Münich, left-center), 1 September, 1961.

25. *Westfälische Rundschau* (Dortmund, pro-SPD), 1 September, 1961. See also *Stuttgarter Zeitung* (independent), 1 September, 1961 and *Neue Rhein Zeitung* (pro-SPD), 1 September, 1961.

26. *Der Tagespiegel* (Berlin, independent), 1 September, 1961.

27. *Neues Deutschland* (East Berlin, Pro-SED), 1 September, 1961.

28. *Emnid Institute* (September 3, 1961), Nr. 35/1961 13 Jahrgang, p. 9.

29. *Ibid.*

30. *Ibid.*

31. *Emnid Institute* (3 September, 1961), Nr. 35/1961, 13 Jahrgang, p. 10.

32. *Ibid.*, p. 10.

33. *Hannoverische Presse* (pro-SPD), 3 September, 1961.

34. *Stuttgarter Zeitung* (independent), 3 September, 1961; *Frankfurter Zeitung* (right-center), 3 September, 1961; *Frankfurter Rundschau* (left-center), 3 September, 1961; *Kölnische Rundschau* (pro-CDU), 3 September, 1961.

35. *Allgemeine Zeitung* (Mainz, independent), 5 September, 1961.

36. *Die Welt* (Hamburg, independent), 6 September, 1961.

37. *Ibid.*

38. *Rheinische Post* (Düsseldorf, pro-CDU), 6 September, 1961.

39. *Ibid.*

40. *Die Welt* (Hamburg, independent), 7 September, 1961.

41. *Hannoverische Presse* (pro-SPD), 5 September, 1961. See also *Allgemeine Zeitung* (Mainz, independent), 5 September, 1961.

42. *Westfälische Rundschau* (Dortmund, pro-SPD), 5 September, 1961.

43. *Die Welt* (Hamburg, independent), 6 September, 1961.

44. *Frankfurter Rundschau* (left-center), 6 September, 1961.

45. *Frankfurter Rundschau* (left-center), 6 September, 1961.

46. *Allgemeine Zeitung* (Mainz, independent), 6 September, 1961.

47. *Neue Rhein Zeitung* (pro-SPD), 7 September, 1961.

48. *Rheinische Post* (pro-CDU), 7 September, 1961. However, if India took the step of recognizing the Soviet Zone regime, this would pose a real challenge to the Hallstein doctrine.
49. *Emnid Institute* (3 September, 1961), Nr. 35/13 Jahrgang, p. 4.
50. *Ibid.*, p. 1. By June, Kennedy's popularity had fallen from 84 to 70 per cent.
51. *Allgemeine Zeitung* (Mainz, independent), 4 September, 1961.
52. *Stuttgarter Zeitung* (independent), 3 September, 1961.
53. *Stuttgarter Zeitung* (independent), 3 September, 1961.
54. *Ibid.*
55. *Frankfurter Rundschau* (left-center), 3 September, 1961.
56. *Frankfurter Rundschau* (left-center), 12 September, 1961.
57. *Die Zeit* (Hamburg, weekly, right-center), 8 September, 1961.
58. *Die Zeit* (Hamburg, weekly, right-center), 8 September, 1961.
59. *Hannoverische Presse* (pro-SPD), 15 September, 1961.
60. *Westfälische Rundschau* (Dortmund, pro-SPD), 15 September, 1961.
61. *New York Herald Tribune* (independent), 12 September, 1961.
62. *New York Herald Tribune* (independent), 12 September, 1961.
63. *Stuttgarter Zeitung* (independent), 14 September, 1961.

Chapter 14

AFTERMATH OF GERMAN ELECTIONS—
BONN INTERREGNUM

1. *Meaning of Parliamentary Elections*

Bonn foreign policy evoked increasing criticism from the German opposition press for being unrelated to the facts of the international situation. It was argued that past policies were predicated on contradictory objectives—membership in NATO and ultimate reunification. Under pressure from both East and West the independent West German press saw an opportunity to formulate a realistic German policy even if on a more limited and narrow basis. Both Chancellor Adenauer and his Defense Minister, Strauss, stated that the Berlin Crisis could not be mastered by military means alone.[1] This was interpreted as a critical evaluation of their own NATO policies. Disarmament alone, on the other hand, without a constructive foreign policy would serve no useful purpose. When Bonn failed to act, therefore, the *Bundeswehr* (West German Army) lost its value while Soviet nuclear power was increasing in the view of the opposition press.

The Berlin Crisis produced one favorable result in that it strengthened independent thinking on the part of German voters. Never before had a similar election campaign been waged in Germany. Never before had American election methods been imitated so slavishly. At first the politicians left the field to public relations experts and public opinion polls. This suddenly changed with the events of August 13, which compelled politicians to switch tactics and act on their own initiative regardless of public opinion polls.[2] The independent *General Anzeiger* stressed the idea that the parliamentary campaign had changed from a struggle of ideas to one of personalities, with publicity experts leading party ideologists.[3] But the fact remained that all public opinion polls showed the persistence of a high percentage of undecided voters. This posed a problem for both government and opposition politicians. In the main, the persistence of this large group was at the expense of the CDU/CSU and was regarded as an asset for both opposition parties which hoped to win over new supporters from this group. The opposition press maintained that a more responsible German Government should make a greater effort to convince both the West and the USSR of Germany's peaceful intentions. Heretofore, the Bonn Government had taken countless measures bound to create the wrong impression in Moscow.[4] Bonn had not even attempted to reconcile differences with Moscow, but instead had disparaged all Soviet feelers. Hence Germany and Soviet Russia again faced each other as rigid opponents.

After August 13 the West German press, whether pro-government, right-center, independent or left-center, showed a greater willingness to face reality. Above all there was clear evidence of a strong trend toward re-evaluation of foreign policy aims and objectives in the light of the Berlin Crisis even if it was manufactured by Khrushchev as a tool in the East-West power struggle. The 28 per cent of undecided voters immediately before the election proved that Germans were thinking hard and coming to question past precepts of policy-makers. More West German papers were confronted with the need to face up to hard realities, to recognize the results of the lost war and that politics is the art of the possible. This applied to both internal and external politics.

It was asserted in *Frankfurter Allgemeine* that U.S. determination to defend West Berlin might not conflict with de facto recognition of the Soviet Zone regime as per the Dulles "Agent Theory." This right-center paper warned Germans to recognize the consequences of World War II.[5] On the other hand *Deutsche Zeitung* warned against domparing the Berlin Crisis to the Munich Conference of 1938 for the following reasons: 1. Rearmament proved the West was well aware of the graveness of the

Soviet challenge in Berlin. 2. The heavily armed Soviet Bloc feared nuclear war as much as the West. 3. Both the East and West respected each other's sphere of interest.[6] This was evident in both the East German and Hungarian uprisings of 1953 and 1956, as well as in Korea and Lebanon after U.S. intervention there in 1958. Even if the Soviet Bloc aimed at world domination, it was still anxious to avoid direct provocation. Khrushchev's primary concern seemed to be to eliminate the Western opportunity to use West Berlin as a base for political propaganda, not to interfere with its freedom. Whereas Hitler's mission was to destroy the post-Versailles *status quo,* Khrushchev proclaimed that he wanted to "stabilize" the present status in Europe. It would be the task of Western diplomacy to demonstrate to Khrushchev that he could not determine the status of either Berlin and Germany or Europe by unilateral action.

Der Mittag, also right-center, chided Germans for political inconsistency in requesting that Western Powers defend Berlin at any price, whereas Germans themselves did not want to run the risk of war. This paper concluded that Germans were "still a sick nation not knowing whether they dared to have patriotic feelings *(National Bewusstsein)* or not." [8] *Frankfurter Presse* noted the complex imponderable factors influencing German voters, who were primarily attracted only by star candidates. This pro-CDU organ regretted that many papers had suddenly shifted from objective reporting to partisanship at a crucial time. This was definitely true of *Der Spiegel* and partly true of *Die Welt,* both of which leaned more toward the Social Democratic Party.[9] *Frankfurter Rundschau* explained Adenauer's efforts to exert a moderating influence on Moscow as a vital part of his diplomatic two-front war to prevent Khrushchev from pushing things too far and to urge Americans against yielding too much.[10] The real cause of the current international crisis, in the view of this paper lay in the recent change of power relations in favor of Moscow, who by nuclear "blackmail" could put great pressure on the Western position in Berlin without running the risk of war if U.S. vital interests were not interfered with.[11]

278

a. No Kanzlerdämmerung

Few political observers in Bonn expected the 1961 election to become another "Adenauer election." Brandt's skillful campaign tactics could make it an "anti-Adenauer election," by announcing its willingness to form a coalition with the CDU/CSU with Erhard, Bundestag President Gerstenmaier or Dr. Krone—but not Adenauer. This scheme proved unworkable when neither Erhard, Gerstenmaier or Krone showed any inclination to lead an "anti-Adenauer fronde. With *der Alte's* determination to remain Chancellor for at least another two years, West German politicians did not rule out an Adenauer offer of a coalition with the SPD.[12] After three electoral victories in 1949, 1953 and 1957, Adenauer continued to tower over his ministerial colleagues by virtue of his long experience, force of character and unequalled prestige both in Germany and the West. When the Western Powers accepted Adenauer's demand for free elections throughout Germany, a solution which neither the USSR nor its East German satellite could accept, the German Chancellor prevented any negotiated solution of the partition of Germany.

Despite assertions of election computers on September 18th that the Adenauer era had ended, the old man refused to give up without a fight. His party had won 45 per cent of the total vote, nearly 10 per cent more than his nearest rival, Mayor Brandt's Social Democratic Party. The Free Democrats' total vote was less than 13 per cent, while Brandt's landslide, greatly feared by the Christian Democrats in the crucial days after August 13, had failed to materialize. According to Chancellor Adenauer the results signified merely a return to the *status quo* of 1953, while the free Democratic Party recovered its loss of 1957. So CDU losses were attributed to natural attrition after 12 years in office.[13]

Obviously those who predicted an "anti-Adenauer election" had failed to consider Adenauer's skillful campaign tactics in calling for negotiations in the last days of the election, while accusing Brandt of Cold-Warlike obstinacy. Nevertheless, Adenauer's explanation of the CDU losses would not hold water. Natural attrition did not prevent a continuous rise in the CDU vote in the 1950s, though most of the dangers imminent in one-party rule were already evident. Adenauer's long rule began to

279

alter profoundly the workings of the Bonn Constitution. In place of a true parliamentary or cabinet system, it substituted the government of one outstanding personality, which reduced the Ministers to mere clerks and the opposition to impotent frustration. Rather, the CDU vote had increased at each election because of Erhard's *Wirtschaftswunder* (economic miracle) and Adenauer's pro-Western foreign policy.

After 17 September, 1961, the vote for Adenauer was no longer a vote of national self-confidence because the CDU/CSU lost 5 per cent of its 1957 vote, in effect 8 per cent since the *Deutsche Partei* (German Party), now weakened after its ill-fated coalition with the weakened Refugee Bloc, was in 1957 a mere appendage of the Government Party. Such a direct blow against the authority and prestige of the CDU meant a drastic fall in national self-confidence.[14]

In spite of the shock of August 13, the confidence crisis was bound to be slow in finding concrete political expression. Despite Dr. Mende's repeated refusal to enter a coalition with Dr. Adenauer, the Free Democrats were pledged to a pro-Western policy. The nationalistic wing of the FDP under Dr. Thomas Dehler and Reinhold Maier, extremely articulate in the foreign policy debate of 1957, was well under control. Any future Erhard-Mende coalition would be committed to political continuity with the policies of Dr. Adenauer, except that Mende strongly disapproved the Hallstein Doctrine—i.e., no diplomatic relations with states which recognized the so called "East German Democratic Republic" (DDR).

Emotional nationalism, resentful of Western inactivity after August 13, did not save the right-wing splinter parties from virtual extinction. Nor was it likely that the neo-Nazi German Reich Party and the Refugee Bloc, in alliance with the German Party, would survive their ignominious defeat in 1961.

For Social Democrats, the election results fell far short of expectations aroused by the Berlin Crisis and the Chancellor's mishandling (in electoral terms) of the domestic situation it created. Some had talked confidently of 40 per cent or more. At least Mayor Brandt had overcome the 30 per cent barrier of the three previous elections. The traditional inhibitions of German middle class voters towards the SPD proved far more stubborn than party leaders supposed. SPD tactics were to maneuver toward a grand coalition of all parties to meet the national crisis in Berlin. There was a growing feeling both in Germany and abroad that no Government even with a Bundestag majority would dare risk making crucial decisions for the future of Germany without Social Democratic cooperation, in order to prevent the growth of a new legend of a "stab in the back."[16] Above all, SPD leaders were most concerned that all parties be given the key information, regarding the international situation. This must be available even to an opposition party if it were to perform its function as a loyal opposition.[17]

b. Editorial Opinion of Post-Election Situation

The pro-CDU press in West Germany interpreted FDP and SPD gains as due to CDU tactical mistakes rather than to FDP and SPD virtues. The greatest gains were made by the smallest party (FDP) by its aim to break the CDU absolute majority rule by promising voters it would form a coalition with the CDU.[18] The pro-government press pointed out that the decisive factor in negotiations for a new cabinet would be foreign policy, an area where FDP ideas were imprecise because of lack of agreement among Free Democratic leaders. Hence, it would be dangerous to renounce Adenauer's leadership in foreign affairs.[19]

Right-center papers admitted the CDU setback was greater than anticipated and attributed this to tactical errors in the campaign after 13 August, 1961 and to increasing opposition in middle class quarters against "welfare state aspirations" of the leftist wing of the CDU.[20] Even pro-government papers criticized the Chancellor for his cool and not always correct relations with Professor Erhard and his attitude in the constitutional struggle over the use of TV in the campaign. Dr. Adenauer had criticized the Supreme Court at Karlsruhe for a "wrong decision." Free Democratic gains, on the other hand, were attributed to FDP fairness in the campaign, reluctance of liberal groups to elect a "Christian" party and the pastoral letter whereby Catholic bishops urged Catholics to vote for a "Christian" party—that is, for the CDU/CSU.[21]

The independent press was primarily concerned with the constitutional responsibility of all three parties in preserving cabinet responsibility and in respecting the intent of voters.

Therefore, the FDP was urged to make no coalition with the Christian Democrats at the expense of the Social Democrats with their impressive 36.3 per cent of the vote. September 17 in the view of the independent press had restored the three-party system and passed a death sentence on both right and left extremist parties.[22] The events of August 13 had made clear to everyone the real meaning of the lofty slogan "reunification in peace and freedom." The independent *Stuttgarter Zeitung* declared: "until the Federal Republic has completed its transition from the realm of wishful thinking into that of necessities, no one party should be permitted to hide in the reservation of pretended opposition. Nor should any one party be excluded from coresponsibility.[23]

Opposition papers stressed the role of strong opposition groups within the CDU who desired Adenauer's withdrawal and a change in the Federal Republic's Berlin and German policies. Their spokesman was Bundestag President Gerstenmaier, author of the historic Bundestag Declaration of 30 June, 1961, on the Berlin and German question at the invitation of all parties in the Bundestag. Strauss seemed more interested in power than in politics. Intimate coalition talks between Strauss (CSU) and Mende (FDP) occurred during and immediately after the election campaign. However, these two groups were too weak to play a decisive role without support in CDU quarters according to the *Westfälische Rundschau*.[24]

2. Coalition Problems in Bonn

Foreign reaction to West German parliamentary elections was reported by *Frankfurter Allgemeine* as follows: Although the United States considered continued cooperation between Bonn and the West of vital importance, Washington expected the New West German Government to present plans for the reappraisal of Western policies. British socialist and other groups welcomed the end of the CDU/CSU absolute majority and would certainly demand that Western lip service for German reunification be replaced by a more realistic attitude.[25] The independent *Stuttgarter Zeitung* reported that in the forthcoming East-West negotiations on central European problems the U.S. Government would show more readiness for concessions and a greater will for flexibility than any previous U.S. Government had ever intended. Among the subjects reported discussed by Western Foreign Ministers in Washington were: 1) an atom-free zone or one of restricted armament in central Europe; 2) West Berlin as an "open city" of the United Nations; 3) relations with the Pankow regime in the Soviet Zone of Germany and 4) the question of Germany's future borders.[26]

Future responsibilities of foreign policy were bound to play a decisive role in all coalition negotiations in Bonn. After conversations between special Ambassador Clay and Foreign Minister von Brentano a series of implications were admitted. Accordingly the three Western Allies had reached a consensus of views for pending problems:

1) The Oder-Neisse Line was not recognized.
2) Propositions for immediate reunification were not considered feasible.
3) Berlin's situation may be prejudiced in so far as the Federal Republic was created out of the Zone of the Western Allies. Any negotiations over Berlin, therefore, could only pertain to West Berlin.
4) Discussion of the size and armament of the *Bundeswehr* must come under the subject of general disarmament and relaxation of tensions.[27]

The Western Allies expected, on the other hand, an understanding of Bonn's ideas for future relations between Bonn and Pankow—to compare with allied concepts prior to a final formulation of the Western position.

a. Speculation on a New Cabinet

Election of the Federal Chancellor had become a complicated mathematical problem because none of the bourgeois parties had agreed on a strategy for handling the Adenauer-Erhard rivalry. The question was even raised whether either of them would become Chancellor. It was noted that individual predictions of a new Adenauer Chancellorship was predicated on the idea that Adenauer should assume the responsibility for future foreign policy developments.[28] Consequently his successor would be relieved of these heavy burdens. Moreover, it was argued that President Lübke would prefer Adenauer as Chancellor, particularly if he headed a great coalition.

Bundestag President Gerstenmaier had convened the new Bundestag for 17 October, 1961. According to the election returns the distribution of seats would be as follows: Christian and Social Democrats (CDU/CSU)—241; Social Democrats (SPD)—190; Free Democrats (FDP)—66. The FDP was on record favoring a coalition with the CDU/CSU without Adenauer. In certain CDU quarters were suggestions for replacing Adenauer with Erhard. However, political observers in Bonn believed that the CDU/CSU Bundestag fraction would hesitate to withdraw Adenauer immediately.

In the first election, people counted on Adenauer's success because with the strong stand of the FDP, the CDU/CSU vote would not suffice to elect a Chancellor. For the second election within 14 days no other result was expected. In the following third election, besides Adenauer and Erhard, Brandt could also be a candidate. A simple majority (plurality) would suffice to elect a Chancellor according to Article 63 of the Bonn Constitution. In this event there would be two possibilities:

1) Adenauer would be prepared for a coalition with the SPD. Brandt would become Foreign Minister and the Free Democrats would be in opposition. 2) A CDU/CSU coalition with the free Democrats under Erhard. In that case, it was noted that SPD politicians emphasized that they would assume no joint responsibility for decisions, for under those conditions they would not participate. However, the Social Democrats declared that they were prepared to undertake responsibility for decisions provided: 1) they were given a part in the Cabinet or 2) were assured access to vital inside information on the international situation and consideration for SPD viewpoints.[29]

"Adenauer for Coalition with Free Democrats" was headlined in many West German papers reporting Adenauer's news conference statements on the day after the elections of 17 September, 1961. Dr. Adenauer declared:

1) that he would not form a coalition with the Social Democratic Party.
2) An all-party coalition in peace-time was inconsistent with the rule of democracy.

3) He had no objections to forming a coalition with the Free Democrats.

4) It would be wrong to firm a "minority government" of the CDU/CSU alone because "disappointed hopes" in the field of foreign policy would then have to be coped with by the CDU/CSU alone.[30]

b. Problems of Forming a Coalition Government

The CDU/CSU decision that Adenauer should head the new Government and the FDP stand against Adenauer were top news in most West German papers on Wednesday, September 20. The CDU had yielded primarily to considerations of foreign policy. However, hundreds of letters and telegrams from Free Democratic voters and FDP local and *Land* organizations warned the FDP Executive Committee against joining an Adenauer Government.[31] This proved to be the most difficult coalition problem in the history of the Bonn Republic and left only three possibilities:

1) Formation of a "minority" government under Adenauer, tolerated by the FDP. 2) A "grand coalition" between the CDU/CSU and SPD. 3) A CDU/CSU coalition under Erhard or Gerstenmaier.[32]

Under these circumstances the SPD was reported planning to ask President Lübke to use his influence in an attempt to bring about an all-party coalition government.[33] On the other hand, the independent papers expressed strong opposition to dropping Dr. Adenauer as politically unwise and undignified, while a minority government would be unstable and an awkward solution to the problem.[34] The independent *Westdeutsche Allgemeine* criticized the FDP as the weakest of all parties because it made two commitments to voters: 1) not to join an Adenauer Government and 2) not to form a coalition with the SPD. Moreover, the composition of the FDP contributed to its weakness. According to Adenauer: one third of the FDP were pro-CDU-ers, another third SPD-ers and the rest did not know what they wanted.[35] Strauss and the CSU delegates originally wanted a new Chancellor. This encouraged Mende. Later the CDU/CSU shifted its position and asked Adenauer to remain Chancellor.

c. Bonn Tug-of-War over Cabinet

With the CDU/CSU resolved to retain Adenauer as Chancellor and the FDP determined not to join an Adenauer Cabinet, a deadlock resulted—a deadlock which continued for nearly seven weeks. This deadlock led to the intervention of President Lübke in coalition talks, which was without precedent in the history of the West German Republic. Foreign policy considerations caused Lübke to favor Adenauer for Chancellor and if that failed, he was reported to favor an all-party government advocated by the SPD.

Events at the CDU Executive Committee meeting on September 19 made headlines in all West German papers. Under the headline "Adenauer in Tears: 'Will Resign in 16 Months,'" *Abendpost* asserted: "The news had leaked out that Adenauer shed tears when urged to resign and that he finally agreed to withdraw after 16 months."[36] After the CDU Executive Committee had accepted this and asked Adenauer to form a government, he took the initiative and called in the SPD leaders for a conference. The already emerging hint of coalition feelers between Adenauer and the SPD was like a shot in the air to frighten the FDP, in order to induce it to enter negotiations. There was no doubt that Adenauer preferred to form a coalition with the FDP rather than the SPD because he preferred to govern with the Free Democrats than have them as opponents.[37] *Bild Zeitung* reported a clash between Adenauer and Erhard when the latter urged the Chancellor to state publicly that he would withdraw and that he considered Erhard a qualified successor. Adenauer reacted so vigorously that CDU delegates were intimidated and agreed to everything Adenauer asked.[38] The continued tug-of-war over the coalition became top news by September 21 in West German papers whose headlines included:

"CSU in Role of Mediator," "Dr. Adenauer to Remain Chancellor for Another Year," "Lübke Intervenes—Strauss Gives Adenauer Another Year," [39] "SPD Offers Cooperation" and "SPD Also Ready for Coalition with CDU/CSU—Possibly under Adenauer." [40] This struggle over a coalition confirmed the close relationship between domestic politics and German foreign policy —a relationship which made the West German parliamentary election of 1961 unique in the postwar era. German voters gave

286

top priority to the basic issues of foreign policy after the events of 13 August, 1961 for fear that the Great Powers might liquidate the war at German expense. The West German Press revealed varied solutions for the coalition deadlock, which came from the pro-CDU, right center, independent and left-center papers.

By Thursday, 21 September, 1961, Washington and London papers were speculating over the eventual outcome of the West German Cabinet crisis. Hanson Baldwin, writing in the New York *Times,* noted that neither German citizens nor U.S. soldiers were as concerned over the danger of war as was the American public. Although the British and French Governments were still committed to the defense of Berlin, they did not have the strong support of either British or French public opinion. The Washington *Post* expressed relief at General Clay's arrival in Berlin, lest the Cabinet Crisis would result in a minority government which could cause political instability in West Germany during a serious international crisis. Gaston Coblentz of the New York *Herald Tribune* reported that Adenauer's political future was at stake with the political impasse caused by the Bundestag elections of 17 September, 1961. If the deadlock continued into November, it could cause disunity and confusion at the height of the Berlin Crisis. Columnist Drew Pearson reported a split among key advisers on Berlin—with Secretary Rusk, Dean Acheson and Charles Bohlen advocating a "hard line" and Adlai Stevenson, Ambassador Lewellyn Thompson, Chester Bowles and Senators Fulbright and Mansfield advocating compromise.[41]

Reports in the West German press that von Brentano was ready for concessions on recognition of the Zone regime and Oder-Neisse Line or renunciation of nuclear weapons for the *Bundeswehr* (army) or that he was under pressure by the West to make such concessions were vigorously denied in Bonn.[42] In making these denials, however, Press Chief von Eckhardt left unanswered the question why Adenauer, in his press conference on Monday, 18 September, 1961, had referred to "inevitable disappointments."[43]

Both pro-government and right-center papers urged the FDP to participate in an Adenauer Cabinet for the sake of a consistent foreign policy and in order to avoid the weakness of the Weimar Republic. Jürgen Tern in *Frankfurter Allgemeine* warned against creating the impression that there was any alternative to the basic lines of Adenauer's foreign policy. He even suggested von Brentano's replacement to assure firm support for "Adenauer's own determination and energetic advice."[44] George Schröder in *Die Welt* maintained that since Adenauer had polled 45 per cent of the total vote, he could not be dismissed by the CDU and CSU deputies, who believed that he should be in charge of difficult East-West negotiations. In a theoretical analysis of cabinet possibilities Schröder mentioned: 1) Adenauer's resignation in favor of Erhard; 2) a CDU/CSU offer to the SPD to form a coalition and 3) intervention by President Lübke who might appoint a minority Chancellor and dissolve the Bundestag.[45] *Frankfurter Allgemeine* welcomed the CDU-SPD contacts, but warned against believing that this would force the FDP to shift its ground. It was clear that Adenauer was fighting for his policy and his office, which were merged into one. The resistance within his own ranks was subdued, but intermingled with feelings of loyalty, political aspirations and party tactics. Dolf Sternberg in *Frankfurter Allgemeine* reminded his readers that after all the Bundestag had the constitutional function of electing the Chancellor and that all the maneuvers in Bonn showed disrespect for Parliament.[46]

Heinz Schiegel proposed a grand coalition government headed by Adenauer. Admitting that an all-party coalition would be awkward in a democracy, he argued that this was demanded by the international crisis, claiming that both Moscow and Washington were ready to liquidate the war at German expense. All parties, he maintained, should bear responsibility for the final settlement of Germany's future—not a minority government. Otherwise certain party leaders could later boast that they would have acted differently.[47]

The opposition press attacked Adenauer for blocking the way to the most natural and logical consequences of the parliamentary elections—a CDU/CSU—FDP Coalition Cabinet. Otherwise a government could be formed under Erhard as Chancellor, Mende as Vice-Chancellor and Interior; Gerstenmaier—Foreign Affairs and Strauss—Defense.[48] The opposition press contended that Germans would have to pay not only for the lost war, but also for the foreign policy pursued by the Bonn Government for twelve years. It was argued that the failure of this policy was ignored by von Brentano and Adenauer, who wanted to remain in power in order to complete this policy. The FDP, however, refused to enter a cabinet where it would only play the role of assistant liquidator. In case of the probable failure of CDU/FDP negotiations, the CDU would have to choose between a grand coalition under Adenauer or the sacrifice of Adenauer for a small coalition under Erhard or Schröder.[49] *Frankfurter Allgemeine,* on the other hand, warned against creating the impression that there was any real alternative to the basic tenets of Adenauer's foreign policy.[50]

d. Factors Behind Coalition Maneuvers in Bonn

Although the CDU/CSU authorized coalition negotiations with the Free Democrats, Adenauer at the same time arranged a meeting with the Social Democratic leaders: Ollenhauer, Wehner and Brandt. According to Ollenhauer, Dr. Adenauer had replied immediately to an SPD resolution in which the Chancellor was called on to furnish "frank and honest" information about the international crisis and the "difficult decisions" confronting the West German Federal Republic.[51] This move was interpreted in Bonn as one of tactics, which would make it difficult for the FDP to adhere to its decision not to join an Adenauer Government.[52]

Nevertheless, a radio address by FDP Deputy Dehler, in which he referred to the need of a new course in foreign policy, created a sensation in CDU quarters, lest this compound the difficulties of a CDU/CSU coalition. The Young Free Democrats were reported to have urged the FDP Executive Committee not to join an Adenauer Government and to provide for the replacement of von Brentano.[53] Nevertheless, the bargaining over coalition terms continued, with reports of tentative offers of the Vice Chancellorship to Mende. However, the FDP position continued unchanged for various reasons: loss of face after a unanimous vote of all 66 deputies against a coalition under Adenauer and the conviction that the FDP would lose prestige by joining a "bankrupt undertaking." CDU quarters, therefore, argued that if the FDP adhered to its rejection of a coalition under Adenauer, the latter would form a coalition with the Social Democrats because the international crisis required that

289

Adenauer be backed up in Parliament by a solid majority giving him a mandate to act as authorized spokesman for Germany as against the Soviets and the Western Powers.[54] Political observers in Bonn, however, continued to believe that eventually the Free Democrats would yield and accept a coalition under Adenauer because of the deeply intrenched feelings within the FDP against the idea of a "red-black" or clerical-socialist coalition.[55] As stated above, Dr. Adenauer insisted that his Weimar experience had taught him to stand right of center and avoid an opposition party on his right. At the same time the Chancellor had reaffirmed his great confidence in the Social Democratic Party as a loyal opposition on his 85th birthday, when he told the Bundestag that a strong Chancellor needs a strong Parliament to support him when he is right and to oppose him when he is wrong. Meanwhile the Social Democrats hinted that they might support an Adenauer Coalition, formed on a broad basis with a responsible post for Willy Brandt.

3. *The Federal German Republic and Its Allies*

a. Reaction to Remarks of General Clay

Sydney Gruson of the New York *Times* reported from Bonn that recent events caused a severe strain in U.S.-German relations, which no amount of denials could change after the original remarks of General Clay at a cocktail party on 23 September, 1961. The remarks attributed to Clay were that West Germans would eventually have to accept the Oder-Neisse Line, de facto recognition of the Zone regime and a Free City status for Berlin. This raised a storm of protest in the West German press on the part of pro-CDU, right-center and independent papers against what were regarded as premature concessions to the Soviets at German expense. There was much discussion about Germans having to pay for the lost war and of US readiness to compromise on Berlin by recognition of East Berlin or the Soviet Zone and other sacrifices.[56]

Despite von Brentano's optimism after returning from the Conference of Foreign Ministers in Washington and vigorous denials by Press Chief von Eckhardt of any change in West German foreign policy, the American press continued to describe these very concessions as necessary and more or less agreed upon. Johannes Gross concluded that American journalists were usually well informed by high authorities and, therefore, identical reports by serious correspondents of serious American newspapers would certainly be based on at least semi-official information.[57] The pro-CDU *Ruhr-Nachricten* was embittered by reports of a nuclear-free zone between the two blocs and plans to equip the *Bundeswehr* with only conventional weapons as unrealistic in the face of Soviet aggressions. It was noted that Washington would inform Bonn as to what issues it considered negotiable and Bonn would have to drop many of its coalition problems and tell Germans unpopular truths. With strong pressure for negotiations, the United States was expected to assure the Soviets that it would not try to roll back the Soviet sphere of influence.[58]

Dieter Cycon in the *Stuttgarter Zeitung* analyzed the relation of the West German Republic to its Allies as follows:

1) Secretary Rusk, realizing his heavy responsibility, had joined that wing of the U.S. Administration favoring a U.S.-Soviet compromise in Europe. 2) Whereas in 1959 the West gave priority to German reunification in any central European settlement, Washington in 1961 was considering recognition of the Oder-Neisse Line and some kind of recognition for the "German Democratic Republic and a German armament limitation as the main basis for negotiations over Berlin. 3) Such an accommodation would come close to Soviet desires for a peace treaty with both Germanies—at a most inopportune time, with insecurity and confusion in the Western camp, while Soviet aggression was increasing. 4) Committed on Berlin, the West was turning to the German problem to win a basis for negotiations and thus falling into a Soviet trap. 5) The West appeared ready to pay a high price in order to avoid choosing between the loss of prestige in Berlin and nuclear war.[59]

b. German Reaction to Kennedy Speech at UN

Soon after the tragic death of United Nations Secretary Dag Hammarskjold in Central Africa, President Kennedy prepared to address the UN Assembly on urgent issues confronting East and West. American papers emphasized the following points of the speech:

1. On disarmament the U.S. was no longer insisting on the completion of one stage before the next was approached.
2. Non-transfer of atomic weapons to other powers was taken as an offer to the Soviet Union that with genuine negotiations on disarmament, atomic weapons for the *Bundeswehr* (West German Army) and Red China could be renounced.
3. Although Berlin's freedom and economic well-being were not negotiable, a new settlement could be found to guarantee the vital interests of the West as well as European security. This meant the Oder-Neisse Line, de facto recognition of the Soviet Zone and its control over access lines could be negotiated.[60]

The Kennedy speech met with high approval in the West, while East Bloc diplomats saw in it American willingness to recognize the partition of Germany. After the speech praise could be heard from members of the European, Latin-American and some Asian and Commonwealth delegations. The only negative reactions came from Africans, who regarded the anti-colonialist declarations and references to economic aid as too weak. They wanted strong declarations about Algeria, Angola and South Africa, but showed no concern over Soviet imperialism in Central and Eastern Europe. Yet no one could doubt the deep effect produced by the President's speech and the strong applause he received on entering and leaving the hall, for certain passages on Berlin and for his powerful appeal for peace at the end of the speech.[61]

President Kennedy's speech was received with great gratitude by the West Berlin Senate and Mayor Willy Brandt as well as by Foreign Minister von Brentano, speaking on behalf of the West German Government. He appealed to West Germans to have confidence in the West before the forthcoming East-West negotiations.[62] Pro-government and right-center papers in West Germany praised the American President for his well conceived plan for general disarmament despite tremendous obstacles. Committed to no rigid formula for negotiations with Moscow over Berlin, Kennedy did "recognize that troops and tanks can, for a time, keep a nation divided against its will."[63] The more influential independent papers showed a willingness to accept the fact that German reunification had ceased to be the primary aim of US policy and that top priority was given to the security of free nations throughout the world. Although the United States would not sacrifice free people, it felt unable to peacefully change existing facts.[64]

The independent West German press hailed the Kennedy address as historic due to the pathos with which he described the danger of self-annihilation through nuclear death. His disarmament plan took the wind out of Moscow's sails in the opinion of the *Allgemeine Zeitung* which predicted it would be approved by a two-thirds majority of the UN General Assembly.[65] For the first time the United States had asked neutral nations, non-atomic powers to help control nuclear weapons. This could weaken Soviet arguments against genuine control as espionage. Above all Kennedy had shown great civic courage *vis-à-vis* the prevailing mood in the United States which had led to outbursts of emotional nationalism.[66]

The American President was commended for his clear outline of the goals and possibilities for Washington's future foreign policy. He laid down precise limits for American concessions and outlined the scope for negotiations with the Soviets. Kennedy wanted to indicate to world public opinion what course the US would pursue in this period of permanent crisis and to win the support of neutrals for his policy. This, however, did not rule out a willingness to face facts, including the partition of Germany. Although the United States would sacrifice neither West Berlin nor West Germany, it would refuse to use atomic weapons in an offensive sense, that is, to roll back the Iron Curtain, but only in defense of those nations which are still free. Just as Kennedy had come to believe there was no perfect solution for the German problem, so the West German pro-government and independent press showed a willingness to accept the fact that German reunification had ceased to be the primary aim of United States policy.[67]

In contrast to the generally favorable reaction of pro-government and most independent West German papers, the tabloid left-center and certain other papers were unrestrained in their criticism of parts of Kennedy's speech. *Abendpost* was embittered over the President's reference to the anticipated Moscow-Pankow

293

peace treaty as a mere "paper arrangement" and called it the first step toward recognition of the Soviet Zone regime.[68] The most trenchant critique came from *Bild Zeitung* which argued that in the years 1933-45 Germany violated all treaties while Germans kept silent and had to pay dearly. This time they would not keep silent, but stand by the German-Allied treaties of 1952 and 1954 which definitely stipulated German reunification as a Western policy aim.[69] *Der Mittag* noted that these treaties described reunification as a "cardinal goal" of Western policy. Hence Western concessions making this goal even more difficult would constitute a betrayal of the spirit of the Allied-German treaties. This paper concluded that articles 2 and 7 of the 1954 treaties made it clear that the Bonn Government agreed to reunification of the Oder-Neisse territories and that the Western Powers could not make any concessions here without violating the treaties.[70]

The left-center *Frankfurter Rundschau* criticized the Kennedy speech for increasing the confusion of the German public over recent impressive American statements on Germany and Berlin. If Washington formulated its German policy without consulting Bonn or the American diplomats stationed in West Germany this paper argued it was time for the Bonn Government to take the initiative. Adenauer however was exclusively concerned with how to remain Chancellor.[71] Everything else was apparently subordinated to him and his ministers. This paper regretted that except for a few generalities no statements had been made of the current international situation by either the Federal Government or the German Foreign Office. "Only Ambassador Grew . . . wages a lonely struggle against the windmill of Washington's Berlin policy, a windmill which is about to grind to pieces German status quo thinking."[72] Therefore *Frankfurter Rundschau* called for a joint foreign policy.

4. *Post-Election Foreign Policy*

a. What Germany Dare Not Concede

Despite the continued deadlock over a coalition cabinet and even before the meeting of the New Parliament called for 17 October 1961 by Bundestag President Gerstenmaier, intensive conferences were taking place in Bonn to clarify the Western position on Berlin and Germany. On October 12 the German

Ambassador in Washington, Dr. Wilhelm Grewe, was called to Bonn for consultations with Ambassador Hasso von Etzdorf from London and Ambassador Herbert Blankenhorn from Paris. Chancellor Adenauer also conferred with the Mayor of Berlin, Willy Brandt, who reported on the outcome of his recent talks with key officials in Washington. At a meeting of the Christian Democratic Party (CDU/CSU), von Brentano outlined the points Germany dare not concede as follows:

1. A *de facto* recognition of the Communist regime of the Soviet Zone by the Federal Government as tantamount to *de jure* recognition and as too dangerous for the West.
2. Any negotiations on a so called European security zone unless combined with a political solution—no "Zones of Relaxation" in Central Europe while Germany remained partitioned.[73] Quarters close to Bonn welcomed a speech on 11 October, 1961 by the British Foreign Secretary, Lord Home, in support of German needs—such as the rights of self-determination, peaceful reunification and the freedom of Berlin.

On the same day Federal President, Dr. Heinrich Lübke, addressing NATO officers in Hamburg, assured them that Germans were linked by culture and tradition to the Free World— to all peoples who valued freedom, human dignity and human rights. Moreover, Germany's unique geographical position increased her obligation to warn the West against yielding to pressures from the East. Using war and peace as interchangeable instruments of politics, Communists sought to undermine public order in free societies as a prelude to their final absorption into the Communist power orbit. President Lübke concluded that historical factors in the last 15 years frustrated the high hopes of the Soviets to absorb all of Europe into their power sphere:

1. The Federal Republic's unequivocal rejection of Communism;
2. The continued coalition of the Western Powers after 1945 and
3. The creation of the North Atlantic Defense Pact.[74]

Arguing that the Soviet objective was to lure the United States into leaving Europe, Defense Minister Strauss summarized the goals of Soviet strategy in the past decade as primarily:

1. To tip the balance of nuclear strength in her favor;
2. To dissipate the nuclear deterrent of the West by atomic "territion," and
3. To break up or jump over the Western system of bases around the periphery of the Soviet Union in order to be able to encircle the United States.[75]

Strauss warned that if the Soviets could prevent Western Europe from uniting or could neutralize it by stages and "if a politically weak and militarily helpless, but economically important Europe should come under Russian control, then the entire Mediterranean area, Near and Middle East and Africa will be lost to the free world." [76] In that case the American fortress would be limited to America and the Soviet military potential would be greater than the American potential.

b. "We Are Assembled Here to Speak for a Single German People"

On 17 October, 1961, one month after the parliamentary elections, the new Bundestag, consisting of 520 deputies, met for the first time to elect its President and four Vice Presidents. By an overwhelming majority, Dr. Eugen Gerstenmaier (CDU) was re-elected President. To assist him four Vice Presidents were elected: Professor Carlo Schmid (SPD), Erwin Schoettle (SPD), Dr. Thomas Dehler (FDP) and Richard Jaeger (CSU). Dr. R. Pfermerges, the 81 year old Chairman of the Bundestag by seniority stressed the current international tensions and attributed the peace and freedom of West Germany to its alliance with the West.

Dr. Gerstenmaier then reminded the deputies that their constitutional mandate made them responsible for all the German people regardless of their party affiliation. Furthermore, the London agreement of 1954 made the Federal Republic the only legitimate government to represent the German people in international affairs. The Bundestag President declared that during the next four years decisions of this House might involve the destiny of all the German people, the question of war and peace and, indeed, the existence of millions of people beyond Germany herself. He warned the free world against permitting Soviet declarations on the avoidance of war to lull it into calm slumber. With the Soviets reaching out to engulf Berlin, Communist Party programs and Kremlin speeches in themselves were no guarantee of peace and might even be instruments of international deceit.

Apart from military defense and guarantees of the Western Powers on Berlin, Gerstenmaier urged the new Bundestag to launch the forces and ideas by which the cause of peace and freedom can be carried forward in the political and diplomatic realm. The German people, he declared, were determined to take a new road of peace and freedom within the community of free nations. Above all they wanted to live as peaceful neighbors of the Russian people. Nevertheless, Article 38 of the Constitution forced on Germans the duty to safeguard the ancient right of every people to self-determination and unity. Dr. Gerstenmaier's concluding words were:

> During the next four years, this House will learn that it is stern work to serve the cause of freedom. We see ourselves faced by a challenge that concerns not Berlin alone, not Germany alone, but practically everything that, by our common conviction, makes life in this world worth living. We must accept the challenge. We propose to stand the test in the community of the free world—fearlessly, prudently and with trust in the God who loves justice.[77]

5. Dr. Adenauer's Re-Election As Federal Chancellor

During the parliamentary session of the new Bundestag from October 17 to November 7 the elevated seats for cabinet members were empty. Konrad Adenauer and other members of the previous cabinet who had been re-elected to the Bundestag sat in the seats for deputies. During this interim period until a new cabinet was formed, affairs of state were handled by the old cabinet. Meanwhile negotiations over terms of a coalition between the Christian Democrats (CDU/CSU) and Free Democrats (FDP) continued.

The new Bundestag consisted of 521 deputies, of whom 129 were newcomers to Bonn and one in twelve were women. Over half of the deputies were between the ages of 45 and 65, while the average age was 50 as against 52 in the previous house. As to professional occupations: farmers led with 57, followed by civil servants and then jurists.[78] Industry and business were heavily represented in all parties: to the CDU/CSU were added Gustav Stein (director of Federation of German Industries) and Itasso Dieghans (director of a large steel plant); to the FDP came Alexandre Menne (on the board of a large chemical concern) and Albrecht Aschoff (of the coal-mining Employers Association of the Ruhr). In the Social Democratic group (SPD) was Alex Möller, a director in the insurance business, who had a reputation since World War II as budget expert in the Baden-Württemberg *Landtag*.

Article 63 of the Federal Constitution (Basic Law) provides that: 1) The Chancellor is elected by ballot on the proposal of the Federal President. 2) Whoever has a majority of the Bundestag members is elected. 3) If the candidate nominated by the Federal President is not elected, the Bundestag can within 14 days elect a Chancellor with more than half of its members. 4) If no one gets a majority this time, a new election is held without delay and whoever receives the most votes (plurality) is elected.[79] On 7 November, 1961, therefore, 490 of the 499 elected representatives of the Fourth German Bundestag assembled at 5:00 P.M. in the great hall (*Plenarsaal*) of the Bundeshaus to elect a new Federal Chancellor. The Bundestag, on the proposal of the Federal President, elected Konrad Adenauer as Chancellor for a fourth time by a vote of 258 to 206 with 26 abstentions—an absolute majority.

Adenauer's re-election was generally interpreted as an assurance that West German foreign policy would be carried on consistently. Several days later in a televised broadcast to the nation, Dr. Adenauer stated:

This Coalition Government (CDU/CSU and FDP) will pursue the same policies in foreign affairs as did the previous Government. And that is of special importance because other countries will see that there is no truth in what a few papers abroad have again begun to print

298

about the instability and unreliability of the German people.[80]

Dr. Adenauer emphasized that West Germans were neither militarists nor revanchists notwithstanding the propaganda of Soviet Russia, who never negotiates with weak peoples, but only strong peoples. The peace of the world, the Chancellor insisted, would depend upon a strong NATO.

Chancellor Adenauer indicated the main topics that he would soon discuss with President Kennedy: the Berlin question, the question of the extent of defense measures and general matters concerning Germany and Europe. He stated that he had some ideas of his own on Berlin and Germany, which he preferred to discuss in private with the American President. But before his departure for Washington, the Chancellor emphasized that he would consult with key officials not only in the coalition parties, but also with leaders of the Social Democratic opposition in the Bundestag and with Mayor Brandt of Berlin.[81] Before departing for Washington, the Chancellor indicated he would confer with the German Ambassador to the United States, Dr. Wilhelm Grewe, and the German Ambassador to the Soviet Union, Hans Kroel. Meanwhile it was reported that political circles in Bonn found nothing in Ambassador Kroel's report on his talk with Khrushchev on 8 November 1961 to indicate any change in the course of Soviet policy toward Germany.

In commenting on Adenauer's forthcoming visit to Washington in November, 1961, the pro-CDU press claimed that:

1. The attitude of the Federal Government was not influenced by either the election campaign or by the struggle to form a coalition.
2. The domestic struggle arose from differences over how best to protect the common interests of the whole free world, with which German interests were completely identical.
3. Actual differences between Washington and Bonn were greatly exaggerated by misinterpretations and distortions.
4. The assumption that the Kennedy administration believed it could satisfy Russia and bring about peace

with "concessions" was sheer nonsense. Any illusions emerging from the period of governmental paralysis in Bonn could be dispelled by Adenauer in talks with Kennedy.

5. On decisive issues of foreign policy all major political parties in Bonn were basically in agreement.[82]

Münchner Merkur (close to the CDU) urged Germans to look forward to the road ahead, not backward to the seven weeks of coalition negotiations. If then Dr. Adenauer seemed unyielding to the point of inflexibility during the long battle over negotiations for a coalition, it may well have been because he wanted to avoid future stumbling blocks.

On the other hand, the Free Democratic Chairman, Dr. Erich Mende, was just as firm in his convictions that he himself would not accept a cabinet position under Adenauer. His Free Democratic Party (FDP) is close to certain sections of big business. No doubt the big industrialists who helped finance the costly campaign of the FDP in 1961 shared both the basic liberal principles of the party along with conservative economic tenets and the party's strong political nationalism.[83] In fact, Dr. Mende saw no contradiction between his opposition to a major Government policy position and his party's presence in the Coalition Cabinet of the Fourth German Bundestag.[84] The Free Democrats have a long tradition of individual freedom and do not enforce party discipline over deputies as do both major parties—Christian Democrats (CDU/CSU) and Social Democrats (SPD). Even though rebuked in public by Dr. Adenauer for his stand, Mende ignored the rebuke.

The mere fact that before going to Washington to confer with President Kennedy in November, 1961, the Chancellor conferred not only with key members of both coalition parties, but with leaders of the Social Democratic opposition and the governing Mayor of Berlin, Brandt, indicated a most significant change in procedure—showing regard for the purpose of the Bonn Constitution. Its framers had envisaged a responsible cabinet form of government. But Dr. Adenauer, after increasing majorities in the parliamentary elections of 1949, 1953 and 1957, stood high above his colleagues, whom he tended to regard as mere clerks. Even members of his own CDU/CSU party and his committee of foreign affairs repeatedly complained of being ignored. In fact, both the former Chairman of the Bundestag Committee of Foreign Affairs, Kurt Kiesinger, and Bundestag President, Eugen Gerstenmaier, both CDU, had been continually pressing for a larger role in the formulation of West German foreign policy. Many factors account for Adenauer's dominant role in policy determination, such as his dual role as Federal Chancellor and head of the strongest party, the CDU.[85]

Historic circumstances have largely determined the significant role of the Chancellor, who was not plagued by large Communist minorities nor by the extreme right-wing nationalists, militarists and armed groups, who eventually ruined the Weimar Republic. Even Social Democratic opponents of Adenauer's foreign policy are staunch supporters of German democratic institutions. Even their opposition to rearmament and compulsory military service prior to 1958 increased his bargaining power with the West. Another powerful factor contributing to the success of Adenauer's foreign policy has been East-West cold war tensions, dominated by the conflict between the United States and the USSR over the future of Germany.

German foreign policy after Adenauer may not be so dependent on the United States. This became increasingly evident in the West German parliamentary elections of 1961, particularly after the erection of the Berlin Wall on 13 August, 1961, followed by the "Confidence Crisis" in Berlin and Germany, just before the arrival of Vice President Johnson and the appointment of General Clay as President Kennedy's Special Ambassador to Berlin. Above all, the persistence of a high percentage of undecided voters from August 13 right up to the end of the parliamentary campaign proved that more and more Germans were beginning to question the basic assumptions of Adenauer's foreign policy and calling for a re-examination and re-evaluation of foreign policy aims and objectives.

NOTES TO CHAPTER FOURTEEN

1. *Frankfurter Rundschau* (left-center), 7 September, 1961.
2. *Frankfurter Neue Presse* (pro-government), 12 September, 1961.
3. *General Anzeiger* (Bonn, independent), 12 September, 1961.
4. *Frankfurter Rundschau* (left-center), 8 September, 1961.

5. *Frankfurter Allgemeine* (right-center), 12 September, 1961.

6. *Deutsche Zeitung* (Cologne, right-center), 12 September, 1961.

7. *Ibid.* See also Symposium; "Is Khrushchev Another Hitler?" in *U.S. News and World Report,* 30 October 1961.

8. *Der Mittag* (Dusseldorf, right-center), 12 September 1961.

9. *Der Mittag* (Dusseldorf, right-center), 12 September, 1961.

9. *Frankfurter Neue Presse* (left-center), 12 September, 1961.

10. *Frankfurter Rundschau* (left-center), 12 September, 1961.

11. *Ibid.*

12. *Die Welt* (Hamburg, independent), 12 September, 1961.

13. *New Statesman* (London, independent), 12 September, 1961.

14. Ibid.

15. *Süddeutsche Zeitung* (Munich, left-center), 22 Sept., 1961.

16. *The Times* (London, independent), 9 September, 1961.

17. This was pointed out to the author in a personal interview with Herr Anders, Director of the SPD Election Campaign.

18. *Rheinische Post* (Düsseldorf, pro-CDU), 19 September, 1961.

19. *Kölnische Rundschau* (pro-CDU), September, 1961.

20. *Frankfurter Allgemeine* (right-center), 19 September, 1961; *Deutsche Zeitung* (Cologne, right-center), 19 Sept., 1961; *Der Mittag* (Düsseldorf, right-center), 19 September, 1961.

21. *Ruhr-Nachrichten* (Dortmund, pro-CDU), 19 Sept., 1961. See also *Frankfurter Neue Presse* (pro-government), 19 Sept., 1961.

22. *Die Welt* (Hamburg, independent), 19 Sept., 1961.

23. *Stuttgarter Zeitung* (Ind.) 19 Sept., 1961.

24. *Westfälische Rundschau* (Dortmund, pro-SPD), 19 Sept., 1961. See also *Neue Rhein Zeitung* (Cologne, pro-SPD), 19 Sept., 1961; *Süddeutsche Zeitung* (Munich, left-center), 19 Sept., 1961.

25. *Frankfurter Allgemeine Zeitung* (right-center), 19 September, 1961.

26. *Stuttgarter Zeitung* (independent), 19 September, 1961.

27. Editorial: "Coalition Maneuvers," in *Politik und Wirtschaft,* Nr. 75/1961 (10. Jahrgang), Bonn-Bundeshaus (22 September, 1961).

28. *Ibid.* Cf. *Der Mittag* (Düsseldorf, right-center), 20 September, 1961. See also *General Anzeiger* (Bonn, independent), 20 September, 1961.

29. *Politik und Wirtschaft*, Nr. 75/1961 (10 Jahrgang), Bonn— Bundeshaus (22 September, 1961).
30. *Neue Rhein Zeitung* (Cologne, pro-SPD), 19 September, 1961.
31. *Der Mittag* (Düsseldorf, right-center), 20 September, 1961.
32. *Stuttgarter Zeitung* (independent), 20 September, 1961.
33. *Westdeutsche Allgemeine* (Essen, independent), 20 September, 1961.
34. *Die Welt* (Hamburg, independent), 19 September, 1961; *Der Mittag* (Düsseldorf, right-center), 19 September, 1961.
35. *Westdeutsche Allgemeine* (Essen, independent), 20 September, 1961.
36. *Abendpost* (Frankfurt, tabloid), 20 September, 1961.
37. *Politik und Wirtschaft*, Nr. 75/1961 (10 Jahrgang), 22 September, 1961. Herr Robert Borchardt, Adenauer's Press Counselor in the German Embassy in Washington, D.C., told the author that the Chancellor's Weimar experience had taught him that it would be unwise to have an opposition party on his right. Therefore, Dr. Adenauer formed a right-center coalition with the Free Democrats, leaving the Social Democrats in their role of loyal opposition.
38. *Bild Zeitung* (Hamburg, tabloid), 20 September, 1961.
39. See *Münchner Merkur* (pro-CSU); *Ruhr-Nachrichten* (Dortmund, pro-CDU); *Stuttgarter Zeitung* (independent); *Wiesbadener Kurier* (pro-government) for 21 September, 1961.
40. *Deutsche Zeitung* (Cologne, right-center), 21 September, 1961; *Westdeutsche Allgemeine* (Essen, independent), 21 September, 1961.
41. See especially New York *Times*, New York *Herald Tribune* and the Washington *Post* for 20 September, 1961.
42. *Der Mittag* (Düsseldorf, right-center); *Frankfurter Rundschau* (left-center) for 20 September, 1961; *Deutsche Zeitung* (right-center), 21 Sept., 1961.
43. *Allgemeine Zeitung* (Mainz, independent), 20 September, 1961.
44. *Frankfurter Allgemeine Zeitung* (right-center), 20 September, 1961.
45. *Die Welt* (Hamburg, in dependent), 20 September, 1961.
46. *Frankfurter Allgemeine Zeitung* (independent), 20 September, 1961.
47. *Stuttgarter Zeitung* (independent), 20 September, 1961.

48. *Süddeutsche Zeitung* (Munich, left-center), 20 September, 1961.

49. *Ibid.*

50. *Frankfurter Allgemeine Zeitung* (right-center), 20 September, 1961.

51. *Kölnische Rundschau* (pro-CDU), 21 September, 1961.

52. *Frankfurter Rundschau* (left-center) and *Deutsche Zeitung* (Cologne, right-center), 21 September, 1961.

53. *Frankfurter Allgemeine Zeitung* (right-center), 21 September, 1961.

54. *Die Welt* (Hamburg, independent), 21 September, 1961.

55. Not even Adenauer's decision to operate with a minority cabinet if the FDP declined to join a coalition frightened Erich Mende, who on Wednesday repeated the unanimous decision of his 66 deputies not to enter a coalition cabinet under Dr. Adenauer.

56. *Kölnische Rundschau* (pro-CDU), 21 September, 1961.

57. *Deutsche Zeitung* (right-center), 21 September, 1961.

58. *Stuttgarter Nachrichten* (independent), 21 September, 1961.

59. *Stuttgarter Zeitung* (independent), 21 September, 1961.

60. *Frankfurter Allgemeine Zeitung* (right-center), 27 September, 1961.

61. *Neue Züricher Zeitung* (independent), 26 September, 1961; *Frankfurter Allgemeine Zeitung* (right-center), 26 September, 1961.

62. *Kölnische Rundschau* (pro-CDU); *Deutsche Zeitung* (Cologne, right-center) 26 September, 1961.

63. *Frankfurter Neue Presse* (right-center); *Deutsche Zeitung* (Cologne, right-center, 26 September, 1961.

64. *Die Welt* (Hamburg, independent), 26 September, 1961.

65. *Allgemeine Zeitung* (Mainz, independent), 26 September, 1961.

66. *Ibid.; Die Welt* (Hamburg, independent), 26 September, 1961.

67. *Stuttgarter Nachrichten* (independent); *Die Welt* (Hamburg, independ.), *Allgemeine Zeitung* (Mainz, independent) for 26 September, 1961.

68. *Abendpost* (Frankfurter tabloid, independent), 26 September, 1961.

69. *Bild Zeitung* (Hamburg, mass tabloid), 26 September, 1961.

70. *Der Mittag* (Düsseldorf, right-center), 26 September, 1961.
71. *Frankfurter Rundschau* (left-center), 26 September, 1961.
72. *Frankfurter Rundschau* (left-center), 26 September, 1961.
73. *The Bulletin:* Weekly Survey of German Affairs, issued by the Press and Information Office of the German Federal Republic, 17 October, 1961.
74. *Ibid.* (24 October), 1961.
75. *Ibid.*
76. *The Bulletin:* Weekly Survey of German Affairs (24 October, 1961).
77. *The Bulletin:* A Weekly Survey of German Affairs (24 October, 1961).
78. *Ibid.* (14 November, 1961.
79. *Das Parlament* (Bonn, independent), 15 November, 1961, 11 Jahrgang/Nr. 46, p. 1.
80. *The Bulletin:* A Weekly Survey of German Affairs (Bonn, independent), 14 November, 1961.
81. *The Bulletin* (Bonn, independent), 14 November, 1961.
82. *Ibid.* Cf. *Frankfurter Allgemeine* (right-center); *Münchener Merkur* (close to CDU) and *Hachener Volkszeitung* (close to CDU) 11 November, 1961.
83. Dr. Mende told the author in a personal interview in June, 1961 that he was forced to pursue a strong nationalist course in order to checkmate a trend toward extremist parties of the right.
84. *New York Times* (independent), 18 February, 1962.
85. For the best analysis of factors which explain the meteoric rise of Konrad Adenauer in postwar German politics, see Hans Speier, "Introduction: The German Political Scene," in Speier and Davidson, *West German Leadership and Foreign Policy,* p. 3. Compare Gerald Freund, *Germany Between Two Worlds,* pp. 54-57, 59-61; 65-66 and 69-73 for a more detailed analysis.

PART V.

PROTRACTED CONFLICT

Chapter 15

FOREIGN POLICY DEBATE IN BUNDESTAG
—7 DECEMBER 1961—

1. *West German Foreign Policy Objectives*

Having reviewed the momentous events in Berlin during the crucial week of August 13-20, 1961, the impact of the Berlin Wall upon the West German press, parties and public opinion, the parliamentary election itself and the tug-of-war over the Chancellorship, it now remains to discuss the first formal foreign policy debate. Officially this was referred to as the First Great Debate on Vital Questions before the Nation. An analysis of the replies of various party leaders to the Government Declaration will reveal points of difference as well as agreement on basic foreign policy objectives. The lack of sharp issues allowed for only subtle differences of interpretation or in methods of implementing basic foreign policy aims.

In view of the Communist-incited crisis over Berlin, the Adenauer-Kennedy talks of November 20-22, 1961, aroused great interest throughout West Germany and Berlin. Here again President and Chancellor reaffirmed the ultimate goal of their governments to achieve peace and freedom on the basis of self-determination. Above all they agreed that this objective could be realized without prejudice to the legitimate security interests of the Soviet Union and of Germany's eastern neighbors. President and Chancellor reaffirmed their belief in a united Europe and the need for aiding underdeveloped countries. In reply to

309

Soviet charges of the aggressive intentions of NATO, they re-affirmed its defensive nature and the complete integration of all West German defense capabilities into the multi-national NATO framework, meeting the resuirements of the UN Charter.[1]

Following von Brentano's resignation as Foreign Minister to become floor leader of the Bundestag fraction of the CDU/CSU, Dr. Adenauer appointed Gerhard Schroeder as his new Foreign Minister, to forestall Strauss's ambitions for the Foreign Office to the delight of the Adenauer loyalists in the CDU/CSU.[2] As the Crown Prince waiting in the wings to inherit Adenauer's mantle by succeeding Erhard, Strauss by his maneuvers to limit Adenauer's chancellorship to one or two years, had fallen out of grace with *Der Alte*. In an address to the National Press Club in Washington, D. C., on 22 November 1961, Herr Schroeder pointed out that the new German Government based on a coalition of parties, continued to uphold "old and tried principles" of West German foreign policy:

1. Maintenance of the close link with the free world and NATO;
2. continued efforts "for European integration in the economic and political sphere";
3. "Maintenance of our claim that the Germans in the Soviet-occupied part of our country, too, must be given the right of self-determination." [3]

Likewise on the touchy issues of the Eastern territories under Polish administration and "even de facto recognition" of the Soviet Zone of Germany, Schroeder reaffirmed the same stand the Bonn Government had taken prior to the parliamentary elections of 1961. During the battle for the Chancellorship (Bonn Inter-regnum) Adenauer and the CDU/CSU had insisted on the continuation of their old foreign policy as their minimum demand for a coalition with the Free Democratic Party (FDP).[4]

In a report to the *Bundestag* on the 29th of November 1961 the new Coalition Government outlined the policies it would follow during the four-year term of office, namely, close ties with the free peoples, world wide development aid without political strings and sacrifices to strengthen NATO. Moreover, in future East-West negotiations, the Government Declaration emphasized three unalterable principles: 1) German security, 2) strong ties between Bonn and Berlin and 3) reunification, non-recognition of the Soviet Zone regime and settlement of frontier questions in a peace treaty with an all-German Government.[5] New nations emerging in Africa were promised economic aid and German support for their aspirations. More specifically the Government Declaration reaffirmed:

1. The question of European security had no connection with the Berlin Crisis, but could be discussed only in connection with the restoration of German unity.
2. Rejection of regional security measures in Europe, since the principal demand of the West can only be fulfilled on global lines.
3. General and controlled disarmament, therefore, continues to be one of the supreme aims of German foreign policy.
4. The establishment of a NATO atomic force . . . is necessary to raise the defensive power of NATO to the same level of military technique as that of their opponent. The Federal Government has never made a demand for atomic weapons of its own.[6]

2. United Stand of Parties on Basic East-West Issues

Soon after Chancellor Adenauer's return from a visit to General de Gaulle in Paris the three Bundestag parties issued important pronouncements on crucial issues of foreign policy that faced the free world in general and Germany in particular. All three parties warned the free world that it could not afford a retreat in Berlin or Germany.

Mayor Brandt, speaking in behalf of the SPD in the debate of 6 December 1961 pointed out that the only immediate prospect of German reunification lay in the surrender of freedom in both West Berlin and West Germany. The sacrifice of individual freedom, however, was too high a price to pay for national unity. Despite the deadlock between German insistence on freedom and Communist insistence on partition, Brandt concluded that German reunification must remain high on foreign policy agenda. Moreover, the Bundestag would continue to uphold the consti-

311

tutional ties between Berlin and West Germany. Hence, Brandt maintained, there could be no isolated solution for Berlin.[7]

The second speaker in the Bundestag Debate was the Chairman of the CDU/CSU fraction, Dr. Heinrich von Brentano, who deplored UN silence on the German question, supported the Government Declaration for negotiations with the Soviets and, like Brandt, regarded an isolated solution for Berlin as unthinkable, lest it lead to a 3-way splitting of Germany. Hence, a final solution for the problem of East and West Berlin could only be found within the scope of the German problem as a whole. Brentano emphatically rejected discussing European security together with the Berlin question as absurd. "It is impossible to offer a decrease in the security of the Federal Republic as an object of exchange for Berlin." [8] Although Brentano noted that the CDU would welcome good relations with East European states, especially Poland, except for the fact that diplomatic relations were not advisable because Poland had expressed approval of the partition wall in Berlin. When Dr. von Brentano resigned his position as Minister of Foreign Affairs to become chairman of the CDU/CSU fraction in the Bundestag, he not only allayed criticism from his opponents in press and parliament, but won great respect and admiration from Germans of all classes. In parliament he could exert a more positive influence on the formation of policy, whereas in the foreign office his opportunity for leadership was restricted by critics inside and outside the foreign office, as well as by the Chancellor and his close advisors.

The chairman of the Free Democratic Party (FDP), Dr. Erich Mende, agreed with Brandt and von Brentano that all plans to solidify the partition of Germany by the separation of West Berlin from the Federal Republic were doomed to failure. Only if some *modus vivendi* between East and West Berlin could be found, might international tensions be relaxed to permit an approach to the far more difficult problems of Central Europe. Mende stated that the Free Democrats expected from the Bonn Government and its Allies a serious effort to gain the initiative in the German problem.[9]

3. Position of SPD Opposition on Government Declaration of 29 November 1961

Because of the serious international crisis over Berlin, Mayor Brandt (SPD) believed that all political and moral forces of the nation should be mobilized behind an all-party cabinet to make Berlin the intellectual and cultural center of Germany. Nevertheless, the SPD leader expressed the loyalty of the Social Democratic opposition to the new Government of Chancellor Adenauer, although it was not as broadly based a government as the SPD would have preferred to meet the national crisis over Berlin. Finally the SPD chairman welcomed the parts of the Government Declaration pertaining to the following:

1. Government aid for the underdeveloped countries.
2. Strengthened parliamentary cooperation and control in the European community, expanded to include England, Finland and Scandinavia.
3. Acceptance of the obligations of NATO so far as they are reasonable, meaningful and compatible with the treaty—with no German power of disposition over atomic weapons—as stipulated in the Declaration of the Fourth Adenauer Government.
4. There is no isolated Berlin solution. We welcome the long awaited guarantee of the three Western Powers for the vitality, security and freedom of West Berlin.
5. Relations between Berlin and the Federal Republic are a question of the political desire of the free Germans, as it is expressed in both the Federal Constitution and the Constitution of Berlin.
6. We are all interested in reaching a common basis for negotiations with the West. The West must adjust itself to the Soviet aim in order to end the isolation of the Federal Republic in world politics and a decisive weakening of the West in general—but not at the price of a foul compromise with the East.
7. We demand with the Government the end of the violation of law undertaken on 13 August 1961. The Wall must go.
8. Ulbricht, in order to perpetuate tensions in Central

Europe, under which all suffer, goes even further than the Soviet advised and allows all possible chicaneries.

9. Berlin must not and will not become a third state on German soil, with the Allied promise that no such agreement will be made against the will of the people concerned. Berlin has become the problem of all free Germans.[10]

Directing his attention to the implications of the sixth item above, Brandt argued that after 12 years the old reunification policy of the Federal Government was shattered because there was no conceivable price for German national unity except the sacrifice of freedom. In any case reunification had always meant more to Social Democrats than mere lip-service.[11] The Social Democratic Mayor of Berlin reminded West Germans that:

The thirteenth of August 1961 goes much deeper than the 17th of June 1953 (date of East German uprising, suppressed by Soviet Tanks) That is the tragic reality of our Nation, that we, the free Germans, must consider. We will preserve our freedom only when we are prepared to fight for the freedom of 17,000,000 Germans in the Soviet Zone and are ready to concentrate all our activities, wealth and economy, our civil courage and our friendship in the world for this cause.

The Federal Republic must become accustomed to an all-around view to which Berlin was forced for years. For we can not ignore the fact that we are neighbors of the Communistic East and will remain such. Above all we dare not turn our backs on our countrymen. . . . Lethargic inactivity will never stop a dictatorship from making new demands. The remains of the old reunification policy must not lead to frivolous reproaches against our friends in the Western world.[12]

To confirm his thesis Brandt reminded the Bundestag that President Kennedy in his interview with *Izvestia* rightly declared that German reunification could not be achieved against the desires of the USSR. From this it would follow that in order to achieve reunification, we Germans would have to improve our relations with the Soviet Union. In view of the international situation that seemed impossible. Nevertheless, Mayor Brandt noted that we ourselves are certainly agreed on this:

> that we conceive of no one as a friend of the German people whose policy enslaves our countrymen over there and prevents our political reunification. . . . The present crisis makes our primary task to come to an understanding with the great Power of the East, which, in complete harmony with our Allies in the West, leads us nearer to a solution of the German question on the basis of the right of self-determination and thus facilitates the interests of both sides in normalizing relations.[13]

The Social Democratic Chairman criticized the Government Declaration for giving undue weight to military considerations without a political counterweight. Instead Social Democrats would have preferred to hear frank and if possible friendly words directed towards some future accommodation with the neighboring states in the East. Brandt won the applause of the entire house when he declared that the Social Democratic opposition in the Bundestag stood at the head of those who were against the Soviet campaign of vituperation, directed against West Germans as if they had been or may be revanchist, war-mongering or neo-Nazi. Although this was not true, it was all part of a deliberate Communist campaign not only to discredit the Federal Republic but also to destroy the very foundations of democracy. In short Brandt maintained that the Federal Republic of Germany must be prepared to make its own contribution to principles of a peace treaty—contributions which result from its own love of peace and that of its people. On this score the Social Democratic leader contended that heretofore the Federal Republic had played no important role. It will now be relentless in developing German ideas on the problem of armament reduction and controls—but above all in working out principles of a peace treaty. If only the Federal Republic had heretofore taken the right of self-determination as its point of departure, the inevitable result would have been "to formulate our internal affairs and our legitimate security needs in harmony with the interests of all our neighbors."[13]

As if to underline the vital importance of positive ideas for a peace treaty to be put forth by both the West and Bonn— ideas which would not only relax tensions in central Europe and counter Soviet proposals, which misuse the word *peace* and, therefore, only worsen international tensions—Brandt concluded that with such a policy we not only could relieve the anxiety of our friends, but win new friends.[14] In order to clarify and strengthen his position, the Berlin Bürgermeister cited the Berlin Resolution of 1 October 1958 and the Declaration of Bundestag President Eugen Gerstenmaier on 30 June 1961. The first part of the latter document bears quoting:

This is the twentieth anniversary of the German attack on Soviet Russia in the decisive phase of World War II (22 June 1941). I understand very well, therefore, that the Russian people recalls with great bitterness these tragic events which caused such a heavy sacrifice and severe loss. There is no one in this parliamentary house who does not look back with grief and sorrow on this misfortune, which the war of Hitler has brought upon the people of the East. I am sure that I speak for all intelligent and rational persons in the entire German nation when I say that we are prepared to do all in our power to overcome the effects of this tragedy and to establish a new relationship between Germany and her neighbors in the East.

We thank God that, after so much blood and tears, we live not only in peaceful, but also friendly relations with France and other nations of the free world. . . . We would be glad for a similar relationship with our neighbors to the East and Southeast as well, for we believe that world peace is so precious a commodity that it should be based not only on systems of alliance and the deterrence of weapons, but on the feeling of peace and good will.[15]

Dr. Gerstenmaier, in this same Declaration of 30 June 1961 referred to an evil catastrophic error—that is, the idea that the security of Europe or at the least of Germany's eastern neighbors would be best guaranteed by the partition of Germany—an error perpetuated not only on Moscow, Warsaw and Prague, but also prevalent West of the iron curtain. Gerstenmaier stated:

The history of the last fifteen years fully demonstrated that the division of Germany was not only a misfortune for the German people, but that it had become a perennial cause of disturbance in international politics. Meanwhile it had grown into a shocking threat to world peace.

Certainly the partition of Germany is in the last analysis the result of Hitler's attack on Russia. But even so, it is equally clear that the German is not responsible for the fact that this result was not in the meantime overcome. We were and still are prepared to give every guarantee that the German people, united and freed by a just regulation of its vital needs, would be a reliable partner of all its neighbors in East and West, North and South.[16]

This historic declaration had the support of all parties— CDU/CSU, FDP and SPD and throughout the campaign both Dr. Erich Mende and Dr. Thomas Dehler (Chairman and former Chairman of the FDP) referred to it as a practical basis for a coalition agreement between the CDU/CSU and FDP. Mayor Brandt expressed the belief that the Government Declaration of Chancellor Adenauer, presented to the Bundestag by Vice Chancellor Ludwig Erhard, in many ways fell far behind Bundestag President Gerstenmaier's Declaration of 30 June 1961.

On the other hand, the fraction chairman of the SPD expressed agreement with the government parties when he stated that the question of the Eastern frontiers could only be determined in a peace treaty with an all-German Government. Mayor Brandt repeated his warning that we dare make no policy without consideration for the views of the millions of German refugees expelled from their homes in the Soviet Zone or the territories east of the Oder-Neisse line.[17] Thus the three major parties, represented in the Bundestag, took a united stand on the main goals and objectives of foreign policy: eventual reunification, the right of self-determination and non-recogni-

317

tion of the Soviet Zone regime and of the Oder-Neisse line. No important German politician would dare renounce any of these general objectives of German foreign policy, regardless of how remote their attainment might appear to more realistic persons, including Germans. Thus the hard facts of Germany's geographic location, in the heart of the East-West conflict limit and restrain German politicians, leaving them little room to maneuver.

This point had been emphatically driven home to General Clay in late September, 1961, when he was reported to have suggested at a cocktail party that West Germans might eventually have to recognize the results of World War II and make concessions on the status of Berlin, give *de facto* recognition to the Soviet Zone regime and accept the Oder-Neisse line.

4. *Statement of Von Brentano (CDU/CSU)*

Von Brentano observed that the CDU/CSU fraction approved and consented to the Declaration of 29 November 1961 in which the new Government placed its program before the fourth German Bundestag. While aware of the need for any coalition government to compose differences over issues of internal and external policy, the CDU/CSU fraction at the same time recognized that the cabinet bears responsibility to the entire parliament and in turn to the whole German people. In reply to questions over the much discussed coalition agreement between the CDU/CSU and FDP, von Brentano replied that it was not a state secret, but merely a type of agreement which was common between coalition parties on both the state and federal level. Like the SPD leader, Brandt, von Brentano emphasized the freedom of Christian Democratic deputies to vote independently, free of any party discipline. Moreover, all deputies, whether in the government coalition or the opposition had a mandate from the individual voters and together represented the entire German nation, both in the part of the German Fatherland where freedom could be re-established and in that part of the Fatherland where a one-party totalitarian system still denied the opposition parties the right to perform their normal function.[18]

Von Brentano took issue with Brandt on the idea of an all-party cabinet, strongly advocated by the SPD opposition. First, the CDU/CSU Chairman posed the question whether or not

318

the serious international crisis might force political parties to sacrifice the lively and fruitful exchange between majority and minority, between Government and Opposition in the interest of a United Front to overcome more difficult political problems. Brentano expressed the hope that this decision would be reserved for a really serious danger. Rather the responsibility on all parties was already so great that they should demonstrate the highest degree of cooperation on vital issues facing the German people. Finally von Brentano appealed in behalf of the Government and his political friends to declare that in the practical work of Parliament they were prepared to do everything to show their complete confidence in cooperation with the opposition.

In the course of his comments on the Government Declaration, von Brentano chose to emphasize the following items:

1. In the midst of many proposals and plans for the Berlin and German questions, the Government—in contrast to the Opposition—was consistently concerned with contributing to the defense of the free world, including the defense of Berlin, which is and should be a part of the free world.

2. Germans are embittered that the great UN Organization becomes involved in long discussions over deplorable disorders in other parts of the world and that this organization is equally obligated to preserve peace and freedom in all parts of the world; but is silent on the German problem.

3. Despite the discussion of colonialism in the UN, no stand was taken against the most brutal form of neo-colonialism in our time. It remained for the U.S. delegate, Adlai Stevenson, to demonstrate in an outstanding paper, with what methods the Communist Bloc suppresses freedom and human rights.

4. We are most grateful to the United States and to our many friends in the world: our Allies, the states of Latin-America and the Afro-Asian realm, who have in past months referred to this unparalleled suppression of people in the Communist-ruled realm and especially in Germany.

5. It is not good that the UN is not concerned that over

in the Soviet Zone of Occupation live 16,000,000 German people, who have the same right to live in freedom as we in the Federal Republic and hundreds of millions of men in other nations of the free world.

6. The Government Declaration in its analysis of Soviet objectives pointed out that an attack on Berlin was an attack on Germany. Therefore, the Federal Government has rightly declared that the question of European security must not be discussed in connection with the Berlin Crisis.

7. We have always taken the position that the question of European security can only be discussed in connection with the problem of the re-establishment of German unity—a position represented in the peace plan of 1959.

8. The stronger we in the European Community and the Atlantic Community become, the stronger is our common capacity, which we build up not in order to make war, but rather in order to be able to prevent it.[19]

Both Mayor Brandt (SPD) and von Brentano (CDU/CSU) referred to the need to develop a genuine spirit of sacrifice in the German people, which in turn called for more political consciousness, an awareness on the part of people of their relation to the whole political community. Von Brentano raised the question whether it was not the task of our pluralistic society to develop in the realm of adult education and particularly the youth movement a universally valid kind of humanitarianism. He pointed to a certain political weariness and political frustration which had frequently weakened efforts toward practical and worthwhile ideals. This directly concerned the rising generation. First of all, German youth had a sober mental attitude toward its environment. This, Brentano believed, should be encouraged, for with such an attitude these people would be conditioned against demagogic enticement and also against nationalistic seduction. "But we must be clear about this," he insisted, "that even this younger generation has still found no substantial foundation for its obligations to the state and to society." [20] The CDU/CSU Chairman recalled how in the time of the Third Reich under Hitler the rebellious mind of German Youth was so shamelessly misused and how much of it had been led into an insoluble conflict between duty and conscience. Many were broken by this and many had suffered spiritual defects and deformities from this and even to this day have not recovered. "Others object that for a part of the Fatherland there is no national feeling nor feeling of patriotism. They do not know—or do not wish to know—that the German who loves his country and his freedom is joined in this feeling by millions in the Soviet Zone, who only await the hour when they will also dare to express it." [21] Von Brentano informed the Bundestag that he had no intention of appealing to nationalistic instincts or overemphasizing feeling; but he continued his discussion of the need for political consciousness with an analysis of freedom: which is worth quoting:

> Freedom is a question of responsibility for the whole. We believe that responsibility is borne only by one who consciously lives in freedom. But freedom, so I believe, is not a concept of public law. Freedom is a moral postulate. The state can and must, through the Constitution and law, create and maintain conditions so that men can live in freedom. But it can not define the concept of freedom and it can not negotiate freedom.

> It can only designate the outer limits of the sphere of freedom within which the individual must be concerned with his own responsibility and limitations which lie where the freedom of others or the legitimate interests of the community are concerned.

> Because we believe that freedom is a moral concept, we reject unconditional freedom, the boundless individualism, whose use or misuse leads to anarchy. Likewise the civic freedom of the individual man needs the moral corollary.

> Naturally, therefore, we reject every kind of collectivist freedom which pretends to make man free, whereas it actually leads to tyranny. . . . We are convinced that politics and *Weltanschauung* (world outlook) must not be separated, but joined together and we believe that the

321

moral foundation, which determines political thinking and activity must rest upon the obligatory traditions of Christian thinking.[22]

With respect to German foreign policy, von Brentano noted that its basic goal was to end the forced partition of Germany and to unite the nation. However, the spokesman for the government party recognized that the Bonn Government could never accomplish this task alone. In the Paris Treaties and in various declarations of the Federal Government and of the Bundestag, just as in many declarations of the Western Allies in sessions of the Ministerial Council of NATO or of the West European Union, forcible means were always explicitly and necessarily rejected.

Hence, it was concluded that the victorious Powers in World War II in negotiations would together find a way to end the unjust partition of Germany, whose continued existence endangered peace in the whole world. Although von Brentano admitted that German hopes had not yet been fulfilled, he took issue with Mayor Brandt, who had argued that the Federal Government's unification policy, pursued for 12 years, was shattered. The CDU/CSU Chairman challenged anyone in the Bundestag to reproach Germany's Western Allies for not having made every effort to settle the German question by negotiations with the Soviet Union, which for 12 years had answered all these various offers and proposals with a rigid No.

Both major parties, throughout this first debate of the fourth German Bundestag, showed a deep concern over the methods for achieving or attempting to achieve reunification. In any case both parties were completely determined to permit no far-reaching change in the status of Berlin—a change which could prove disastrous to this outpost of the Western world. Whereas the Free Democrats in February, 1956, under Thomas Dehler pulled out of the Government Coalition over differences of foreign policy, the Social Democratic Party both in its Bad-Godesberg program of 1960 and in the foreign policy debate in parliament on 30 June 1961 moved closer to the position of the governing CDU/CSU party of Adenauer.

5. *Statement of Erich Mende (FDP)*

To understand the full import of the remarks of the FDP Chairman in the debate of 7 December 1961, it is essential to review the high points of the recent history of the Free Democratic Party. Formed in 1945 from remnants of old German liberal parties, the FDP attracted both liberal and conservative forces. Its main sociological strength came from Protestant, urban middle classes: professions, trades, small and medium-sized industries. Without influence among manual workers and rural voters, its 12.7 per cent of the total vote polled in 1961 showed wide geographic distribution.[23]

Fear of an unduly powerful CDU is strong in the Rhine-Ruhr where conservative financial interests are aware of elements in the CDU fraction that after Adenauer's death might align with the SPD. The conservative wing of the FDP in the Rhine-Ruhr, Lower Saxony and Schleswig-Holstein is balanced by a Left-wing group of old-style German liberals, led by Reinhold Maier, which is strong in Hamburg and in southwest Germany. The official party position reflects the middle-of-the-road point of view.[24]

The views of German business are reflected in those FDP deputies who mistrust Adenauer's pro-Western orientation and consider themselves the guardians of German national interests. They insist that those interests should not be forfeited by sacrificing to the West and burning bridges to the East. In January 1958 Erich Mende berated the Adenauer Government for its failure to give serious consideration to any of the various plans for disengagement, as proposed by Anthony Eden, Hugh Gaitskell, the Polish Foreign Minister, Rapacki and by George Kennan. He then pointed to the offer of Soviet Minister President Bulganin in a note of December 1957 to reduce Russian troops in Germany or to withdraw them completely in proportion to withdrawals by the NATO Powers—France, Great Britain and the United States.[25]

At its March 1961 Convention the FDP still held to its policy of disengagement, stronger efforts to negotiate reunification, regard for the military factor as only a means of foreign policy and support of NATO only until after Germany's reunification when her future geographic, military and political status could be geared to a broad European system of mutual guarantees.[26]

However, the chances of implementation of such foreign policy objectives of the FDP are limited by a number of factors:

1) Loss of all financial support from German industry between 1956 and 1959 after FDP threats to align with either the CDU/CSU or the SPD;

2) Concentration of powerful groups of domestic economic interests, balanced and mutually reinforced by the skillful tactics of Konrad Adenauer;

3) Steady retreat of the FDP from its arbitrary stand against Adenauer in the parliamentary selections of 1961, cavalier treatment by Adenauer and the resulting tensions within the FDP;

4) Powerful economic forces, creating a steady trend towards a two-plus party system, unless checked by overriding issues of foreign policy;

5) Possibility that Right-wing elements in the CDU that switched from Adenauer in 1961 to the FDP might return to the CDU.

The above factors help to explain why the Free Democratic Party finally agreed to form a coalition with the CDU/CSU despite its failure to displace Konrad Adenauer as Chancellor, to negotiate or enforce an effective coalition contract or to effect any immediate change in Adenauer's foreign policy objectives. Of the utmost significance in the FDP Chairman's statement on behalf of his party was the emphasis he gave to President Kennedy's views on the problem of normalizing life in both parts of Berlin:

> The American President, Kennedy, in his interview with the Soviet Government paper, *Izvestia*, limited the first aim of negotiations in the coming East-West Conference over Berlin to an assurance from the Soviet Union that the Western Powers be allowed their rights in West Berlin by virtue of existing Four-Power agreements and be guaranteed freedom of access to and from the city.

> "The only thing we desire," said President Kennedy, "is the maintenance of limited—and of course numerically *very* limited—military forces of the three Powers in West Berlin and for instance an International Administration for the Autobahn so that persons and goods could come

in and out without interference. Then we could secure peace in this area for many years." [28]

The above quotation is most significant because within six months the suggestion of an International Administration for the Autobahn, consisting of representatives of 13 European States, including East and West Germany, caused a temporary crisis in relations between Washington and Bonn, after the proposal was "leaked" to the West German press through the indiscretion of some West German official.[29] Dr. Mende expressed his belief that "We Germans—as obviously also the Americans—could consider such conversations over Berlin as merely preliminary negotiations, which must as soon as possible be combined with the principal negotiations over the questions of "Germany," and "European security." [30] The proximity of Mende's position to that of Kennedy and MacMillan in urging East-West negotiations on a broad basis in contrast to the Adenauer-De Gaulle formula for resisting both Soviet and Western pressures to negotiate is better understood in the light of Dr. Mende's refusal to accept any Cabinet position himself in the new coalition between the FDP and CDU/CSU. Mende preferred to maintain his freedom to criticize the Coalition Government his party had entered even though publicly rebuked for this by Chancellor Adenauer.

The FDP Chairman supported the Federal Government in warning that the present unnatural partition of the German nation could only worsen international tensions and militated against any hope of peace or security in Europe. Mende clinched his argument when he concluded that it was necessary to emphasize this state of affairs in Europe in order to counteract those voices both in Germany and abroad which equated the just demand of our people for political unity and the ending of slavery for 17,000,000 Germans in the Soviet Zone with national, nationalistic, German-national or even pan-German irredentism.[31] He further argued that the partition of Germany was entirely incompatible with the UN Charter, with the first Declaration of the United Nations on 1 January 1942, the Declaration of the Allies at the Yalta Conference of 12 February 1945 and with the UN Assembly Resolution of 14 December 1960, passed by a large majority, in which the claim to self-determination and free,

325

secret elections for all nations, victor and vanquished of World War II was made a legally binding right. In the remainder of his parliamentary address, Dr. Mende renounced the use of force by the Germans and their Allies, peaceful competition of intellect as well as of the social-economic systems of East and West.

Finally Mende found a useful point of departure for serious East-West negotiations in the Four-Power Declaration of 23 July 1955 and the Herter package plan of 1959, if adapted to the latest advances in international politics and military technology. The basic element in all these recent proposals was the close relation between the German problem and that of European security. The CDU/CSU party in contrast placed a priority on German reunification before any serious consideration of East-West negotiations. Mende not only found the shameful wall of Berlin an act of inhumanity and a new blow against German national unity, but an admission of the superiority of Western Capitalism to Eastern totalitarian Communism. Hence, he had to reject Khrushchev's offer of "peaceful co-existence" as unrealistic and dangerous.

Dr. Mende's remaining remarks were mainly concerned with less crucial but yet important issues of internal politics: economic, social and cultural policy, liberalism and trade unions and a new orientation of agriculture. He justified the decision of his party to form a coalition with the CDU/CSU on the basis of the need of parliamentary democracy for a parliamentary opposition in contrast to an All-Party Government, strongly favored by Social Democrats. Although the international crisis obligated all political forces in Germany to cooperate in vital questions effecting the nation, this cooperation need not mean that all parties in the Bundestag must bear a joint responsibility of government. "An All-Party Government can never be the rule; it must be the exception. A government without an opposition in a parliamentary democracy is only justified in unusual circumstances." [32] Amid shouts of protest from the SPD opposition Mende continued:

> This would above all be valid for a case of defense, which we hope will not occur, just as for other possible phases of immediate threat to life, limb or property. (Renewed shouts of the SPD) An all-party government now, Gentle-

men of the Opposition, would have meant that we ourselves would have increased the scale of a possible reaction
to the already increased tensions. Hence, we would have
run the risk of having contributed to a dramatization of
the present doubtless serious international crisis, which
could actually become still more dangerous in the future.
[Rep. Mattick (SPD): Unheard of!]

Herr Colleague Mattick, that is no underestimation of
the Wall; but over the Wall there is a still far more
dangerous development, which only under very extraordinary circumstances should be taken into account. In internal politics an All-Party Government would eventually
lead to a neutralization of economic, social and political
forces. Such a government would finally be paralyzed by
discussion at the moment the crisis had ended and with
this, the reason for its existence. . . . Who would then
undertake the role of opposition? [33]

The FDP Chairman concluded by stating that the coalition negotiations (seven-week interregnum) between the CDU/CSU and
FDP were the subject of severe criticism. However, he maintained
that the Free Democrats in the Bundestag held a key position
between the Christian Democrats and the Social Democrats. They
are aware of their great responsibility in this position before
the whole German nation. It was, therefore, the wish and desire
of the Free Democrats to work together in a loyal partnership
with the CDU/CSU in the joint responsibility of Government.
"Likewise, it is our intention to strive for harmony among all
three parties in the Bundestag in the fateful questions before our
nation. Our relation to the SPD opposition will to the same
degree, therefore, be animated by the desire and the will to place
above parties our Common German Fatherland. . . . We Free
Democrats place our decisions and our work in the Fourth Federal Government before the judgment of history." [34]

6. Final Rebuttal Arguments in Bundestag Debate of 7 December 1961

Having analyzed the pronouncements of the Chairmen of
each of the three parties in the Fourth German Parliament, it

now remains to summarize the main rebuttal arguments put forth by key leaders, noted for their skill in polemics, repartee and parliamentary strategy. Erich Ollenhauer, Chairman of the Bundestag fraction of the Social Democratic Party since the death of Kurt Schumacher, summarized the position of the SPD, emphasizing the following points:

1. It can not be denied that influential West German institutions and leading newspapers after 17 September 1961 (parliamentary elections) had repeatedly urged the Free Democrats not to prevent the formation of a bourgeois government by the refusal to form a coalition with the CDU/CSU party.
2. The decisive historical fact was that a government was formed without Social Democracy, thus excluding 11½ million voters, over 36 per cent, who on 17 September 1961 decided in favor of the Social Democratic Party.
3. This Government both in its historical origins and actions is a government without and against Social Democracy. However, we do not wish to assume that no other solution would have been possible.
4. If in West Germany normal democratic principles had prevailed, the answer to the election results would have been that both previous opposition parties (SPD and FDP), which together would have still commanded a majority, would have made an effort to form a coalition. That did not happen and for that the Free Democratic Party must answer.
5. Many Germans know that the CDU/CSU-FDP coalition under the conditions of internal politics and foreign policy was certainly not the most fortunate solution—and no solution which corresponds to the vital interests of our people.
6. The present Government therefore does not correspond to the ideas of Social Democracy and above all to the extraordinary circumstances under which we now and in the immediate future will have to work and live.[35]

As the spokesman of the loyal opposition, Ollenhauer offered to respect the wish of the Government in the coming difficult negotiations not to be burdened by public parliamentary debates, which under the circumstances could limit its freedom to maneuver. At the same time the SPD Chairman could not suppress apprehensions of his party over the course of negotiations and in the name of his party expressed a desire to be informed of the leading discussions of the Federal Government in the coming international negotiations in the appropriate parliamentary committee [36] and to work with it with complete knowledge of the state of affairs at the time of final decisions. Otherwise the reference in the Government Declaration to "common responsibility" would amount to nothing more than a mere declamation. Amid applause from both the SPD oppositions and government parties, Ollenhauer warned the Bundestag never to forget in the weeks and months ahead that in our relations with Berlin and the whole German question and reunification, decisions should be made not on the basis of political expediency or party tactics, but rather in accordance with our obligations to the Constitution.

Fritz Erler, foreign expert of the SPD, speaking on behalf of his party, stated that discussions between the Government, government parties and opposition were the salt of democracy. In fact, he argued, it would be a very poor opposition which by its critical objections would not force the majority parties and also the Government constantly to re-examine the justification for its position. Hence, the importance of parliamentary debate, even though the group not in possession of the information of the government would be at a great disadvantage. Parliament, he said, should be a model for the nation—not as an executive organ of government, but rather as a counterbalance not only to the majority party, but against the Government itself, in order to preserve the freedom and independence both of the legislature and the people outside, who were not *subjects,* but *citizens* with rights and obligations. The SPD spokesman regretted that the young German democracy lacked the long history and traditions of thriving democracies in many other European and overseas lands. Hence, Germans still had much to make up for and would have to test the ground under their feet. Both Erler (SPD) and Von Brentano (CDU/CSU) had noted that the political consciousness of the younger generation was not as developed as it should be to realize that Berlin and the Soviet Zone were also Germany. Every young man must and can know that what West Germans do affects not only the free part of Germany, but all of the German people and the whole German Fatherland.

Defense of Berlin, Germany and the West in the view of Social Democrats was more than merely a military problem of making NATO the fourth atomic power. Erler reminded the Bundestag that Willy Brandt had urged all Germans to form a United Front if Soviet politicians and their East German comrades tried to defame the German people and the West German Republic as an affair of revanchists, militarists and war-mongers. Above all, Brandt emphasized that Germans after the bitter experiences of their recent history were permitted the insight of no other people in order to realize what a military conflict would mean even for us and for our capital city, but at the same time to realize that the love of peace is part of a determination to preserve freedom against any outside threats and to help restore freedom to East Germans now under foreign rule.

Erler regretted the meager statement in the Government Declaration on the significant world problem of controlled disarmament and limitation of armaments. After conversations with many, many Europeans, Erler warned that other Europeans expected much more than mere general support of controlled disarmament, but rather to bring pressure through original thought and literature to overcome the power wielded by a few men in government offices. For instance the formula, which had appeared in the Government Declaration, used the hard words of Defense Minister Strauss, who, when in the United States had urged the Allies to make NATO a fourth atomic power. This would only give nourishment to Communist propaganda against us, which unfortunately also capitalized on the somewhat frivolous utterances of the Chancellor in the campaign, who failed to distinguish between atomic weapons and their carriers.[37]

The SPD spokesman pointed out that defense problems were not immune to the requirements of parliamentary discussion in quest of the best solution particularly in times of crisis. Yet only nine days after the Berlin Wall (13 August 1961), Erler had requested the parliamentary Defense Committee for a report of the Foreign Ministers Conference in Paris just after the erection of the Wall. Although the Foreign Affairs Minister, von Brentano, was perfectly willing to report to the parliamentary committee, he was not permitted to do so.

As foreign affairs expert of the SPD, Erler noted several other differences between the Government and his party: handling of the Berlin question in the UN and the connection between the Berlin question and European security. Von Brentano had warned against connecting the Berlin question with that of European security, whereas Erler contended that the Berlin question was deeply imbedded in the German question and therefore in the question of European security. Pointing out the interrelation of all three questions, as set forth by NATO in December, 1958, immediately after the proposals of the Russian ultimatum, Erler concluded that it was well that the Bundestag in the past had always emphasized the inextricable connection between Berlin, the all-German question and the problem of over-all European security. The SPD spokesman indicated he had no reliable information on the handling of the Berlin question in the UN. He had merely noted that Mayor Brandt was heavily attacked for bringing the Berlin problem before the UN because of the violation of human rights. Brandt then volunteered the information that the Foreign Ministers Conference had reached a deadlock over this question. Brandt also stated that the Bonn Government had set itself strongly against a proposal to discuss the violation of human rights in Berlin in the United Nations against all considerations of the Americans.

The Federal Government according to its Declaration would concentrate all its efforts for bringing about a peace treaty. This, Erler stated, leaves open a whole chapter. How? What preparation was being made? Was a coalition treaty envisioned or not? Like Bundestag President Gerstenmaier and Brandt earlier, Erler noted that, in view of the growing European community, it was fitting that the foreign policy of the Federal Republic should not be limited merely to concern about matters in which Germans are passionately interested.

Social Democrats were most pleased with Bonn support for Great Britain's entrance into the Common Market and urged all continental partners to act not only to remove any barriers to Britain's economic cooperation, but at the same time to work for political cooperation. Trying to separate the two, Erler maintained, would be disastrous, particularly for defense problems. Above all the impact of the thriving democracies of Great Britain and several Scandinavian countries would be most wholesome for the whole political climate within the European community. Erler also recommended showing consideration for the plans of our French friends to strengthen the institutions of the European community. Erler continued:

> It would be worthwhile to reduce the Executive and to take care that it be counter-balanced by a functioning parliamentary control. The parliament has a vast integrating function. The work of our socialist fraction illustrates this and perhaps we will reach the point where a parliament, also chosen by direct election of the representatives, will be bound closely with our people.

> Then it will come about that the European communities will be communities of peoples and not merely organized bureaucracies. It is important, therefore, that the West German Federal Government clarify the German viewpoint in this area and that Parliament be informed.[38]

With this Fritz Erler (SPD) concluded his review of German internal and foreign policy. He then added a word in reply to von Brentano's statement that the moral principles, so vital to parliamentary democracy must be based on strong traditions of Christian thinking.

In the period of persecution by the National Socialist dictatorship Christians of both confessions, Catholic and Protestant, found themselves together and thus prepared the way for their later union (CDU). Erler then recalled that on 15 September 1939 that he along, with a Protestant clergyman, was sentenced to ten years imprisonment by the People's Court of Berlin for working against Hitler. Erler agreed that Christians of all denominations suffered from Nazi persecution, but in the resistance against the *Third Reich* and in the work for a new Germany were found both Christians and non-Christians. Since there were various forces in democratic Germany, it could not be assumed that all Christians somehow were to be found in one party. On the contrary, Erler concluded that for the sake of moral principles, Christianity was not obligated toward the building of any particular social order; rather there were conservative, liberal and social democratic Christians. Erler wanted to avoid a false emphasis when he maintained that Christians work as the salt of the earth in various political parties. "For as soon as Christians are all found in one party in a nation with our tradition, essentially stamped by Christianity, there would again be a One-Party State, which none of us would want." [39] Thereupon, Erler concluded his warning observation from his own personal experience in both the Weimar and Hitler periods because he was convinced that the Bonn Democracy needed a strong manifestation of work and devotion by Christians in all democratic parties.

7. Dynamic Political Forces

Social Democracy in Germany is a tradition with millions of workers, intellectuals and a way of life dating back to Karl Marx and the revolution of 1848. After the discouraging defeat of the Liberals and Democrats in 1848/49 the German middle class generally cooperated with reactionary and imperial forces. Unlike the liberal, progressive governments of Western Europe, the pre-1914 Governments of Germany, Austria-Hungary and Russia geared foreign and domestic politics to the interests of the army, the Church and the landed aristocracy. In consequence the Social Democratic Party always had to bear a double burden of supporting both liberal-democratic and socialist policies.

It is an axiom that a nation's social structure and internal political processes affect the reliability of its foreign policy. It is, therefore, essential to study and analyze the current development of democracy in West Germany as well as the dynamic forces in East Germany (*Mittel Deutschland*). Germans regardless of party, whether Right, Left or Center agree that the key problems are the partition of their nation and its reunification in peace and freedom. But these German problems are closely bound up with other issues: such as "relaxation of East-West tensions," regulation of armaments, the safety of Berlin, European security and the relation between Berlin, the all-German question and the problem of European security.

The United States, because of her powerful position in world affairs since World War II, finds herself involved in the contemporary German problem. In general Americans, many of whom have only recently become cognizant of its complexities, find numerous aspects of German history and political development unintelligible. This is particularly true when these complexities are expressed in the various and often conflicting pronouncements of propagandists for the East and West Germans, the administration and opposition parties in West Germany, the Free Democrats and Social Democrats, the German Party and the Refugee Bloc, the internationalists, neutralists and nationalists and finally the outlawed Neo-Nazis and West German Communists.

The multi-party system, with its major and minor parties, splits and realignments, has also proved confusing to Americans. Notwithstanding the increasing evidence in contemporary Germany of a trend toward a two-party or two-plus party system, the roots of German development lie deep in the past. Unlike American political parties, German parties are steeped in ideologies, past traditions and differences of class, religion and geography.[40] Recent studies, such as those of Professor Merkl, purporting to show that the merging of powerful ecomic forces, skillfully balanced by the astute leadership of Konrad Adenauer constitute only one basic factor—the economic.[41] The opposite thesis, to which this writer holds, is that which emphasizes other factors—religious, social and cultural, ideological and intrenched patterns of the past. Apart from the equilibrium of forces of powerful economic groups, Adenauer's success as "honest broker" of these forces was in no small measure due to his ability to marshal support from the southwest regions of Germany in contrast to the central, eastern and northeastern old colonial regions, untouched by Roman Civilization and less influenced by the Renaissance. Moreover, the remarkable fact about German voters except for the refugees in the early fifties was the orderly and consistent way in which they voted their class or religious interests in normal times.[42] For instance the combined vote of Socialists and Communists in the total vote remained about the same in the national elections of 1912, 1928, 1949 and 1961—about 36 per cent. Only in July, 1962 did the SPD in North-Rhine-Westphalia succeed in polling over 40 per cent by bourgeois appeals for prosperity, moderate reform and NATO.

334

1. *The Bulletin* (Bonn, pro-government), 28 November 1961, IX, 1-2.

2. Peter Merkl, "Equilibrium, Structure of Interests and Leadership: Adenauer's Survival as Chancellor," *American Political Science Review*, LVI (September, 1962), No. 3, 641-2.

3. *The Bulletin* (Bonn, pro-goverment), 28 November 1961, IX, 3.

4. Despite the impressive gains of the FDP from 7.7 to 12.7 per cent of the vote, the position of the FDP gradually weakened during seven weeks of negotiations on the issues of: 1) Adenauer's continuation as Chancellor, 2) coalition policy and the FDP share in cabinet portfolios, 3) the coalition contract between the two parties. At the height of the crisis Professor Theodor Heuss and Reinhold Maier, two former chairmen of the FDP, gave their support to the decision of the Main Committee of the party to enter a coalition with the CDU/CSU despite all campaign promises to the contrary. See Peter Merkl, *loc. cit.*, p. 646.

5. *The Bulletin* (Bonn, pro-Govt.), 5 December 1961, IX, 1.

6. *Ibid.*, p. 2.

7. *The Bulletin* (Bonn pro-Government), 12 December 1962), IX, 1.

8. *Ibid.*, p. 2.

9. *The Bulletin* (Bonn, pro-government), 12 December 1962, IX, 2.

10. Der erste grosse Debatte: der 4 Bundestag zu den Lebensfragen der Nation," in *Das Parlament* (Bonn, independent), 13 December 1961, p. 1 ff.

11. *Das Parlament* (Bonn, independent), 13 December 1961, p. 1. Applause from the Free Democrats and center benches.

12. *Ibid.*

13. *Das Parlament* (Bonn, independent), 13 December 1961.

14. *Ibid.*

15. Deutscher Bundestag: *Sperrfrist:* 30 June 1961. 15 Uhr, bzw. Ende der Plenersitzung.

16. *Ibid.*

17. *Das Parlament* (Bonn, independent), 13 December 1961.

18. *Das Parlament* (Bonn, independent), 13 December 1961, p. 3.

19. *Das Parlament* (Bonn, independent), 13 December 1962, 11 Jahrgang, Nr. 50, p. 5.
20. *Das Parlament* (Bonn, independent), 13 December 1961, p .4.
21. *Ibid.*
22. *Das Parlament* (Bonn, independent), 13 December 1961, 11 Jahrgang/p. 4.
23. For further details on FDP and its role see John W. Keller, "Current German Political Scene," in *Current History*, XXXVIII, 221 (January, 1960), 35-36; reprinted as Chapter 2 in this work.
24. Gabriel Almond, "The Politics of German Business," in ans Speier and W. Phillips Davidson, *West German Leadership and Foreign Policy* (1957), 209.
25. *Das Parlament*, VIII, 4 (29 January 1958), 3.
26. *Ordentlicher Bundesparteitag der FDP*, 23/25 März 1961 in Frankfurt/Main (Bundesparteileitung der FDP, Bonn, date omitted), XII, 20-23 ff.
27. Peter Merkl, loc. cit., 644-49.
28. *Das Parlament* (13 December 1961), XI Jahrgang/Nr. 50, p. 5.
29. "Out in the Open—A U.S. Battle with Allies: Terms for a Deal on Berlin," *U.S. News and World Report*, LII, 21 (21 May 1962), 38-39.
30. *Das Parlament* (13 December 1961), XI Jahrgang/Nr. 50, p. 5.
31. *Das Parlament* XI, 50 (13 December 1961), p. 5.
32. *Das Parlament*, XI, 50 (13 December 1961), p. 6.
33. *Das Parlament*, XI, 50 (13 December 1961), p. 6.
34. *Ibid.*, p. 7 Cf. Peter Merkl, "Equilibrium Structure of Interests and Leadership," in *American Political Science Review*, LVI, 3 (Sept., 1962), 646-8. Professor Merkl contends that the balance of interests so successfully maintained by Chancellor Adenauer in the CDU/CSU militates against future chances of the FDP or any third party to the right of the SPD. He finds that the same powerful industrial interests supported by the FDP are even more dependent on the much larger CDU/CSU party. Although the complete loss of financial support from heavy industry, 1956-59 did reduce FDP strength from less than 10 per cent to 7.7 per cent in 1957, the remarkable comeback of the Free Democrats in

1961 would seem to indicate that a third party in the future could play an increasing role in German politics. The intellectual acumen, the war record and brilliant leadership of Erich Mende—far more astute than the former chairman, Dr. Dehler—seems to have worked miracles in Free Democratic Party. Powerful industrial interests of the Ruhr always have to consider the common interests of the labor, Left-wing of the CDU and the Social Democratic Party. A movement of these interests over to the FDP, which already commands strong national support as well as the backing of German liberals could result in giving Germans a third choice between two big mass parties, as Konrad Adenauer freely admitted to Erich Mende prior to the election of 1961.

35. *Das Parlament,* XI, 50 (13 December 1961), p. 7.
36. i.e. Defense or Foreign Affairs or All German Affairs Committee.
37. As for instance in his Press Conference in Bundeshaus on 16 September 1961 when Adenauer had to be corrected by his campaign manager on this point.
38. *Das Parlament,* XI, 50 (13 December 1961), 9-11.
39. *Das Parlament,* XI, 50, (13 December 1961), 15.
40. See John W. Keller, Current German Political Scene," *Current History,* XXXVIII, 221 (January, 1960), 30-31.
41. Peter Merkl, "Equilibrium, Structure of Interests and Leadership," in *American Political Science Review,* LVI, 3 (September, 1962), 638-42.
42. Otto Kirchheimer and Arnold Price, "An Analysis of the Effects of West German Elections on First Bundestag of 14 August 1949," in *U.S. Dept. of State Bulletin,* Vol. XXI, No. 537 (17 October 1949), p. 563.
43. *Time,* LXXX, 25 (20 July 1962).

Chapter 16

UNRESOLVED ISSUES—PROTRACTED CONFLICT

The problem of German reunification is provokingly complex. Both the Government Coalition and Opposition parties in the Bundestag agree that the goal should be unity and freedom. But radical solutions of the problem by war are ruled out because neither Germany nor any other nation would want to lose its life for German unity. Thus, the Western German Republic, the three Western Powers and the Soviet Union all accept the *status quo* of a divided Germany rather than go to war to change it. Naturally the three Western Powers and the Federal Government in Bonn all would prefer to see Germany united and allied with the West; whereas the Soviet Union and its puppet regime in the Soviet Zone would prefer to see Germany united and allied with the Eastern Bloc.

This East-West deadlock has persisted through so many conferences that an increasing number of Germans are becoming restless, lest the *status-quo* of a partitioned Germany become permanent. So both the West German Government and opposition parties warn the Occupation Powers that the longer reunification is delayed the more opportunity will the Communists have to indoctrinate the youth in their zone. While it is true that the spontaneous revolts of 17 June 1953 proved that the vast majority of the population is against the Communists, it is also true that half the population of East Germany had had no personal experience with democracy in action. All Germans in the Soviet Zone who are 42 today (1963) were only 12 when Hitler came to power.

Through debate after debate in the West German Parliament in the years since 1949 speakers for all parties—Government and Opposition— have admitted over and over again that after all reunification is a problem for all four Occupation Powers to agree upon. No one openly argues for a military solution of the problem. A peaceful solution requires the acceptance of all four Powers and the Germans.

The present policies of East and West on this problem seem irreconcilable. "The over-all Sino-Soviet objective is consolidation of post-war territorial gains in order to firm up the base for future expansion in Asia and Africa—in all probability by economic and political rather than overtly military means." [1] Recent events, including maneuvers of Khrushchev, warrant no belief in the relaxation of the basic Soviet objective of Soviet foreign policy to weaken and eliminate capitalism.[2] The present uncertainty of Western policy evolves from its unwillingness either to muster sufficient force to effect a rollback of the Communist frontiers or to accept those frontiers and disengagement.

Both sides must revise their positions if they hope to break the military deadlock in Germany and Central Europe. Prior to the Berlin Wall (13 August 1961) Willy Brandt, Social Democratic Mayor of Berlin, had taken a much more moderate, middle-of-the-road stand on Berlin and the German problem than Dr. Adenauer. In a radio broadcast on 25 January 1959 he stated that he did not want Germany to have nuclear weapons. He also indicated a willingness to see some plan of disengagement between East and West explored in talks with the Russians.[3] Early in February 1959 both President Eisenhower and Prime Minister Macmillan were anxious for Big Four Talks to relieve the tensions and fears of the "cold war." Yet the German Chancellor opposed all Anglo-American suggestions for breaking the deadlock in Berlin and Central Europe in general. Adenauer remained adamant to any of the Dulles-Macmillan solutions—Confederation of East and West Germany, acceptance of East Germans as Russian agents, demilitarization and neutralization of all Germany, or withdrawal of allied troops.[4]

Naturally Germans are the most interested element. But certainly the desires of all concerned for security must be respected, i.e., what each side conceives to be security for itself—not what one side considers to be security enough for the other. Even Dr.

Adenauer for all his firmness finally recognized Russian anxieties over security. In a press interview in Hamburg on 15 May 1957 the Federal Chancellor stated that in the event of German re-unification, he would agree to a zone of military inspection in the heart of Europe, demilitarization of the Soviet Zone of Germany and exemption of it from military service.[5]

To Germans, Soviet fears may seem illogical in the light of 175 Soviet divisions posed against the few NATO divisions in Europe. Nevertheless, Soviet leaders recall how German troops marched to Moscow, Leningrad, Stalingrad, in spite of the fact that the United States was then an ally of Russia. They fear what German troops, backed by Americans as allies, might be able to accomplish. Do any reputable Western diplomats maintain that the Russians are not frightened by German rearmament or that they might not even risk a war to prevent this rearmament? The eminent American correspondent, Drew Middleton, saw the staggering destruction of Stalingrad, Voroshilovgrad, Zaporozhe, Minsk and numerous Russian villages in 1946/47— destruction more complete than anything seen in the West; yet it was done by Germans in retreat. He wrote:

> No one who went through the last war can be complacent over the rearmament of the Germans. The military, po-litical and economic integration of Germany into Western Europe is a great goal and worthy of implementation provided the democratic forces in Germany are given full support by the West against the militant nationalists and militarists.[6]

The original intention of SHAPE was to use Germans in Europe only as a holding operation, not to expect them to bal-ance 175 Russian divisions in a real war. Behind this decision to rearm the Germans was the desire so to shift the military bal-ance in favor of the West that the Soviets would, first, be deterred from a military attack on the West and, second, would seek an end to "prolonged political crises of intimidation, political pene-tration and propaganda in Western Europe, which we call the cold war."[7]

Unfortunately, a grave mistake was made in treating German rearmament as a purely military matter. In fact, General Eisenhower, on a visit to Germany in the fall of 1950, told the leader of the parliamentary opposition, Dr. Kurt Schumacher, that German rearmament was not a military, but a diplomatic and political question. At the very time when the Western Powers were engaged in delicate negotiations to bind the West German Federal Republic to the West, German rearmament was proposed. This premature suggestion without taking full cognizance of French views and the bad timing delayed both objectives— European integration and German rearmament. Naturally the Kremlin lost no time in playing up the natural fears of German militarism entertained by both French and German politicians. Numerous public opinion polls in the fall of 1950 showed that many Germans of all classes—Protestant and Catholic, men and women, former Nazi soldiers and officers—were strongly opposed to rearmament.

Moreover, negotiations between the Western Powers and the Bonn Government were complicated by German concepts of neutrality and reunification. Germans of all political parties believe that all efforts should be made to end the division of the Fatherland in peace and freedom. Many Germans were and still are convinced that Germany should play a neutral role in the power struggle between East and West. The close connection between the two basic German desires for neutralism and reunification affect German rearmament, despite all efforts to the contrary of both the Western Powers and the Adenauer Government. In fact, President Theodor Heuss, first President of the Federal Republic pointed this out in his address before both houses of the U.S. Congress on 5 June 1958. He stated:

> Believe me, it was not easy in Germany to explain the duty to perform military service to the man-in-the-street who had been persuaded by propaganda that his military service had been some sort of crime because the supreme command had been in the hands of criminals. . . . National reunification remains not only the object of German longing but also the prerequisite for Europe's recovery. . . .
>
> This much is evident; the Germans know where they belong. Their history, their intellectual and Christian-religious traditions have made them an integral part of

what is called the Western World. On this point there can be *no neutrality* for us. (italics supplied) . . .

Believe me that our Germany will never again depart from the path of democracy and freedom. It is our sincere resolve to be good and dependable allies. . . . What we must aim at is to ease the social, economic, military and political problems causing tension in the world—problems which have always existed, but which have been aggravated since 1914.[8]

The Head of the West German State, in the course of his remarks, pointed out to the Congress how reassuring President Eisenhower was in characterizing Germany's tragic partition as a heavy mortgage on Europe. Nor did Dr. Heuss fail to emphasize the undying gratitude of his people to President Truman and the American people for saving Germany's old capital, Berlin, by means of the airlift in 1948/49. Moreover, Germans regarded it as their duty to participate as free and active partners in NATO. Finally, President Heuss assured the Congress that never again would German and American soldiers fight each other. Holding no illusions about the urgent questions connected with European cooperation and safeguarding the Free World against totalitarian threats, he concluded that experience had shown that these difficult issues were capable of solution.

In the decade of the sixties the most dynamic force in international politics is the Cold War, with the Free World still committed to resist Communist aggression, expansion and subversion. The Cold War began soon after the end of World War II on the ruins of the military coalition which had defeated Hitler. The most significant heritage of World War II was the partition of Germany. This German division reflects the division of Europe and the world into Eastern and Western blocs, creating sharp friction in the center of Europe.

When, on the 13th of August 1961, Berlin was divided by a wall of barbed wire and cement, constructed by forty thousand troops of the East German Communist *Volksarmee, Volkspolizei* and factory militia, the world stood aghast. World public opinion, already confronted by a divided Germany and a divided world, now witnessed a divided Berlin. West German papers, whether

342

pro-government, right-center, independent or left-center, were united in their reaction to the incredible situation. Meanwhile key leaders of all political parties flew into Berlin to register their protests against this unilateral, arbitrary action, which clearly violated the four-power agreements of 1944 and 1949 over the status of Berlin. The Western world was shocked at the desperate efforts of Ulbricht to stem the flow of refugees out of the Soviet Zone of Germany by resorting to completely totalitarian tactics—use of violence and blackmail—to gain his point.

The immediate result was a loss of confidence in both the Bonn Government and its Western Allies. This confidence crisis, which engulfed West Berlin and most West German newspapers in general and West Berliners in particular, was only mitigated by the alert tactics of the Mayor of Berlin, Willy Brandt, who had inherited much of the prestige acquired by his predecessor, the renowned Mayor Reuters, Social Democratic Mayor of Berlin during the Berlin Blockade of 1948/49. Addressing a vast throng of several hundred thousand West Berliners in a giant protest rally before the City Hall, Mayor Brandt promised that he would write a personal letter to President Kennedy. In this much discussed letter, which later became an issue between the two major German parties—Adenauer's Christian Democrats (CDU/CSU) and Brandt's Social Democrats (SPD)—the Bürgermeister gave President Kennedy a first-hand, on-the-spot appraisal of an increasingly dangerous situation. As the leading official of Berlin —an enclave within the Soviet Zone of Germany—Brandt made use of Berlin's special status to inform the President of the leading Western Power that paper protests would not stop tanks and that the United States would have to take strong counter-measures to meet the Soviet challenge.

The impact of the visit to Berlin of Vice President Johnson as President Kennedy's special envoy, followed by 1500 American troop reinforcements and tanks, met the confidence crisis head on. When the Vice-President spoke before the Berlin Senate, flanked by General Clay, Charles Bohlen, Mayor Brandt and von Brentano, he promised that "we pledge to Berlin our lives, our fortunes and our sacred honor." The effect on Berlin was electric. Like a shot heard round the world the impact on the Great Powers and on world public opinion was immediate. Johnson had won the undying gratitude of those inside and outside Germany who value freedom, human dignity and the right of self-determination.

After four days of strong protest in both the West Berlin and West German press, followed by mass demonstrations, the wall still stood. Now began a painful process of self-introspection, re-examination and re-evaluation of postwar foreign policies pursued by both the Western Powers and the West German Federal Republic, established in Bonn in 1949. Meanwhile leading officials in Washington, Bonn and Moscow pursued cautious tactics. Neither side wanted to see violent resistance develop on the scale of that in the East German uprising of 17th of June 1953 or of the Hungarian revolt of 1956. Large, conservative newspapers in Washington, London and Bonn joined in warning against the danger of mass slaughter. East of the Iron Curtain no less caution was shown when the East German puppet, Walter Ulbricht, backed up by his obedient Socialist Unity Party (SED) and the East European states of the Warsaw Pact, took every precaution against violent resistance by the deployment of 40,000 East German troops, backed up by Soviet tanks stationed in and around Berlin.

During the remaining weeks of August all major German parties went through a process of complete metamorphosis with respect to their campaign tactics in the great electoral contest for seats in the West German Parliament. This change of tactics proved to be a *sine qua non* in the effort to win over the undecided West German voters who on the 28th of August 1961 still numbered 28 per cent. This proved to be a great asset to the opposition Free Democrats (FDP) and Social Democrats (SPD), but at the same time was a liability to the ruling Christian Democratic Party (CDU/CSU). The stakes were enormous in this election campaign, by far the most interesting in postwar German history. Whereas before the 13th of August 1961, Christian Democrats confidently expected Adenauer to increase his absolute majority of 50.2 per cent in 1957 by a vote of 52 or 56 or even 60 per cent; public opinion polls showed a 5 per cent drop of the CDU/CSU party from 50.2 to only 45 per cent, with a Social Democratic increase from 31.8 to 38 or 39 per cent. In any case political observers in Bonn saw no chance of Adenauer's Christian Democrats retaining their absolute majority. Even CDU deputies were conceding that the events in Berlin might well lead to some kind of coalition government not unlike that of 1949 or 1953, which included three parties—Christian Democrats, Free Democrats and the small conservative German Party (DP), which drew its strength mainly from Mecklenberg and Schleswig-Holstein.

The West German parliamentary elections of 1961, if not a clear case of a no confidence vote for the governing CDU/CSU party, were certainly a confirmation of von Ranke's thesis of the primacy of foreign policy over domestic issues *(Primat von Aussenpolitik)*. Leopold von Ranke, eminent nineteenth century German historian, had strongly emphasized the overpowering impact of foreign policy issues upon domestic policy, particularly in Germany, situated in *Mittel-Europa* and always confronted therefore with the nightmare of a war on two fronts. This hypothesis had enjoyed wide support among both German and European historians. In fact the dean of twentieth century German historians, Friedrich Meinecke, held firmly to this thesis until shortly before his death. When confronted with the opposite thesis of the grass roots approach or the impact of domestic politics upon foreign policy, pioneered by Professor Sigmund Neuman, Meinecke insisted that this was incorrect and that the truth lay with the Ranke thesis. Some time later, however, when the aging Meinecke came over to the United States to receive an honorary degree from Princeton University, he wrote Sigmund Neuman that he, not von Ranke, had discovered the right approach. Yet prior to the erection of the Berlin Wall on the 13th of August 1961 both major German parties—the ruling CDU/CSU and the opposition SPD—based their electoral campaigns primarily on domestic issues: prices, wages, living standards, unemployment insurance and insurance against sickness *(Krankengeld)*. At the Nürnberg Congress and election rally of the SPD party, Willy Brandt stated that until then (12 August 1961): "ninety per cent of my campaign focused on domestic rather than foreign policy issues." Brandt further stated that his speech at the Nürnberg Congress was the first one in which he had attacked the Chancellor's foreign policy.

On the other hand Professor Peter Merkl attributes Adenauer's survival as Chancellor in November, 1961 during the bargaining over a coalition to his unique capacity as broker of the policy trends developed by dynamic forces within his CDU/CSU system of equilibrium. The CDU/CSU represents a double compromise between Catholics and Protestants, big business and trade unions, Bavarian particularists and refugee nationalists—an amalgamation of nearly all elements in the body politic—merged together on the basis of pragmatic compromise. With reference to the equilibrium of domestic forces Merkl continues:

> By equilibrium among the group forces we mean a relative state of balance among several pairs of distinct and antagonistic groups within the CDU/CSU which tends to operate in favor of the *status quo*. . . . There can be shifts of emphasis or orientation owing to the changing weight of individual groups. It is essential to this concept of equilibrium, however, that there is a consensus among the groups not to wipe out one another at times of superiority and to give each group its due voice, according to its size in the formation of the policy of this whole organization. . . .
> Once a leader or policy has become accepted and managed to unify the whole system behind it, however, efforts at overthrowing the leader or the policy face the same obstacle: the opposition of a single group, albeit a small minority, can frustrate them once and for all.[9]

The role of broker between the policies developed by dynamic groups within the CDU/CSU is essentially a passive one, calling for a leader who is basically uncommitted to any one group. Adenauer, in fact, has never displayed a pronounced position on issues of domestic policy either as a member of the old Center Party or as head of the more recent CDU/CSU party. In foreign policy, however, Adenauer, as a strong Chancellor, exercised the prerogative given him by the Basic Law (Constitution) to make foreign policy. Here his main objective has been to honor his commitment to NATO and European unity via a Franco-German *rapprochement*.

On 8 May 1962 Chancellor Adenauer made it unmistakably clear in rather blunt terms that American proposals for an International Authority to control access routes to Berlin were "unworkable." At the same time Dr. Adenauer insisted that he was not opposed to negotiations with the Soviet Union on Berlin. The feeling of West German officials was that the Kennedy-Rusk proposals gave too many concessions to the Russians with nothing significant in return. The U.S. State Department countered by stating:

> Both the President and the Secretary of State have repeatedly stated ... that in view of the potentially dangerous nature of the Berlin problem and the personal sacrifice which the American people have made and may be called upon to make in connection with the fulfillment of our commitments to West Berlin, it was incumbent upon the U.S. Government to explore the possibilities of reaching some measure of agreement with the Soviet Union on the Berlin problem. We are still convinced of the soundness of this policy and will continue our exploratory conversations with our Western Allies.[10]

On the 8th of May 1962 the Federal Republic of West Germany announced the recall of its ambassador to Washington, Dr. Wilhelm Grewe. Reports indicated that the Ambassador had become *persona non grata* because of his public criticism of the way the Berlin problem was being handled in the United States. The net result of this diplomatic clash was to bring Adenauer and De Gaulle closer together and to push both of them further away from Britain and the United States. Adenauer was reported as becoming cold toward Britain's entrance into the Common Market and at the same time moving toward De Gaulle's concept of a Continental Coalition of West European nations, independent of both the United States and the USSR.

De Gaulle has always been cold toward East-West negotiations, lest the West bargain away its rights in Berlin under early postwar agreements. Behind the German desire for reunification is the fear that signing any agreement that seemed to seal partition of Germany would delay indefinitely any hopes of reunification. Thus American proposals to include East Germany as one of the 13 nations in the "International Authority" to control access to Berlin would be tantamount to recognition of East Germany as a legitimate nation. In the same category would be the proposal to set up "mixed commissions" of East Germans and West Germans to negotiate broad issues such as reunification and trade. Germans considered it useless to negotiate with the Eastern Bloc an agreement not to give nuclear weapons to its satellites because Russia would not dare do this anyway. On the other hand a non-aggression pact between NATO and the Warsaw Pact States would result in undue recognition of the status of Soviet satellites in Eastern Europe, particularly East Germany.

This cleavage between West Germany and its Allies in May, 1962 resulted in an East-West stalemate. President Kennedy and Prime Minister Macmillan both realized that their vital national interests called for negotiation and some sort of *modus vivendi* over access to Berlin to relieve the dangerous situation in Berlin where Russian and Allied troops faced each other across the street—a tinder-box. De Gaulle and Adenauer, however, refused to recognize this situation and even tried to torpedo efforts of President Kennedy to initiate negotiations for some sort of accommodation with the Soviet Union.

The basic objectives of American foreign policy have not changed with the Kennedy administration: to guarantee the freedom of Berlin, access to it and a vital economy. But instead of dealing with one man—Dr. Adenauer—President Kennedy wisely insisted on working with leaders of both the Coalition and Opposition parties as well. There have been White House meetings not only with Chancellor Adenauer but Mayor Brandt, leader of the Social Democratic Opposition, and Dr. Erich Mende, the astute leader of the rising Free Democratic Party. Mende has no use for the Hallstein Doctrine, whereby Bonn refuses to extend diplomatic recognition to any nation which has diplomatic relations with the Soviet Regime of East Germany, except the USSR. This doctrine has evoked increasing criticism from West German newspapers and political leaders, particularly since the Belgrade Conference of so called "neutral states" in September 1961, when the Bonn Government found itself with no diplomatic representative in Belgrade, yet trying to influence the delegates. Adenauer, Brandt and Khrushchev all wrote letters in efforts to influence the delegates.

The Chairman of the Free Democratic Party, Erich Mende, visited Washington on 21 March 1962 for long talks with President Kennedy in order to explain the foreign-policy position of his party in matters that concerned both the United States and West Germany. Speaking on the German television later, Dr. Mende noted that since 13 August 1961 the three parties represented in the Bundestag—FDP, CDU/CSU and Social Democratic opposition had come much closer together on issues of foreign policy. All three were convinced of the importance of closer cooperation with the West, particularly the United States. With regard to relations between Bonn and the States of Eastern Europe, Dr. Mende stated:

> President Kennedy had wanted to know how the FDP Chairman sees the situation. I think there was understanding for the fact that my party tends to want a normalization of relations with the countries of Eastern Europe. But, of course I believe that the improvement of those relations should not be paid for with territorial concessions. Only an all-German Government freely elected by the entire German people can make territorial concessions in a peace treaty.[11]

In December 1961 Dr. Mende was publicly reprimanded by Chancellor Adenauer for criticizing the Government of the Federal Republic, which consisted of a coalition between the CDU/CSU and the Free Democratic Parties. However, the FDP Chairman himself accepted no cabinet position, preferring the freedom to criticize.

The English historian, H. R. Trevor-Roper sees only three approaches to the basic issues raised by the Berlin Crisis: the Russian response to end the "anomaly" of West Berlin and eventually absorb the whole city into a separate, internationally recognized East German state; second, the hard Western view to maintain the *status quo* in West Berlin, even at the risk of nuclear war, pending reunification, as originally advocated by General Lucious Clay and Robert Murphy during the 1948 Berlin Blockade and by Dr. Adenauer, General de Gaulle and ex-President Truman in December, 1958. The third approach is the soft Western view: to detach Berlin from the general problem of Europe, in order to avoid a general war for an anomaly by compromising with the Russians at the expense of the Germans.

The soft Western view is held by many European socialists: British and French. Advantages claimed for this plan are that it would reduce a great danger with a small change—changing Berlin's status, without removing its non-Communist freedom.[12]

One must try to understand the problem of political leadership in present-day Germany in its complex ethical and political ramifications. Dr. Adenauer had a special German problem which was essentially a world problem, the restoration of Germany to its rightful place in Christian Civilization. Adenauer's mission was to replace the materialistic philosophy of an idolized absolute state, whose only ethics were power and aggrandizement with the values of Judaeo-Christian, Greco-Roman ethics. The basic tenet of Adenauer's foreign policy was to follow a course of firm solidarity with the West, whereas the Social Democrats in 1957 denied that solidarity with the West would lead to reunification and urged the Federal Republic, as well as a future reunited Germany, to occupy a position by itself, in between the two big power blocs. With Germany located in the very focus of the European high-tension area between East and West, Adenauer regarded this Social Democrat position as most naive and utopian.[13]

Beginning with the Hanoverian program in November 1959, followed by the Bad-Godesberg program of 1960, the SPD made a right-about-face from its old Marxian tenets in a bid for middle class votes and also ceased its strong and continued opposition to government foreign policy. In fact, in the foreign policy debate of 30 June 1960 Herbert Wehner (SPD) proclaimed the full support of his party for the foreign policy objectives of the Federal Government, including support of NATO and conscription, which it had opposed in the great foreign policy debate of March 1958.

Back in the 1950's the first two Chairmen of the Bundestag Foreign Affairs Committee, Eugen Gerstenmaier (now President of the Bundestag) and Kurt George Kiesinger continually urged that parliament should be given a more important role in the formulation of foreign policy and insisted that the Foreign Affairs Committee should be kept currently informed of the Government's action in foreign affairs. Dr. Gerstenmaier, Bundestag President and leading Protestant layman in the CDU, wanted the Bonn Government to play a more important role in determining the policies of the Western Allies. Moreover, he opposed the Chancellor's abrupt rejection of the Rapacki Plan for a denuclearized zone in Central Europe and was not opposed in principle to disengagement of military forces in Europe. Although he supports the major objectives of the West German Government's pro-Western policies, Gerstenmaier, nevertheless, favors a more flexible handling of major issues. Having served a prison term under the Nazi tyranny, Gerstenmaier feels a very great responsibility towards the peoples of Central Europe who now suffer under the Communist dictatorship because of the Hitler war.

In June 1961, because of the critical international situation, following the Vienna meeting of Kennedy and Khrushchev, Adenauer did not want a foreign policy debate. So the steering committee of the Bundestag proposed instead that leading members of each party agree on a general Bundestag Declaartion on foreign policy, which all parties in parliament could accept. The net result was that a group of leading deputies, including Dr. Thomas Dehler and Dr. Mende of the FDP, Professor Carlo Schmid and Erich Ollenhauer of the SPD and Dr. Krone of the CDU/CSU, invited Dr. Gerstenmaier to issue a Bundestag Declaration on foreign policy in behalf of all the parties. So the President of the Bundestag prepared a pronouncement and discussed the main ideas with the Chancellor, who approved them in substance.[14] On 30 June 1961, therefore, Dr. Gerstenmaier read this Declaration before the full assembly of the West German Parliament amid lively applause from all parties and the galleries. In a most impressive introduction, he referred to the 20th anniversary of the German attack on Soviet Russia (22 June 1941) and showed deep understanding for the bitterness of the Russian people over these events, entailing heavy sacrifices and severe losses. He continued: "There is no one in this house who does not look with grief and pain upon the misfortune which the war of Hitler also brought upon the peoples of the East." [16]

This Declaration of the Bundestag President so impressed leaders of all parliamentary parties, that Dr. Thomas Dehler (FDP) and Dr. Erich Mende, Chairman of the FDP, both considered it a fair basis for some sort of coalition agreement with the CDU/CSU later in the 1961 parliamentary campaign. And yet immediately after the ringing ovation that Gerstenmaier

351

received from the Bundestag and the visitors, a few CDU politicians and Swiss newspaper reporters attempted to insinuate that this Declaration was tantamount to disengagement and a soft neutralism. Although this was vigorously denied by Dr. Mende and others, Chancellor Adenauer himself a few days later stated that this Declaration, to which all parties in parliament had agreed, was only Gerstenmaier's own opinion. Adenauer stated that the Constitution made the Chancellor responsible for making policy and that the Bundestag could only advise. In any case this historic Declaration of the Bundestag President in behalf of all the parties represented made a deep and lasting impression on the West German press and on world public opinion and was referred to many times during the 1961 parliamentary campaign by both Free Democrats and Social Democrats, although Dr. Gerstenmaier is and always has been a staunch member of the Christian Democratic Union party of Dr. Adenauer. This whole affair would seem to confirm a statement made on television by Walter Lippman (7 June 1962) that "Germany inside is not nearly as inflexible as Dr. Adenauer makes it sound, and we know and we are interested in a lot of Germans, both on the Right and Left, and in the Center of his own party."

In the twilight of his career, Dr. Adenauer is sure that his place in history will be determined not by domestic [16] political issues and events, but rather by his role in building a new Europe and a new Germany. He is somewhat obsessed by the fear that the fruits of his diplomacy—notably a united Franco-German front against Communism—could be weakened by his successors. For over 40 years Dr. Adenauer has worked to improve Franco-German relations—ever since 1919, in fact, when he became convinced that a reconciliation between France and Germany should be the first law of European politics. Speaking before the Washington Press Club on 15 November 1962 Chancellor Adenauer took the opportunity to explain briefly the aims and objectives of his policy vis-à-vis those of France. He reviewed the close relations between Germany and Russia directed against France in the time of Bismarck; after Bismarck relations between France and Russia (1894) were directed against Germany. In 1944 General de Gaulle went to Moscow to sign a Franco-Russian treaty directed against the Germans to safeguard against French fears of a German war of revenge. But later De Gaulle convinced himself that the German people of today were no longer the German people of former times and that there were no trends in Germany toward revanchism. The Chancellor, therefore, concluded that the present Franco-German *rapprochement* would prevent a repetition of an alliance either between Germany and Russia against France or between France and Russia against Germany. Dr. Adenauer concluded:

> We want—and that is also the view of General de Gaulle —to establish a dike, a dam, in the heart of Europe by bringing together these two nations, not only by treaties but also by strengthening the human bonds, the human ties, and we want to erect this dike against any Russian attempt to communize Europe, to draw Western Europe over into the Communist orbit.[17]

In other words the Chancellor felt that the Communist threat, emanating from Russia would continue for some time and that no European countries could object to Franco-German friendship, which serves the cause of liberty and peace in Europe and the whole world. In his brilliant Epilogue, "Germany and the Western World," written for a recent book, Konrad Adenauer quoted the great liberal Spanish historian, Salvadar de Madariaga:

> Reunification is not a German problem because the Iron Curtain extends from the Baltic to the Adriatic Sea. If Germany should embrace nationalism, the future of Europe would look dark indeed. But if Germany should rise to the level of what she can attain, she will achieve the place, within a united Europe, to which she is entitled, thanks to her intellectual vigor. . . . Time demands great decisions of everyone, most of all the Germans.[18]

Dr. Adenauer's press conference in Washington gave him an opportunity to explain the position of his Government in the recent *Der Spiegel* controversy. First of all, he found it very deplorable that here in the United States it was said in the press that there was a revival of the Gestapo spirit in Germany. The Chancellor explained that he supported the action of his

Government in arresting several editors of the weekly news magazine, *Der Spiegel,* for publishing information, which constituted an act of treason—a crime against a nation—which could cost the lives of hundreds of thousands of people. This, however, had nothing to do with freedom of the press. "The press is free in Germany and the press will remain free. We are far from applying Gestapo methods. I was arrested twice by the Gestapo and I know the methods which the Gestapo applied."[19] The Chancellor explained that the main decisive question was not why *Der Spiegel* had published this or that, but where did it get the information? Who were the civil servants, the officials, the officers who handed the information to *Der Spiegel?* As evidence of the very generous freedom of the German press, Adenauer cited two incidents: First, the circulation of the edition in which the questionable article appeared was 500,000; the next edition sold 750,000 copies. "In another edition you may see how free the press is in Germany by the fact that while Herr Augustein is in prison, was in prison, arrested, he was authorized to write an article in prison, which was published in *Der Spiegel,* an article which he directed against Herr Strauss."[20]

A coalition crisis resulted from the aftermath of the "Spiegel affair" which aroused lively debates both in parliament and among the public. A new cabinet became necessary after the FDP members, and shortly afterwards the CDU/CSU members as well resigned. The new Cabinet had 21 members, including the Chancellor: 12 from the CDU, 4 from the CSU and 5 from the FDP. Most of the previous Cabinet kept their positions, including Ludwig Erhard, Minister of Economic Affairs, and Gerhard Schröder as Foreign Minister. Seven new Cabinet members included: Defense: Kai Uwe von Hassel (CDU), succeeding Franz Joseph Strauss (CSU); Justice: Ewald Bucher (FDP), succeeding Wolfgang Stammberger (FDP); Finance: Rolf Dahlgrün (FDP), succeeding Heinz Starke (FDP); All-German Affairs: Rainer Barzel (CDU), succeeding Ernst Lemmer (CDU); Bundesrat and Länder Affairs: Alois Niederalt (CSU), succeeding Hans Joachim von Merkatz (CDU), Family and Youth Affairs; Bruno Heck (CDU), succeeding Franz Würmeling (CDU); Federal Property: Werner Dollinger (CSU), succeeding Hans Lenz (FDP).[21]

After a series of party maneuvers, Dr. Adenauer and his

party advisers realized that rather than form a coalition with the Social Democrats, they would have to meet the demands of the Free Democrats:[22] 1) to expel Franz Joseph Strauss, the controversial Defense Minister, whom the FDP had accused of engineering the "Spiegel affair" for personal vengeance. 2) that Dr. Adenauer announce when he planned to resign. He complied and announced at a party meeting he would retire some time in the fall of 1963. Heretofore, he had always dodged being pinned down on his retirement—except to set some time prior to the 1965 elections. Ludwig Erhard, Economics Minister in the West German Government, was said no longer to be the assured successor to Adenauer when he retires. Erhard was said to have lost ground when he first attacked the Chancellor's policies on the Franco-German treaty and then pulled back.[23]

In early December, 1962 there was a brighter German outlook when Premier Walter Ulbricht indicated his regime was ready to compromise on the Berlin and German question. He and Adenauer have symbolized the forces of the Cold War that for 17 years have kept Germany divided. In East Berlin Mr. Ulbricht who has continually pursued a "hard" line on Berlin and generally seems to represent Soviet policy, issued a "soft" statement on Berlin, omitting any reference to a separate peace treaty and even called for compromise between East and West to bring about a reunified Germany. At the same time there was speculation in the West over the foreign policy line of Adenauer's successor. His Foreign Affairs Minister, Gerhard Schröder was regarded by the West as more flexible in his approach to cold war issues. Ever since the Soviet Union withdrew from Cuba, there was speculation as to the effect this would have on Soviet policy toward Berlin. But even if the Kremlin is unwilling to risk a showdown over Berlin in the present strategic situation, neither can it afford to drop its Berlin plans, now four years old. Although officials in Washington and Bonn do not consider the Berlin Crisis over, the current era of "peaceful coexistence" could lead to plans for some kind of *modus vivendi* between East and West over Berlin. Among the prospects were a reduction of tensions in Central Europe, or a non-aggression pact by the NATO and Warsaw Pact countries.[24]

Nevertheless, the role of Konrad Adenauer in any East-West negotiations over Berlin can not be discounted. West Germany in a sense holds a trump card, which is neither French nor American—but a bilateral agreement with Russia, another Rapallo Pact with a "de-Stalinized" East Germany. West Germans today are convinced, despite all denials from Washington, that Americans and Russians may contemplate a deal at Germany's expense—involving "*de facto* recognition of the Zone regime, recognition of German partition and the "minimization" of Berlin. The Germans have let it be known that "if the United States goes ahead playing a lone hand with Soviet Russia, Bonn may have to turn directly to Moscow and ask for terms.[25]

NOTES TO CHAPTER SIXTEEN

1. William F. Frye, "Are We Realistic about Communist Power?" in *Foreign Affairs Policy Bulletin* (5 January 1959), p. 1.
2. Michael T. Florinsky, "The USSR and West Europe," in *Current History*, XXXVI, 209 (January, 1959), 6.
3. Pittsburgh *Post Gazette* (10 February 1959), 8.
4. Brownsville *Telegraph* (9 February 1959), 4.
5. Heinrich Siegler, *Reunification and Security of Germany* (Bonn, 1957), pp. 173-179.
6. Drew Middleton, *Defense of Western Europe* (New York, 1952), 190.
7. Drew Middleton, *op. cit.,* 190.
8. Congressional Record: House of Representatives, CIV, 90, (5 June 1958), 9182-3.
9. Peter H. Merkl, "Equilibrium, Structure of Interests and Leadership: Adenauer's Survival as Chancellor," in *American Political Science Review*, LVI (September, 1962), No. 3, 63, 638.
10. "Out in the Open—A U.S. Battle with Allies," in *U.S. News & World Report*, LI, 21 (21 May 1962), 38-39.
11. The Bulletin: Weekly Survey of German Affairs XI, 13 (12 March 1962), p. 2.
12. H. R. Trevor-Roper, "Berlin: The Large and Basic Issue," *New York Times Magazine*, III, 6 (25 February 1962), 13 ff.
13. Edgar Alexander, *Adenauer and the New Germany: The Chancellor of the Vanquished*, with a preface by Alvin

Johnson and Epilogue by Chancellor Adenauer (New York, Farrar, Straus and Cuday, 1957), p. 293.

14. From a personal interview with Dr. Fritche, Secretary of Dr. Gerstenmaier.

15. Deutscher Bundestag, *Erklärung des Herrn Bundestag-Prësidenten vor dem Plenum des Deutschen Bundestages am 30 Juni* 1961, p. 1. (Sperrfrist: 30 Juni 1961. 15 Uhr, bzw. Ende der Plenarsitzung).

16. A sharp regional election in July, 1962 upset the CDU in North Rhine-Westphalia, West Germany's richest state, comprising ⅓ of the whole West German electorate. The CDU lost its absolute majority and had to form a shaky coalition with the FDP. The only gainers in votes were the Social Democrats, who increased their percentage from 39 to 43% by bourgeois appeals for prosperity, moderate reform and NATO. *Time,* LXXX, (20 July 1962), 25.

17. Stenographic Transcript: National Press Club, Washington, D.C.: Press Conference of His Excellency Konrad Adenauer, Chancellor, Federal Republic of Germany, Thursday, 15 November 1962, pp. 12-13.

18. Edgar Alexander, *A History and an Estimate: ADENAUER and the New Germany,* New York, Farrar, Straus and Cudahy, 1957), p. 296.

19. Stenographic Transcript: National Press Club, Washington, D.C.: Press Conference of His Excellency Konrad Adenauer, 15 Nov., 1962, pp. 16-17.

20. *Ibid.,* 17.

21. *The Bulletin* (Bonn, pro-Government), X, 50 (18 December 1962), 1. Negotiations for this fifth Cabinet under Konrad Adenauer were completed after several weeks and the new Cabinet was sworn in before the Bundestag on 14 December 1962.

22. *Sunday Star* (Washington, D.C., conserv.)

23. *U.S. News and World Report* LIV, 7 (18 Feb. '63).

24. *The Sunday Star* (Washington, D.C., conservative), 9 December, 1962.

25. Martin Painelle, "European Chess Game," in *America,* CVIII, 4 (26 January 1963), 143.

Chapter 17

GERMAN POLITICS AND THE CRISIS IN THE ATLANTIC ALLIANCE OF 1963

I

American postwar foreign policy as laid down by Presidents Roosevelt, Truman, Eisenhower and Kennedy was predicated on the thesis that in both world wars and the later cold war Europe could not defend itself without U.S. intervention. This basic fact brought about the transformation of the United States from nineteenth century isolation to a twentieth century world power. This basic aspect of American foreign policy was reconfirmed on 15 November 1962 by the Kennedy-Adenauer talks on Cuba, Berlin and Germany. The basis for these talks was found in common German and American interests in the aftermath of the Cuban crisis and the need for "contingency planning" by NATO to guarantee the freedom and security of West Berlin in all circumstances. Among other important international problems discussed by the President and Chancellor were: Germany, including Berlin, political and military aspects of NATO and developments relating to the economic and political integration of Europe.[1]

Yet only three months after the Cuban crisis, American foreign policy faced many dangers and difficulties. Our policies were being challenged in Cuba, generally regarded as a Kennedy diplomatic victory; in Latin America where the Alliance for Progress showed negligible results, in Canada where anti-Americanism threatened to be a major issue in parliamentary elections, in New York where the talks on banning nuclear weapons had failed, in NATO with France determined to pursue an independent course, in Britain with widespread dissatisfaction over the Nassau decision against Sky bolt and over De Gaulle's veto of Britain's request to join the Common Market.

What caused these challenges to American leadership, threatening our position in world affairs? To find an answer one must re-examine the basic trends in postwar international politics and the opinions of leading statesmen as to the meaning of events. In General de Gaulle's judgment we were at the end of the postwar era with the United States as the defender and banker of Western Europe.[2] The over-all effect of the Cuban crisis was to weaken the control of the two Super Powers (U.S. and USSR) to control their respective camps. Both NATO and the Warsaw Pact were confronted by divisive forces. Above all the Cuban crisis had demonstrated that neither Moscow nor Washington would unleash a nuclear war in behalf of a third party. To all intents and purposes this limited nuclear warfare to the one instance of self-defense involving massive destruction. Khrushchev's primary objective in the Cuban venture seemed to be to convince world public opinion that neither he nor Kennedy would dare use atomic weapons in an offensive sense, only in self-defense, which would bring massive retaliation as long advocated by John Foster Dulles.

So the lesser partners on either side of the Iron Curtain became increasingly more assertive. This was particularly true of Tito, knowing how vital Yugoslavia is to Soviet strategic plans in the Mediterranean, and De Gaulle, fully aware that France is essential to American military power in the West.[3] U.S. foreign policy predicated on the assumption of a strongly integrated Europe, backed by Anglo-American nuclear power with Britain in the Common Market was now confronted with the need to reappraise past policies and readjust them to the postwar era. De Gaulle would neither allow Britain a few years to readjust its agriculture to the Common Market nor allow the United States time to reappraise and revise its policies. Instead, he confronted Macmillan and Kennedy not with a diplomatic argument but with a *fait accompli*.

Three events at the turn of the year seemed to foreshadow a turn of the tide in international politics—events that were bound to increase the fascination of the international chess game in 1963: the deepening rift between the Soviet and Chinese Communists, the signing of the Franco-German Treaty and De Gaulle's veto of Britain's request to join the European Common Market.[4] By mid-December, 1962, De Gaulle was reported to have decided to bring to a head the issue of the Common Market on the basis of three developments: Adenauer's rather perilous position in Germany after the *"Spiegel* Affair," widespread dismay in Britain over the Skybolt affair, aggravated by Dean Acheson's speech minimizing her world position and reports of the softening of Russian positions and deeper differences between the Soviets and the Chinese Communists.

The Franco-German pact provided for close and constant cooperation—military, political, economic and cultural—and marked a vital stage in a long overdue *rapprochement* between two warring lands. But as developments were to show De Gaulle's design called for an exclusive European club that Britain could not join and in which the United States was not welcome. Washington generally regarded the dispute with De Gaulle as one of internationalism *vis-à-vis* nationalism. When American and British newspapers suggested that powerful German business and banking interests wanted to keep Britain out of the Common Market and that Adenauer did not really try to convert De Gaulle, a right-wing German paper, *Deutsche Zeitung,* asked how Adenauer could be expected to do what neither Roosevent nor Churchill could do in World War II.[5]

A brief resumé of the evolution of De Gaulle's views is most intriguing. In the 1930's he was talking in Machiavellian terms of men of action with a strong dose of "egotism, pride, hardness and cunning" [6] and of glory reserved for a race created by brilliant deeds. In the 1940's the General attributed his wartime leadership to his acting as the inflexible champion of the nation and state and predicted that England and France together would create peace. Nor did he overlook the prospects of a new Franco-Russian solidarity in order to checkmate Anglo-Saxon efforts at hegemony, and to curb the German danger (1944) as he later told Konrad Adenauer.[7] He firmly believed that the equilibrium of Europe from the Rhine to the Balkans plus an organization of nations would be more than a mere area for disputes between America and Russia.

In the early 1950's De Gaulle became convinced that French primacy in Western Europe with German help could change the entire European atmosphere from the Atlantic to the Urals and create an economic, political and strategic bloc in Western Europe, which could prevent the rise of a new Reich and, if need be, arbitrate between the Soviet and Anglo-American camps.[8] By 1959 De Gaulle contended that only a united Europe could assure world peace and dissuade the two nuclear Super Powers from the temptation either to divide the world into spheres of interest or to destroy Europe in the process, that is, if Western Europe were wiped out from Moscow and Central Europe from Washington.

In the early 1960's De Gaulle complained that the very basis of integration on which NATO was predicated was destroyed because the whole defense of Europe was commanded by the Americans. The diversity of American and French interests would be even greater in the future and therefore give greater weight to Europe *vis-à-vis* the United States (1963). "Following Britain, other states would want to enter the Common Market." [9] In that case a colossal Atlantic Community under American leadership would engulf the European Community.

II

Future historians will say that the American blockade of Cuba and the Chinese attack on the Himalayas did not accidentally occur at the same time. Through two events at two far distant points near the end of October, 1962, the world had fallen into the most serious crisis since the end of World War II. Through the direct confrontation in Cuba of the two Great Powers we stood dangerously near the brink of World War III, whereas heretofore all postwar crises were resolved by representatives of the two Super Powers and were always limited to a local or regional character. After Khrushchev on October 28th had decided upon a strategic retreat from Cuba, the immediate danger was over. But since he had also undertaken a change of course in another type of crisis, in the quarrel between India and China, there emerged in October a shifting of the whole world scene. Moscow had abandoned its previous concept of politics in the underdeveloped areas. Khrushchev will no longer be able to restore the state of affairs prior to 20 October 1962, since the Chinese mounted their massive attack in the Himalayas.[10] Six months later the full import of this Chinese attack in the battle for Asia became clear. Writing in West Germany's leading Protestant weekly, Dr. Giselher Wirsing concluded:

When the worst famine conditions [1959-1962] had ended, the Chinese took no steps to improve matters further, but immediately launched a military invasion of the Himalayas that gave their Asian neighbors a staggering display of power and surprised the Russians even more than it did the Americans.

The war against India, short as it was, stands as a classic maneuver in the field of Asian policy. The short but brilliantly prepared advance, the halt and then withdrawal after Nehru had lost face as an Asian leader—all this was not primarily directed against India. Its purpose was to whittle the Soviet Union down to size in the eyes of the Asians, for the Soviet Union's sympathies lay with India. From his own position of weakness, Mao—who could not fight a real war with a major power like the United States—fascinated all Asia with his master stroke.[11]

In Hong Kong it was noted how the Chinese even resorted to the Asian racial issue against the Russians. In fact, the Russians were berated for their failure to understand the Chinese and for trying to judge the Chinese by their own standards as the Europeans had done and failed.[12]

India as well as Cuba had apparently been a part of the ideological discussion between Moscow and Peking. First of all the Russians had advocated the thesis that the East should cooperate with the national revolutions in Asia, Africa and Latin America, i.e., the revival of national revolutions in the social sense, socialist and communist revolutions, must be given priority. The Chinese, on the other hand, had no use for a strategy of cooperation with what is known in the Communist program as the national democratic regime. Rather they recommended both before and after independence an active Communist battle against the non-Communist leaders of the independence movement. They insisted upon direct support of Communistic parties, in order to set in motion the social revolution immediately after the winning of independence, in any case in order to bring the Communists into leadership from the start. In cases where independence had already been won, a national democratic regime should not be supported.[13] According to Peking, the weakness of the West permitted such a strategy.

In Moscow, on the contrary, it was said that this strategy conjures up war and that an atomic war must destroy its own substance. Originally Soviet aid to Cuba was used to refute Chinese charges that the Russians had betrayed the cause of world revolution. The Cuban venture, which was the counterpart of the Soviet's Indian policy, came into direct confrontation with Washington, leaving Moscow no other choice but to encircle India, since Russia needed China as an ally in the Cuban crisis. In India Khrushchev had brought a great sacrifice to the Chinese.[14] In fact, he had given up the policy which he had announced in 1955 in India and beyond in the direction of all Asia, Africa and Latin America. Without regard to the status and chances of respective Communist parties, to cooperate with national-democratic regimes, i.e. with non-Communist or even outspoken anti-Communistic governments, to support them with economic and military aid and to divert them from the West, if not able to woo them into a Front position with the West. The achievements of this policy had been impressive even if the material aid of the Soviets proved less than the promises. In the United Nations were prospects of a coalition of Communist and neutralist states, if somewhat irregular, especially if it came to a question of resistance to former colonial powers or the United States. For years Khrushchev had held to this policy. In all cases where an opportunity came to establish a completely Communist regime, Khrushchev had renounced the opportunity. This was the case in Egypt and Iraq, in the Congo as well as Ghana, Guinea and Laos. In all these cases Khrushchev estimated the disadvantage to be greater than the advantage. This disadvantage for him was primarily the defeat of his over-all policy. With this formula there was only one exception: in Cuba he was overwhelmed by the temptation to transform a nationalistic revolution into a Communistic revolution. With the daily increasing tension around Berlin, Cuba posed the question as to whether a strategic base of Russia in Cuba might become either an object of exchange in connection with Berlin or a direct military threat in the sense of pressure against Washington. Soviet Government declarations and letters in the week prior to October 28 confirmed the fact that Khrushchev needed about four weeks to make his trump card available and then to play it. But President Kennedy destroyed this trump card by his quick and decisive action. Although Khrushchev could not afford to risk nuclear warfare with the United States, he was able to observe in these October days that his basic formula was correct: as soon as a completely Communistic regime arose in a developing region and this Communist regime showed an expansive, even militaristic potential, the deterrent effect set in the whole region.[15] Despite all preparations of the Latin Americans, to allow them to yield to Castro and thus prevent a new precedent for North American intervention may have seemed to Khrushchev the best justification for his policy *vis-à-vis* that of Peking. The concept of the Chinese had proved itself useless in Cuba.

As late as October 20, 1962, Khrushchev was still ready to follow his previous Indian policy. His ambassador assured Nehru that with the continuation of Soviet neutrality, it was possible that Moscow could mediate. The Roumanian party chief, Gheorghiu-Dej, on a visit with Nehru in New Delhi on October 24th still considered it right to support Nehru in his resistance against China. But on October 25th Moscow made a complete switch and adopted the Chinese interpretation of the Himalayan war as stated in Pravda and Izvestia.[16] Now Moscow falsified on its part the Indian defense on Indian territory as an Indian attack against Chinese territory. This event of October 25 in the long run may prove more significant than October 28 when Khrushchev announced withdrawal of missiles from Cuba. For the Indians October 25 was the greatest disappointment. Peking of course fully exploited the situation. She completely encircled India politically and diplomatically through treaties with Burma and Nepal, through negotiations with Pakistan and Ceylon and through a new approach to Indonesia. No non-Communist Asiatic country at a crucial moment has raised its voice for Jawaharlal Nehru, who should be the symbol of emancipation of the people of Asia and Africa.[17] With the Cuban crisis, Khrushchev was no longer in a position to burden his relations with China by pursuing his old policy with India. Thus ended the fiction, which Khrushchev had built up, that only the Soviet Union could lead the liberation of the peoples of Asia and Africa. Although viewed from Hong Kong the Chinese Communists appeared to be gaining in influence over the Russian Communists; viewed from Europe, Khrushchev appeared to have Mao-Tse-tung on the run. Early in 1963 the Chinese seemed to be getting the upper hand in most of the underdeveloped countries in Asia, Africa and Latin America. But, according to the Zürich correspondent, Lorenz Stucki, Khrushchev's Cuban venture was a "complete success" as shown by the speeches, proclamations and agreements signed by Khrushchev and Castro during the latter's visit to Moscow. These agreements underlined Khrushchev's policy of peaceful coexistence:

> Castro has attested to the fact that the first "Socialist" state in the Americas developed from a "democratic, anti-imperialist people's movement" that later fell into Communist hands and not from a communist revolution of the sort that Peking demands in all under-developed lands.[18]

By the end of May, 1963 this writer predicted that since Krushchev's battle with Peking had been a draw, he would adopt a hard anti-Western policy rather than relax tensions and that this might benefit the Western Alliance at a time when its unity had become precarious.

III

Origins of Franco-German Treaty

The immediate origins of the Franco-German Treaty of 1963 are to be found in the France of De Gaulle, not in the Germany of Adenauer, despite the latter's abiding interest in a *rapprochement* between these two whose warring goes back to 1919. Hence this treaty must be regarded not merely as a symbol of international brotherhood, but rather as another move of De Gaulle in the international game of power politics. An indication of this was the timing: the treaty was signed on 22 January 1963 only eight days after De Gaulle's press conference in which he vetoed Britain's request to join the Common Market and lashed away at Americans with his veto of President Kennedy's Polaris offer.

In July, 1959, one year after De Gaulle's rise to power, the

French Plan for the coordination of foreign policies was presented to the Common Market (EEC). When neither the Commission of the EEC nor the Dutch or Belgians would approve the plan, it fell into the background. A year later at Rambouillet, the French President sought Dr. Adenauer's approval for his French Plan on the basis of the "weakness and irresolution" of American diplomacy under Eisenhower, its careless regard for European interests and softness toward Soviet Russia. After further study the scheme was blocked in April, 1962 by the Dutch and Belgians who demanded an answer to Britain's request to join the EEC as the price of their support. But since General de Gaulle wanted a political union without Britain, he postponed his plan until the fall of 1962 on his tour of Germany. This time the plan was presented in the form of an Association of France and Germany alone, so the British would be excluded regardless of whether they eventually joined the Common Market or not. The other four members of the EEC could fall into line later. The Treaty signed in Paris on 22 January 1963 by the heads of state and government and foreign ministers of France and West Germany was essentially the same French plan of 1962, except that any notion of true European union was scuttled by brutal French treatment of the EEC over Britain's entry. Despite the fact that De Gaulle had made plain his desire to rid the European continent of the American military presence at his press conference of 14 January 1963, West Germany signed a pact with Paris providing for "close, constant and far-reaching military collaboration." [19] The signing of this Paris Pact posed a serious question for Konrad Adenauer: how reconcile this action with his other foreign policy principle that German security against Russia depended on American support? What would be the future relationship of France and West Germany to the remainder of the Atlantic Alliance? Had De Gaulle any designs for some kind of entente with Moscow to follow the American withdrawal from Europe? Only thus could a new Franco-German power, cut off from its Atlantic partners, hope to maintain itself. How could an entente with Moscow be reached without imposing greater national sacrifices on Germany than the Germans would accept? The independent British journal, *The Economist*, stated:

What in the meantime happens to Berlin, to NATO, to the strong European link in the American world-wide system of defense, and the free European countries that had not knuckled under to Paris, are matters to which the North Atlantic nations, all but France and Germany, must soon address themselves.[20]

Accordingly the whole design of De Gaulle seemed predicated on the assumption of cooperation with Moscow and on America remaining passive, neither of which could be counted on. Germans friendly to Britain joining the Common Market pointed out that the French Treaty, providing for political and military as well as economic and cultural collaboration, would have to be ratified by the German Bundesrat and Bundestag, which could always refuse. To this argument *The Economist* retorted:

In the absence of a major political convulsion in West Germany . . . this is simply self-deception. The German majority parties, like the German ministers, were perfectly well aware of what was going on, and if they wanted to know what it meant, General de Gaulle had told them. Since they acquiesced in the signing of the treaty, they are not likely to refuse ratification of it. Nothing short of a wave of national alarm could force a change of course.[21]

Before turning to a consideration of German political reaction to the crisis in the Atlantic Alliance, it is essential to have a clear idea of American views on Europe in January, 1963. Basically Americans wanted Britain in Europe as a bridge between the two continents, but also as a means of strengthening parliamentary democracy, particularly in West Germany, where Chancellor Adenauer was said to have resented any potential domination of the European Economic Community by the inclusion of the Social Democratic governments of Scandinavia.[22] Senator Morse, no isolationist, deplored the idea of a fragmented and divided NATO, with the disproportionate contribution of American men, money and military equipment. Many in Congress might follow Morse's suggestion of a friendly separation of America from European affairs. In any case General de Gaulle had no interest in the Kennedy design of an Atlantic Community linked with Japan and Latin America. Meanwhile the Kennedy Administration continued its cool, calculated approach, looking beyond Adenauer and De Gaulle to the future when a new generation of politicians might be more likely to share the American view. It was even doubtful if the aged Chancellor could take Germany completely over to De Gaulle in view of the delicate, domestic political state in Germany.[23]

The American solution to NATO problems consisted of submarines with Polaris missiles and mixed crews for the atomic age. The United States favored the concept of both national and multinational components within NATO's strategic force. Plans included provisions for a separate nuclear command under the supreme European Commander, with its own headquarters. Completing all the details would require months, but Washington considered this task would be highly educational for American and Congressional public opinion as well as for Europeans. This would involve trends toward de-sovereignty in the atomic age.

Torn between his old loyalty to the United States and his new Gaullist affections, Konrad Adenauer's influence still pervaded the West German political scene. Most Germans regarded the Paris Pact as a legitimate agreement, not prejudicial to German relations with Britain or the United States. Independent and pro-CDU papers both noted the warmth of De Gaulle's desire for a *rapprochement* and closer solidarity with the Federal Republic and his references to Adenauer as a "great statesman.[24] Competing for headlines in the West German press was President Kennedy's State of the Union message, appealing to Europe for economic and military cooperation, while avoiding nuclear anarchy with a balanced military strategy and warning the EEC not to jeopardize the Atlantic Alliance by high protective tariffs.[25] Several West German papers noted Republican criticism of the Kennedy message for being too optimistic over the general international situation, "for courteous but acid" criticisms of America's allies and for allowing the Russians to take the initiative in international politics.[26] Certain UN diplomatic observers were disappointed.

All three political parties represented in the Bundestag were deeply concerned over De Gaulle's statements. In fact, all three floor leaders urged Chancellor Adenauer to try to influence De Gaulle to reconsider his opposition to Britain's membership in EEC. Erich Ollenhauer, SPD Chairman, wrote Adenauer advising him to exert every effort to save European unity.[27] Moreover, the Social Democratic Opposition gave full support to the U.S. position that European NATO members should intensify their conventional armaments rather than seek nuclear weapons, a position long advocated by the SPD.[28]

Whereas pro-government and right-center papers showed deep understanding for De Gaulle's reasoning, independent, left-center and pro-SPD papers were more critical of De Gaulle and sympathetic to British membership in the Common Market and to Kennedy's new strategy. Thus the influential right-center *Frankfurter Allgemeine* defended De Gaulle for his belief that he, not the U.S. President, should decide on France's national defense system. Nor could Germans overlook Great Britain's independence in rejecting statutory provisions of the EEC, as if the Six should be expected to amend them in deference to the desire of a new applicant.[29] The very influential, but independent *Die Welt* carried a trenchant critique of De Gaulle for slamming the door against the British, for narrowly scrutinizing the Moscow-Peking conflict and for his frank espousal of Europe without Britain and anti-American trends. Reminding Germans that as the Adenauer era was drawing to a close, none of the Chancellor's potential successors wanted Britain excluded from Europe or U.S.—German cooperation lessened. Apart from Adenauer himself, neither his Cabinet ministers, the coalition parties nor the opposition would agree to the exclusion of Britain from Europe. Moreover, a declaration of the Bonn Government in November, 1961 supported Britain's entrance into EEC and nothing happened since to cause any deviation from this goal.[30]

The pro-SPD *Neue Rhein Ruhr Zeitung* was even more severe in criticizing De Gaulle for rudeness to the United States over the Bahama offer, for not supporting Britain and for making it difficult for the Federal Republic. It contrasted De Gaulle's stiffening position with the flexible course of Kennedy, who, as head of a state in control of 90 per cent of the West's military, nuclear potential, could not be expected to be even more obliging.[31] The left-center *Frankfurter Rundschau,* commenting on conflicts within both the East and West Blocs, wondered if the key to better international relations might not be found in the "extraordinarily cordial" talk between Kennedy and Kuznetsov.[32]

After a four-hour cabinet meeting in preparation for the Adenauer-De Gaulle meeting, Adenauer did not say a word about De Gaulle's statements of January 14th and all discussion of this subject was taboo. The German Chancellor could see no reason for dramatizing things. However, many Bonn ministers and parliamentary deputies of all parties were greatly concerned over De Gaulle's veto of British EEC membership. The great majority of Adenauer's own Cabinet were said to be in favor of British EEC membership: Erhard, Krone, Schröder, von Hassel, Heck, Dollinger, Seebohm, Schwarz and the five FDP ministers were believed to favor Britain. Only five or six of Adenauer's own ministers would support him if he decided with De Gaulle on this issue. Such a step by Adenauer would lead to another cabinet crisis, in the view of some deputies.[33] On the eve of his Paris negotiations with De Gaulle, Adenauer was most careful to avoid anything that might trouble the atmosphere and he strongly criticized any negative comments on De Gaulle's statements by German delegates to the EEC meeting in Brussels. Even Foreign Minister Schröder was said to have been reprimanded by the Chancellor.[34]

Editorial opinion in the West German press became increasingly critical of Paris as EEC negotiations on Brussels slowed down to a snail's pace. Not only left-center and independent papers, but even right-center and pro-CDU journals joined in this mounting criticism of Gaullism. How could Paris remain indifferent to a deterioration of the European climate which would affect Franco-German relations adversely? Did De Gaulle expect Adenauer to bring pressure on the British to prevent them from joining Europe? Even if some officials in Bonn did approve De Gaulle's policy, the Bonn Government had already committed itself on promoting British membership in EEC as of November 1962. Not even Adenauer could change this, no matter how much he favored De Gaulle and questioned Foreign Minister Schröder's idea of admitting Britain to EEC.[35] Left-center papers were amazed at French Foreign Minister Couve de Murville's open dissatisfaction with other EEC members negotiating with Britain at Brussels after De Gaulle had once spoken. What a tragedy would follow if De Gaulle smashed Europe with German aid. De Gaulle was said to make things difficult for both friends and foes.[36]

The French newspaper *L'Express* saw France at the crossroads. The western course would involve British membership in the EEC, broadened to include all of Western Europe, in close cooperation with the U.S.A. as the leading power. But De Gaulle preferred a different course, leading ultimately to a greater Europe, extending from the Atlantic to the Urals, with Berlin as a center and symbol. With the deepening Sino-Soviet split Russia might need the backing of Europe, acting as a third force. In any case Chancellor Adenauer could never condone the Brest-Vladivostok line envisaged by certain leftist forces in France.[37] French diplomacy had been able neither to break up the EEC negotiations in Brussels nor to isolate Great Britain. Rather De Gaulle's "offensive" might have isolated France and led to a "crisis of cooperation" within the EEC over French interest in the association of African countries—especially former French colonies—with EEC. It was feared that Adenauer's three secret meetings with De Gaulle might result in committing Adenauer's successors to Franco-German cooperation.[38]

IV

Difficulty of Adenauer's Paris Mission

Adenauer's Paris mission became increasingly difficult. De Gaulle's arguments could not be easily brushed aside. To Adenauer a Franco-German *rapprochement* represented the core of his life work. His desire to commit France was as deep as the desire of De Gaulle to commit Germany. The Chancellor wanted the Bundestag to ratify the new agreement, thus to leave it to his successors as his will. However, the Chancellor's parliamentary position was not strong enough to override the will of the people, of his parliament, his cabinet and powerful industrial leaders—all of whom implored Adenauer to use his influence with De Gaulle.[39] Why should Adenauer risk his life work in order to support De Gaulle's Greater Europe policy? Faced with De Gaulle, pursuing anti-American goals, Germany had reached its crossroads. Her security was deeply involved.[40] Even CDU deputies said frankly they would not forget what their Chancellor had been teaching them for fourteen years. They argued for a continuation of Adenauer's foreign policy at the crucial moment when he seemed to abandon it for De Gaulle's grand design.[41] Were the Americans right in equating Gaullism with revived French nationalism and Adenauer's past policy with internationalism? De Gaulle, on the other hand, equated American policy in World War II with national egoism. The French President interpreted U.S. commitments in Asia and South America to mean that American statesmen could not predict today how the United States ten years later would act in case of an armed conflict in Europe. De Gaulle saw Britain as the Americans' Trojan Horse in Europe, whereby the British could transform the EEC into a colossal Atlantic community dependent upon the United States.[42] Yet Germans, unlike De Gaulle, could ill afford the luxury of an outright anti-American policy. The announcement of Kennedy's later visit to Bonn indicated to De Gaulle that this might enhance German prestige in Washington.[43]

Despite Franco-German differences over military integration—with Adenauer for it and De Gaulle against it—common feelings of insecurity regarding U.S. plans made Franco-German relations more intimate. McNamara's unfortunate emphasis on nuclear weapons as a shield and NATO ground divisions as the sword increased Franco-German fears that the new American strategy might give priority to U.S. self-defense *vis-à-vis* all-out nuclear protection of Europe.[44] Both the SPD and the Bonn Government supported the American plan for a multilateral nuclear force in NATO with German participation. But the SPD went even further than the Federal Government with its all-out support for the American desire that Bonn should raise more conventional divisions.[45] Thus the SPD was fighting a rear-guard action because the Federal Government objected to the increased cost of stepped-up recruitment of conventional forces plus the increased costs of the new multilateral nuclear force. Fritz Erler, SPD defense expert, while supporting a multi-national nuclear force, called for a European-American "two-key system" to give the European partners a voice and a veto in the use of nuclear weapons. He also proposed a reform of the "NATO apparatus," especially the NATO Council. While Erler wanted the *Bundeswehr,* like the U.S. "front units" in Germany, equipped with nuclear carrier weapons, he insisted that control of the nuclear war-heads for these carrier weapons should be vested not in local troop commanders, but in the hands of the NATO commander.[46]

Count von Guttenberg (CSU), in contrast to Erler, criticized the multi-national nuclear project envisaged at Nassau because, he argued, it would only increase the American nuclear weapons "monopoly." Such efforts at American "hegemony" would not sufficiently protect European security. Von Guttenberg saw no objection to De Gaulle's plans for an independent French nuclear force because this could be the "germ" to lead to Erler's desire for a "two-key" system." [47]

At a news conference the SPD press officer, Franz Barsig, was asked if the Social Democratic opposition would call for a "constructive no confidence vote" against Adenauer in the Bundestag if the Chancellor went over to De Gaulle's idea of a united Europe without Great Britain. Barsig called this a mere "hypothetical question," pointing out that Adenauer's task was to try to influence De Gaulle to reconsider his opposition to Britain in the EEC.[48]

To make doubly sure that the signing of the Franco-German agreements would not imply German approval of De Gaulle's Europe policy, the influential *Die Welt* advocated tactics of delay or threats of a German veto of the agreement on the association of the former French colonies with the EEC if De Gaulle insisted on blocking the policies of the other five EEC members.[49] Yet despite all the misgivings expressed in the West German press, Chancellor Adenauer on his Paris mission proved to be a very astute statesman. Not only did he refuse to fall into any morass, but he showed great tact and diplomacy in working with and not against the will of the German press and industrial circles and reflected in the cabinet and in the leadership of both coalition parties and the SPD opposition. When West German papers, whether independent, pro-government or left-center focused public opinion on vital German institutions in the Atlantic and European communities, Adenauer had to temper his enthusiasm for the Franco-German Treaty with *Realpolitik*. The Chancellor could not and would not sacrifice German vital interests by all-out support of De Gaulle's narrow European policy. Rather he showed more concern over the Common Market negotiations continuing in Brussels than had been attributed to him.

German Reaction to the Signing of the Treaty

Nearly all West German papers on Wednesday carried headlines on the signing of the Franco-German Treaty in Paris on 22 January 1963.[50] In a joint declaration Adenauer and De Gaulle characterized the Treaty as an "historical event" which would bring a basic change in Franco-German relations by intensifying cooperation. Franco-German rivalry of the past 400 years would be replaced by close solidarity between the two peoples— in foreign affairs, economic and cultural developments—an important step toward a unified Europe. The Franco-German agreement was directed against no one and all other European partners were free to join it.[51] Instead of a Protocol, a formal treaty reflected efforts to commit both countries more strongly than an executive agreement. French quarters emphasized that the agreement did not provide for "integration" but for "association." This simply meant the two countries were pledged to consult each other on all important matters of mutual interest.[52]

Recent events had prompted serious concern in all political parties. All parliamentary groups insisted on seeing Adenauer and Schröder. In fact the Bundestag committees on foreign affairs and Common Market problems were meeting to discuss events in Paris and EEC negotiations in Brussels. Both Erhard (CSU) and Mende (FDP) maintained it would be impossible to continue the European policy if Britain were excluded.[53] The SPD opposition would insist that Adenauer and Schröder inform the Bundestag and its foreign affairs committee on the outcome of the Paris negotiations. In fact SPD deputy Mommer suggested that his party might even withhold its parliamentary approval of the Paris Pact until De Gaulle ceased his opposition to British EEC membership.[54] While recognizing that fears of the SPD opposition were not unfounded, the pro-government papers advised against such parliamentary pressure as unwise, lest it impair the Franco-German alliance even before it started. After all the treaty provided for joint consultation, which would in itself prevent France from rejecting Britain's entry into the EEC without previously consulting Bonn, it was argued.[55] However, De Gaulle'e veto had occurred on January 14, 1963, one week before the Treaty was even signed. In any case the treaty represented a climax in Franco-German relations, but only the beginning of a politically unified Europe. The pro-SCU Munich *Mercury* warned that parliamentary refusal to ratify the French Treaty would undo the work of ten years, climaxed by newly won confidence existing in large groups in both countries. After all public confidence was vulnerable. After Dean Rusk had characterized the French Treaty as a work of peace on the road to European progress, why should Germans be more papal than the Pope? A choice of alternatives between the United States and France was called inappropriate, if not impossible, in the light of German security needs.[56]

The left-center press regretted that the Chancellor and most political leaders in Bonn regarded Franco-German friendship as inviolable and almost sacrosanct.[57] The independent press was, if anything, more critical of what it called a new European "axis" prompted partly by resentment and nationalism. There were mixed feelings of skepticism and deep concern lest Gaullism split Western Europe into two camps. The key problem was whether a Europe without America could be created. When De Gaulle revived the old struggle between maritime and continental interests, the young German Republic was caught up in a maelstrom.[58]

Right-center papers, in contrast to the moderate pro-government and pro-CDU journals, bitterly resented James Reston's editorial in the *New York Times,* asking Adenauer to choose between France and the United States. Reston was chided for pretending not to know that Germany had no real power of choice because it depended primarily on the United States for its security. Reston, a prominent editorial writer, knew perfectly well that only France—not Germany—could make the decision on British membership in EEC. Nevertheless, he made the American people wrongly believe that after De Gaulle vetoed Britain's membership in the Common Market, everything depended on Adenauer.[59] *Deutsche Zeitung* recognized that the British press had praised German public opinion and German political parties for backing Britain's admission to the Common Market. Nevertheless, certain British editorial writers surmised that Britain's absence would be welcome to Bonn because German industrialists and big bankers close to Adenauer might hope, after De Gaulle's withdrawal, to make Germany the leading industrial power in continental Europe.[60]

Sharp criticism in Bonn of De Gaulle's refusal to permit Britain to join the EEC prompted Adenauer to hold his first press conference since 18 September 1961, the day after the Bundestag elections. The Chancellor dodged all questions regarding EEC negotiations in Brussels, but to ease the work of the EEC ministers and to give the EEC staff some democratic basis, proposed the election of a European parliament, which would represent people rather than governments. Although skeptical of an Atlantic economic community, Adenauer favored close cooperation between the U.S.A. and EEC. He and Foreign Minister Schröder emphasized that intensified joint consultation would coordinate French and German foreign policies.[61] Joint foreign and defense policies were justified because a political union of the Six seemed impossible. The German bipartite alliance was said to go far beyond conventional military alliances. Therefore, the Bundestag would have to study all possible effects of the Paris Pact upon European institutions and NATO. The majority of the Bundestag and the German public were already convinced that German security depended primarily upon good U.S.-German relations.[62] The major part of the German population and world opinion were predominantly critical of the Paris-Bonn Alliance because of fear of Franco-German dominance, because of concern over De Gaulle's veto of British membership in EEC and the general belief that western defense must be indivisible.[63] All three parliamentary parties, despite their support of Franco-German cooperation, voiced concern lest ratification of the Paris Pact might prevent progress in EEC negotiations with Britain. In contrast to the SPD and FDP groups, CDU/CSU quarters rejected the idea of linking ratification of the Franco-German Treaty with British EEC membership. Members of the Bundestag foreign affairs committee directed many "piercing questions" to the Chancellor.[64]

Several West German papers reflected the growing criticism of De Gaulle's role in Europe, expressed by officials in Washington, despite recognition of the historical significance of the Franco-German Treaty. The State Department warned the German Embassy in Washington of the Kennedy administration's concern that De Gaulle's efforts were aimed at isolating western Europe, including Germany, from the United States. Washington's reactions to Adenauer's letter from Paris and to the explanations of Ambassador Knappstein showed U.S. "bitterness." The Kennedy administration was convinced that De Gaulle's direct attack on British membership in EEC was really a blow against the United States. Thus Bonn seemed to be caught between the millstones of the opposing goals of De Gaulle and Kennedy.[65] Whereas Adenauer seemed willing to tolerate De Gaulle's policy in Europe, Ministers Erhard and Schröder stressed positive proposals for continuing EEC negotiations with Britain in Brussels the following Monday.[66]

Editorial opinion in the West German press, except for progovernment papers, continued critical of the Franco-German Treaty. CDU papers defended the Federal Government because it was not strong enough to mediate between France and Britain. It had no alternative to a united West and could not afford discord with even one single partner.[67] American reactions to the Franco-German Treaty were compared to the grumbling of an irritated giant by the *Rheinische Post,* which placed the blame for Anglo-American discontent not on France or Germany, but rather upon the developments emerging in Bermuda back in 1961 when Kennedy and Macmillan began negotiating with Moscow without De Gaulle. This paper argued that later events in Cuba proved that De Gaulle's analysis was correct. Then Kennedy and Macmillan again met in the Bermudas to make a decision on the western alliance without consulting De Gaulle, who was merely asked to approve it. Hence, De Gaulle's veto of Kennedy's Polaris offer on 14 January 1963. So Kennedy's reaction to the Franco-German Treaty was simply regarded as a reply to De Gaulle.[68]

More objective than the pro-CDU press was the analysis of *Die Zeit,* which appeared in an article interpreting James Reston's editorial of January 21: "What Do They Think We Are?" in the *New York Times.* According to *Die Zeit* Americans expected the German Federal Republic, particularly Adenauer, to seal the rifts in the Western Alliance, attributed to De Gaulle. In attempting to force Adenauer to decide between French and American nuclear weapons, Kennedy was said to be preparing for a diplomatic two-front war in Europe. *Die Zeit* concluded that the American President was strong enough to force Bonn to choose the United States, but hoped that this would not be necessary.[69] America could not give up Europe because both were mutually dependent upon each other for security.

More critical of De Gaulle were the independent and right-center and pro-CSU papers. The influential *Frankfurter Allgemeine* warned that De Gaulle should not compel the Federal Republic to choose between the U.S. and France. Regardless of what had been said in the face-to-face talks between Adenauer and De Gaulle in Paris, all three parties in the Bundestag and the major part of German public opinion would decide in favor of the United States. And if the Chancellor took any other line, he would cause domestic conflict and another cabinet crisis. In fact the SPD was moving for a no-confidence vote and had found parts of the FDP and CDU/CSU supporting this motion.[71] For the past fourteen years Adenauer had emphasized that alliance with the United States was indispensable. After he had failed to make De Gaulle face facts, the Bundestag had the responsibility to put De Gaulle in his place in the opinion of Cologne's *Stadt Anzeiger*. This paper concluded that a "no" to De Gaulle would not necesarily mean "no" to France. Such parliamentary independence would protect rather than destroy Adenauer's life-work.[72]

VI

German and Foreign Reaction to EEC Failure

Several Monday papers carried previews of the "crucial" conference on British EEC membership opening in Brussels. Professor Erhard called the situation very serious, not only for France, Germany and the EEC, but for all Europe and the Atlantic community. Washington felt that Erhard and Schröder had understood Bonn's role in this, whereas Adenauer's position was considered ambiguous.[73] Both Secretary Rusk and President Kennedy had warned the German Ambassador Knappstein against any Franco-German special agreements which might weaken NATO.[74] At his press conference the previous week, President Kennedy had used all arguments of history, strategy and mutual interest to convince Europeans of the advantages of Atlantic unity. Several West German papers on Saturday carried the following headlines:

378

"Kennedy: Only United Are We Strong" (*Frankfurter Neue Press*, pro-Gov.); "Kennedy: Western Alliance Is Stronger than Communism" (*Kölnische Rundschau*); "Kennedy Pleads for U.S.-European Cooperation" (*Muenchner Merkur*, pro-CSU); "Kennedy Demands Western Unity" (*Frankfurter Allgemeine*, right center); "Kennedy Calling for Unity" (*Deutsche Zeitung*, Cologne, right-center); "Kennedy's Serious Appeal to Europe (*Süddeutsche Zeitung*, left-center); "Kennedy Reprimands De Gaulle" (*Stuttgarter Zeitung*, independent); "Kennedy Warns De Gaulle" (*Neue Rhein Ruhr Zeitung*, pro-SPD); "Kennedy Exhorts Europeans" (*Hannoverische Presse*, pro-SPD).

All Europeans interested in the Common Market realized that the basic question raised by De Gaulle was the question of the whole future of the Western Alliance.[75] Centrifugal force always favors national rather than community interests. On the previous Wednesday a Belgian socialist, Leo Collard, announced that European socialists had no use for De Gaulle's authoritarian design for Europe.[76] Hence President Kennedy's urgent appeal for European unity at his press conference on Saturday, 26 January 1963.

When the five EEC members insisted on meeting the French delegation again on Monday there were reports of a *"Fronde* against De Gaulle,"* based on statements in favor of British EEC membership made by the Italian Premier Fanfani, the Belgian Foreign Minister Spaak, former U.S. Secretary of State Christian Herter and SPD party whip, Herbert Wehner.[77] Chances of success of the special EEC meeting were regarded as very poor by *General Anzeiger,* which reported a visit to Franco's Spain of French ministers and military leaders. Other papers reported "massive threats" to Spain by Khrushchev in an effort to influence U.S.-Spanish negotiations over U.S. bases.[78]

Several papers on Monday reported on signs of growing isolationism in Congress, reflected in the President's statements—tendencies which resulted from De Gaulle's policy and which might mean withdrawal of U.S. troops from Europe unless Europeans would assume more of the financial burden of defense of Germany and Berlin.[79] President Kennedy's "public reprimand" of De Gaulle was called a "climax in the polemical war of words over the Atlantic." [80] Former Secretary of State Acheson and former U.S. Commissioner for Germany John McCloy both wired Adenauer urging him to warn De Gaulle against threatening European unity.[81] All this demonstrated official America's annoyance and alarm over the future of the Atlantic Alliance. No responsible European statesman would have denied the impossibility of defending Europe without U.S. aid. But even so, how could Germany be expected to influence the policy of a European nation, which had only recently ended its rivalry with her? In this dilemma, Bonn officials regarded the task of German diplomacy to make all parties to the conflict see its real proportions, for without the Atlantic Alliance both Europe and the United States would be lost. Chancellor Adenauer, therefore, rejected the idea of acting as an "American buffer" in Paris. Instead he proposed the United States itself take the diplomatic initiative in both Paris and London to overcome the crisis in Brussels. The opinion was voiced in Bonn that De Gaulle had caused the crisis in Brussels not over the British attitude toward the EEC, but rather because of the Bahama deal. Intensive diplomatic pressure, therefore, was exerted by Bonn on the U.S. to use its direct influence on Paris and London rather than using indirect pressure through Bonn.[82]

That Adenauer was not standing alone within the CDU/CSU was shown at a Friday meeting in which a broad majority backed the Chancellor's request for early ratification of the Franco-German agreement, with only a small minority for postponement. Among the majority were Bundestag President Gerstenmaier and Foreign Minister Schröder, who rejected any link between ratification and British EEC membership. Adenauer's preference for early ratification was also supported by CDU Chairman Dufues and Strauss (CSU), whereas Erhard, Furler and Majonica within the CDU preferred that ratification be delayed, as did the SPD opposition.[83] Bonn-Washington relations were further strained by reports of several U.S. Senators, including Mansfield, calling for a "radical revision" of U.S. foreign policy unless West European Allies contributed more to Western defense and development aid. This was reflected in headlines of several West German papers.[84]

Part of the misunderstanding between Bonn and Washington was attributed to the SPD opposition for pretending to be more

380

American than the Americans in order to win voters' confidence according to the *Deutsche Zeitung*. This paper also enumerated other factors of mistrust: German fears of the consequences of an American-Soviet understanding in Europe; certain miscalculations of German feelings by President Kennedy, McNamara and their advisers; need of more frankness on nuclear questions and over-simplification of the problem of European unity by Americans equating this with their own past history. Whereas the Kennedy Administration stressed joint American-European development aid in Africa, Asia and Latin America, De Gaulle and Adenauer gave European security priority in the Atlantic partnership.[85]

On Tuesday Adenauer's press chief, von Hase, defended the Bonn Government against U.S. charges with respect to the Franco-German agreement by emphasizing that Germany's friendship with France was a natural right, which could not be denied her; that in the past the U.S. had raised no objections to Franco-German cooperation, but on the contrary had encouraged it. Bonn having already endorsed the Bahama agreement, could not be held responsible for France taking a different attitude.[86] Astonished and concerned over U.S. criticism of the Franco-German agreement Adenauer decided to write Allied statesmen and key political leaders urging them to help preserve Western unity. In the Chancellor's view this unity was being jeopardized by personal attacks and exaggerated demands.[87]

The conservative Swiss paper *Neue Züricher Zeitung*, highly regarded by Europeans for its objective treatment of international issues, directed sharp criticism at Washington for threatening countermeasures such as special Anglo-American relations or withdrawal of U.S. troops from Europe, which would only confirm De Gaulle's thesis. This trenchant critique was focused on U.S. political leaders for personal diatribes against Chancellor Adenauer, concluding that strange reactions were to be expected from U.S. "technocrats" until serious forces" in the United States took a more objective approach.[88] More restrained was *Süddeutsche Zeitung*, which stressed the dilemma of the German delegation in Brussels, striving to maintain good contacts with all parties involved: France, the United States and the other five EEC partners to save the Common Market.[89] The Brussels meeting involved much more than British membership in EEC; the very future of the European Economic Community and the solidarity of the West were at stake. The United States was said to have thrown in its political weight to make Europe respect the American idea of Western unity. America considered Britain her trustee in Europe, whereas De Gaulle regarded Britain as America's "fifth column." [90] But De Gaulle's continental European policy proved unacceptable to Belgium, Holland and Italy primarily because he lacked the military power vis-a-vis both the East Bloc and the United States.[91] Germans could ill afford to overlook such basic factors as the nuclear balance of power when thinking of the perennial questions of divided Germany and Berlin. They could not ignore the basic geographic and strategic factor by reason of their location in *Mittel Europa*. Even though Adenauer's cabinet gave unanimous approval to Britain to join EEC, Washington continued its pressure on the Chancellor to make De Gaulle change his mind. Germans countered by noting that De Gaulle exercised his right of veto under the EEC Treaty signed in Rome, which had no relation to the Franco-German agreement.[92] Actually Bonn had no interest in siding with either France or the United States, for the reason that it would need both in the event of war. Moreover, American supply lines to West Germany ran through France. Yet the pressure from Washington continued because of its mistrust of the Franco-German agreement, lest it strengthen the position of De Gaulle who was against NATO, against Britain and against the United States.[93] Worried by foreign criticism and U.S. wrath, Bonn tried to avert a sharp clash by mediation, a most thankless task.

The breakdown of the Brussels negotiations caused the greatest disappointment to Washington and the Pentagon since the end of World War II—referred to as a "Black Day" for the Western Alliance. In Washington's view Adenauer had only half-heartedly supported British EEC membership and therefore it would be up to the Bundestag to make Germans aware of the consequences if German foreign policy were geared to the ideas of De Gaulle. In that case forebodings of an approaching storm in Congress were already evident in statements of Senators Mansfield, Morse and Fulbright, suggesting a possible revision of American military and alliance policy.[94] The possible consequences of the failure of EEC negotiations in Brussels were outlined by official quarters in Bonn as follows:

1. Ambiguous position of Walter Hallstein, President of EEC Commission.
2. British membership in EEC, Euratom and Coal and Steel Authority impossible for the time being.
3. Continuation of EEC, but limited to an economic association, with no hopes of political integration.
4. Plans for associating African and Commonwealth territories irrelevant.
5. Revival of European Free Trade Area (EFTA) of the Outer Seven and trends toward an economic division of Europe.
6. Fear of new economic blocs militated against German export interests.
7. German concessions to France on joint agricultural policy and association of African territories meaningless, with ratification of "African Convention" doubtful.[95]

Most West German papers on Wednesday fronted the failure of EEC negotiations, despite Chancellor Adenauer's final effort at mediation through a meeting of Foreign Minister Schröder with Couve de Murville. Typical headlines included the following:

"De Gaulle's 'No' Prompts Alarm and Concern—Adenauer and Schröder Do Not Believe Britain Permanently Excluded" *General Anzeiger* (Bonn, Ind.). "Black Day in Brussels Is Heavy Setback for Europe" *Der Mittag* (right-center); "Rupture with Britain Final" *Neue Rhein Zeitung* (Cologne, pro-SPD). "Bonn Tried in Vain to Help London; Europe Bus to Run without Britain. Paris Remains Hard; London Bitter; America Disappointed" *Bild Zeitung* (Hamburg, mass tabloid) 30 January 1963.

U.S. quarters suspected De Gaulle of planning a diplomatic revolution, nothing less than a reversal of alliances, aimed at a continental bloc from the Atlantic to Kamchatka Peninsula, north of Japan. Paris quarters rejected this report as fantastic.[96] Adenauer and De Gaulle were said to have agreed to use any interruption of the Brussels negotiations with Britain for strengthening the organic structure of EEC. DeGaulle was said to have been ready to accept "certain supra national developments" within European institutions.[97] Meanwhile Paris quarters argued that neither Britain nor the U.S. could afford an "economic war" against France or the Common Market. In 1962 the Common Market had become Europe's best customer, while France alone could block U.S. efforts at tariff reductions.

Spokesmen of all three political parties in Bonn voiced deep regrets over the failure in Brussels and predicted this would impede European unity and Atlantic solidarity. SPD Chairman Ollenhauer charged De Gaulle with complete responsibility, while a CDU deputy urged the continuation of efforts at European integration. *The SPD opposition argued the thesis that European unification was the only guarantee of German economic and political stability and military security.* It was generally agreed that Chancellor Adenauer's Bundestag Declaration on 6 February 1963 would provoke a violent domestic dispute over German foreign policy.[98] In any case the breakdown of negotiations in Brussels left a heavy responsibility for the Bundestag, which Washington hoped would either refuse ratification of the Franco-German Treaty or delay or modify it in order to permit U.S. influence in Europe to continue.[99]

More and more attention was focused on the parliamentary debate set for February 6-7, 1963, as West German opinion began to crystallize. The majority opinion in the West German press was sharply critical of De Gaulle, although several pro-government papers defended the French President on grounds that Kennedy and Macmillan had agreed on a NATO nuclear force without consulting De Gaulle or because Britain was not yet ripe for EEC membership.[100] *Frankfurter Allgemeine,* which usually leans towards the Federal Government, warned that domestic criticism of the Government would not be restricted to the opposition SPD party. This paper warned that any attempt of the Chancellor to counter this criticism by continuing in office beyond October, 1963 would fail.[101] *Die Welt* warned that Black Tuesday in Brussels was a body blow against Europe and Western cooperation, which pleased Khrushchev to no end, but might conjure up another German domestic crisis.[102] The impact of this crisis in the Western Alliance in January, 1963 upon German domestic politics was powerful, demonstrating *Primat von Ausenpolitic* (primacy of foreign policy) thus reconfirming the thesis of the eminent nineteenth century German historian, Leopold von Ranke.

The left-center West German press continued its previous warnings against the dangers of De Gaulle's grand design and his hard gestures *vis-à-vis* Moscow and, therefore, warned the Bundestag against ratification of the French Treaty if it could be construed as Bonn taking a stand against Britain and the United States.[103] Taking a middle-of-the road position, the independent *Stuttgarter Zeitung* argued that Bonn could not mediate between Britain and France because De Gaulle was not exclusively responsible for the Brussels fiasco. Rather it urged President Kennedy himself to mediate with De Gaulle, a mission similar to that performed by Anthony Eden in 1954 when the French National Assembly rejected the European Defense Community (EDC). Anthony Eden immediately persuaded France to accept Germany as a signatory of the Brussels Treaties resulting in the West European Union (WEU). The important thing to avoid in any case was an undeclared diplomatic war against France within the Atlantic Alliance, with Germany as the scapegoat merely because Adenauer had not succeeded in doing what Roosevelt and Churchill had failed to do in four years, i.e. to make De Gaulle shift his ground. Finally this paper concluded that Washington should be willing to reappraise the role of France and Europe in the alliance, whereby France could play a greater part in Europe and Europe could play a greater role in the Atlantic Alliance. For every move designed to checkmate De Gaulle, France could reply with moves to block the United States in Europe, ranging from economic and financial reprisals against U.S. exports and investments to military countermeasures.[104]

Poles apart were the two independent papers, *Stuttgarter Zeitung* and *Die Welt,* in their analysis of the issues of German foreign policy. Whereas the former called on Washington to revise its policy on Europe and De Gaulle, *Die Welt* argued the thesis that Bonn would have to face the hard fact that Washington regarded the Franco-German agreement as a diplomatic declaration of war. So Americans put pressure on Bonn and via Bonn on Paris. Such drastic tactics were used to make Germans realize that they were reaping the fruits of Adenauer's foreign policy, which had cast a twilight on priorities. This paper noted the differences between Adenauer and his Foreign Minister Schröder, who had a broad parliamentary majority behind him. Washington interpreted De Gaulle's embrace of Adenauer in Paris to mean political support, which Adenauer could not deny in the view of Die Welt. The Chancellor's offer to Secretary Ball of his support for Kennedy's proposed multilateral nuclear NATO force was hardly sufficient to dispel American concern. Americans would accept no bloc within NATO. Die Welt concluded that in the last analysis the Federal Government in Bonn would have to re-evaluate its foreign policy. This would mean recognition of Bonn's absolute dependence on the U.S. when confronted by the German problem, Berlin and vital security interests. France on the contrary was the only ally of Germany to recognize the Oder-Neisse line, which no German politician except Carlo Schmid (SPD) and Dr. Thomas Dehler (CDU) could afford to recognize. And yet De Gaulle referred to Germans across the wall as "Prussians," "Saxonians," and "Thuringians." [105] With its deep concern over basic issues facing a divided Germany and a divided Berlin, *Die Welt,* though independent, was moving close to the position of the SPD opposition party. This paper observed that the Bundestag would play a very decisive role in determining the fate of the Franco-German agreement. Any immediate or premature ratification, it warned, would be interpreted as a serious affront to the U.S.[106]

Differences between West German Catholic and Protestant papers over the Franco-German Treaty were even greater than the differences between the views expressed by pro-government as against pro-SPD and left-center papers. The Protestant weekly *Christ und Welt* noted that De Gaulle, unlike the British and Americans (except for Harold Wilson, British Labor leader) had recognized the Oder-Neisse line. This Protestant paper cast suspicion on Adenauer for accepting De Gaulle's interpretation of the Franco-German agreement.[107] In contrast, the Catholic weekly *Rheinische Merkur* strongly objected to the tone of the West German press in general for taking such a dark and foreboding view of Adenauer's life-work and for mad suggestions to the Federal Government and the Bundestag, such as delaying ratification of the Franco-German Treaty until De Gaulle revised his stand against Britain. This Catholic organ defended Adenauer against such scare headlines as the following: "This is the End of Europe," "EEC is falling apart," "The Bonn-Paris Axist disrupts NATO" and other outcries prompted by anti-Adenauer sentiments of recent years with the leitmotif "The old man should go." [108]

By the end of January 1963 the climax of the Atlantic Crisis was reached. At the end of the week following the Brussels fiasco, U.S. reactions were, if anything, less pessimistic than say on "Black Tuesday." Though disappointed, Washington was more inclined to a calm philosophical view of the European situation, with Bonn in a key position. Europe's future would now depend on the attitude of the Bundestag toward the Franco-German agreement. Washintgon, of course, hoped that the forces pressing for European integration would prevail and isolate De Gaulle. The West German Parliament was expected to discuss the question whether France had the military capability to assume a "forward defense" of Central Europe and West Berlin.[109] Would the Bundestag delay ratification of the Franco-German agreement? Did Germans realize that their national aim of reunification could not be promoted without U.S. protection? Numerous Declarations of the Federal Government and public opinion polls showed that Germans gave priority to these basic questions.

Nationalism was reviving in Germany as a result of two factors: the ever-increasing economic prosperity, with German industrial production in 1960 at 276 per cent above the level of 1936,[110] and as a reaction to Gaullism. This trend was more evident in certain right-center papers in contrast to the more restrained headlines appearing in both pro-government and SPD or left-center papers, which were more positive and hopeful of European unity. Headlines of both pro-CDU and pro-SPD papers included:

"European Unity Continues to Be Policy Aim" *Frankfurter Neue Presse* (pro-gov.) ; "Bonn Wants to Get Talks with Britain Going Again" *Rheinische Post* (CDU) ; "Europe Buried" *Rheinische Merkur* (Cologne, Catholic weekly) 31 January 1963. "Bonn Not Giving Up; New Mediation Efforts; Adenauer-Macmillan Meeting?" *Frankfurter Rundschau* (left-center) 31 January 1963. "U.S. Alarmed by De Gaulle; Concern over NATO Solidarity" *Neue Rhein Ruhr Zeitung* (Cologne, pro-SPD) 31 January 1963. "Europe NOT Lost Despite Deep Disappointment over Rebuff to Britain" *Bild Zeitung* (Hamburg, mass tabloid) 31 January 1963.

387

More negative and more nationalistic were the headlines of right-center papers:

"Europe Dissociating Itself from Stubborn De Gaulle"
Der Mittag (Düsseldorf, right-center) 31 January 1963.
"Bonn in No Hurry on Franco-German Agreement"
Deutsche Zeitung (right-center) 31 January 1963.

Der Mittag printed a trenchant critique of De Gaulle for causing an expansion of the EEC crisis, making impossible negotiations over British membership in EEC, Euratom and the Coal and Steel Community and for preventing former Secretary of State Herter from initiating discussions in Paris for tariff reductions. This paper repeated criticisms of De Gaulle's unrealistic dreams of grandeur by Senator Fulbright and even quoted a statement from an East German Communist paper *Neues Deutschland,* which contended that Adenauer wanted to cooperate with De Gaulle and subsequently Spain in order to bring pressure on the United States.[111] Alarmed by De Gaulle's alleged plans for regrouping NATO in order to curb U.S.-British influence in the NATO command and rumors of De Gaulle conspiring with the Soviets for the dissolution of both NATO and the Warsaw Pact, Washington counted on strong resistance to De Gaulle's plans by German political leaders in the Bundestag.[112] Historical necessities were said to make close relations between the U.S. and a powerful Europe mandatory. By its very nature Western nuclear force was indivisible.[113]

VII

Parliamentary Debate on German Foreign Policy,
6-7 February 1963

The signing of the Franco-German Friendship Treaty on 22 January 1963 followed a week later by the fiasco in Brussels furnished the occasion for a full dress parliamentary debate on the aims and objectives of German foreign policy as related to Europe and its American Ally. Chancellor Adenauer, in making the Government Declaration, briefly reviewed the crucial developments in international politics at the turn of the year, including: the Cuban Crisis, the attack on India, the Sino-Soviet split, the NATO Conference in Paris in December, 1962, the Nassau agreements, the signing of the Franco-German Friendship Treaty, the breaking off of negotiations over British membership in EEC, the breaking off of U.S.-Soviet negotiations over an atomic test ban and the order of the American President to prepare for a new series of atomic tests.[114]

Focusing first on the Cuban Crisis of 28 October 1962, the Chancellor stated that more significant than the dangerous, ruthless action of the Soviet leadership, this crisis gave proof that the American Government was prepared to make a hard decision when it came to a question of the existence of freedom. The Cuban Crisis had made a very deep impression on the Federal Government because the American people was solidly behind its government and was ready to stand by its convictions. Hence the solidarity of the Western world. The West had proof of the powerful leadership of the United States.

From the Cuban Crisis, the Chancellor turned to key points of interest in the Franco-German Treaty. Reviewing briefly the 400 years of tensions and wars between France and Germany, bringing death to millions of men and damage to all of Europe, the Chancellor emphasized the special significance of Franco-German reconciliation for both countries and for all of Europe. Closer relations between the two peoples—particularly their youth—were more important than formal agreements. Without this friendship, the Chancellor declared, Europe could not exist.[115] This was the idea which had inspired Robert Schuman, French Foreign Minister, in planning the European Coal and Steel Authority. Nevertheless, the Chancellor emphasized that cooperation between the French and German people was no substitute for European integration, but rather an essential prerequisite.[116]

Turning next to the Brussels Crisis, Dr. Adenauer called it serious, but still curable. Recalling the many disappointments on the way to European unity, the Chancellor assured his audience that in the future also "we will work for Europe despite all hindrances and difficulties." He then cited the Joint Communiqué, signed by De Gaulle and himself on 22 January 1963:

. . . In recognition of the fact that strengthening coopera-

389

tion between both countries constitute a great step on the way to a united Europe, which is the goal of all nations . . .

the negotiations over entrance of Great Britain into the EEC were held to be on ice—but not broken off. All participants— we especially—will exert every effort to resume normal discussions. Moreover, the Chancellor announced that only one week previous his cabinet had given unanimous approval to a resolution to work for closer unity among the EEC partners in order to make it possible for Great Britain to join the Common Market.[117]

The rest of the Government Declaration concerned with foreign policy was essentially a reiteration of the Federal Government's basic objectives in foreign policy: Germany's right of self-determination, close ties with the people of the Soviet occupation zone, active cooperation with NATO—despite strong domestic opposition in the 1950s—and close cooperation with the United States, based on the deepest conviction of the value of the freedom of nations. Europe knows that without the support of the United States it can not defend itself.[118]

Following the Government Declaration on the Foreign and Domestic Situation by the Chancellor, came the discussion and debate by the party chairmen and other key leaders in the Bundestag, beginning with the opposition SPD party. Chairman Ollenhauer argued the thesis that the Government Declaration really was no foreign policy at all. He emphasized that not one word pertained to the origins, background or objectives of Dr. Adenauer's fifth cabinet and referred to the fourth Adenauer Government, set up on 7 November 1961, long after the Bundestag elections of September 17 as a government of the "lost year." He then alluded to the *Spiegel* Affair, which had produced a violent domestic conflict, forcing Dr. Adenauer to reorganize his entire cabinet and weakening his position within his own party, in the Bundestag and with large sections of public opinion. Ollenhauer called for absolute guarantees against the arbitrary arrest of newspaper editors in the future under any circumstances. The SPD Chairman repeated his charge that the Government Declaration had failed to set forth any over-all policy and that a mere cataloging of items that one could or should do was no policy.

Turning to the issues of foreign policy, Ollenhauer announced the full support of the Social Democratic opposition for the Chancellor's statement that: "The Federal Republic stands firmly behind the free part of Berlin, which is inseparable from free Germany." Berlin was and must remain part of Germany. The SPD Chairman evoked applause from both government and opposition benches when he condemned the ruthless policies of exploitation practiced by Soviet Zone officials, denying basic human rights to 17 million Germans, destined to suffer such a cruel fate.[119] Ollenhauer could find no connection between the observations of the Chancellor upon the Franco-German Treaty and the breaking off of EEC negotiation in Brussels vis-a-vis the complex problems of Germany's European policy—especially Germany's treaty obligations in other areas of West European or Western policy. Actually there was a long Social Democratic tradition in support of Franco-German friendship long before the First World War, climaxed by the peace conference of leading French and German socialists in Basel, Switzerland in 1913, with the warm embrace of August Bebel, Chairman of the SPD, and the French Socialist Party leader, Jean Jaures. Ollenhauer emphasized that through all these years the German Socialists had remained faithful to this tradition. Moreover, the French Socialists, who after the Hitler War in their country faced complex problems, were the first to publicly turn against the partition of Germany. "We in Europe can only achieve peace with a Germany which is not unnaturally divided; we can only achieve peace in a Europe in which the French and German people live together in sincere friendship." [120] The SPD Chairman recognized the impossibility in the parliamentary discussion of 7 February 1963 of analyzing all the possible consequences of the Franco-German Treaty and its impact on the European crisis, until the first reading of the treaty, which would come later. However, he did emphasize that De Gaulle's brutal actions against British EEC membership on January 14 and 29 were both related to the question of the further existence of the EEC and the possible development of the European Community and European cooperation as well as the Atlantic Alliance of Free Europe with the United States. More specifically, the Chairman of the SPD opposition called upon the Adenauer Government to clarify the actual meaning of its European policy and explain how the Paris agreements would place common European interests above national or group interests within the community. Was this French Treaty really compatible with the great European idea of the French Foreign Minister, Robert Schuman, who had worked out the Treaty of the Mountain Union, known as the Coal and Steel Community (ECSC) so highly revered by Adenauer? This Schuman Treaty, in Ollenhauer's view, went far beyond other European Treaties in its supra-national character. When challenged by Count Guttenberg (CSU), Ollenhauer admitted that the provision for joint consultation on important mutual problems, contained in the Franco-German Treaty was not incompatible with Robert Schuman's idea. But everything would depend on how this formal treaty was implemented. The decisive question, therefore, was where Bonn stood in its foreign policy and what line it wished to follow in the future. So the SPD opposition party in the coming weeks and months would undertake to examine carefully all aspects of the Franco-German Treaty and its possible consequences for Germany's other international or European treaty obligations: the EEC, the Coal and Steel Community and NATO. Near the end of his discourse Ollenhauer drew applause from all sides of the house with a ringing appeal to those in the Government and the Coalition for a close understanding with the United States, on whom Germans must depend to protect Berlin and Germany's position on the crucial question of recognition of the Soviet Zone regime.[121]

Dr. Heinrich von Brenatano, floor leader of the ruling CDU/CSU party, followed SPD Chairman Ollenhauer with a discussion on "The Creed of Solidarity of the Free World" emphasizing the strengthening of the Atlantic Alliance and the Franco-German Treaty as the kernel of German foreign policy. He contended that the most recent events had not weakened, but rather strengthened Germany's policy of European integration. The Franco-German Treaty was called the historical result of the Adenauer Government's European policy, which began with Robert Schuman's Treaty for the Mountain Union and ended with the Rome Treaties for the EEC—a policy not always supported by the SPD party. In reply to Ollenhauer's question as to the effect of the French Treaty upon other treaty obligations, von Brentano stated that the Federal Government's main goal of multilateral European integration remained unchanged. The Government wished to use the Franco-German Treaty as a means of strengthening its over-all European and Atlantic policy.[122]

The CDU/CSU Chairman called the Soviet Note of 28 August 1962 in response to the Chancellor's note of February 21st protesting the murder of Peter Fechter at the Berlin Wall a cynical and inhuman document. And yet he agreed entirely with his SPD opponent, Ollenhauer, that it was the responsibility of the Federal Government to do everything within its power to increase contracts with the 17 million Germans living in the Soviet Zone. He gave full support to Ollenhauer's protest against violations of human rights in East Berlin, on the Berlin Wall and along the zonal border, also protested by the Free World as inhumanity. On the other hand the Chairman of the CDU/CSU fraction took issue with his SPD opponent on the *Spiegel* Affair. In order to balance the SPD demand for an absolute guarantee against any future arbitrary arrests of newspaper editors, von Brentano called for a guarantee that no secret documents would fall into false hands.[123] Von Brentano answered Ollenhauer's complaint that a mere cataloging of aims and objectives in the Government Declaration was no policy with a statement that the mere enumeration of unattainable demands by the opposition was no policy.

Following von Brentano's discussion of the Government Declaration came the discourse of the dynamic Chairman of the Free Democratic Party, Dr. Erich Mende, entitled "Coalition Calls for Compromise." He began with a rebuttal against SPD Chairman Ollenhauer's arguments. Dr. Mende characterized Ollenhauer's speech as a series of admonitions, good advice, apprehensions and a confession of communal spirit. The FDP Chairman emphasized that for the first time in the fourteen years of this parliament, the Chancellor, after completing the Government Declaration, had invited the opposition to become a vital element—in fact the only occasion when the Head of the Government had to ask the opposition to be an opposition. He then observed that one had often had the impression that the Social Democratic opposition was more and more on the way to becoming a coalition party in a look-out tower, still exerting every effort to join the Government Coalition. This seemed to Mende a contradiction—for on the one hand the SPD spoke of a lost year and deplored this bad government. On the other hand it had continually tried to join it as a participant.[124]

In the first half of his discourse Mende discussed such crucial questions as: the Cuban Crisis, efforts toward European unity, relations with France and the United States, defense needs and problems of Germany and Berlin. He saw three positive elements in the Cuban Crisis:

1. The solidarity of the Atlantic Alliance and the determination of the American President and the American people to show the Soviet Premier the limits of U.S. self-respect—also in the Berlin question—to beware of making any false calculation.

2. The second positive element was the sobering effect on part of the German people—that no one can withdraw into a private realm of self-imposed isolation, but that public and private affairs were inseparably bound together, that the fate of an individual and his family was joined to the fate of the nation, indeed, of the whole continent and finally that everything was bound up with the question of war and peace.

3. Finally the 28th of October 1962, especially in the thinking of the Soviet Premier, Khrushchev, probably marked an historical date in the realization by the world powers that severe conflicts today could no longer be settled by atomic war, but in the atomic age war had to give way to policy carried on by other means.[125]

The FDP Chairman took pains to emphasize the endless efforts of the early Coalition Governments of the CDU/CSU and FDP to encourage European unification through such organizations as the Strasburg European Council (1950), the Coal and Steel Community, the European Defense Community (though most unpopular with many Germans, who bitterly resisted it with such expressions as "Ohne mich"), the West European Union and NATO. The FDP hesitated at first to support the European Economic Community of the Six, but only out of consideration for the Outer Seven countries, including Great Britain, in the European free Trade Association (EFTA). After a period of misunderstanding over the Saar, a Franco-

German understanding won the respect of the French Government and the French people. Then the FDP hailed the Franco-German harmony and friendship as a point of departure for even greater efforts toward European cooperation, as an historical event, after 400 years of tragic civil war.

After the set-back of the EEC at Brussels on 29 January 1963 new situations would call for new efforts at cooperation, such as tariff agreements, closer contacts in the West European Union, the Organization for Economic Cooperation and Development (OECD) and the Atlantic Alliance. The question whether German policy would have to make a choice between the United States and Great Britain *vis-à-vis* Franco-German friendship, as suggested especially in the foreign press, was regarded by Mende as an absurd alternative. Germans should avoid anything which could force them to make such a choice. Franco-German friendship, European integration—including Great Britain—and Scandinavia—and the Atlantic Alliance were all children of the same spirit and not in opposition. Dr. Mende next turned to the question of home defense with pointed emphasis upon quality rather than quantity of troops in the military buildup. He stated that the strategic concept within NATO would, indeed, occupy the parliament and its defense committee. Mende supported the SPD Chairman Ollenhauer, who had said it was expedient not to overstress this defense issue, but rather to give the new Defense Minister Kai von Hassel, who had replaced Strauss after the "Spiegel" Affair, an opportunity first to orient himself in the military realm.

The FDP Chairman concluded his discussion of the foreign situation with pointed references to the German and Berlin problems. The world should realize that all three political parties, represented in parliament, demand no less than the natural right of self-determination. This is a right now exercised by even the newly emerging nations in Asia and Africa necessary to regulate their own political and economic, social and cultural affairs. All three parliamentary parties were, therefore, determined that the German people, particularly its youth, should never resign itself to accept the partition of Germany. The dynamic fraction leader of the FDP recommended a permanent German Conference to meet continually in Berlin in keeping with a resolution of the Bundestag on 12 October 1962.

It appealed to all four occupation powers to set up an all-German technical commission on the ministerial or ambassadorial level in order to deal with economics, trade, commerce, sports and culture.[126] In this proposal and in his continued and consistent opposition to the Hallstein Doctrine (of severing diplomatic relations with any state that recognized the Ulbricht regime of the Zone) the political astuteness, imagination and dynamic force of the Chairman of the FDP fraction was shown. Most pronounced was his willingness to work patiently toward a solution of the perennial German problem along pragmatic lines rather than through ideological dogmatism.

The parliamentary debate on foreign policy was continued by Fritz Erler (SPD), who discussed the "Standard of the Opposition." To FDP Chairman Mende's diatribe that the SPD had become a party of government watchers, Erler asked who then was the opposition party watcher? Certainly the capacity of the SPD to take over governmental responsibility was more developed than the capacity of the FDP to go into opposition. Although the SPD with 40 per cent of the parliamentary seats was not part of the Government Coalition, Erler concluded, "What is not can still become." He chided the FDP Chairman for claiming credit for any accomplishment, but attributing no action to the fault of the opposition.

After the Brussels failure, Erler warned that no Franco-German alliance or network of bilateral consultations could replace real community cooperation. It would be dangerous if a Franco-German strategic concept would contradict the strategic concepts not only of the United States, but of the majority of states in the Atlantic Alliance. To strengthen the solidarity between partners on both sides of the Atlantic, Erler considered that the Forum of the OECD would be even better than the West European Union (WEU). The SPD speaker deplored a European economic autarchy, which would be as absurd as that which emerged in Hitler's Third Reich before 1939. Since West German exports totaled 50 billion DM annually, German vital interests required a world market. But apart from economic advantages of British membership in the EEC, Erler argued that the European Community would also benefit from closer contact with English principles of free, constitutional, parliamentary democracy. He felt encouraged by Chancellor Adenauer's promise that the Federal Government at the very next session of the EEC Ministers would undertake to strengthen the democratic-parliamentary character of the Community.

The SPD Chairman turned to the question so often asked in and out of parliament as to why the Social Democrats had formerly opposed the European Defense Community (EDC) and the Coal and Steel Community, whereas later they gave full support to building up the European Community and strengthening Atlantic solidarity. His answer was that the former were so bound up with military problems. Social Democrats had always asked how much the fusion of half of Germany into Western organizations would affect chances of German reunification. Whoever says European unification must wait until German unification is achieved not only torpedoes European unity, but hands a prize to the Soviet Union.

Erler strongly emphasized the great change in world power relations with the ending of the U.S. monopoly of nuclear weapons, which led to the brutal sharpening of the Soviet's German policy. By 1958 the USSR had sufficient nuclear capacity to issue the Berlin Ultimatum. People must understand this transformation of world power relations. For Germans this meant close solidarity with the great world power, the U.S.A.—even though back in 1955 the SPD had opposed West German membership in NATO, in accordance with German public opinion. Rather than face two terrible alternatives: atomic holocaust and death *vis-à-vis* capitulation, a broader scale of defense possibilities might reduce the risk of atomic war present in any world conflict. Hence, the great anxiety in the Western Alliance: How should these defense possibilities be established? After the West united its atomic potential, it turned to the area of a conventional striking force. But even here Germans could not take over because they knew their limitations in man-power, financial and economic resources. So the Chancellor in his Government Declaration had stressed the strengthening of quality, not quantity of troops recruited for home defense. This concept, Erler noted, contradicted the ideas of the former Defense Minister Strauss on territorial defense. Finally the Western Alliance must create security for all. Naturally there was some apprehension as to whether the strongest partner (U.S.A.) in the hour of danger would sacrifice all in a life and death struggle.

397

Whoever weakens confidence in the Western Alliance destroys its practical military effectiveness and encourages other ventures. What Erler considered most dangerous were senseless discussions charging that the leading world power wanted to push Europeans into the rank of ground troops, while it retained its monopoly of nuclear power. This was false because the U.S. knew what the destruction of Europe would mean for it. Moreover, it maintained 400,000 of its ground troops in Europe—a greater number of foot soldiers than most European states.

Regarding military arrests of editors in the *Spiegel* Affair, Erler emphasized that German public opinion was rightly aroused over the flagrant disregard of free constitutional principles. The arrest of five editors at night was not because the soldiers wanted it, but merely because the civilian responsible for the military arrests acted in defense of his own political power. This point was made clear by the action of Parliament and the storm of public opinion against Strauss. What further annoyed Parliament was the fact that this house had to endure this from a responsible Minister who had acted in so underhanded a manner and then lied to the Bundestag. *Before this high house, all the truth must be told—above all by the Government.* In the background stands the relation of the Government and Parliament to the pros and public opinion. To draw a careful line of demarcation between the legitimate needs to protect the security interests of the state and the legitimate basic right of information and freedom of opinion on the other hand is a difficult task, but we must make the effort. Only thus can our citizens when they enter the voting booth be fully informed and able to make decisions. Also between elections the citizens must be able to act. They are sovereign, not we in Parliament. Without democrats there can be no democracy.[127]

Following the rebuttal of Erler, Adenauer returned to the rostrum to state that De Gaulle had promised him in Paris that after the Franco-German Treaty had been ratified the first subject of consultation would be the entrance of England into the Common Market. Adenauer continued that he told De Gaulle: "We Germans are on good terms with Britain because of Berlin and reunification and, therefore, apart from all other considerations I am in favor of taking Great Britain into the Common Market." In reply to a previous question from the SPD Chairman Ollenhauer, the Chancellor said that on 11 October 1962 he had made the same statement, which had found recognition in the British press. Adenauer concluded that in his opinion it was not good for foreign policy for a head of government to be always questioned, for people to exaggerate various shades of opinion within the Cabinet or to speak of a twilight government. The Chancellor expressed the desire that Britons would believe him. Above all, he could not lead the way to negotiations with Britain, if here in Parliament his word was doubted.[128]

Following the Chancellor's statement, Erler rose to state that the Chancellor had made unmistakably clear the position of his Government on the entrance of Great Britain into the Common Market and that if he followed through on this commitment, he would have the support of this entire house.

Dr. Ernest Achenbach, speaking for the Free Democrats, carried the Chancellor's idea of confidence in our good will one step further and called for negotiations with the Soviet Union on the basis of the Soviet Note of 3 August 1961, which was still unanswered. In this note the Russians said their proposals were not an ultimatum and that the West Germans should make proposals and they "would prove it." Before all the world and the Soviet Union we should make clear: that we are ready to state what political problems stand between us—East and West. We might make clear that the German problem poses no threat to world peace. The Russian Note states that if we ourselves ever obtain atomic weapons, they would have to consider this as an immediate threat to their vital interests and would then take counter-measures. In this lay a certain parallel with the threat of Cuba to the U.S.A. On such a vital matter, the FDP spokesman continued, we naturally should consult our allies, particularly the United States. But, together with our allies we should say: Eighteen years after the ending of hostilities, it is high time to discuss problems which still confront us. In such negotiations we should, of course, support our allies, but with a firm will say "no" if anything should arise, which is not compatible with our vital interests and self-respect. Twice within the twentieth century the German people have been involved in two frightful world wars. Therefore, it is our responsibility, the FDP speaker concluded, to do everything within our power to spare the people from a new World War. No future historian then would dare say, Herr Chancellor, you were in agreement with those Germans who destroyed peace with the East. *We want peace—above all there where there is a possibility of maintaining world peace,* there where it is a question of settling an outstanding political problem in a just manner or of bringing it near to a solution. The world should know that the German Federal Republic and the Federal Government are prepared to do whatever is necessary.[129]

Foreign Minister Schröder followed Dr. Achenbach and urged the Bundestag not to delay ratification of the Franco-German Treaty any longer than was absolutely necessary. Dr. Schröder first expressed his agreement with the SPD spokesman, Erler, on several items relating to past efforts toward European integration as a way for Germany to get back into the community of free nations. He took occasion to dispel the legend that for a short time back in 1945 the Germans would have had the chance to become a free Germany with Soviet support. Schröder argued that the merits of the Franco-German Treaty were in no way affected by its unfortunate timing, that is, being signed on 22 January 1963, just one week after De Gaulle's press conference of January 14 and one week before the Brussels fiasco on 29 January 1963. In any case, the Paris Treaty provided a special kind of future cooperation, the essence of which was consultation. "This does not mean that we signed a blank check for French policy." [130]

VIII

Bundesrat Resolution of 1 March 1963

Immediately after the general foreign policy debate in the lower house (Bundestag), the upper house (Bundesrat) urged the entrance of Great Britain into the Common Market in terms of a resolution expressing anxiety for European unity by the representatives of the 11 states (Länder):

The Bundesrat observes with great anxiety the difficulties which resulted from the interruption of discussions over the entrance of Great Britain into the European Economic Community.

400

If these discussions were not resumed, the danger of a split of free Europe into two economic blocs would emerge and through this the political relations of the European states with one another would be impaired.

The Bundesrat, therefore, urges the Federal Government, in cooperation with the governments of the various member states and the specialized agencies of the EEC to do everything to avoid the obvious dangers and to work for negotiations with Great Britain in the spirit of the preamble of the EEC Treaty, which contains an invitation to other European nations to join as soon as feasible.[131]

On 1 March 1963 the Bundesrat passed a resolution introduced by Mayor Brandt of Berlin endorsing the Franco-German Treaty with certain qualifications:

a. The Bundesrat requests the Federal Government to work to the end that through the application of the Franco-German Treaty the great goals which determine foreign policy for Germany in common with its allies be promoted:

b. The establishment and strengthening of the union of free peoples, especially a close partnership between Europe and the U.S.A.;

c. the realization of the right of the German people to self-determination and the reunification of Germany;

d. the common defense within NATO and the integration of the military forces of the states joined together in this alliance;

e. the integration of Europe through the European Community in which a way was begun for the inclusion of Great Britain and other states;

f. the strengthening of commercial ties through negotiations between the EEC, Great Britain and the U.S.A. along with other states in the General Association for Trade Treaties (GATT).[132]

In the third item above, Brandt explained that the self-determination resolution in the Paris Treaty was valid for the *Land* of Berlin except defense considerations. He called this the normal clause, which was customary to clarify the relation of Berlin to bilateral treaties of the Federal Republic. This normal clause was used in the 1952 Treaty between the Three Powers, the Federal Republic and the Berlin Senate. The Mayor of Berlin explained that the Federal Republic represents the state of Berlin in foreign affairs and that this should not be changed. Therefore, it would be necessary to include the Berlin clause in the ratification law. Finally, Mayor Brandt wanted to emphasize the desire of Berlin that the rights and responsibilities of the Three protecting Powers for Berlin, including France, shall in no way be affected by the foregoing treaty. [133]

Following Mayor Brandt, Chancellor Adenauer addressed the Bundesrat in behalf of the Franco-German Treaty, emphasizing the following items: a. The Treaty would have created no confusion were it not for the unfortunate timing, which was purely accidental. b. In the words of Mayor Brandt the Treaty had finally ended centuries of rivalries between France and Germany in the interest of both nations, in the interest of peace in Europe and of European cooperation and in the interest of world peace. c. This Franco-German *rapprochement* originated with the French Foreign Minister Robert Schuman, founder of the Coal and Steel Community. d. Decades ago there was an alliance between Czarist Russia and the German Reich, an alliance against France, followed in 1891 by a Franco-Russian Alliance against Germany. The Franco-German Treaty would prevent any Russian attempts either to align with Germany against France or with France against Germany. Moreover, it would be a dam against communistic threats from the East—much greater than the threat before 1914—a dam to protect not only France and Germany, but all Europe. e. Germany's rights and obligations under NATO would in no way be impaired by this Treaty as Mayor Brandt had indicated in his report for the Defense and Foreign Affairs Committees of the Bundesrat.

In a powerful peroration Dr. Adenauer emphasized that they had not wanted to make a treaty between governments nor between two "old men," De Gaulle and Adenauer, but wanted to see a treaty concluded between peoples, especially between French and German youth in the faith that strengthening cooperation between their countries would be an important step on the way to a united Europe, the goal of both peoples. In

402

fact, the Treaty was signed by De Gaulle and Adenauer despite their different views on NATO, on the multilateral nuclear striking force and on Britain's entrance into the Common Market. Finally the aged Chancellor concluded with a powerful appeal to his hearers to consider the Treaty for what it was, without regard to what happened at De Gaulle's press conference or the meeting in Brussels in January. There was no connection between these events. Dr. Adenauer asked his hearers to consider the Treaty as the final stone of a structure representing long years of work after all parties in the Bundestag, including the Social Democrats, will have participated in the parliamentary ratification. All parties should consider the Treaty for what it should be, that is, a work of peace, a treaty of peace, a peace between Germany and France, a treaty for the peace of Europe.[134]

Most marked in the parliamentary debate on international politics on February 7 was the unanimity of all three political parties on the basic tenets of German foreign policy: loyalty to the Atlantic Alliance and close cooperation with the U.S.A. to guarantee peace, freedom and security. The Franco-German Treaty was regarded as an important part of this policy. That the Bundestag, the Bundesrat and the Bonn Government all agreed that Great Britain must be admitted to the Common Market was attributed to the cooperation of the SPD opposition speaker, Fritz Erler.[135] Although *Die Welt* had characterized the Chancellor's Declaration of February 6 as "meager, colorless and lacking in inspiration,"—closely parallel to SPD Chairman Ollenhauer's comment—it admitted Adenauer's skillful tactic, which was obviously to avoid a sharp debate in Parliament. In fact both the Chancellor and his Foreign Minister Schröder went out of their way to compliment the SPD opposition, to elicit its support and to point out items of agreement between the Government and opposition. In sharp contrast to this, the West German press had, just prior to the Bundestag debate, emphasized sharp differences within the Bonn Cabinet between Adenauer and Erhard, with Schröder taking a vague stand between them. The CDU/CSU Fraction Chairman von Brentano exerted great efforts to smooth over these differences and wanted to exploit all possibilities for a relaxation of tensions within the EEC and Atlantic Alliance. Prior to the foreign policy debate of February 7 many papers supported the views of the FDP and SPD opposition against early ratification.[136] By this time the Chancellor had shown political astuteness in avoiding discussion of differences with Erhard over bilateral treaties and by declaring his support for British admission to EEC because vital to Berlin and the whole German question.

Following the foreign policy debate in the Bundestag, the United States was struggling to adapt its policy to the facts of the European situation by revising its European policy to allow Europe a greater role, with atom bombers leaving Europe as part of the armament shift. With Polaris missiles replacing IRBMs in Italy and Turkey, the scrapping of rocket bases in Britain and of U.S. bomber bases in Europe and Africa, Germans feared a basic change in U.S. strategy, which might affect NATO planning.[137]

Secretary of State Rusk meanwhile emphasized three basic tenets of U.S. policy:

    a. a multilateral nuclear force within NATO despite De Gaulle,

    b. expansion of U.S. foreign trade by lowering tariffs and

    c. better consultation with states in NATO on foreign policy.

Meanwhile Bonn foreign policy was between two fires as far as its military policy was concerned. Germans could not afford to deviate from NATO strategy or lose U.S. support in Berlin, but was still militarily dependent on France for defense in depth in case of war. Writing in *Die Zeit*, Marion Countess Doenhoff called De Gaulle's European plan Europe's doom. She surmised it would take Moscow some time to decide whether to work toward agreement with Kennedy or to throw the Americans out of Europe. Only in the latter case would Moscow side with De Gaulle, who controlled U.S. supply lines to Germany. This warning against De Gaulle and French power politics was underlined by the reliable Swiss paper *Neue Züricher Zeitung,* which reported the deletion under French pressure of a clause in the Franco-German Treaty (Sec. II B, paragraphs 1 and 3) referring to NATO as the basis of Western strategy. When

Foreign Minister Schröder denied the deletion of this clause in a meeting of the Foreign Affairs Commitee, he suffered violent SPD criticism for the first time from Deputy Chairman Herbert Wehner. Kennedy had to regard the Franco-German Treaty, therefore, as a bilateral treaty, an instrument of French power politics directed against the United States. Thus Adenauer faced a dilemma parallel to that faced by von Caprivi after Bismarck's dismissal in 1890. Caprivi allowed the Reinsurance Treaty with Russia to lapse in 1890 because Berlin did not want to hurt Austria. To protect Adenauer against a mistake similar to that of Caprivi, Erhard requested the Bonn Cabinet prior to ratification to determine whether the Treaty might in any way conflict with Germany's NATO commitments. But he and four FDP Ministers were voted down. The Protestant weekly *Christ und Welt* noted that the Chancellor had received emphatic warnings from General Clay and John McCloy against any false moves. Hence, Washington's fear that Adenauer might switch alliances was as well founded as Russian distrust of Germany in 1890.[138]

In the meantime De Gaulle's European concept was being challenged by Prime Minister Macmillan's speech in the British Parliament, criticizing De Gaulle, praising the Germans for their stand on the EEC problem and calling for Anglo-German friendship. On the other hand the Scandinavian Governments were deeply concerned over statements by the new German Defense Minister, Kai von Hassel. He was reported to have stated at a CDU meeting in Schleswig-Holstein that Adenauer feared the possible participation in EEC of Scandinavian countries with Social Democratic governments might result in Social Democratic countries having a predominance in Europe. CDU/CSU headquarters in Bonn interpreted the controversial statements attributed to von Hassel as reflecting attempts of the SPD opposition to break the CDU/CSU—FDP Coalition and bring about a coalition with the SPD. These sources claimed that such efforts were made by Ollenhauer and Herbert Wehner in interviews with *Berliner Morgenpost* and *Rundschau Am Sonntag*.[139]

German Internal Politics—Events in Berlin

The close interrelationship between German domestic and foreign policy in 1963 was shown by the impact of the Berlin parliamentary elections upon politics in Bonn. Press reports of Dr. Adenauer's interview with the Berlin *Morgenpost* reflected the Chancellor's recognition of the decisive role of U.S. military power for the security of Germany and Berlin. He emphasized the advantage of the Franco-German Treaty for Berlin because it was the basis of a united Europe and, therefore, vital to the Atlantic Alliance. The best evidence of this, according to Adenauer, was the bitter Soviet reaction. The Chancellor's Berlin radio address, criticizing the illusions of Brandt's SPD party, was described as intervention in the Berlin elections of 17 February 1963. SPD deputy chairman Herbert Wehner called for an all-out political offensive by all three political parties in Bonn. Meanwhile the Indivisible Germany Organization urged Bonn to make reference to German partition in all future treaties. Reports in the West German press of a long interview with Khrushchev reflected the belief of the Soviet Chief that German reunification was pure imagination and not desired by any Western Power—U.S.A., Britain or France because they feared a reunited Germany. At the same time Mayor Brandt in Berlin rejected an offer by SED Chief, Walter Ulbricht to negotiate with the West Berlin Senate, except on technical matters of traffic and interzonal trade.[140]

On 17 February 1963 came the Berlin elections for the City Parliament, the first since the erection of the Berlin Wall on 13 August 1961. The overwhelming defeat of the Berlin CDU with the loss of nearly one fourth of its seats contrasted with the impressive victory of Willy Brandt's SPD. Mayor Brandt thanked Berliners for their large turnout and assured them that the SPD would prove itself worthy of their trust. The Berlin FDP, which in 1958 could not even clear the 5 per cent hurdle, now doubled its vote with an increase from 3.6 to 7.9 per cent. To Erich Mende this vote reflected the political maturity of Berliners and their faith in the three party system. Foreign observers interpreted the switch of about 9 per cent of the voters away from the Berlin CDU over to the SPD and also to the FDP as reflecting their high morale despite the Berlin Wall, their impatience with the EEC failure in Brussels and their protest against the Berlin CDU's interference with the projected meeting between Khrushchev and Willy Brandt. At the instigation of Vice Mayor Amrehn (CDU), Brandt cancelled the interview, although Chancellor Adenauer in Bonn had told Brandt over the telephone he had no objection to his meeting the Soviet Chief and that it might relieve tensions. Headlines in the West German Press included:

"Heavy SPD Gains in Berlin" (*Rheinishce Post,* Düsseldorf, pro-CDU); "SPD Strongest Party in Berlin" *(Frankfurter Allgemeine,* right-center); "Berlin Confirms That Brandt's Policy Was Correct; Heavy Defeat for CDU; FDP Clears Hurdle" *(Der Mittag,* Düsseldorf, right-center); "Triumph for Willy Brandt; Big SPD Victory; FDP, Too, Successful; "CDU Defeated" *(Bild Zeitung,* mass tabloid) 18 February 1963.

Results of the Berlin elections were as follows:

	1963	1958
Total Registered Voters:	1,749,368	1,757,842
Total Votes Cast:	1,571,820	1,632,540
Turnout of Voters:	89.9%	92.9%
SPD	61.9	52.6
CDU	28.9	39.7
FDP	7.9	3.6
SED (Communist Zone Party)	1.3	1.9

After Khrushchev's Berlin Ultimatum of 27 November 1958, Berliners responded with a 3 per cent larger turnout than in 1963. Prominent CDU papers attributed SPD success to voter disapproval of the Berlin CDU leader Amrehn's veto of Brandt's meeting with Khrushchev. The conservative *Mittag* went even further in its criticism and admitted that Berliners had indicated their desire for a strong SPD government or an SPD-FDP Coalition to back their mayor in efforts to protect their interests *vis-à-*

vis the mighty power to the East.[141] The independent *General Anzeiger* emphasized that the clear loser was the CDU which suffered heavy losses even in the strong CDU districts of West and Southwest Berlin. Deputy Mayor Amrehn pointed to outside influences, such as the hard attack by West German CDU party leader Dufues against Brandt, which Berliners considered unfair. Other papers warned that the special situation in Berlin would prevent any real policy change in Bonn because decisions on Berlin would now as before be made primarily by the U.S. and the Soviet Union.[142] Even the pro-CDU/CSU press admitted that voters were showing impatience with the lack of a consistent German foreign policy, as well as sharp differences within the Cabinet over domestic issues. Above all Berlin needed a government of action lest it again become an international sore spot. Tensions between factions in Berlin and among the Western Powers could only benefit Khrushchev in East-West negotiations over Berlin.[143]

Nevertheless, differences continued within the ranks of both the CDU and SPD parties. Whereas Wehner (SPD) favored an SPD-CDU coalition both in Berlin and Bonn, Brandt wanted to continue cooperation with the CDU only if the latter would accept a minor role. The SPD leadership in Bonn, however, urged Brandt to seek a coalition with the CDU in Berlin. Ollenhauer feared that snubbing the CDU in Berlin would militate against chances of a grand coalition government in Bonn after Adenauer's resignation in the fall of 1963. Brandt personally favored a coalition with the FDP. The big SPD vote in Berlin undoubtedly improved Brandt's position as potential candidate for the Chancellorship in 1965. The big SPD vote in Berlin of 61.9 per cent would also enable Brandt to build up his closest political adviser in the Berlin Senate, Heinrich Albertz, as the logical candidate to succeed Brandt as Mayor of Berlin, if Brandt should win the chancellorship in 1965. Albertz had already demonstrated bold and unconventional traits, initiative and a capacity for responsibility in critical situations.[144]

In any case Brandt's Berlin triumph placed him in a strong position to decide Berlin's future policy without depending on a coalition. His readiness to cooperate with the CDU or FDP was only to check extreme demands of his own party. Brandt was expected to continue efforts toward a *modus vivendi* for Berlin by future contacts with East Berlin, despite CDU opposition. The Berlin election results showed that Berliners were more aware than most West Germans of the primacy of foreign policy over domestic issues and the priority of close relations with the U.S.A. Both the failure in Brussels and trenchant American criticism of the Franco-German Treaty were important factors in the heavy CDU losses. In fact the Bonn CDU expected further setbacks in coming Landtag elections in lower Saxony and Rhineland Palatinate in the spring of 1963. Apart from the reaction of voters against the *Spiegel* Affair and Adenauer's loss of prestige was the fact that the SPD was changing from a socialist party to a people's party. Although Adenauer himself preferred an SPD-CDU Coalition in Berlin, CDU Chairman Dufues and most CDU politicians in Bonn wanted the Berlin CDU to go into opposition.[145]

Frankfurt papers began speculating on new U.S.-Soviet Berlin talks. Reports from Washington indicated the U.S.A. was basically in favor of continuing contacts with the Soviets in Berlin through negotiations between Secretary Rusk and Soviet Ambassador Dobrynin. Whereas the British Ambassador was said to give full support, the French Ambassador indicated De Gaulle would not obstruct such talks, but had little faith in them. Bonn quarters considered the time inopportune after the Cuban crisis, but still expected Khrushchev would propose direct negotiations between Bonn and Moscow to settle the Berlin problem. Meanwhile *Der Spiegel* reported Khrushchev's willingness to remove the Berlin Wall provided: a. allied troops in West Berlin were placed under a UN Command, b. Berlin access routes were under UN control and guaranteed by both the U.S. and USSR, c. the Western Allies gave *de facto* recognition to the Ulbricht regime, d. the West would accept a nuclear test ban with a limit of three annual inspections. The Berlin elections, however, showed that Berliners were still adamant in their opposition to the Ulbricht regime. Therefore, Berlin needed a strong government to guarantee close cooperation between Berlin and Bonn. Meanwhile SPD deputy chairman Wehner was urging Bonn to open discussions with Moscow on the basis of the Soviet Memorandum of 27 December 1961 and Bonn's reply of 21 February 1962. While admitting that Berlin was primarily a problem for the four Powers, they needed Bonn's support to

409

get the German problem off dead center. As long as Bonn and Moscow continued their polemics, the situation would become more critical, according to Wehner.[146]

In the meantime, the new British Labor leader, Harold Wilson frightened Germans with a speech in support of the Gaitskell plan of calling for disengagement and a *détente* in Central Europe and *de facto* recognition of the Soviet regime. Wilson called for intensified East-West German trade, a nuclear-free zone in Europe and recognition of the Oder-Neisse line. Wilson's statements evinced less alarm in Washington quarters because many Americans considered the Oder-Neisse line as a *fait accompli.* Anyhow the U.S.A. had been calling for intensified trade between East and West Germany even if this should lead to practical *de facto* recognition. At the same time SPD deputy chairman Fritz Erler, who had been invited to London to discuss the German problem, was expected to brief Wilson on SPD views on Germany and Berlin. Meanwhile Sebastian Haffner, eminent British journalist writing from Berlin for West German papers, found the Soviet plan for peace treaties with both German states preferable to the U.S. policy of including the two parts of Germany in the two alliance systems. The Soviet plan, he argued, called for mutual withdrawal of foreign troops from Germany within one year and, therefore, could lead to political changes in the Zone regime and encourage eventual inner-German understanding. He reminded Germans that the two alliances—NATO and Warsaw Pact—were concluded for an East-West war, which had been called off as suicidal for both sides. He chided Germans for being more American than Americans and for clinging to an alliance which they had hoped was the way to reunification. Such wishful thinking, Haffner concluded, enabled Germans to ignore the present and overlook the facts of World War II.[147] In contrast to Bismarck's *Realpolitik,* Chancellor Adenauer was pursuing a policy of *Fiktionspolitik* with respect to: a. the cold war fiction, b. repeated demands for access to atomic weapons and c. the fiction that Germany was not divided and that the German Democratic Republic did not exist.[148]

Several conservative papers reported that Mayor Brandt in Berlin had received letters from President Kennedy and General Clay. Brandt merely said the letters had increased his concern over the crisis in the Western Alliance and that he would express his concern to the *Bundesrat* (upper house) on Friday, 1 March 1963. In contrast to reports of the Berlin CDU going into opposition, Chancellor Adenauer was said to favor continuing the SPD-CDU coalition in Berlin if necessary to prevent Brandt from having a free hand in solving the Berlin problem. Other papers reported that Adenauer felt uneasy over new U.S.-Soviet Berlin talks, lest the Soviets try to pressure Kennedy to balance Soviet concessions on Cuba with a *quid pro quo* of Western concessions on Berlin. Bonn continued skeptical after U.S.-Soviet exploratory talks in 1961 and 1962 had caused a near crisis between Washington and Bonn with the recall of the German Ambassador in Washington, Dr. Wilhelm Grewe, who had become *persona non grata*. It was feared that a new round of talks would only rehash old problems, old plans and old worries. Bonn warned that when Moscow said Berlin, she really meant Germany. In view of Berlin's exposed position, Bonn preferred the status quo.[149]

Public opinion polls showed the Social Democrats steadily gaining at the expense of the Christian Democrats. In February, 1963 44 per cent of German voters favored the SPD as against 42 per cent for the CDU with the trend continuing strongly in favor of the Social Democrats. Recent setbacks in state (*Länder*) elections showed that the CDU was no longer in good shape. The CDU/CSU was weakened by bad management, whereas in the years 1962/1963 the SPD had gained 1,306,000 votes in state elections. In elections in eight *Länder* between 1957 and 1959 the Union party still had 755,000 more votes than the SPD, whereas in the same elections four years later the tables had turned. The SPD won the confidence of more and more voters. By the spring of 1963 the SPD led the CDU/CSU with 645,000 votes. Four years before the CDU/CSU held 488 seats in these eight *Länder,* while the Social Democrats had only 469 or 19 seats less. The SPD had managed to forge ahead with 57 new mandates, while the CDU/CSU had lost 37. Thus voter statistics disproved ineffective propaganda. In short the SPD was definitely turning from an ideological party to a people's party. Voters did not unconditionally oppose Adenauer, but no longer did they unconditionally support him. Although voters were no longer anti-clerical as in the nineteenth century, some had recently observed clerical aspects. Although voters favored the

411

Franco-German Treaty and the Atlantic Alliance, they had a vague feeling that something was wrong with German foreign policy. Therefore, they no longer felt unable to vote SPD, whereas before many Germans young and old just automatically voted CDU in order to prove that they were bourgeois. Voter confidence in the CDU/CSU would reach a new low if any struggle for power should develop within the Union party.[150]

The steadily weakening position of the CDU in many *Länder* and the heavy defeat in the Berlin elections became a powerful factor in bringing about efforts to solve the problem of Adenauer's succession before the end of the parliamentary session in June 1963. Toward the end of February efforts of the Union party in this direction reecived wide coverage in the West German press. After Erhard's article in *Süddeutsche Zeitung* opposing Adenauer on bilateral treaties and the controversy between von Brentano and Erhard over the latter's failure to attend the EEC meeting in Brussels, there was growing doubt among CDU leaders that Erhard should succeed Adenauer. Many preferred Schröder as the next chancellor candidate. Others mentioned Krone, Dufues and von Brentano. Adenauer was believed to favor von Brentano. But other voices in the CDU/CSU wanted Adenauer to carry on until 1964 to allow time for building up his successor. Adenauer was said to favor continuing the SPD/CDU coalition in Berlin and not to have abandoned the idea of a grand coalition between the CDU and SPD in Bonn in order to prolong his chancellorship until the spring of 1964.[151]

On April 1 most papers led with articles on the Rhineland-Palatinate Landtag elections in which the CDU lost its absolute majority, with heavy SPD gains at CDU expense. The switch of about 4 per cent of the vote away from the CDU over to the SPD was seen as a reaction to events in Bonn. The very conservative population of Rhineland-Palatinate expressed its resentment at the numerous mistakes in Bonn. To the CDU this result represented another warning to shift its course or expect further setbacks.[152] All Bonn parties interpreted the election results as prompted by CDU problems on a nationwide level rather than by local issues in Rhineland-Palatinate. All parties welcomed the defeat of extremist parties of the right and left unable to clear the 5 per cent hurdle, demonstrating again that radicalism has no chance in the West German Federal Republic. The SPD inferred from the election results that it was on the right course and could look forward to increasing gains in coming elections.

It was an "open secret" in Berlin that Mayor Brandt largely shared President Kennedy's views on Berlin and that the West Berlin Senate fully supported efforts to achieve some kind of *modus vivendi* with the Soviets on Berlin.[153] Brandt was said to seek support for these plans from Foreign Minister Schröder. During his projected visit to Paris, Brandt would try to prevent a French veto against a possible U.S.-Soviet agreement on a *modus vivendi* on Berlin. Meanwhile *Die Zeit* reported that Washington and the Soviets both realized that there was no chance of changing the *status quo* in Berlin for the time being. Hence the Berlin Ultimatum of 1958 was no longer on the table. As to whether this could be interpreted as a settlement of the Berlin crisis, the American answer was yes, except that the Berlin problem as part of the German problem would remain unsettled as long as Germany remained divided. Hence a new Berlin crisis may break out whenever Khrushchev wants one or decides to use the divided city to demonstrate a Soviet policy of strength.[154] The real significance of the projected Kennedy visit to Berlin was said to be the rousing welcome which Berliners would give the President. This then might be considered by Kennedy as a direct authorization for the continuation of talks with the Soviets in efforts at a Berlin settlement and, if possible, a general East-West settlement on a world-wide basis.[155]

Pro-SPD papers placed great emphasis on the April 24 meeting between President De Gaulle and Berlin Mayor Brandt. Brandt was expected to discuss not only Berlin problems, but basic problems of German foreign policy. At his press conference in Paris Brandt was reported to have called the Franco-German friendship Treaty indispensable to Franco-German understanding, but that it must be included within the framework of existing German-Allied agreements. Brandt expressed himself for extending the non-military clauses of the Franco-German Treaty to Berlin and said he was deeply satisfied with his discussion with President de Gaulle. Brandt said he shared Khrushchev's view that there could be no peace in Europe without settling the German problem. However, a settlement of this problem against the will of the German people would not be a settlement.[156]

A lively controversy arose among party politicians in Berlin over a "New Line" of the Berlin Social Democrats. The lively discussion in both Berlin and Bonn resulted from a radio speech by the Deputy Mayor of Berlin, Heinrich Albertz (SPD), on 13 August 1963. The Berlin Christian Democrats were so shocked that they introduced a No-Confidence Resolution, which was to be discussed on 3 September 1963 in the Berlin House of Representatives. Extracts from this very significant radio speech follow:

> Today, two years after Black August Sunday, the bitter truth remains that a world power, two great powers and also we Germans have tolerated the most sordid satellite state of Moscow in complete disregard of existing inter-allied arrangements—a state that decided if and where they could enter East Berlin. . . .
> It is true that Ulbricht and no one else has built the wall with the consent of his employer and therefore is responsible for it. It is also true that we Germans in the free part of our land and our friends in the West have neglected doing many things which otherwise possibly could have been done to prevent the erection of the wall.
> More important than this, however, is to realize that even today, two years after 13 August 1961, there is still no common policy in the free part of Germany. Immediately after Black Sunday in Berlin most German politicians were too involved in the parliamentary campaign to concentrate on the really vital questions before the nation. Had the majority of German politicians nothing better to do than to deepen the cleavage over internal political differences and thus limit the chances for a common responsibility of a new Federal Government? . . .
> But one consolation remained. In divided Berlin, despite all difficulties, the relation between the ruling party and opposition was in sharp contrast to that in Bonn. In Berlin both sides attempted to reach a common understanding

414

on basic questions and did not accuse their political opponents of heresy.

The Berlin Wall has not only advertised to all the world the complete failure of the Zone regime, but also revealed its true meaning, that is, what those in West Berlin have been representing for others—not because they are heroic or holy, but because they live in this city—*in a capital without land in a* Land *without a capital,* 40 square kilometers in the place in which it will be decided whether in the unforeseen future there will be a Rhine Confederation of States and Middle Germany as a Soviet Colony or one Germany again a self-contained unit.

And now here in the core of this problem since 13 August 1961 we have become stronger and more assured. No one any longer dares to doubt that one World Power together with both of the other protecting powers will remain in this part of the city.

After what President Kennedy has declared in Frankfurt and Berlin, there is no longer any doubt that one World Power sees in common with us much more than only this half of the city when it comes here.

Along with this conviction certainly goes the courage to handle our own affairs. I can not even speak over a radio in West Germany without expressing my deep anxiety over this—with how much timidity and mistrust even the smallest advance is accompanied, which is found in the peace strategy of the U.S.A., our most powerful ally, and which should be the beginning of a way bound up with more hope for peace and with more room for freedom. Here is the fatal attitude, the entirely provincial timidity with which the past years were so heavily burdened. Instead of examining carefully the best claims, which the prison wardens in East Berlin make for their statehood, responsible officials in Bonn played up the question of "recognition" of the Zone regime in a public discussion and, therefore, have now achieved exactly what they had wanted to prevent: the presence of Ulbricht in international negotiations.

When will we finally stop in order to overcome every ob-

415

stacle which is holding us back? Where is there in the Western part of our Fatherland a serious person who could consider it right to give legal-constitutional [*de-jure*] recognition to the Zone? Is "recognition" the contact, which Interzonal Trade Commission has with the Ministry of the Zone Regime? Has "recognition" become such a horrible fact that within Berlin and Germany an insurgent army of German citizens shoots down those who wish only to go from Germany to Germany? Why then all the ideal talk? Before us lie the tasks of the hour:

a. to secure civilian access to Berlin, b. to restore intercity intercourse in the German capital, c. to make possible intercourse between the two parts of Germany and c. with all this to prevent making the division of Germany permanent.[157]

The Social Democratic deputy mayor of Berlin urged Germans to initiate their own proposals for attaining peace and freedom while the world was showing strong desires for peace. This would require complete confidence in those who have combined their fate and destiny with our fate and destiny. Above all Germans must realize and declare publicly that not even the German Federal Republic is all of Germany. Athough we speak for the others, we can not set forth their desires immediately. The perfectionist state which we have recently constructed between the Elbe and the Rhine can not be final according to our constitution.

John Baptist Gradl (Bundestag member of the CDU) objected to Senator Albertz's reference to Bonn discussions of the international appearance of the Soviet Regime in the Test Ban agreements as "provincial timidity and idle talk." Gradl pointed out that the anxiety in Bonn was not over legal recognition of the Zone regime, but that discussion had focused on the behavior of Ulbricht as a negotiator and its possible effect upon the noncommitted states between the two power-blocs. The CDU spokesman also attacked the Berlin Senate Press Chief Bahr for a speech in Tutzong, in which he had referred to the question of recognition of the Zone as if it were *de jure* recognition, despite the absolute refusal of Bonn to even consider this Soviet

416

thesis of the so called "two German States." Gradl chided the Senate Press Chief for recommending that the Berlin Senate accept the principle of "Change through the Approach" as German policy in the All-German question. This principle had been formulated by President Kennedy, but only as the leading proposition of a global political strategy in the long view. This principle could scarcely apply to a divided Germany with Ulbricht as a close partner. Such an inappropriate German policy, in Gradl's opinion, could only encourage certain tendencies in international politics, which were all too prone to shelve the difficult question.

Finally the CDU spokesman argued that Mayor Brandt himself was not entirely blameless for the confusion over Berlin policy. Brandt through ambiguous formulation and declarations had given rise to certain doubts and misinterpretations. However, Gradl contended that the parliamentary action of the Berlin CDU had nothing to do with the motives or good opinions of SPD speakers. Nor was there any question about the common resoluteness of the Berlin parties for the unconditional defense of their city. The basic question, he said, was whether a second foreign policy should be put forth by Berlin or whether one man in the Berlin Senate, despite the different stand of the SPD opposition in Bonn, should be fully recognized as the only decisive foreign policy spokesman for the free part of Germany and Berlin. After all Berlin political declarations commanded a special hearing and attention in both the friendly and hostile world. This was only natural and gratifying. But, Gradl continued, this should cause every responsible speaker in Berlin to pay more attention to the primacy of the Federal Government in foreign policy. Otherwise, Gradl feared, the real force of German foreign policy would be weakened by its friends and that in Moscow and Pankow false hopes and hardened fronts would be released. The CDU speaker had in mind the Soviet two-state thesis and the isolation of the so called "Free City." This was not to say that Berlin should abstain from all criticism of Bonn. Naturally the foreign policy of Bonn and its German policy needed critical observation and comment. But, Gradl concluded, Berlin's criticisms and demands should be discussed in the appropriate agencies in Bonn and Berlin and

417

not placed in more or less sentimental public declarations. Finally the CDU spokesman advised that Berlin should value its integration with the Federal Government and not impair this by special pronouncements on foreign policy, particularly to avoid any discord between Bonn and Berlin in view of the present unstable phase of international politics, lest this weaken Germany's position in world affairs.

William Borm (*Land* Chairman of the FDP in Berlin) was unimpressed by the No-Confidence motion brought in by the Berlin CDU, considered the charges against the ruling SPD party as petty and disposed of them in short order. He began by emphasizing 13 August 1961 as the day when the German postwar tragedy reached an unforeseen high point, when Berliners, representing all of Germany, witnessed the erection of a horrible wall through the legitimate German capital. "Any man who has not felt the urge to tear down this monument to inhumanity has not understood and never will understand the doctrine of *Mahnungmale* (Timely Warning) in the state of the brown tyranny." With inexorable logic the FDP spokesman developed the thesis that it was the task of German politics to examine every possibility to overcome the dangers to world peace which the wall demonstrates out of hatred, fear and helplessness. In this task all Germans were united in good will. Berliners were daily confronted with the gruesome effects of the wall upon intimate family life. Therefore, it was the obligation of Parliament and the Berlin Senate on the anniversary of the tragedy of 13 August 1961 to admonish, to warn and also to criticize, wherever any doubt and confusion made criticism an internal obligation. We should have expected that reaction, since the German need for everyone of good will is conceded—apart from any supposed advantage of party politics.

It was, therefore, surprising to the FDP spokesman when the Berlin CDU, standing in opposition, declared the SPD deputy mayor Heinrich Albertz unbearable because:

    a. He had abandoned the basis for common action in the vital questions before the nation;

    b. on 13 August 1963 in a radio address he had used formulations which the Federal Government should renounce;

c. besides he had acted irresponsibly when he raised strong doubts against the reunification policy of Bonn.

The FDP Chairman in Berlin cautioned against assuming that in fact foreign policy and the All-German policy was determined by the Federal Government from the ideas of the CDU. This same CDU, therefore, must not wonder if it is criticized, because success in the question of reunification of our nation could not be firmly determined. The parliamentary elections in 1961 and the Berlin elections in February 1963 should have made clear to the blindest in the CDU that there are Germans who are not followers of this party. So the Free Democrats exercise their right of appeal in any appropriate manner with every possibility to state their opinions and to appeal to the judgment of the citizens.

The FDP spokesman explained that a judgment on this whole affair would be rendered in Parliament where everything will be expressed that is necessary. So far he welcomed the injudicious no-confidence motion of the CDU opposition against Mayor Albertz. Meanwhile it could be said that the most fateful days such as August 13 are not days of conventional speeches for Berliners, but days for meditation for ourselves and the German peoples. Therefore, whoever continually endeavours in public to interpret the changed situations occurring in the world and looks for possibilities to appraise them for German desires will find us understanding. We appraise any good intentions and reject over-zealous and petty criticisms of individual formulations. Moreover, if on 13 August 1963, the day of Albertz's speech, any special criticism was to be made, it should have been directed against the CDU opposition for not deploring the fact that similar speeches had not already been made five or more years before.

Continuing his closely reasoned argument on a higher level, Borm concluded by noting that the world and what happens therein does not follow the laws of statistics, but dynamic forces. Whoever fears dynamics and characterizes them as "experiments" forgets that the most fatally disastrous experiment was to separate the German people. Here lie serious dangers for freedom and world peace. We will therefore undertake with our friends in the free world to investigate every possibility, which could re-

419

move this danger here. This must rightly be expected of German politics—perhaps to consider the fixed fronts of world politics in motion. It would be unpardonable if the Federal Republic were to not prove itself elastic.

Kurt Mattick (*Land* Chairman of the SPD in Berlin) began by emphasizing that it was not normal procedure in parliamentary history to introduce a No-Confidence Motion against a Minister for the contents of a speech, which at that time had no immediate connection wtih his office, but was intended as a reproach. If the Social Democratic Bundestag group had followed such practice in the years 1953-1959, they actually would have overburdened the calendar. According to the Constitution (Basic Law) a motion against a Minister is not possible; it must always be directed against the entire Government. The Berlin CDU had not done that. This was not good parliamentary form. The No-Confidence Motion of the CDU seemed to the SPD spokesman a case of running amuk (*Amoklauf*), as if after the electoral defeat of 17 February 1963, it was searching with a telescope for some way to make a stronger sound than the opposition.

Mattick continued, that immediately after the announcement of the CDU motion, the SPD declared:

The speech of Deputy Mayor Albertz on 13 August 1963 contains nothing which has not already been covered in current discussions between the CDU and SPD on many levels. The presence of Minister Dr. Krone and Minister Plenipotentiary Dr. Eckhardt at the night session of the CDU Executive Board shows that the No-Confidence Resolution against Mayor Albertz is not concerned with Albertz alone, but a greater action over Berlin.[160]

The *Land* Chairman of the Berlin SPD drew the conclusion that actually it was all a question of preparations of the CDU in Bonn for the parliamentary election campaign of 1965 directed against Willy Brandt. Mattick explained the CDU campaign strategy thus: By consideration of the No-Confidence Resolution the Executive Board of the CDU, as was well known, would be followed up by the Berlin CDU fraction, whose abstinence from voting—as it was called in the press report of the CDU Executive Board—wanted to have a fair chance.

Mattick noted that according to the press report of the CDU, it had shown a desire to elevate August 13 to a day of meditation and stated that it certainly was no day for fixed speeches, but a day of the saddest balance after the tragedy of 9 September 1948. At that time the Governments of the Western Powers had resigned themselves to the political split of Berlin when the Soviets ejected from the Berlin City Hall the Mayor, duly elected by all Berlin. August 13 was a day when people ask: Had we really done everything possible in order to protect the 17 million across the Demarcation Line before the step of August 13. Mattick noted that the CDU had apparently taken pleasure in again raising this question. He then quoted from the speech of Mayor Albertz, criticized by the Berlin CDU: "More important . . . is to recall that even today, long after 13 August 1961, there is still no common policy in the free part of Germany." It was Willy Brandt who in the evening of 13 August 1961 had appealed in vain to the CDU to break off the parliamentary campaign in order to unite all active democratic forces of the nation, in view of the wall, behind a common platform. And it was the Chancellor himself who did not come to Berlin then, but instead went off on another gay campaign and made use of the wall to insult Willy Brandt in a most disgusting manner. The remainder of the SPD spokesman's statement was focused on international politics:

The "hard fighters" against the Berlin Senate still did not seem to understand that the Kennedy Government after accepting the dangerous neglect of the past had built up and re-established the military superiority of the West by an unusual exertion, involving the maintenance of one million American soldiers overseas, just in order to be better able to match the new efforts of the Soviet Union. Only one who sees the background will also comprehend that Kennedy's effort is not retreat, nor softness, but bold politics in the interest of freedom. And only with this background can the effort be understood along the line of a military relaxation of designs of power politics and also the

421

effort to set the German problem in motion. And it will come to this, whether German politics understands the international situation well enough to profit by it or lets itself be washed over by this wave.[161]

These observations seemed just as important to Kurt Mattick as the admonition before the "great" discussion in the small realm of Berlin politics.

The lively debate initiated by the Berlin CDU opposition over the so called "New Line" of the Berlin Social Democrats in no way interfered with the determination of the Berlin Senate to project its future policy for easing world tensions. Through its elected representatives, the Berlin Senate proclaimed its policy for relieving tensions in divided Berlin, divided Germany and divided Europe. The projected program presented by Governing Mayor Brandt before the Berlin House of Representatives on 4 September 1963 included the following items:

a. An effort to decrease human misery in Berlin, despite the Wall;

b. Guarantee of free access to Berlin on the ground and in the air, possibly supervised by an International Authority;

c. More technical contacts between East and West Berlin;

d. The four Occupation Powers to continue their reponsibility for Germany and Berlin as a whole;

e. Relaxation of cold war tensions caused by the partition of Germany and its traditional capital.

In addition the Berlin Senate's nine-point program emphasized:

1. Berlin's future is linked with the struggle for self-determination for all Germans and reunification in freedom;
2. Berlin is part of the German Federal Republic by German law and by the will of the people, notwithstanding the superordinate rights of the Four Protecting Powers.

3. The Berlin Senate is prepared to cooperate in an interim solution to improve the lot of its citizens in terms of the Federal Government's statement of 18 March 1963.
4. The Senate approves efforts to increase technical intercourse within the entire city of Berlin without extending legal recognition to the Soviet Zone regime.
5. The Senate favors efforts to modify the inhuman effects of the Wall upon family ties between the two parts of the city, while avoiding political extortion.
6. An International Access Authority to guarantee free access to Berlin on the ground would represent a decided improvement of conditions.
7. The Senate believes German policy should harmonize with international efforts for control of armaments and relaxation of tensions, aimed at better living conditions and political changes in the Soviet Zone as steps toward a solution of the German problem.
8. Emphasis on the superiority of democracy means there can be no pause in the ideological controversy with Communism. There is no substitute for the all-German policy.
9. The Berlin Senate's responsibility is to mould public opinion and represent the special interests of Berlin. At the same time it wants the greatest degree of common action between Berlin and Bonn on all vital national issues.[162]

The first five items of the Berlin Senate's policy closely paralleled the main tenets of Bonn's past foreign policy, whereas the last 4 items showed more initiative and independence on the part of the Berlin Senate. Apart from the powerful impact of the Berlin *Land* elections of February 1963 and the switch of about 9 per cent of the voters away from the CDU over to the SPD and FDP, there was clearly evident a willingness to experiment and search for some interim solution to the Berlin problem. This search for some *modus vivendi* was the result of a slow but steady evolution from the inflexible position of Bonn in the spring of 1962 when U.S.-Soviet negotiations over Berlin led to sharp clashes between Bonn and Washington. Certain officials in Bonn seem to have leaked to the West German press inside information of a proposed detente, including a 13-nation international authority to guarantee access to Berlin. Adenauer raised strong objections to this plan and called it unworkable. But much had happened between March 1962 and September 1963: continued losses of the CDU party in state (*Land*) elections, the steady loss of public confidence in the Federal Government's foreign policy, the deterioration resulting from the *Spiegel* Affair in the late fall of 1962, an SPD report on the *Spiegel* Case in March charging the Government with 16 lies, the struggle over Adenauer's succession—not settled until 23 April 1963—and the crisis in the Western Alliance, which continued through the winter and spring of 1963.

The lively debate carried on both in Parliament and in the West German press over these issues gradually oriented German public opinion to re-examine and re-evaluate the basic tenets of German foreign policy. According to the eminent European scholar, Hans Kohn, the great achievement of the Adenauer Era was the Western orientation of Germany: its prominent role in the Atlantic Alliance and European cooperation through good relations with France and membership in the Coal and Steel Community, the Common Market, Euratom, European Assembly, West European Union and Organization for European Economic Cooperation and OEED. The Franco-German Treaty climaxed Adenauer's life work. Perhaps the post-Adenauer Era would see the implementation of an Eastern policy to promote inter-zonal and East-West trade and gradually ease tensions in Central Europe through a step-by-step process along lines of military relaxation of designs of power politics in order to raise living standards of Central European peoples as well as to protect the legitimate security interests of these people and of the German and Russian peoples.

X

Parliamentary Ratification of the Franco-German Treaty

By its resolution on 1 March 1963 the upper house (*Bundesrat*) prevented the possibility of the French Treaty being used by the Federal Government to support a pro-French policy at the expense of the U.S.A., Britain or NATO. Not even the presence of the Chancellor and his eloquent plea for the treaty could remove the reserve of the Bundesrat. This body simply paralleled efforts of the lower house (*Bundestag*) and leaders of all three political parties to achieve a solid balance and avoid the risk of a sudden shift in German foreign policy.[163] It may have been painful for the Chancellor to see his crowning life-work overshadowed by criticism. But numerous factors dictated no other course: the *Spiegel* Affair, the overwhelming SPD victory in the Berlin elections of February 17, a series of CDU losses in local state elections, a growing impatience of voters with Bonn's foreign policy and the struggle within the CDU over Adenauer's succession—all these were factors. Future historians may note with satisfaction Adenauer's heroic fight against all these obstacles to complete his life-work. The aged Chancellor had clearly demonstrated that politics, whether domestic or international, is the art of the possible. Never is there a complete victory by any one idea, cause or movement, but rather a compromise between that idea, cause or movement and its opposite.

Internal political differences played a large part. The Chancellor wanted to let his and De Gaulle's European concept prevail, despite the opposition of a majority in both the Bundestag and the CDU.[164] SPD deputy chairman Wehner called for additional clauses in the Franco-German Treaty in order to place it within the framework of all other European treaties, especially NATO and WEU. Wehner's request was important because in the recent Bundesrat debate (1 March 1963) two SPD-governed States (*Länder*) had approved the ratification bill in its present form.[165] The successive visits to Washington of State Secretary Carsens, Defense Minister von Hassel and CDU/CSU fraction chairman von Brentano had failed to eliminate U.S. misgivings over the Franco-German Treaty. Finally even CDU leaders admitted that U.S. misgivings could only be overcome if it became unmistakably clear in the Bundestag debate that the Franco-German Treaty would in no way weaken previous German-Allied treaties.[166]

When EEC Commission President Hallstein warned against any "blocs" within the EEC, the Bonn parties were convinced that the Bundestag would refuse to ratify the French Treaty without an additional clause to the act of ratification. CDU/CSU floor leader Von Brentano seemed ready to comply with this demand of the SPD and FDP in order to get as large a majority for the treaty as possible. Both Adenauer and Foreign Minister Schröder, however, voiced misgivings over Hallstein's criticisms of the French Treaty. Schröder preferred a Bundestag resolution to inserting another clause in the ratification act.[167] The "tug-of-war" in Bonn over the French Treaty later shifted to the timing of the Bundestag debate, with the SPD proposing May 15 for the first reading and the CDU/CSU accusing the SPD of delaying tactics. The government party preferred April 24 for the first reading. The latter date was used, just one day after a CDU/CSU caucus had voted by a large majority in favor of Erhard succeeding Adenauer as Chancellor in October 1963. Out of a total of 225 votes, 159 were cast for the Economics Minister and Vice Chancellor, with 47 deputies voting against the proposal and 19 abstaining.[168] Thus 66 CDU deputies could later block Erhard and let it be known that if the Chancellor ever changed his mind, they would make it impossible for Erhard to succeed him. Dr. Thomas Dehler later questioned whether Adenauer would really resign in October, 1963.[169]

Historians are well aware of the difficulties confronted by any attempt to analyze human motives, even when limiting their task to one historical character. This is doubly difficult for writers of contemporary history who try to analyze the motives of various political groups or special interests within a country. And yet this is important to attempt particularly when certain élites exercise a decisive influence upon the formulation of foreign policy. Thus Countess Marion Doenhoff, brilliant columnist writing for *Die Zeit*, deplored the tendency of Germans to split up into more factions: the Protestants and Catholics, the Centralists and Particularists, the native residents and refugees and finally what she hoped would not develop into a pro-American and pro-French group. The latter was in turn composed of three groups of Germans: a. All-Germans who demanded reunification at any price, b. advocates of military disengagement in central Europe to ease tensions and c. German Nationalists. The latter seemed to be stronger as a result of the long debate in the press and Parliament over the French Treaty, De Gaulle and Gaullism. In any case spokesmen of these three schools of

German thought argued that efforts to integrate the Federal Republic too closely with the West would only weaken, if not destroy, chances for eventual reunification. Members of these groups commonly believed that De Gaulle would eventually seek a disengagement in Central Europe and that this was the only chance to reunite Germany. Doenhoff, of course, disparaged such wishful thinking on the part of too many Germans.[170]

At a meeting in Cadenabbia, Adenauer and leaders of both the CDU and FDP agreed upon the form of a preamble to be affixed to the ratification act: a. to express a determination to strengthen Franco-German friendship, b. to bring about reunification, c. to support the European communities and NATO and d. to continue the work of European unification. SPD deputy Mommer stated that the planned text of the preamble was in harmony with SPD desires. FDP deputy Dehler noted that the method of preceding laws with a preamble was a Nazi method.[171]

On 24 April 1963, while the Mayor of Berlin was in Paris exploring chances of a *modus vivendi* for Berlin, the aged Chancellor, mellowed somewhat by crucial developments in both German domestic politics and world politics, was in the Bundestag, making a final appeal to all parties in Parliament for the completion of his life work—a solid treaty of friendship between the French and German people. The Chancellor evoked applause from both the government and opposition parties when he praised the similar efforts of Stresemann and Briand in the Weimar period (1924/25) over a decade after the pioneer efforts of August Bebel, pre-1914 Social Democratic fraction chairman in the old Reichstag. Adenauer continued, emphasizing that we and the world might have been spared the misfortune of National Socialism, which was rooted in Franco-German mistrust after the war of 1914-1918 and have been spared World War II. Relations between France and Germany were unique because determined by geographical proximity, with a common frontier of 450 kilometers and both countries were highly industrialized. France was Germany's most important commercial partner in Europe. In 1961 German trade with the U.S.A. totaled 9.5 billion marks, while that with France was practically the same: 9.4 billion marks. The full significance of the Franco-German Treaty Adenauer continued was to be found in the recent history of Europe:

427

the Russo-German Treaty against France,
the Franco-Russian Treaty of 1892 against Germany,
the Versailles Treaty of 1919, against Germany,
the Franco-Soviet Treaty of 1935, against Germany,
the Russo-German Pact of 1939 against France.

De Gaulle's Treaty with Russia in 1944 was directed against Germany and in 1946 came French Foreign Minister Bidault's proposal to internationalize the Rhine and Ruhr and to block the formation of a new central German Government. But in 1950 French Foreign Minister Robert Schuman proposed and concluded the Mountain Union or Coal and Steel Community. This Schuman Treaty transformed French anxieties and fears of a rearmed and vengeful Germany into feelings of confidence, understanding and warm friendship, strengthened by a common destiny to protect Western Europe from political pressures from the East. The warm reception given to President Lübke in Paris in 1961 and to Chancellor Adenauer in 1962 was reciprocated by the warm feelings expressed by the Germans for De Gaulle when he toured Germany in September 1962 and visited Bonn, Cologne, Düsseldorf, Hamburg, Munich and Ludwigsburg. The friendship of all classes in Germany for the French President was expressed in mighty ovations. The Chancellor concluded his Bundestag statement with a plea that without Franco-German harmony and friendship there could be no peace either in Europe or the world. The Treaty would be a pillar of peace between France and Germany and of peace in Europe and peace in the world.[172]

The following day most papers described the three hour Bundestag debate when spokesmen of all three political parties recalled the disastrous consequences of Franco-German tension. Adenauer's speech won him warm applause, with Erhard moving up to congratulate the Chancellor, whom he had criticized recently for certain aspects of the Treaty. Adenauer emphasized that the Treaty did not interfere with other contractual agreements of the Federal Republic. The ratification bill was referred to the appropriate committees which formulated the preamble to this bill along the lines laid down by the Bundesrat on 1 March 1963 in its resolution on the Franco-German Treaty.[173]

428

The Bundestag passed the ratification law for the Franco-German Treaty on 16 May 1963. Two weeks later the Bundesrat passed this law with a unanimous vote, joining with the Bundestag in expressing its belief that the Treaty was an historical event, coming at a most significant time in the spirit of Franco-German friendship. When the Bundestag voted the preamble to the ratification law it adopted the wording proposed by the Social Democratic fraction in Parliament.

NOTES TO CHAPTER SEVENTEEN

1. *The Bulletin* (Bonn, pro-Govt.) X, 46 (20 November 1962), 1-2. Cf. Stenographic Transcript: Press Conference of Konrad Adenauer at the National Press Club, Washington, D.C. (15 November, 1962), 3-10.
2. Walter Lippmann, "Today and Tomorrow," *Washington Post* (31 January 1963), A 19.
3. Martin Painelle, "European Chess Game," *America,* CVIII 4 (26 Jan. 1963) 142
4. *Washington Post* (16 December 1962), A 19
5. Quoted in the *Economist* (London, independent), 26 January 1963), p. 311.
6. "The Vision of Charles De Gaulle," *Time* LXXXI, 6 (8 February 1963) 23
7. *Ibid.* Cf. Stenographic Transcript of Adenauer's Press Conference in Washington, D. C. on 15 November 1962, p. 12
8. "Since 1940 my every word and deed has been dedicated to establishing these possibilities." (1955).
9. *Ibid.*
10. Heinrich Bechtoldt, "Theme des Monats, *Aussen Politik: Zeitschrift Für Internationale Fragen,* XIII, 11 November, 1962), 721.
11. *Christ und Welt* (Stuttgart, 17 May 1963), quoted in *Atlas,* VI, 1 July 1963.
12. *Ibid.*
13. H. Bechtoldt, "Thema des Monats," *Aussen Politik,* XIII, 11 (Nov. 1962), Moscow Retreats in Cuba and India," 721.
14. *Ibid.*

16. Heinrich Bechtoldt, "Moscow Retreats in Cuba and India," in *Aussen Politik*, XIII, 11 (November, 1963), 722.

16. Heinrich Bechtoldt, "Moscow Retreats in Cuba and India," *Aussen Politik*, XIII, 11 (November, 1963), 723-724.

17. Ibid., 724.

18. *Die Weltwoche* (Zürich, independent), 31 May 1963).

19. Editorial: "Reversal of Alliances," *The Economist* (26 January, 1963), 294-5.

20. *Ibid*, 295.

21. *Ibid*, 294.

22. *Ibid*.

23. *The Economist* (26 July 1963), 318.

24. *Die Welt* (Hamburg, independent); *Kölnische Rundschau* (CDU) 15 Jan. 1963.

25. Headlines included: "Kennedy Appeals to Moscow for Negotiations" (*Frankfurter Allgemeine*); "West Berlin Remains Free" (*Kölnische Rundschau*, CDU); "We Are Seeking Victory of Man" (*Die Welt*, independent); "Kennedy Optimistic on International Situation" (*Deutsche Zeitung*, right-center) ; "Kennedy: Present Calm Does Not Lull Us To Sleep" (*Der Mittag*, right-center); "Kennedy: Changes in East and West" (*Frankfurter Rundschau*, left-center); "Kennedy for Alertness and Confidence" (*Neue Rhine Ruhr Zeitung*, pro-SPD) 15 January 1963.

26. *Deutsche-Zeitung* (Cologne, right-center); *Frankfurter Rundschau* (left-center) 15 January 1963.

27. *Stuttgarter Zeitung* (independent) 15 January 1963.

28. *Frankfurter Neue Presse* (pro-Gov.); *Frankfurter Rundschau* (left-center) 15 January 1963.

29. *Frankfurter Allgemeine* (right-center) ; *Der Mittag* (right-center) 15 January 1963.

30. *Die Welt* (Hamburg, independent), 15 January 1963.

31. *Neue Rhine Ruhr Zeitung* (pro-SPD), 15 January 1963.

32. *Frankfurter Rundschau* (left center) 15 January 1963.

33. *Die Welt* (Hamburg, independent), 16 January 1963.

34. *General Anzeiger* (Bonn, independent) ; *Deutsche Zeitung* (Cologne, right-center) ; *Rheinische Post* (Düsseldorf, pro-CDU) 16 January 1963).

35. *Rheinische Post* (Düsseldorf, pro-CDU); *Frankfurter Allgemeine Zeitung* (right-center) ; *Die Welt* (Hamburg, independent) 17 January 1963.

36. *Frankfurter Rundschau* (left-center); *Süddeutsche Zeitung* (Munich, left-center) 17 January 1963.
37. *L'Express* (Paris newspaper, independent), quoted by *Frankfurter Allgemeine Zeitung* (right-center), 20 January 1963.
38. *Frankfurter Allgemeine Zeitung* (right-center) 20 January 1963.
39. *Frankfurter Neue Presse* (pro-govt.), 20 January 1963.
40. *Die Welt* (Hamburg Ind.), 20 January 1963.
41. *Ibid.*
42. *General Anzeiger* (Bonn, independent), 20 January 1963.
43. *Frankfurter Rundschau* (left-center), 20 January 1963.
44. *Frankfurter Allgemeine Zeitung* (right-center), 21 January 1963.
45. *Ibid.*
46. *Die Welt* (Hamburg, independent), 21 and 22 January, 1963.
47. *Die Welt* (Hamburg, independent), 22 January 1963; *Deutsche Zeitung* (Cologne, right-center), 22 January 1963.
48. *Stuttgarter Zeitung* (independent), 21 January 1963.
49. *Die Welt* (Hamburg, independent), 21 January 1963.
50. Headlines included the following: "Friendship with France Sealed by Treaty" (*Kölnische Rundschau*, CDU); "Franco-German Cooperation on Contractual Basis" (*Stuttgarter Zeitung*, Ind.); "Treaty with France Seals Reconciliation" (*Münchner Merkur*, pro-CSU); "Adenauer Seeks EEC Compromise" (*Die Welt*, independent); "De Gaulle Embraces Adenauer Simultaneously" (*Kölner-Stadt Anzeiger*, Indep.; "Treaty of Historical Significance Signed" (*Frankfurter Neue Presse*, pro-Gov.); "Treaty with Paris" (*Neue Rhein Ruhr Zeitung*, pro-SPD).
51. *Rheinische Post* (Düsseldorf, pro-CDU) 22 January 1963.
52. *Süddeutsche Zeitung* (Munich, left-center) 22 January 1963.
53. *Die Welt* (Hamburg, independent), 22 January 1963.
54. *Süddeutsche Zeitung* (Munich, left-center) 22 January 1963.
55. *Frankfurter Neue Presse* (pro-gov.); *Kölnische Rundschau* 22 January 1963.
56. *Muenchner Merkur* (pro-CSU) 22 January 1963. Cf. *U.S. News*, LIV, 9 (4 March 1963), p. 9.
57. *Frankfurter Rundschau* (left-center) 22 January 1963.
58. *General Anzeiger* (Bonn, Ind.); *Die Welt* (Hamburg, ind.) 22 January 1963.

431

59. *Deutsche Zeitung* (Cologne, right-center) 22 January 1963.
60. *Ibid.*
61. *General Anzeiger* (Bonn, independent), 23 January 1963.
62. *Frankfurter Allgemeine* (right-center); *Deutsche Zeitung* (Cologne, right-center) 25 January 1963.
63. *Frankfurter Neue Presse* (pro-gov.); *Stuttgarter Zeitung* (Ind.); *Der Mittag* (Düsseldorf, right-center); *Die Welt* (Hamburg, Ind.); *N.Y. Times* (Ind.) 23 January 1963.
64. *Deutsche Zeitung* (Cologne, right-center) 25 January 1964.
65. *Stuttgarter Zeitung* (Independent); *Frankfurter Allgemeine* (right-center); *Frankfurter Neue Presse* (pro-gov.) 24 January 1963.
66. *Der Mittag* (Düseldorf, right-center) 24 January 1963.
67. *Kölnische Rundschau* (CDU) 24 January 1963.
68. *Rheinische Post* (Düsseldorf, pro-CDU) 24 January 1963.
69. *Die Zeit* (Hamburg, weekly, right-center) 24 January 1963.
70. *Frankfurter Allgemeine* (right-center) 24 January, 1963.
71. *Muenchner Merkur* pro-CSU) 24 January 1963.
72. *Kölner Stadt Anzeiger* (independent) 24 January 1963.
73. *Rheinische Post* (Düsseldorf, pro-CDU) 28 January 1963; *General Anzeiger* (Bonn, independent); *Die Welt* (Hamburg, Ind.), 28 January 1963.
74. *Frankfurter Rundschau* (left-center) 28 January 1963.
75. "A Clutch at Europe's Heart." *Economist* (London, Ind.) 26 January 1963, p. 309.
76. *Ibid.* See also Max Beloff, *The U.S. and Unity of Europe* Washington, D.C. Brookings, 1963; George L. Lichtheim, *The New Europe: Today and Tomorrow*, New York, Praeger, 1963; Robert Strausz-Hupé et al, *Building the Atlantic World*, New York, Harper and Row, 1963.
77. *Der Mittag* (Düsseldorf, right-center) 28 January 1963.
78. *General Anzeiger* (Bonn, Ind); *Frankfurter Allgemeine* (right-center) 28 January 1963.
79. *Frankfurter Neue Presse* (pro-gov.); *Neue Rhein Ruhr Zeitung* (pro-SPD); *Hannoverische Presse* (pro-SPD) 28 January 1963.
80. *Stuttgarter Zeitung* (Independent) 28 January 1963.
81. *Kölnische Rundschau* (CDU) 28 January 1963.
82. *Frankfurter Allgemeine* (right-center); *Frankfurter Neue Presse* (pro-gov.); *Kölnische Rundschau* (CDU); *Stuttgarter Zeitung* (Ind.) 28 January 1963.

83. *Stuttgarter Zeitung* (independent) 28 January 1963.
84. "U.S. Senators Apply Pressure on Europe; Threaten Radical Change of Policy." "Warning of U.S. Troop Withdrawal—Mansfield Criticizes Military Efforts of European Allies" *Kölnische Rundschau* (CDU) ; *General Anzeiger* (Bonn, Ind.) ; "Revision of U.S. Policy If . . ." *Muenchner Merkur* (pro-CSU) 28 January 1963. "Partial Withdrawal from Europe Possible" *Die Welt* (Hamburg, Ind.) 28 January 1963.
85. *Deutsche Zeitung* (Cologne, right-center) 26 January 1963.
86. *Die Welt* (Hamburg, independent) , 29 January 1963.
87. *Rheinische Post* (Düsseldorf, pro-CDU) , 29 January 1963.
88. *Neue Züricher Zeitung* (Swiss daily, independent), 28 January 1963.
89. *Süddeutsche Zeitung* (Munich, left-center) 29 January 1963.
90. *Rheinische Post* (Düsseldorf, pro-CDU) 29 January 1963.
91. *Die Welt* (independent) , 29 January 1963.
92. *Deutsche Zeitung* (Cologne, right-center) 29 January 1963.
93. *Die Welt* (independent) , 29 January 1963.
94. *Frankfurter Allgemeine Zeitung* (right-center) ; *Westdeutsche Allgemeine* (Essen, independent) 30 January 1963. The American hope was that the Bundestag might delay ratification of the Franco-German Treaty and thus prolong public discussion of critical issues of German foreign policy.
95. *Die Welt* (Hamburg, independent) , 30 January 1963.
96. *Deutsche Zeitung* (Cologne, right-center) ; *Kölnische Rundschau* (CDU) 30 January 1963.
97. *Frankfurter Neue Presse* (pro-Gov.) 30 January 1963.
98. *Kölnische Rundschau* (CDU) 30 January 1963.
99. *Deutsche Zeitung* (Cologne, right-center) , 30 January 1963.
100. *Kölnische Rundschau* (CDU) ; *Frankfurter Neue Presse* (pro-gov.) 30 January 1963.
101. *Frankfurter Allgemeine* (right-center) 30 January 1963.
102. *Die Welt* (Hamburg, independent) , 30 January 1963.
103. *Süddeutsche Zeitung* (Munich, left-center) ; *Frankfurter Rundschau* (left-center) 30 January 1963.
104. *Stuttgarter Zeitung* (independent) 30 January 1963.
105. *Die Welt* (independent) 30 January 1963; *Christ und Welt* (Stuttgart, Protestant weekly) 31 January 1963.
106. *Die Welt* (Ind.) 31 January 1963.
107. *Christ und Welt* (Stuttgart, Protestant weekly) 31 January 1963.

108. *Rheinische Merkur* (Cologne, Catholic weekly) 31 January 1963.

109. *Frankfurter Allgemeine Zeitung* (right-center), 31 January 1963.

110. Hans J. Morgenthau, "Germany Gives Rise to Vast Uncertainties," *New York Times* (8 September 1963) p. 21.

111. *Der Mittag* (Düsseldorf, right-center) 31 January 1963.

112. *Neue Rhein Ruhr Zeitung* (pro-SPD) 31 January 1963.

113. *Muenchner Merkur* (pro-CSU); *Süddeutsche Zeitung* (Munich, left-center); and *Rheinische Post* (pro-CDU) 31 January 1963.

114. Chancellor Konrad Adenauer: Government Declaration on the Foreign and Domestic Situation: *Das Parlament,* 13 Jahrgang, No. 3 (13 February 1963), p. 1.

115. Chancellor Adenauer: Government Declaration: *Das Parlament,* 13 Jahrgang, No. 3 (13 February 1963), p. 1.

116. *Ibid.* (Von Brentano (CDU): "Very good!" Applause from CDU/CSU benches).

117. *Ibid.*

118. *Ibid.*

119. Ollenhauer (SPD): "The Question of an Over-all Policy is Still Unanswered," *Das Parlament,* 13 Jahrgang, No. 7 (13 February 1963), p. 4. (Applause from the benches of the SPD and CDU/CSU).

120. *Ibid.*

121. *Ibid.,* p. 5.

122. *Ibid.,* 5-6.

123. *Ibid.,* 5. Compare Adenauer's version of the *Spiegel* Affair at his press conference in Washington, D.C. on 15 November 1962, discussed in the preceding chapter.

124. *Ibid.,* 5. (Shouting and applause from the government parties—calls from the SPD.)

125. *Ibid.,* 7.

126. *Ibid.*

127. Fritz Erler (SPD): "The Standard of the Opposition," *Das Parlament,* 13 Jahrgang, No. 7 (13 February, 1963), 7. (Applause by SPD and FDP representatives. On 11 March 1963 the SPD published a report accusing the Government of 15 lies in handling the *Spiegel* case in fall of 1962.)

128. *Ibid.*

129. Dr. Ernest Achenbach (FDP) "German-Soviet Relations": *Das Parlament,* 13 Jahrgang, No. 7 (13 February, 1963) , 7.
130. *Das Parlament,* 13 Jahrgang, No. 7 (13 February, 1963) , 8.
131. *Ibid.*
132. Meaning and Value of the French Treaty: Brandt: governing Mayor of Berlin, reporting for Bundesrat Committees of Defense and Foreign Affairs: *Das Parlament,* 13 Jahrgang/No. 10 (6 March 1963) p. 2.
133. *Ibid.*
134. *Das Parlament,* 13 Jahrgang, No. 10 (6 March, 1963) , 1-2. Adenauer's mellowness in the Bundesrat discussion of March 1 and his willingness to agree with Mayor Brandt on several items may have had some connection with the brilliant victory won by Brandt's SPD party in the Berlin elections of 17 February 1963 and the feeling in CDU party quarters of the need to make a decision by Easter on the question of Adenauer's successor.
135. *Frankfurter Rundschau* (left-center) ; *Kölnische Rundschau* (pro-CDU) 8 February 1963.
136. *Frankfurter Neue Presse* (pro-gov.) ; *Frankfurter Rundschau* (left-center) ; *Frankfurter Allgemeine* (right-center; *Die Welt* (independent) 1 Feb. 1963.
137. *Die Welt* (Hamburg, ind.) ; *Frankfurter Allgemeine* (right-center) *Der Mittag* (Düsseldorf, right-center) ; *Frankfurter Rheinische Post* (Düsseldorf, pro-CDU) 15 February 1963; *Neue Presse* (pro-gov.) 15 February 1963.
138. *Die Zeit* (Hamburg weekly, right-center) 14 February 1963; *Neue Züricher Zeitung* (independent), 14 February 1963; *Christ und Welt* (Protestant weekly, Stuttgart) 14 February 1963.
139. *Frankfurter Allgemeine* (right-center) ; *Frankfurter Rundschau* (left-center) ; *Kölnische Rundschau* (CDU) 12 February 1963.
140. *Die Welt* (Hamburg, independent) 13 February 1963; *Hannoverische Presse* (pro-SPD 12 February 1963; *Frankfurter Rundschau* (left-center) 11 February 1963; *Münchner* (pro-CSU) 11 February 1963.
141. *Der Mittag* (Dusseldorf, right-center) ; *Kölnische Rundschau* (CDU) ; *Rheinische Post* (Düsseldorf, pro-CDU) 18 February 1963.

142. *Frankfurter Allgemeine* (right-center) 18 February 1963; *Münchner Merkur* (pro-CSU) 19 February 1963.

143. *Rheinische Post* (Düsseldorf, pro-CDU) *Münchner Merkur* (pro-CSU); *Die Welt* (Hamburg, independent) 19 February 1963.

144. *Süddeutsche Zeitung* (Munich, left-center); *General Anzeiger* (Bonn, Ind.); *Frankfurter Rundschau* (left-center) 19 February 1963.

145. *Der Mittag* (Düsseldorf, right-center); *Süddeutsche Zeitung* (Munich, left-center); *Neue Rhine Ruhr Zeitung* (pro-SPD); *Die Welt* (Hamburg, Indep.); *General Anzeiger* (Bonn, independent) 19 February 1963.

146. *Frankfurter Rundschau* (left center); *Frankfurter Allgemeine* (right-center) 18 February 1963; *Der Spiegel* (Hamburg, weekly); *Die Welt* (independ.) *Neue Rhine Ruhr Zeitung* (pro-SPD) 19 February 1963.

147. *Frankfurter Neue Presse* (pro-Gov.) 25 February 1963.

148. *ATLAS: The World Press in Transition,* V, 6 (June, 1963), 325.

149. *Der Mittag* (Düsseldorf, right-center); *Frankfurter Allgemeine* (right-center); *Die Welt* (Hamburg, independent) 27 February 1963; *Rheinische Post* (Düsseldorf, pro-CDU); *Deutsche Zeitung* (Cologne, right-center) 28 February 1963.

150. *Frankfurter Allgemeine* (right-center) 26 February 1963. *Statistics Prove SPD again Leads;* Herausgeber: Vorstand der SPD Druck NVV, Abt. Bonn-Druck—Verantworthlich W. Koch.

151. *Frankfurter Rundschau* (left-center); *Westdeutsche Allgemeine* (Essen, independent) 21 February 1963.

152. *Rheinische Post* (Düsseldorf, pro-CDU); *Der Mittag* (Düsseldorf, right-center) 1 April 1963.

153. *Frankfurter Rundschau* (left-center) 1 April 1963.

154. *Die Zeit* (Hamburg, right-center) 28 March 1963.

155. *Abendpost* (Frankfurt, tabloid) 24 April 1963.

156. *Frankfurter Rundschau* (left-center); *Abendpost* (Frankfurt, tabloid) 24 April 1963; *Die Welt* (Hamburg, independent) 26 April 1963.

157. "A Controversy over a 'New Line' of the Berlin Social Democrats: Three Politicians Take a Stand," *Die Welt* (Sunday, 31 August 1963), p. 17.

158. John Baptist Gradl, "Foreign Policy Is Made in Bonn,"

Das Forum Der Welt in *Die Welt* (Hamburg, independent) , Sunday, 31 August 1963) , p. 17.

159. William Borm (*Land* Chairman of the Berlin FDP) "We Value Good Intentions," *Das Forum Der Welt* in *Die Welt* (31 August 1963) , p. 17.

160. Kurt Mattick, "In Reality Only an Electoral Campaign," *Das Forum Der Welt* in *Die Welt* (31 August 1963), p. 17.

161. Kurt Mattick, "In Reality only an Electoral Campaign," *Das Forum Der Welt* in *Die Welt* (31 August 1963), p. 17.

162. *The Bulletin* (Bonn, Weekly Survey, pro-government), XI, 34 (24 September 1963), 1-2.

163. *Die Welt* (Hamburg, independent; *Frankfurter Allgemeine* (right-center) 4 March 1963.

164. *Süddeutsche Zeitung* (Munich, left-center) 4 March 1963. The following headlines focused on internal struggles within the CDU/CSU: "War of Nerves over Adenauer Succession" (*Süddeutsche Zeitung,* left-center) "Will Erhard Resign?" (*Stuttgart Zeitung,* independent) 4 March 1963. "CDU Mediates in New Adenauer-Erhard Controversy" (*Westdeutsche Allgemeine*) ; "CDU Disappointed by Both Adenauer and Erhard" (*Kölner Stadt-Anzeiger*) 4 March 1963.

165. *Kölnische Rundschau* (pro-CDU) 6 March 1963.

166. *Frankfurter Rundschau* (left-center); *Rheinische Post* (Düsseldorf, pro-CDU) 27 March 1963.

167. *Der Mittag* (Düsseldorf, right-center) 29 March 1963; *General Anzeiger* (Bonn, independent), 29 March 1963.

168. *The Bulletin* (Bonn, Weekly survey of German Affairs, pro-government) XI, 16 (30 April 1963) , 1.

169. *Die Welt* (Hamburg, ind.) , 5 April 1963. Dehler referred to the time since the 1961 Bundestag elections as one of frustration and speculated that unless put under heavy pressure Adenaure would try to renege on his promise to resign.

170. *Die Welt* (Hamburg, ind.) 4 April 1963).

171. *Ibid.* 5 April 1963.

172. "Harmony or Discrepancy: French Treaty and the Community of the Six: The Bundestag discusses the future of European Cooperation"; *Das Parlament,* 13 Jahrgang, 19 (8 May 1963) 1.

173. *Kölnische Rundschau* (pro-CDU) 26 April 1963.